Contributors

About the author

Robert Loredo is the IBM Quantum Ambassador worldwide lead, a Qiskit Advocate, and a Master Inventor with over 20 years of experience in the technical industry. He is a prolific inventor holding over 250 patents in areas such as: AI, life sciences, and quantum. He taught computer and software engineering at Florida International University and holds both a Bachelors and Masters degree in computer and electrical engineering from the University of Miami. As a philanthropist, he donated the royalties from his previous book to the charity Doctors without Borders.

I would like to thank the following people for their guidance, expertise, and motivational support: Arvind Krishna, Dario Gil, Jay Gambetta, Scott Crowder, Steffen Thoss, Katie Pizzolato, Blake Johnson, Tammy Cornell, Birgit Schwarz, Bob Sutor, Denise Ruffner, Brian Ingmanson, Charles Robinson, Chris Nay, Dan Maynard, Edward Van Halen, Enrique Vargas, Gabe Chang, Hanhee Paik, James Weaver, Jerry Chow, John Buselli, Julian Tan, Kenneth Wood, M. Lewis Temares, Mark Ritter, Matthew Broomhall, Matthias Steffen, Michele Grossi, Mohammed Abdel-Mottaleb, Nick Bronn, Olivia Lanes, Paul Bastide, Pete Martinez, Petra Florizoone, Voica Radescu, Vishal Bajpe, and Zaira Nazario for their continued support.

About the reviewers

Hassi Norlén is a client engagement leader with IBM Innovation Studio. He is also an IBM quantum technical ambassador and Qiskit advocate and has been at IBM for 18 years. He holds an MSc. in physics from Uppsala University, Sweden. He has worked as a science journalist, astronomy teacher, software developer, content designer, and an engagement leader in various places around the world. Since becoming an IBM quantum technical ambassador and Qiskit advocate he has reconnected with his physics roots and has first-hand insights into the rapidly evolving field of quantum computing, and specifically Qiskit/IBM Quantum.

He is the author of *Quantum Computing in Practice with IBM Quantum Experience*, and has also written about exploring quantum computing on non-standard platforms in *Qrasp - Quantum on a Raspberry Pi* on Medium.

Michele Grossi is a senior fellow in quantum computing at CERN. He received his industrial PhD in High Energy Physics from the University of Pavia while working at IBM. Michele has worked as as a quantum technical ambassador at IBM and a hybrid cloud solutions architect, and in his current role he co-supervises quantum machine learning projects within the CERN Quantum Technology Initiative. His focus is the development of QML pipelines for high-energy physics problems with possible extensions to different fields. He is a co-author of several scientific publications, a conference speaker, and a lecturer at various universities. In 2019, Forbes selected Michele as one of the top 30 under 30 young Italian leaders in enterprise technology.

Sean Wagner is a research scientist, Quantum Technical Ambassador, and Accelerated Discovery Ambassador at IBM Canada. As a member of the IBM Canada National Innovation Team, Sean works with researchers at academic institutions and industry partners in Canada, from start-ups to large companies. The projects involve high-performance computing, computer architecture, data science, and artificial intelligence applied to numerous scientific and business domains. His most recent work focuses on hardware acceleration, particularly for deep neural networks, and software tools for machine learning. As a member of the IBM Quantum team, Sean is an advocate for and conducts workshops on quantum computing. He earned a BASc. in Computer Engineering from the University of Waterloo in 2003, and completed MASc. and PhD. degrees in electrical and computer engineering at the University of Toronto in 2006 and 2011, respectively.

Voica Radescu holds a PhD in particle physics from the University of Pittsburgh, PA USA. She currently works as the quantum alliances leader in Europe for IBM, where she is committed to enabling quantum partners to achieve success. Before joining IBM in 2017, Voica worked as a high energy physics researcher at top institutions in Europe, such as DESY, CERN, and the University of Oxford.

Join us on Discord

Join our community's Discord space for discussions with the author and other readers:

https://packt.link/3FyN1

Table of Contents

Chapter 5: Understanding the Qubit 99

Chapter 6: Understanding Quantum Logic Gates 115

Preface

Ever since IBM released their first commercially available quantum system for free on the cloud back in 2016, many researchers, developers, faculty, students, and quantum enthusiasts have been running their experiments on real quantum computers. Since then, many in both academia and industry have been investing time and personnel to investigate the potential that quantum computing has in store. The first step in this quantum journey is education, which I assume is why you purchased this book. In this book, you will learn the basic principles of quantum computing and how to leverage those principles to create quantum algorithms and run them on IBM's powerful quantum computers.

This book provides you with a step-by-step introduction to quantum computing using the **IBM Quantum** platform. You will learn how to build quantum programs on your own so you can discover early use cases in your industry or domain and get equipped with quantum computing skills.

You will start working with simple programs that illustrate how these quantum computing principles differ from classical computing and slowly work your way up to more complex programs and algorithms that leverage advanced quantum computing algorithms.

The quantum computing principles we will explore are superposition, entanglement, and interference, then you'll become familiar on how these are used to create quantum circuits, which you can then run on IBM Quantum systems.

Then, you'll learn about the quantum gates and how they operate on qubits and discover the **Quantum Information Science Kit** (**QISKIT**, depending on who you ask, is pronounced KISS-kit) and its circuit libraries and advanced features to help you build quantum algorithms.

You'll then get to grips with quantum algorithms such as Deutsch-Jozsa, Simon, Grover, and Shor's algorithms, while visualizing how to create a quantum circuit and run the algorithm on any of the quantum computers hosted on the IBM Quantum platform.

Later, you'll explore the basics on how your circuit is run on the quantum hardware by learning about the Qiskit Runtime, which has many functionalities to help optimize your quantum circuits.

By the end of this book, you'll have learned how to build quantum programs on your own and will have gained practical quantum computing skills that you can apply to your industry or domain.

Who this book is for

This book is for Python developers who are interested in learning about quantum computing and expanding their abilities to solve classically intractable problems with the help of Qiskit. Some background in computer science and Python is required. While a background in physics and linear algebra is suggested, it is not entirely required.

What this book covers

Chapter 1, Exploring the IBM Quantum Tools, will introduce you to all the tools available to you on the IBM Quantum platform. These tools will help you get up and running quickly and easily without having to install or purchase anything.

Chapter 2, Creating Quantum Circuits with IBM Quantum Composer, discusses this easy-to-use user interface, which is a great tool for visualizing how the various quantum gates and operations affect each qubit and help build an intuitive understanding of the differences between classical and quantum computing.

Chapter 3, Introducing and Installing Qiskit, explores the **Quantum Information Science Kit (Qiskit)** and its advanced features to develop and implement various quantum algorithms, and noise models. Qiskit has various features that help you build quantum circuits, algorithms, and applications easily and allows you to run them on local simulators and real quantum systems.

Chapter 4, Understanding Basic Quantum Computing Principles, begins our quantum journey by discussing the basic quantum computing principles of superposition, entanglement, and interference, which are used by many quantum algorithms. This will also help you understand what differentiates quantum computing from classical computing.

Chapter 5, Understanding the Qubit, covers what the quantum bit, or qubit, is and how you can manipulate it on a quantum system using the various gates and operators, and how to visualize the results of those operations.

Chapter 6, Understanding Quantum Logic Gates, takes a deeper look at the various quantum gates and operations used to change the state of the qubits and your quantum circuit.

Chapter 7, Programming with Qiskit, is where we start digging into creating quantum circuits using the quantum gates and operations we've learned about so far. You will also learn how these gates and operations are converted into microwave pulse schedules, which are what is used to manipulate the qubits on the quantum system.

Chapter 8, Optimizing and Visualizing Quantum Circuits, discusses sending the instructions from your quantum program to run on a quantum system, which has some interesting work happening in the background. Which qubits are the best for running your circuit? Which connections should we select between the qubits that minimizes the number of gates? All these are taken care of by the preset pass manager generator, which we will cover in this chapter.

Chapter 9, Simulating Quantum Systems and Noise Models, explains that all quantum systems, no matter the technology used to create them, must deal with the issue of noise. In this chapter, you will learn what these noises are and how to create models that simulate them to better understand the effects they have on your quantum circuit.

Chapter 10, Suppressing and Mitigating Quantum Noise, explains how to mitigate the various effects noise has on a quantum system.

Chapter 11, Understanding Quantum Algorithms, takes a deep look at the basic quantum algorithms to help understand how the quantum computing principles of superposition, entanglement, and interference are used. We will also review and code some fundamental concepts and algorithms which will help us understand the more complex algorithms.

Chapter 12, Applying Quantum Algorithms, takes you through applying the quantum computing principles and concepts that we've learned about to some complex quantum algorithms.

Chapter 13, Understanding Quantum Utility and Qiskit Patterns, covers what quantum utility is and why it is the key to getting us closer towards quantum advantage. It will also provide an overview of the Qiskit patterns and how they can simplify your development experience to build complex quantum circuits.

Appendix A: Resources, provides a list of further resources that you can use to explore the topics covered in this book in more detail.

Appendix B, Assessments, provides the answers to the questions that you will find at the end of each chapter.

To get the most out of this book

- You will need to have internet access to access the IBM Quantum systems available to you. Since the platform is hosted on the cloud, you will not need anything more than a browser and to register a free account.

- You will also need an up-to-date browser (Firefox, Chrome, Safari)

- OS requirements (only if installing the software locally): Windows, Mac, and Linux.

Download the example code files

The code bundle for the book is hosted on GitHub at `https://github.com/PacktPublishing/Learning-Quantum-Computing-with-Python-and-IBM-Quantum-Second-Edition`. We also have other code bundles from our rich catalog of books and videos available at `https://github.com/PacktPublishing/`. Check them out!

Download the color images

We also provide a PDF file that has color images of the screenshots/diagrams used in this book. You can download it here: `https://packt.link/gbp/9781803244808`.

Conventions used

There are a number of text conventions used throughout this book.

`CodeInText`: Indicates code words in text, database table names, folder names, filenames, file extensions, pathnames, dummy URLs, user input, and Twitter handles. For example; "Simply run `pip install qiskit-aer` from your command line, or Python environment, and that should be all you need."

A block of code is set as follows:

```
from qiskit_ibm_runtime import QiskitRuntimeService

# Save your IBM Quantum account to allow you to use systems:
QiskitRuntimeService.save_account(channel="ibm_quantum", token='PASTE-API-
TOKEN-HERE', set_as_default=True)
```

When we wish to draw your attention to a particular part of a code block, the relevant lines or items are set in bold:

```
import numpy as np
#Bind the parameters with a value, in this case 2π
```

```
qc = qc.assign_parameters(parameters={param_theta: 2*np.pi})
#Draw the circuit with the set parameter values
qc.draw(output='mpl')
```

Any command-line input or output is written as follows:

```
pip install qiskit
```

Bold: Indicates a new term, an important word, or words that you see on the screen, for example, in menus or dialog boxes, also appear in the text like this. For example: "One of the more popular experiments that have come out of quantum mechanics is the **double-slit experiment**."

> Warnings or important notes appear like this.

> Tips and tricks appear like this.

Get in touch

Feedback from our readers is always welcome.

General feedback: Email feedback@packtpub.com, and mention the book's title in the subject of your message. If you have questions about any aspect of this book, please email us at questions@packtpub.com.

Errata: Although we have taken every care to ensure the accuracy of our content, mistakes do happen. If you have found a mistake in this book we would be grateful if you would report this to us. Please visit, http://www.packtpub.com/submit-errata, selecting your book, clicking on the Errata Submission Form link, and entering the details.

Piracy: If you come across any illegal copies of our works in any form on the Internet, we would be grateful if you would provide us with the location address or website name. Please contact us at copyright@packtpub.com with a link to the material.

If you are interested in becoming an author: If there is a topic that you have expertise in and you are interested in either writing or contributing to a book, please visit http://authors.packtpub.com.

Leave a Review!

Thank you for purchasing this book from Packt Publishing—we hope you enjoy it! Your feedback is invaluable and helps us improve and grow. Once you've completed reading it, please take a moment to leave an Amazon review; it will only take a minute, but it makes a big difference for readers like you.

https://packt.link/r/1803244801

Scan the QR code below to receive a free ebook of your choice.

https://packt.link/NzOWQ

Download a free PDF copy of this book

Thanks for purchasing this book!

Do you like to read on the go but are unable to carry your print books everywhere?

Is your eBook purchase not compatible with the device of your choice?

Don't worry, now with every Packt book you get a DRM-free PDF version of that book at no cost.

Read anywhere, any place, on any device. Search, copy, and paste code from your favorite technical books directly into your application.

The perks don't stop there, you can get exclusive access to discounts, newsletters, and great free content in your inbox daily.

Follow these simple steps to get the benefits:

1. Scan the QR code or visit the link below:

https://packt.link/free-ebook/9781803244808

2. Submit your proof of purchase.
3. That's it! We'll send your free PDF and other benefits to your email directly.

1

Exploring the IBM Quantum Tools

Quantum computing has been growing in popularity over the past few years, most recently since IBM released the first commercially available quantum computer on the cloud back in May 2016, back then referred to as the IBM Quantum Experience, now rebranded as the **IBM Quantum Platform (IQP)**. This release was the first of its kind, hosted on the cloud and providing the world with the opportunity to experiment with quantum devices for free. The platform includes a **user interface (UI)** that allows anyone to run experiments on a real quantum computer. And just recently added was direct access to all documentation and learning resources, such as tutorials and courses, right from the platform, making it easier to run circuits as you learn.

The goal of this chapter is to first introduce you to the IBM Quantum Platform, which contains everything you need to learn how to create and run quantum circuits on real quantum systems. It also provides you with courses and tutorials to experiment with existing quantum algorithms and applications. The IBM Quantum Platform is comprised of the following three applications, which you can see listed in the Application Switcher located at the top-right corner of the platform (see *Figure 1.1*):

- **Platform**: Lists all the jobs and systems (dashboard, systems, and jobs) you have access to on the platform.
- **Documentation**: Provides a list of resources to help you get started. Resources include how to set up your development environment and build/test/execute quantum circuits on quantum systems. It also provides API documentation of the latest version of the **Quantum Information Science Kit (Qiskit)** open-source code.

- **Learning:** Provides quantum courses and tutorials for users of all different levels. These cover topics such as the basics of quantum computing, variational algorithm design, and a new addition: quantum-safe cryptography!

You can select and switch between each of these applications using the top-left applications icon next to your avatar, the switcher is shown in the following figure:

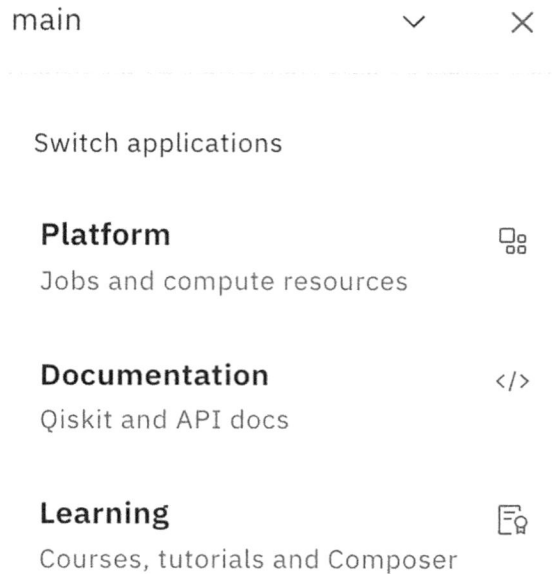

main   ∨   ✕

Switch applications

Platform

Jobs and compute resources

Documentation

Qiskit and API docs

Learning

Courses, tutorials and Composer

Figure 1.1: Application selection

This chapter will help you understand what actions and information are available in each application, each of which we will also cover in more detail in later chapters, to give you an overview of where everything is. This includes creating circuits, running the circuits on both simulators and real quantum devices, viewing information about your profile and available backend systems, and visualizing the results of your experiments. So, let's get started!

The following topics will be covered in this chapter:

- Getting started with the IBM Quantum Platform
- Using the documentation to quickly start up
- Understanding IBM quantum tools

Technical requirements

Throughout this book, it is expected that you will have some experience in developing with Python and, although it isn't necessary, some basic knowledge of classical and quantum mechanics would help. Most of the information will be provided with each chapter, so if you do not have knowledge of classical or quantum mechanics, we will cover what you need to know here. For those of you who have existing knowledge in this area, the information here will serve as a useful refresher.

The Python editor used throughout this book is **Jupyter Notebook**. You can, of course, use any Python editor of your choice. This may include **Watson Studio**, **PyCharm**, **Spyder**, **Visual Studio Code**, and so on.

Here is the source code used throughout this book: `https://github.com/PacktPublishing/Learning-Quantum-Computing-with-Python-and-IBM-Quantum-Second-Edition`

Getting started with the IBM Quantum Platform

As mentioned earlier, the IBM Quantum Platform application is your high-level view of what you will normally see once you log in. It's good to mention here that there may be updates to the tools as the platform evolves with the technology after the time of writing, so some visualizations and results may vary. The platform aggregates multiple views that you can see, and this helps you to get an idea as to what machines you have access to and what jobs you have pending, running, or completed.

In this section, we will go through the steps to get registered. Let's get started.

Registering to the IBM Quantum Platform

In this section, we will get registered and explain what happens in the background once you sign up to the IBM Quantum Platform for the first time. This will help you understand what features and configurations are prepared and available to you upon registration.

To register, follow these steps:

1. The first step is to head over to the IBM Quantum Platform site at the following link: `https://quantum.ibm.com/`

2. You should see the login screen, as shown in *Figure 1.2*. Your individual situation will determine how to proceed from there:

   - If you already have an account or are already signed in, you can sign in and skip this section.

- If you have not registered, then you can select the login method of your choice from the sign-in screen. As you can see, you can register using various methods, such as with your **IBMid**, **Google**, **GitHub**, **Twitter**, **LinkedIn**, or by email.

- If you do not have any of the account types listed, then you can simply register for an **IBMid** account and use that to sign in:

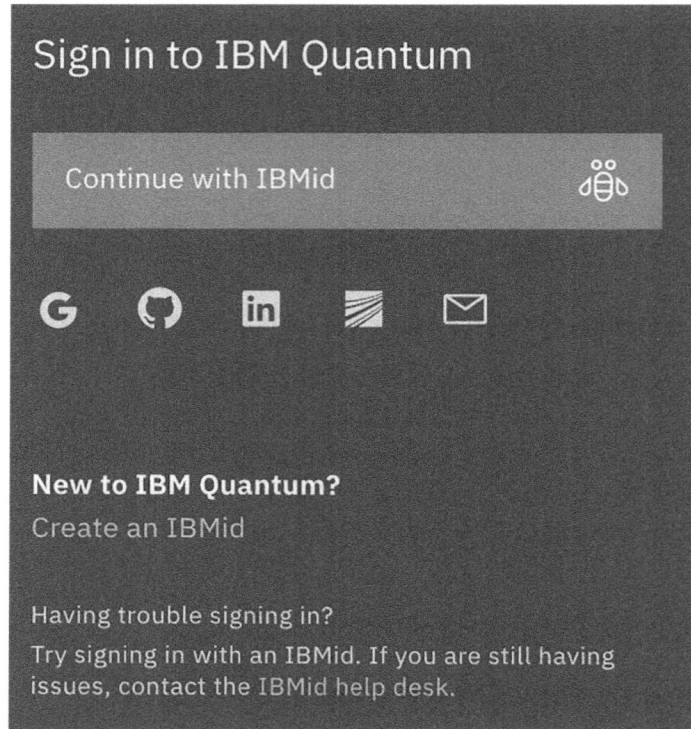

Figure 1.2: The IBM Quantum Platform sign-in page

3. Once you select the login method of your choice, you will see the login screen for that method. Simply fill out the information, if it's not already there, and select **login**.

4. Once signed in, you will land on the IBM Quantum Platform home page. This is the first page you will see each time you log in:

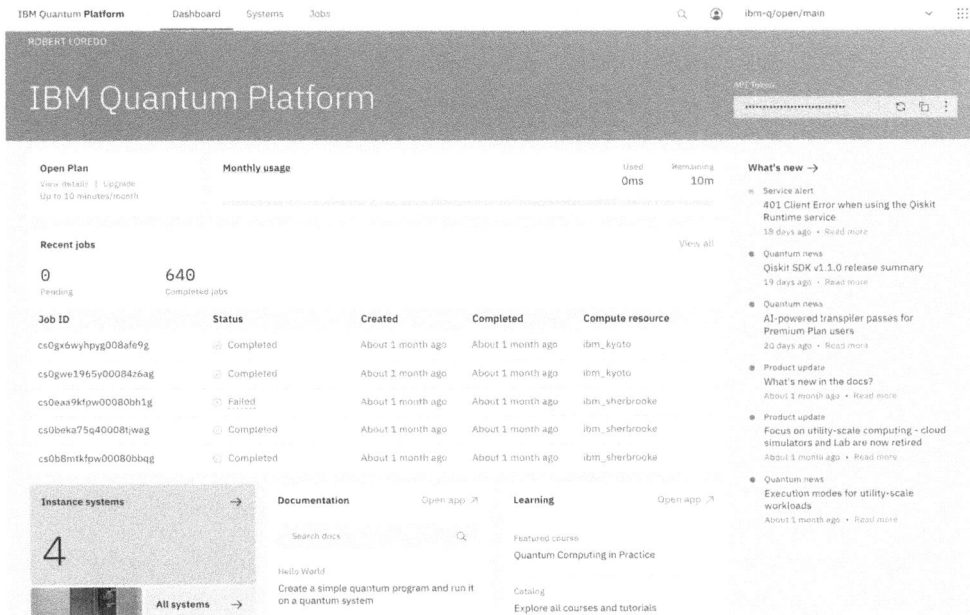

Figure 1.3: The IBM Quantum home page

Now that you have registered with IBM Quantum Platform, let's take a quick tour and delve into some features that make up the home page.

Note first that across the top of the Platform application page you have three tabs: **Dashboard**, **Systems**, and **Jobs**. Each of these provides various information for you, which we will cover in detail in the following sections. But before we get started, let's look at the **Manage account** settings view.

Understanding the Manage account settings view

Let's start by reviewing the home page, specifically the **Manage account** settings view. You can access your user account and settings view via your avatar, located at the top right of the page (as visible in *Figure 1.3*).

This view provides **profile settings** of the logged-in user, as illustrated in *Figure 1.4*:

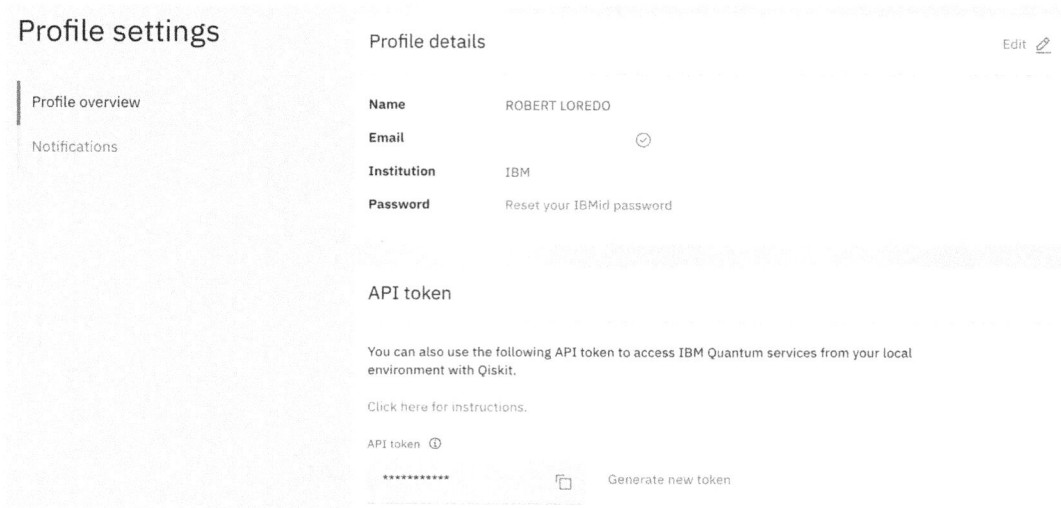

Figure 1.4: The Manage account settings view

This view also provides actions regarding your profile such as setting your password, email, API token, and in-app notification settings.

> The API token is used by the provider to determine which systems you have provisioned for your account. This is autogenerated when you use the platform; however, should you ever decide to run a notebook off the platform, then you will need to save your API token locally. We describe how to save and load your account details locally in *Chapter 7, Programming with Qiskit and the Qiskit Runtime Service*.

Below the **Manage account settings** is the **Instances** list, which allows you to see which instances you are a member of. Instances are used to determine which IBM Quantum systems you have access to based on which hub, project, or group you belong to, as illustrated in *Figure 1.4*. Also, below the list of instances is the option **Delete Account**, which will also remove all your account data.

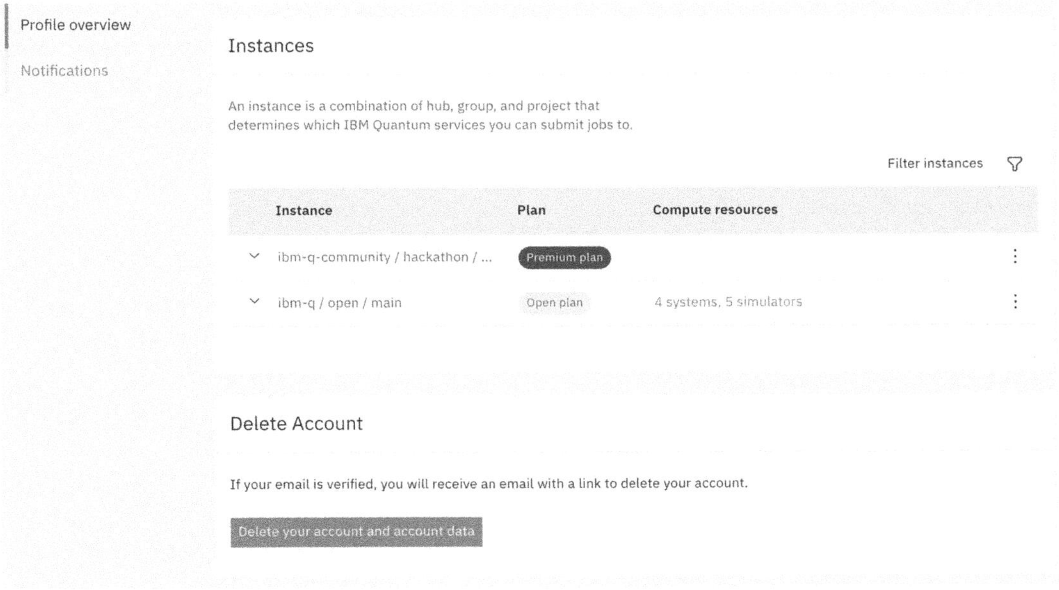

Figure 1.5: Instances and Delete Account views

Finally, at the bottom of the **Profile** settings you will see your **Notification** settings, which you can enable based on your preferences.

Getting familiar with the Compute resources view

The **Compute resources** view provides you with a list of all the various quantum services available to you, which include the quantum systems. You can see all the available services by selecting the grid icon, located at the top left of the IBM Quantum Platform view, and selecting the **Platform** tab.

Once the **Compute resources** page is open you will see a grouping of systems via a pull-down selector highlighted by a box in the following figure. The groupings are of systems that you have access to and a list of all systems including those systems reserved for premium users, as illustrated in *Figure 1.6*:

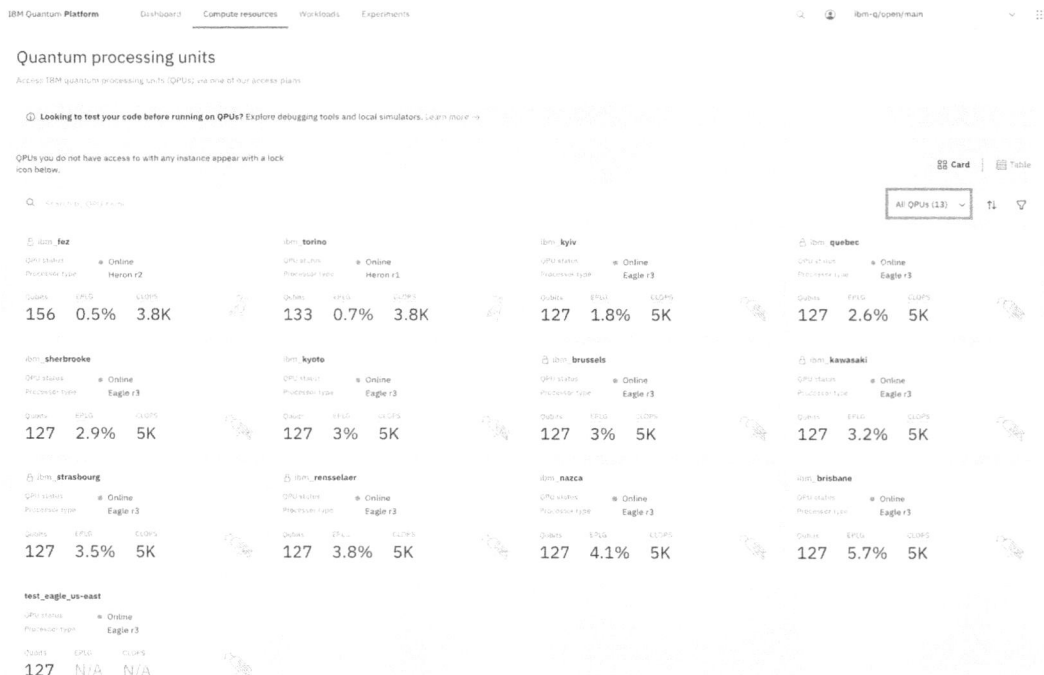

Figure 1.6: The Compute resources view

The view contains all the systems available to you.

Each card (or row if viewing in table mode) represents a different quantum system available to you and details that describe each system. In the previous figure you can see it lists out detailed specifications. Systems with a lock icon next to them are those reserved for premium users such as those who are active members of the IBM Quantum Network.

The details you can see for each system are:

- **Qubits**, which is the number of qubits available
- **Error Per Layered Gate (EPLG)**, which is the latest metric used to measure the quality and performance of a quantum system
- **Circuit layer operations per second (CLOPS)**
- **Status**, which is the availability of the system (Online, Maintenance, etc.)
- **Total pending jobs**, which is the number of jobs waiting to run on the system (queue)
- **Processor type**, which is the type and version of the processor of the system

This information allows you to visualize all the systems and their metrics so you can select an ideal system to run your quantum circuits.

The second selector is to view **All Instances**; this lists all the quantum systems that are available to you, including the open systems as well as premium quantum systems, if you are a quantum network member. To view the list as a table, rather than cards, you can select table view (located just above the system selector) as illustrated in *Figure 1.7*:

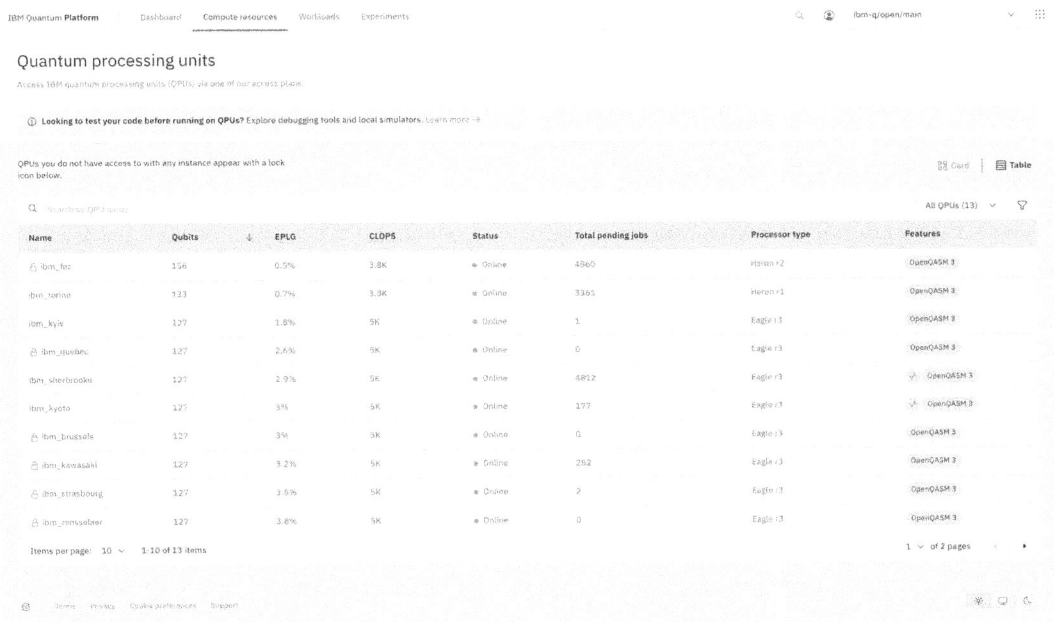

Figure 1.7: A table view of all available systems – shows all available quantum systems, including premium systems

In this view, same as the **Your resources** view, each row represents details about each quantum system's properties such as the status, processor type, number of qubits, quantum volume, and **CLOPS**.

> CLOPS is one of the measurements that is used to determine the performance of a quantum computer. It measures the speed at which a quantum processor can execute layers of a circuit, similar to the parameterized model circuits used to measure the quantum volume of a quantum computer.

The names of the systems do not represent the location of the device; the city names originated from where IBM Research has a lab and have since expanded to include cities where IBM has offices around the world. At the time of writing, the IBM Quantum systems reside in many locations around the world. The largest groups are located at the IBM Research Lab in Yorktown Heights and in Poughkeepsie, NY. There are now many on-prem systems in many locations, such as IBM Ehningen, Germany (via a partnership with Fraunhofer-Gesellschaft), and University of Tokyo. The first on-prem system that is not on an IBM site was recently installed in Cleveland Clinic, with many more scheduled to be installed in other countries such as Spain and South Korea.

Above the rows you have a few features; one is a search window to help you find a specific system and next to that is a filter option, which allows you to narrow down the visible list of systems based on provider, status, or processor types. You can also see them as cards if you select the card selection on the top right of the table.

To view further details of each quantum system, let's select one of the systems; in this case I will select **ibm-brisbane**, as seen in *Figure 1.8*. Keep in mind that systems will continue to evolve and may be replaced after the time of writing this, so if a system is mentioned in this book that you do not see, don't worry; just select any that you like as the details you see will vary per device.

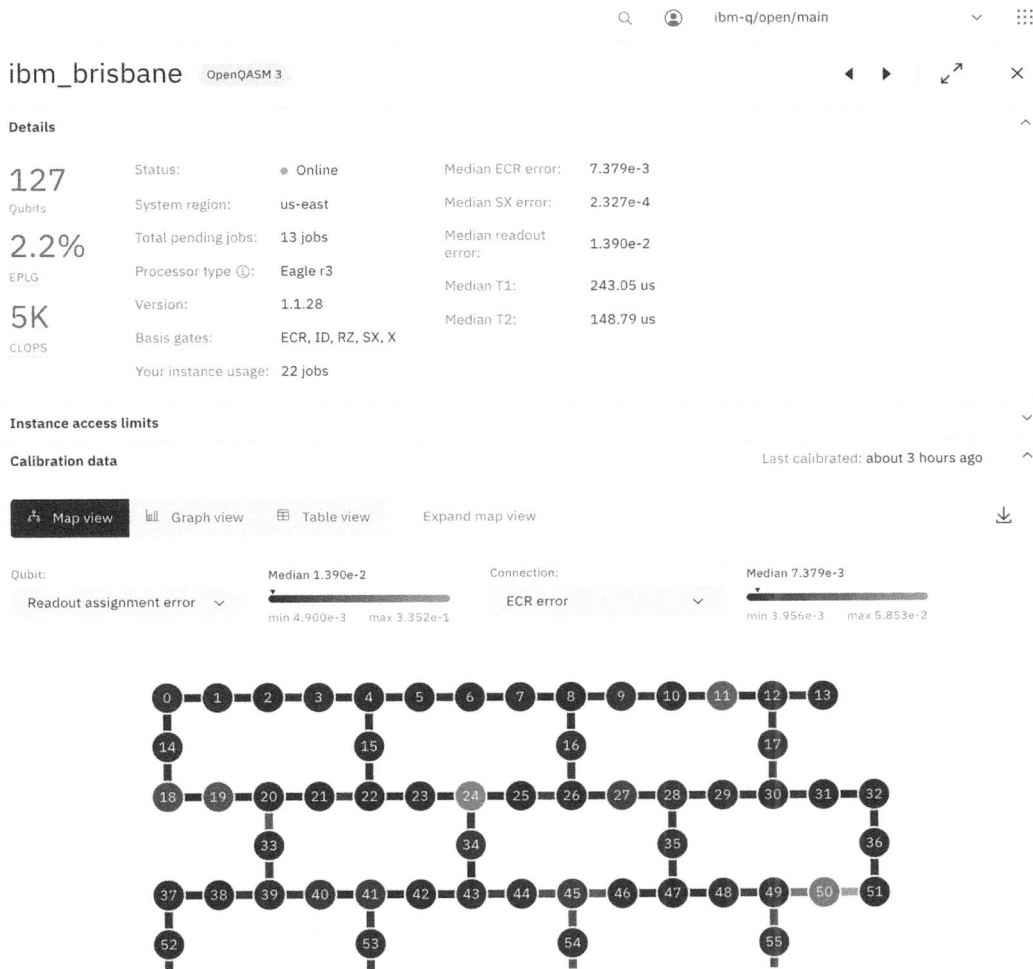

Figure 1.8: The device details view (truncated view of all 127 qubits)

In this view you can examine each system in more detail. Each quantum system has a set of properties that you have access to view. This helps greatly if there are some constraints or requirements to the type of system you wish to run your quantum programs on—for example, the connectivity between qubits, the error rate of each qubit and its physical connection, the basis gates, and other details that we will cover in detail in various chapters throughout this book.

This view also allows you to download a CSV file that contains all these properties so you can analyze them using any analysis tools you wish. To download the properties, simply click on the download icon located below the **Last calibrated** time in the **Calibration data** section.

You'll also notice that there are two pull-down options available just above the qubit map of the system, where one has a set of options for **Qubit** and another for the **Connection** between the qubits. The options provide you with the ability to see what properties you wish to have rendered for each qubit and connection, respectively. In the qubit options you can select to see the details of each qubit, such as its frequency, T1/T2 times, anharmonicity, and readout assignment error. The connection options allow you to view the CNOT error and gate time (in nanoseconds) between each physically connected qubit.

There are of course other ways to obtain these properties programmatically using Qiskit code, but we will get to that later in this book. For now, this is just for awareness, so in later chapters when you learn more about them, you'll know where the information is located.

We are now familiar with the systems, and their details, on which we will run our quantum circuits; let's see how we can view the results after the quantum systems have completed their job.

Learning about pending and latest jobs

When you send a circuit to run on a simulator or a quantum system you will want to know the status of the circuit. This is where the **Jobs** view comes in handy. To get to the Jobs view, go back to the grid icon located at the top left of the dashboard and select **Jobs** from the list of views. Once the view is open you will see a table, as shown in *Figure 1.9*, that contains a complete list of jobs that are pending completion on either the simulators or backend devices. You can use this view to see the status of your circuit or program, the job ID, which provider and service were used, and other details for each job you submitted:

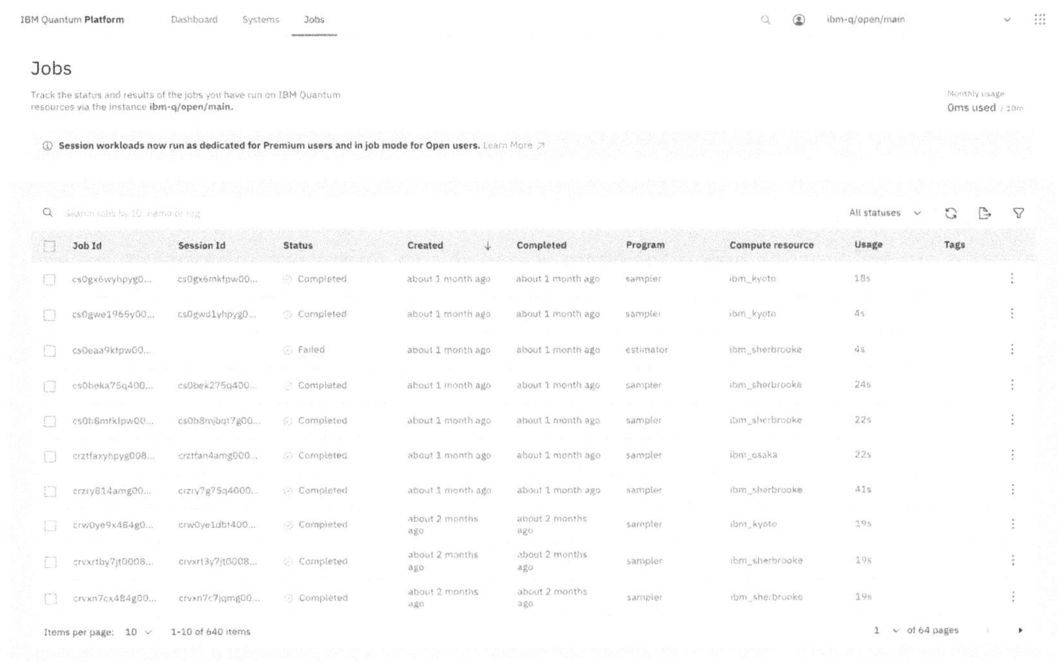

Figure 1.9: The Jobs view list

The job ID is listed so that you can call back the details of that job later. Each job is initially sorted by creation date but can also be filtered by **Status** (completed, pending, or returned), **Session Id** (the unique ID for the session the job was run in), **Compute resource** (which simulator or quantum system was used), or **Usage** (time indicating how long the job took to run).

Details regarding job objects will be covered in *Chapter 7, Programming with Qiskit.*

In this section, you have learned where to find information about your experiments, and hardware details about the quantum devices from the various views available on the IBM Quantum Platform. There are views that also provide you with the tools you need to start programming and running circuits on a quantum computer, in an easy-to-use format that does not include any installation of software.

In the next section we will review what the Documentation application provides you to help get started using the systems we just learned in this section.

Using the Documentation to quickly start up

Earlier in this chapter we covered what systems you have access to and details about each system. In this section we will review the Documentation application, which will provide you with information and guidance on how to get yourself up and running and executing quantum circuits on a quantum computer.

First, from the application selector, select the **Documentation** application. This will open the **Documentation** page as illustrated in *Figure 1.10*:

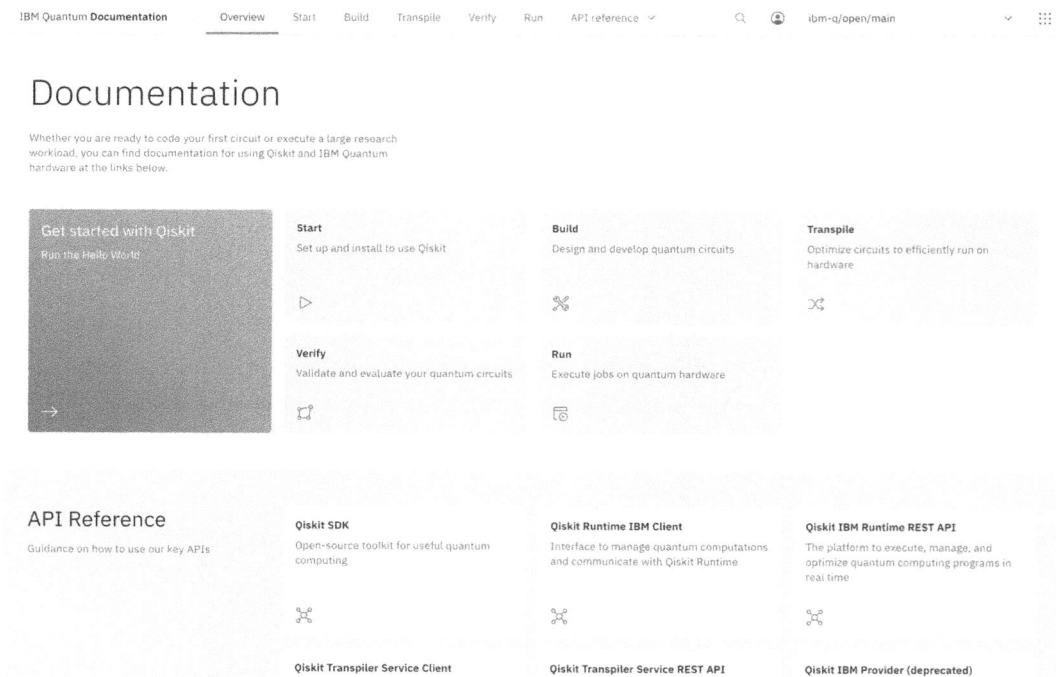

Figure 1.10: Documentation application view

Let's look across the top of the page where you will see seven shortcuts each to help you get started. They are described as follows:

- **Overview**: The view that you see when you first get to the documentation page that has all the options
- **Start**: Directions on how to get your local system set up and install Qiskit
- **Build**: Instructions on how to design and develop your first quantum circuits
- **Transpile**: How to optimize the mapping of your circuit onto the selected device to ensure the highest quality and performance
- **Verify**: As the title indicates, how to test, verify, and evaluate your quantum circuits
- **Run**: Executing your tested quantum circuits on the quantum systems
- API reference: Quick links to key documentation on common objects and functions

Below the **Get started with Qiskit** and **API Reference** section of the page, you will also see the various tutorials available for those of you who already have your system set up and want to dive right into running quantum algorithms on a quantum computer. Each tile represents a different tutorial and they are independent of each other so you can pick whichever you'd like to get started on without worrying about any dependency on another tutorial.

Now that you know where to find the documentation needed to help you get up and running quickly, let's continue and explore the tools you can use to generate quantum circuits using the IBM Quantum Composer.

Understanding the IBM Quantum tools

Understanding the systems and knowing the status of our circuit jobs is great, but knowing how to create these circuits and run them is clearly an important step. In this section we will review both tools that are available to you. Using the application switcher, select the last application listed, **Learning**.

The following figure, *Figure 1.11* is the IBM Quantum Learning application view. This view provides you with a one-stop shop of resources. At first you will see that at the top, it highlights the latest course that was released. At the time of writing this, it was the **Fundamentals of quantum algorithms**. Below that is the catalog of courses available to you on the platform with topics ranging from the basics of quantum information science to quantum-safe cryptography.

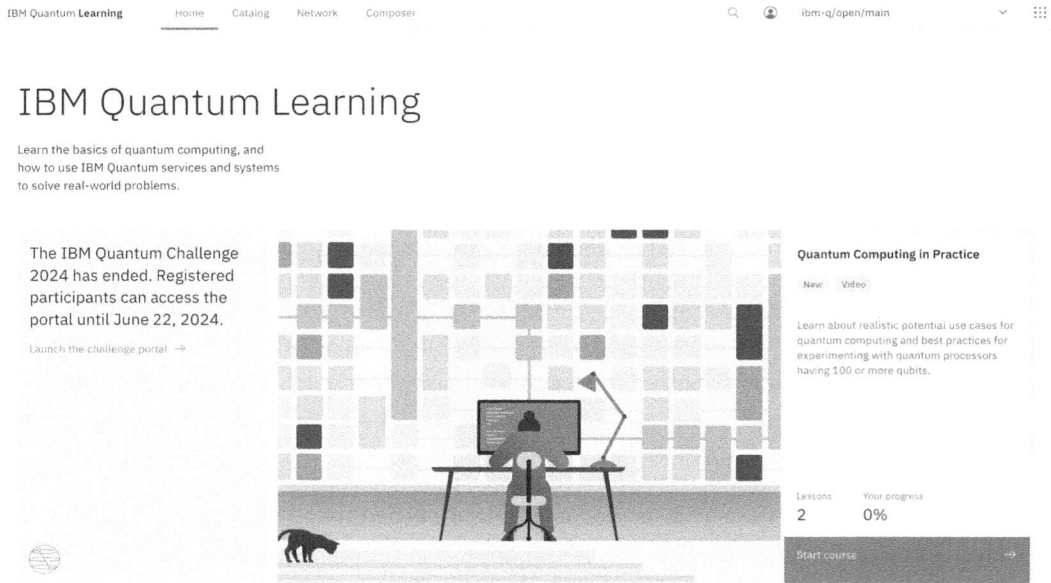

Figure 1.11: IBM Quantum Learning application view

Below the courses you will see three other sections. The first is the list of tutorials. This is the same list you saw in the previous section. It is duplicated in this section for completeness as it is of course the learning application. And at the bottom is the **Resources** section, which lists other helpful learning resources, as illustrated in the following figure:

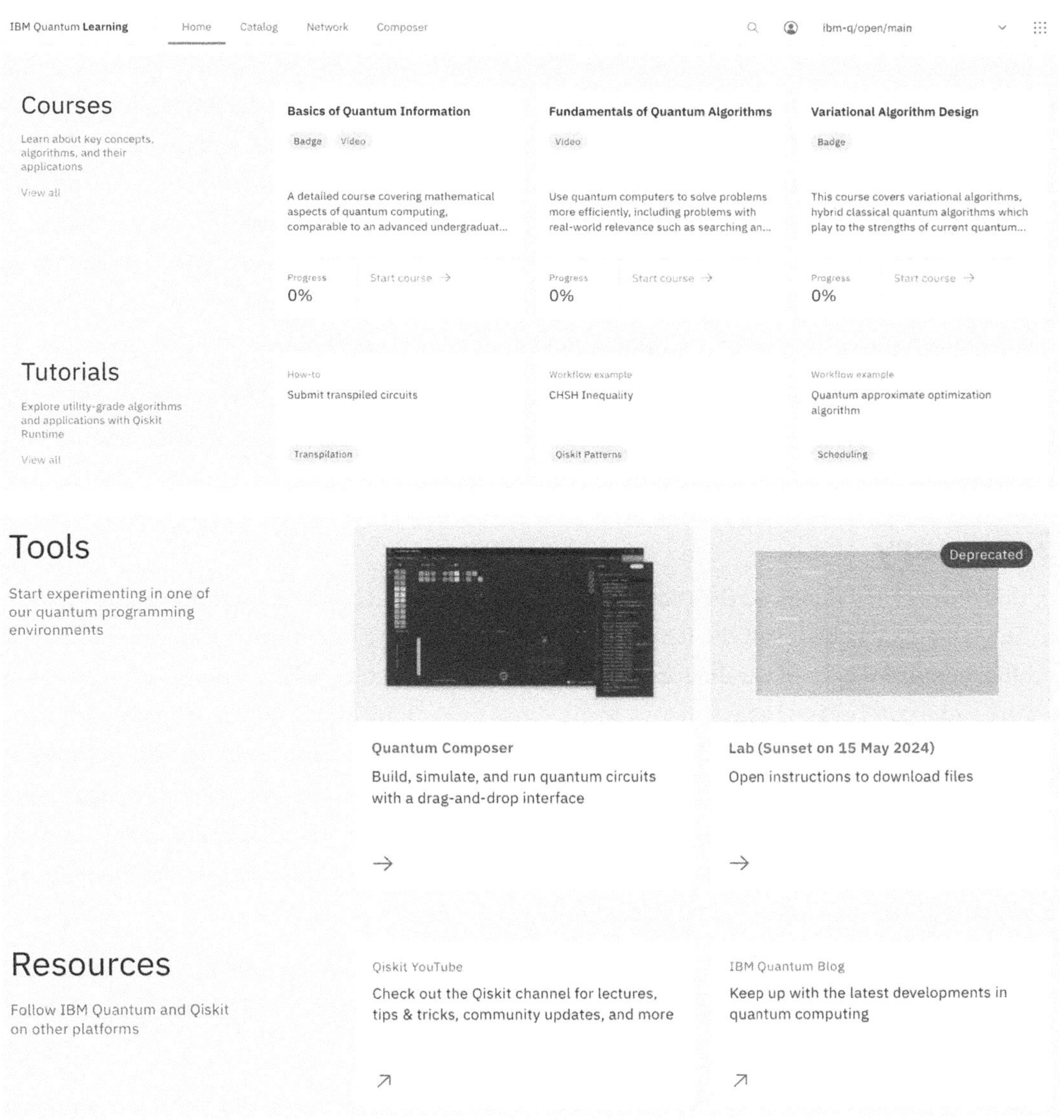

Figure 1.12: Courses, Tutorials, Tools, and Resources sections.

We have two ways to launch each tool. First, as illustrated in *Figure 1.12*, you can launch each tool by clicking on it within the **Tools** section. The second way is by selecting it from the top of the page as illustrated in *Figure 1.11*.

The Composer is a graphical UI where you can create your quantum circuits by dragging and dropping quantum gates onto a quantum circuit. The Composer also provides various visual representations of the results such as the state of the circuit and the expected probability measurements. This makes the Composer a fantastic tool to help you get a visual, and perhaps intuitive, understanding of how the various quantum gates and properties affect the results of both the qubit itself and the overall quantum state. This is a tool I highly recommend you start with as it contains some very nice introductory tutorials that you can follow to create your first quantum circuit and run it on an actual quantum computer. We will create a simple circuit and run it on a quantum computer in *Chapter 2, Creating Quantum Circuits with IBM Quantum Composer*.

Now that we are done with our tour of the IBM Quantum tools, we're ready to get to work. In the following chapters, we will delve further into the Composer and progress to writing quantum programs.

Summary

In this chapter, we reviewed the IBM Quantum Platform, which provides plenty of information to help you get a good lay of the land. You now know where to find information regarding your profile, details for each of the devices you have available, the status of each device, as well as the status and results of your experiments. Some views might look a little different based on the level of provider you have. I have chosen to use the free open provider throughout this book so all users can see the general views. If you are a premium or partner user, then your views may have more information or options that are specific to your provider. Details about those differences are outside the scope of this book; however, you can check with your IBM Quantum representative for details about the additional views and roles.

Knowing where to find this information will help you monitor your experiments and enable you to understand the state of your experiments by reviewing your backend services, monitoring queue times, and viewing your results queues.

In the next chapter, we will learn about the Composer in detail and run our very first quantum circuit.

Questions

1. Which Application contains your API token?
2. Which device in your resources list has the fewest qubits?
3. Which Application would provide you a qubit map of a quantum system?

Join us on Discord

Join our community's Discord space for discussions with the author and other readers:

`https://packt.link/3FyN1`

2

Creating Quantum Circuits with IBM Quantum Composer

In this chapter, you will learn how to use the **IBM Quantum Composer** and what each of its component functions are with respect to creating and running experiments. The Composer will help you to visually create a quantum circuit via its built-in UI, which in turn will help you to visually conceptualize some of the basic principles of quantum mechanics used to optimize your experiments. You will also learn how to preview the results of each experiment and create your first quantum circuit.

The following topics will be covered in this chapter:

- Getting started with the Quantum Composer
- Creating a quantum circuit with the Quantum Composer

By the end of this chapter, you will know how to create a quantum circuit using the **Composer**, and create experiments that simulate classic gates and quantum gates. You will also have learned where to examine the various results of your experiments, such as state vectors and their probabilities. This will help you understand how some quantum gate operations affect each qubit.

Technical requirements

In this chapter, some basic knowledge of computing is assumed, such as understanding the basic gates of a classic computing system.

Here is the full source code used throughout the book: https://github.com/PacktPublishing/Learning-Quantum-Computing-with-Python-and-IBM-Quantum-Second-Edition

Getting started with the IBM Quantum Composer

In this section, we will review the IBM Quantum Composer (hereafter referred to as simply the Composer) layout so that you can understand its functionality and behavior when creating or editing quantum circuits. Here, you will also create a few circuits, leveraging the visualization features from the Composer to make it easy for you to understand how quantum circuits are created. So, let's start at the beginning: by launching the Composer.

Launching the Composer

To create a quantum circuit, let's first start by opening the Composer. To open the Composer view, click on the **Composer** button located at the top of the IBM Quantum Learning (`https://learning.quantum.ibm.com`) application as shown in the following screenshot:

IBM Quantum **Learning**   Home   Catalog   Network   Composer

Figure 2.1: Launch the Composer

Now that you have the Composer open, let's take a tour of what each component of the Composer editor provides you with.

Familiarizing yourself with the Composer components

In this section, we will get familiar with each of the components that make up the Composer. These allow you to do things such as visually inspect the results of your experiments in a variety of ways. Visualizing the construction of the quantum circuit will help you conceptualize how each quantum gate affects a qubit.

Understanding the Composer

In this section, we will review the various functionalities available to ensure you have a good understanding of all the different features available to you.

In *Figure 2.2*, you can see the landing page of the **Composer** view:

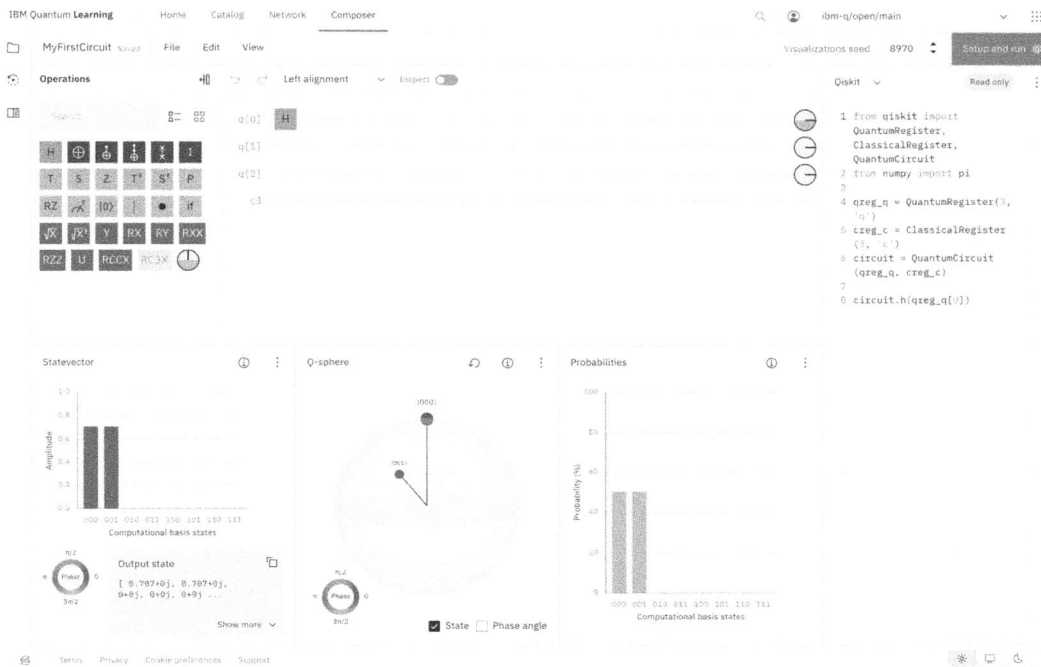

Figure 2.2: The IBM Quantum Composer view

From the preceding screenshot, you can see the **Composer** view, containing three qubits (**q[0]**, **q[1]**, and **q[2]**). This might not look the same when you launch the Composer for the first time. If you would like to add or remove qubits, you can simply select a qubit, for example **q[1]**, by clicking on it, and selecting the plus icon or the trash icon, which will appear over the specific qubit.

> If any of the views are not visible, this just means they have not been enabled. You can enable them by selecting the **View** pull-down menu located across the top of the Composer, hovering over **Panels**, and selecting the views that are not visible: for example, the **Statevector** view.

To reproduce the views used throughout this chapter, simply add or remove the qubits until you only have three qubits left. You can add/remove by clicking on the qubit label. The default is three.

Now that you have your views set up, let's continue to the Composer view itself. In the following screenshot, you can see a series of **gates** and **operations**:

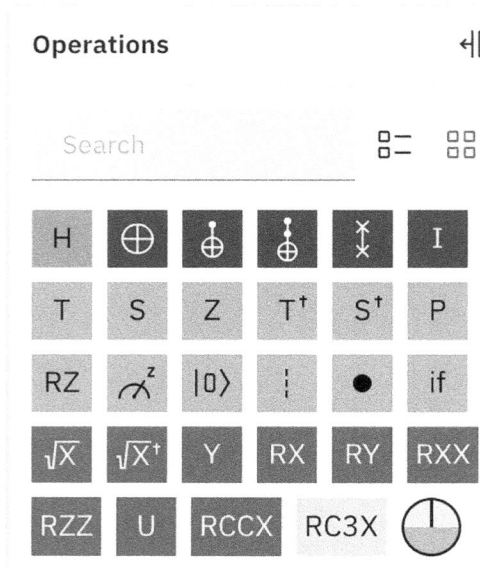

Figure 2.3: Gates and operations

Each of the components shown has a specific function or operation that acts upon the qubit(s), which we will cover in detail in *Chapter 6*, *Understanding Quantum Logic Gates*.

As we can see in the following screenshot, we also have the **circuit editor** itself, which is the part of the Composer where we will create our quantum circuit by placing various gates and operations:

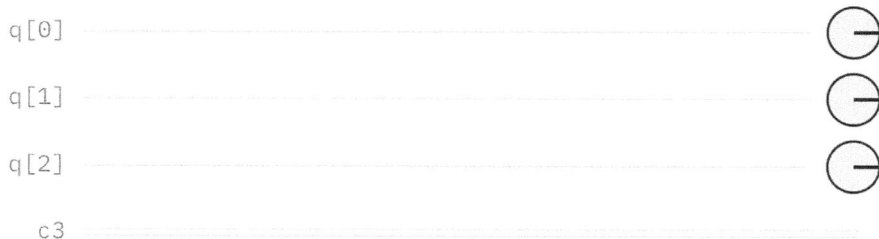

Figure 2.4: Circuit editor

As you can see from the preceding screenshot, the default circuit includes three qubits (though this might change over time) each of which is labeled with a **q**, and the index appended in order from left to right (in this case, **q[2]**, **q[1]**, and **q[0]**). This will be significant when we want to map the results from our quantum circuit. Each qubit is initialized to an initial state of **0** before running the experiment.

The last line is the classical bits, which are what we will map each qubit to so that when we complete running our quantum circuit, the results are then passed to the classical bits according to the mapping. By default, the mapping from qubit to bit is done based on the index of the qubit. For example, q_0 measurement results will be mapped to c_0 via the measurement operator, which we will see when we run our quantum circuit. You can add or remove classical bits in the same manner as qubits.

Next to the qubit you will see a line, which looks like a wire running out from each qubit, in the circuit editor:

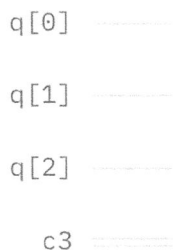

```
q[0]    ----------

q[1]    ----------

q[2]    ----------

 c3     ==========
```

Figure 2.5: Qubits and circuit wires

These lines are where you will be creating a circuit by placing various gates, operations, and barriers on them. This circuit has three wires, each of which pertains to one of the three qubits on the quantum computer. The reason it is called a **Composer** is primarily that these lines look very similar to a music staff used by musicians to compose their music. In our case, the notes on the music staff are represented by the gates and operations used to ultimately create a quantum algorithm.

In the next section, we will review the various options you have available to customize the views of the Composer. This will allow you to ensure that you can only see what you want to see while creating your quantum circuit.

Customizing your views

Continuing with our Composer tour, at the top of the Composer view are the circuit menu options that allow you to save your circuit, clear the circuit, or share your quantum circuit:

IBM Quantum **Learning**   Home   Catalog   Network   Composer

    ▢   MyFirstCircuit *Saved*   File   Edit   View

Figure 2.6: The Composer menu options

First, we will cover how to save your circuit. To do this, simply click on the default text at the top left of the Composer where it currently reads **Untitled circuit**, and type in any title you wish. Ideally, select a name that is associated with the experiment. In this case, let's call it **MyFirst-Circuit** and save it by either hitting the *Enter* key or clicking the checkmark icon to the right of the title, as shown below:

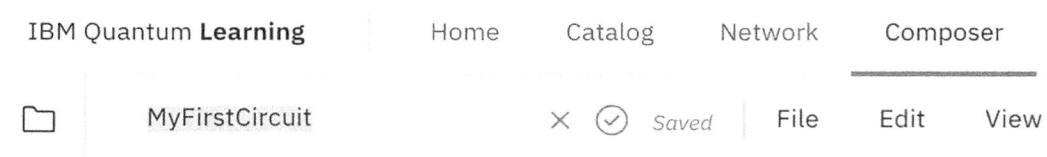

IBM Quantum **Learning**   Home   Catalog   Network   Composer

    ▢   MyFirstCircuit   ✕ ✓ *Saved*   File   Edit   View

Figure 2.7: Renaming the circuit

Across the top of the Composer, you will see a list of drop-down menu options. The menu items in the preceding screenshot have the following options:

- **File** provides options to create and open circuits, as well as copy, export, share, or delete the current circuit.
- **Edit** allows you to manage your circuit and clear gates and operators.
- **View** enables the various view options, which we look at in the following sections.

Let's now look at each of the various views in the following sections.

The Graphical Editor view

The **Graphical Editor** view contains a few components used to create quantum circuits:

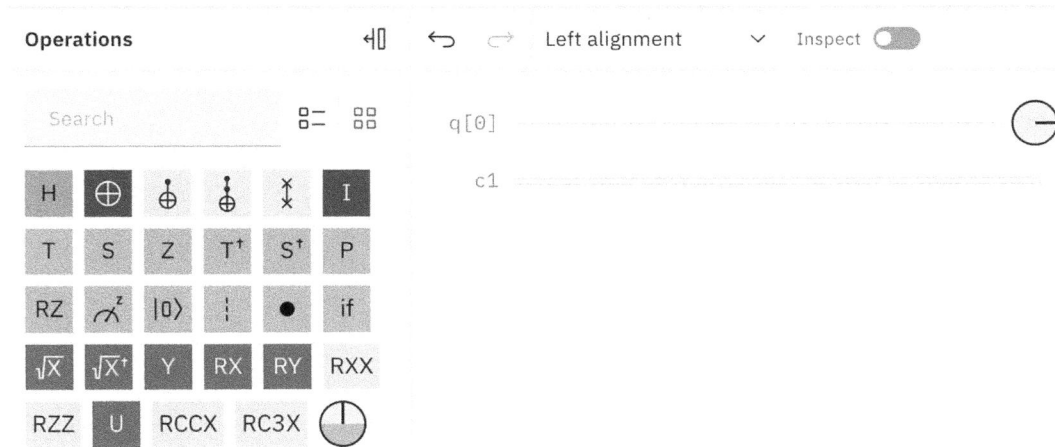

Figure 2.8: The Graphical Editor view options

The components include the following:

- **Circuit Composer**: UI components used to create quantum circuits.

- **Operations**: A list of available drag-and-drop gates and operators to generate a quantum circuit.

- **Options**: The ability to set up the alignment and turn on the **Inspect** feature, which allows you to step through each gate and operation as you would to debug your code on an IDE or browser.

- **Disk**: A disk that is located at the end of the circuit to serve as a visual representation of each qubit as you add gates and operations.

Now that we know where we can create a quantum circuit, let's move on to displays, which provide various ways to visualize the results of our quantum circuit.

The Statevector view

The **Statevector** view allows you to preview the state vector results, which is to say the quantum state result of your quantum circuit. The state vector view presents the computational basis states of the quantum circuit in a few different ways. To simplify the view, I have removed all but one qubit so it is easier to read the values.

You can do the same if you wish, otherwise your x axis may have more than just the two states of 0 and 1, as shown in the following figures:

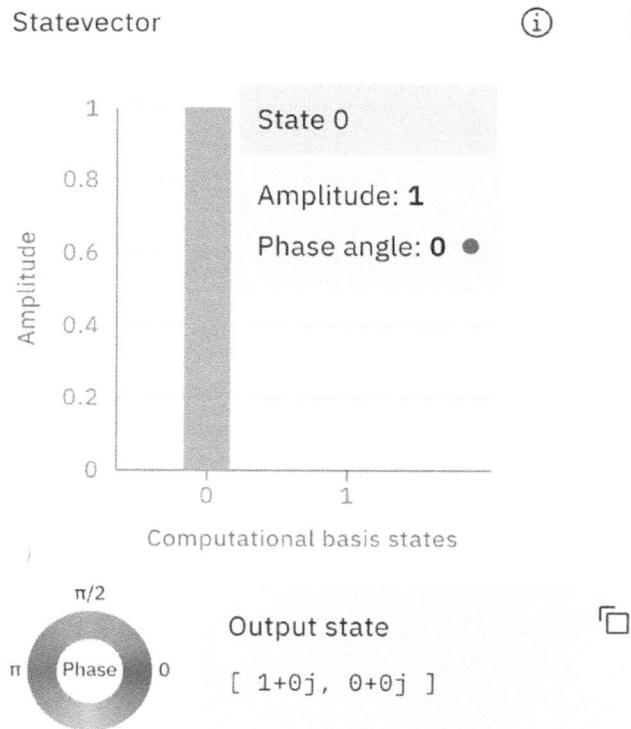

Figure 2.9: The Statevector view

First, we see the **Amplitude** bar graph, which represents the amplitude of the *computational basis states*. In this case, as mentioned earlier, for simplicity we have reduced the number of qubits to just one qubit, for which there are two computational basis states, 0 and 1. These are represented along the x axis. The value of the amplitude of each basis state is represented along the y axis. In this case, since we do not have any gates or operators on our circuit, the state vector representation is that of the initial (ground) state. The initial state indicates that all qubits are set to the 0 (zero) state, indicated by an amplitude value of 1.

At the bottom of the Statevector view we see the **Output state** representing the complex value of each computational basis state. In this case since we are in the initial state, we see the 0 state at `1 + 0j` and the 1 state at `0 + 0j`.

To the bottom left is the **phase wheel**. The phase wheel is a color visual representation of the phase for each basis state, which has a range between 0 and 2π. Since we have not applied any phase gates, we see the default phase of 0 represented by the color blue. As you apply phase shifts to each qubit, the color of the bar will update according to the color representation of the phase.

> We will cover what phases are in more detail in later chapters, but for now just know where they are and how they are indicated, both by value in the state vector results and in the phase wheel by color.

The state vector information is just one of the visual representations of your quantum circuit. There are a couple of others we want to visit before moving on.

The Probabilities view

The next view is the **Probabilities** view. This view presents the expected probability result of the quantum circuit (with the addition of a single measurement operator to the qubit). As mentioned in the previous description, and illustrated in the following screenshot, since we do not have any operators on the circuit, the results shown are all in the initial state of 0:

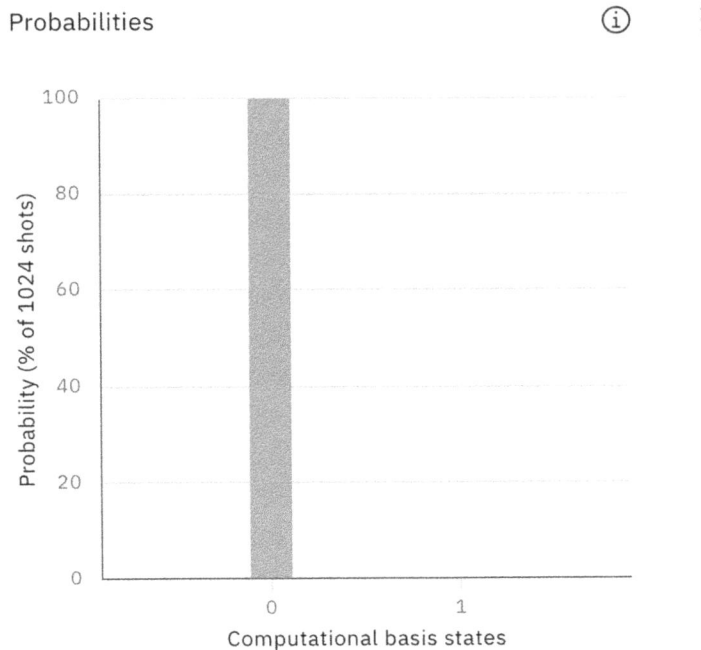

Figure 2.10: The Probabilities view

The probability view is a general representation of the results based on expected values, not the actual results you will get from a quantum system. This view currently represents what the Composer is calculating classically as we have not yet run this circuit on an actual quantum computer. The results you will see as we create this circuit are computed by the classical system and not by a quantum system. The results from a quantum system are received after we send the completed circuit to run.

The Q-sphere view

Finally, the last of the state visualizations we must review is the **Q-sphere** view. The Q-sphere looks similar to a Bloch sphere, which is used to represent the statevector of the current state of a qubit. However, the Bloch sphere does have some limitations, particularly that it can only represent the state of a single qubit. On the other hand, the Q-sphere can be used to visually represent the state information of a single qubit or multiple qubits at once in one sphere, including the phase information. The following screenshot shows a representation of a circuit with three qubits, all of which are in the initial state:

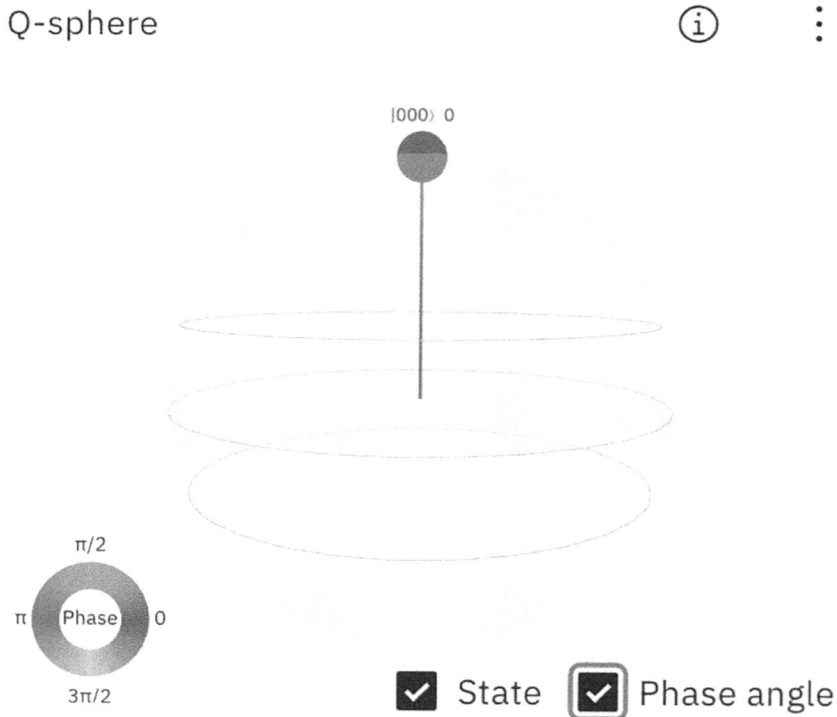

Figure 2.11: The Q-sphere view

The Q-sphere view has two components; the first is the Q-sphere itself, which represents the state vector of the multi-qubit state, represented by a vector that originates at the center of the sphere. At the end of the vector is a smaller sphere, which represents the probability of the state by the radius of the top that lies on the surface of the Q-sphere. The states represented by these small spheres are visible when hovered over. The previous screenshot illustrates the three qubits in an initial state of $|000\rangle$, with a probability of 1, and a phase angle of 0.

> Those fancy symbols around the numbers are referred to as Kets; we will learn about them later in this book. For now, just think of them as labels to differentiate between the number 0 and the quantum state $|0\rangle$, for example.

The second component is located at the bottom left, which is the legend that describes the phase of the states. Since the small sphere represents the phase angle of 0, the color of the sphere is blue, which is the same as what the legend indicates for the phase of 0. If the state had a phase value of π, then the color of the sphere would be red.

There are various options here; on the top right you can see an ellipsis that you can select, providing various options to download visualizations in different image formats, and to move the view to the left or right. At the bottom right you can select whether to enable the state or phase angle information of the Q-sphere.

OK, we went through all of the various views and components that make up the Composer view, so now let's go to the fun part and start creating our first quantum circuit!

Creating a quantum circuit with the Quantum Composer

Now that we know where everything is in the Composer, we will create our first quantum circuit. This will help you to get a better understanding of how all these components work together, and it will show you how these components provide insights such as the current state and its probabilistic estimation as you build your first quantum experiment.

Building a quantum circuit with classical bit behaviors

We are all familiar with some of the basic classic bit gates such as **NOT**, **AND**, **OR**, and **XOR**. The behavior that these classic gates perform on a bit can be reproduced on a quantum circuit using quantum gates. Our first experiment will cover these basic building blocks, which will help you to understand the correlation between quantum and classical algorithms.

Our first experiment will be to simulate a classical gate, specifically a NOT gate. The NOT gate is used to change the value of the qubit, in this case from the $|0\rangle$ state to the $|1\rangle$ state, and vice versa. We will cover details on how this gate operates on qubits in *Chapter 6, Understanding Quantum Logic Gates*.

To simulate a NOT gate on a quantum circuit, follow these steps:

1. From the open Composer editor that you previously created and titled MyFirstCircuit, reduce the number of qubits and classical bits down to just one of each if you have not already. This will simplify the visualization of the results for us. You may have to reopen the other views such as qsphere. to get the updated changes.

2. Next, click and drag the NOT gate, which is visually represented by the $\oplus$ symbol, from the list of gates down onto the first qubit, as shown in the following screenshot:

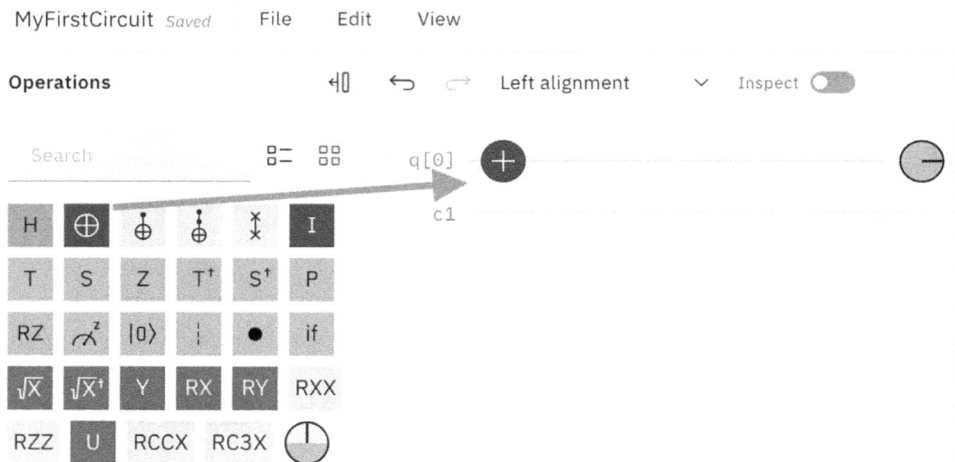

Figure 2.12: Add an X (NOT) gate to the first qubit

3. Next, click and drag the measurement operation onto the first qubit, q_0, just after the NOT gate:

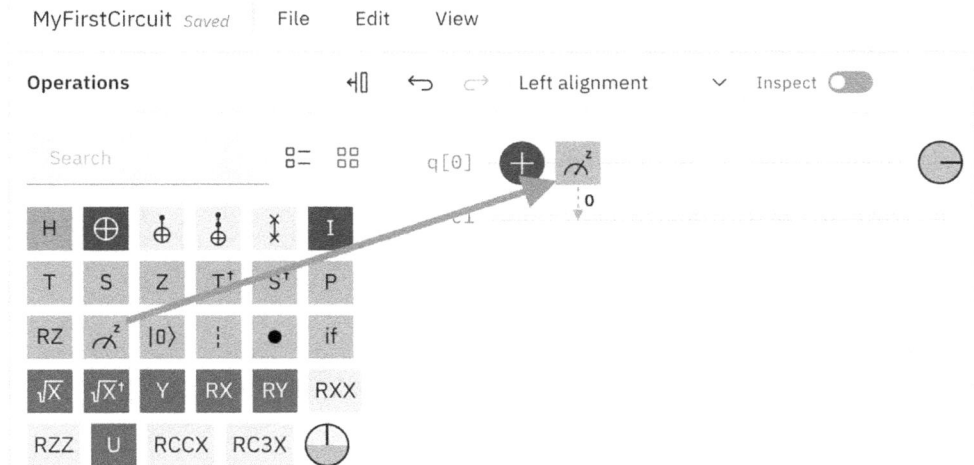

Figure 2.13: Add a measurement operator to the first qubit

4. By taking a measurement of the qubit and having its value sent out to the pertaining classic bit, we are essentially reading the state of the qubit. You can see this by the connecting arrow between the measurement operator and the classical bit. It also includes the index of the classical bit, the result of which the measurement operator will write out, which in this case is the bit in position 0.

> Note that the result bits, similar to the qubits, will be ordered from left to right: $c_2c_1c_0$, for example.

A measurement occurs when you want to observe the state of the qubit. What this means is that we will collapse the state of the qubit to either a 0 or a 1. In this example, it is straightforward that when we measure the qubit after the NOT gate, the reading will be 1. This is because since the initial state is set to 0, applying a NOT gate will flip it from 0 to 1.

Before we run this experiment, let's note a few things. First, note that the classic bits are all on one line. This is mostly to save space. Next is to note that all the views are updated as we add gates and operators. As mentioned earlier, this is the system computing these classically to provide us with an ideal result. We have not yet specified which quantum computer to run this circuit on, hence the results you are seeing are what the classical system is computing and not real-time results from a quantum computer.

1.	Select the **Setup and run** button located at the top right of the Composer view. This will display the run settings, illustrated as follows:

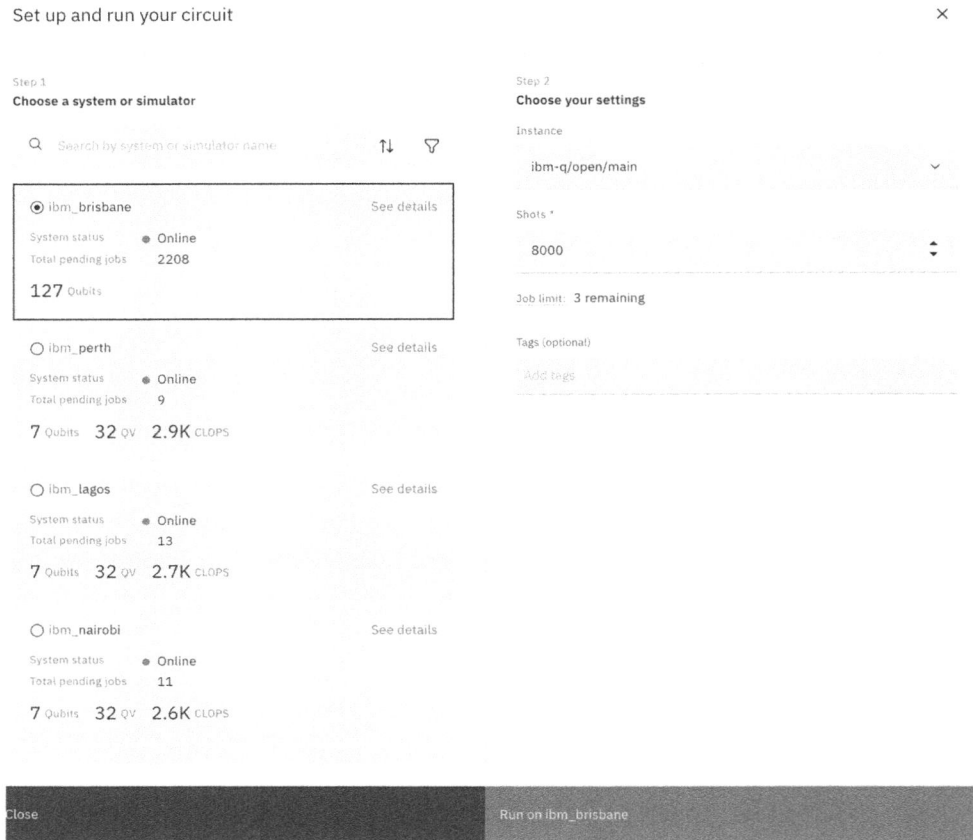

Set up and run your circuit	×

Step 1
Choose a system or simulator

Q	Search by system or simulator name	↑↓	▽

⦿ ibm_brisbane	See details

System status	● Online
Total pending jobs	2208

127 Qubits

○ ibm_perth	See details

System status	● Online
Total pending jobs	9

7 Qubits	**32** QV	**2.9K** CLOPS

○ ibm_lagos	See details

System status	● Online
Total pending jobs	13

7 Qubits	**32** QV	**2.7K** CLOPS

○ ibm_nairobi	See details

System status	● Online
Total pending jobs	11

7 Qubits	**32** QV	**2.6K** CLOPS

Step 2
Choose your settings

Instance

ibm-q/open/main	⌄

Shots *

8000	⬍

Job limit:	3 remaining

Tags (optional)

Add tags

Close	Run on ibm_brisbane

Figure 2.14: The run settings view

2.	The run dialog prompts you to take two steps:

- First, select which quantum system you would like to run the experiment on. Select any of the options you wish to run. In this example, we'll select ibm_brisbane.

- The second step first allows you to select the **Provider**. There are different providers—ibm-q/open/main is for open free quantum devices, and if you are a member of the IBM Quantum Network then you'll have a provider that assigns you to the available premium quantum devices.

For now, leave it at the default setting. This step also prompts you to select a number of **Shots** of the quantum circuit you wish to run. What this means is how many times you wish the quantum circuit to run during your experiment to obtain a reliable overall result. For now, let's set it to 8000.

3. Now that you have selected your run options, let's run the circuit. Click **Run on ibm_brisbane**. If you selected a different device, it will indicate it accordingly.

Once your experiment begins, you should see an entry of this experiment in the **Composer jobs** view in the left panel on the Composer view, indicating that your experiment is **Pending**. While the job is **Pending**, it will display the status of the job, accordingly.

> Note that depending on how busy the selected device is, you may have to wait for some time for your job to complete.

Once completed, you will see the status for the specified job as **Completed**, illustrated as follows:

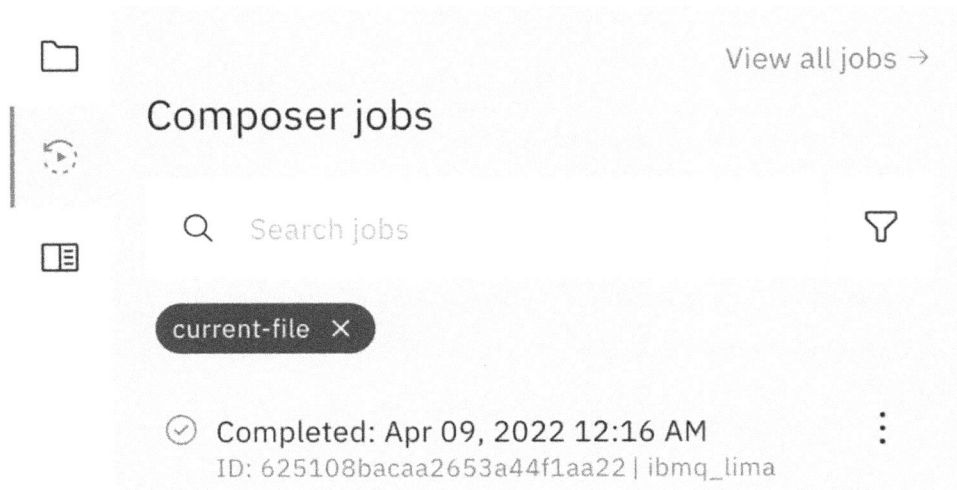

View all jobs →

Composer jobs

Q Search jobs

current-file ✕

⊘ Completed: Apr 09, 2022 12:16 AM
ID: 625108bacaa2653a44f1aa22 | ibmq_lima

Figure 2.15: The Composer jobs view displaying the job status for the selected circuit

1. Upon completion, open your experiment from the list by clicking on the job. This opens the **Jobs** results view:

Jobs /

625108bacaa2653a44f1aa22

⋮

See more details ↗

Completed
Apr 09, 2022 12:17 AM (in 30.6s)

Backend
ibmq_lima

Status timeline   ⊘ Completed ∨

Details   ∨

Result - histogram   ∨

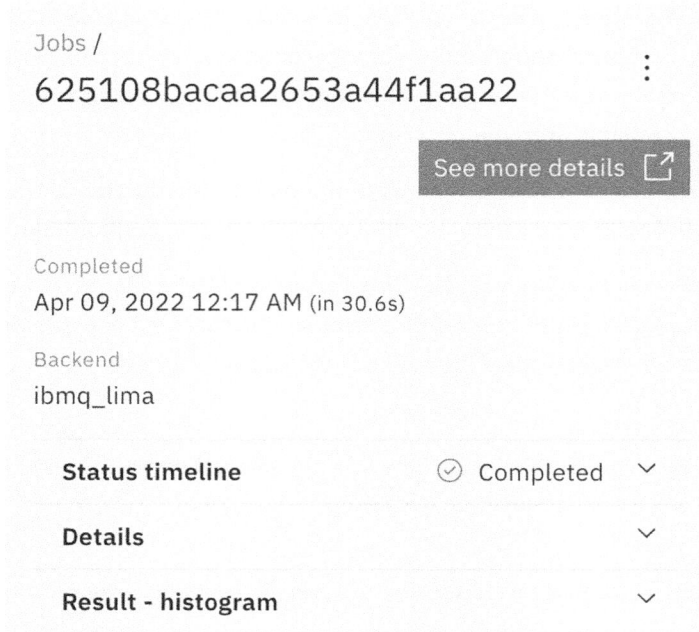

Figure 2.16: The Jobs results view

2. Once you have the job opened, you can see some basic information about the job, such as the job ID across the top, followed by the date and time the job was completed, the backend it was run on, and three views that contain details about the job itself, such as the status, details, and results. You will also see a button at the top right that will provide the same information in the views, only in a separate window. Let's review the views next.

First, we have the **Status timeline** view, as illustrated in *Figure 2.17*:

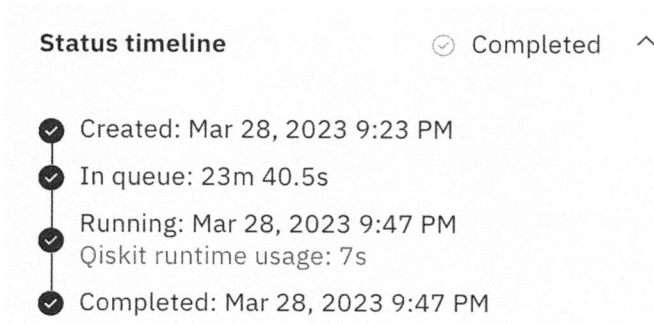

Status timeline   ⊘ Completed ∧

● Created: Mar 28, 2023 9:23 PM
● In queue: 23m 40.5s
● Running: Mar 28, 2023 9:47 PM
  Qiskit runtime usage: 7s
● Completed: Mar 28, 2023 9:47 PM

Figure 2.17: The jobs status timeline view

Here you can see the timeline that represents the time it took to complete your circuit. Each step represents the different processes that your circuit completes as it is executed on the quantum system:

Creatinged: The date and time the job instance was added to the queue to run on a specific quantum system.

In queue: The length of time your job was in the queue prior to running on the quantum system.

Running: The time it takes from moving out of the queue and running on a quantum system before returning the results back. **Time in system** is the actual time that the circuit is running on a quantum system, separate from the time it is on the classical components. For example, transforming the circuit from digital to analog and analog to digital is not included in the *time in system* value.

Completed: The date and time the job had completed running on the quantum system.

Next is the **Details** view, as seen in the following figure, which provides you with the details of the job; in this case it was sent from MyFirstCircuit. It also provides information such as the program, the number of shots, the number of circuits, and the instance. The instance is the provision of the quantum system; since we are using open free devices, this is categorized as an open system.

If you are a premium user, you will likely run in a mode specific to your provider, details of which you can obtain from your administrative provider.

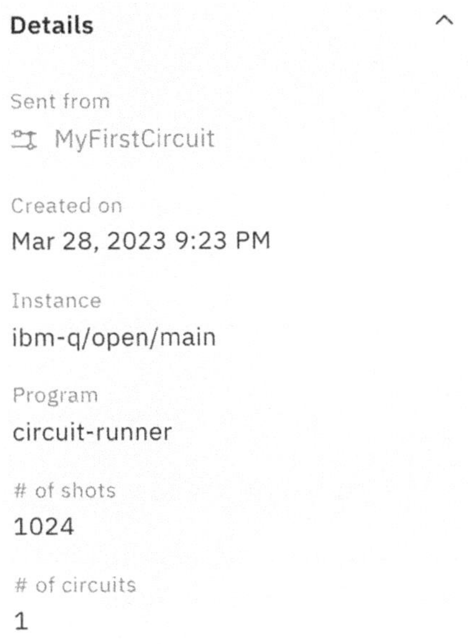

Details   ⌃

Sent from
⚏ MyFirstCircuit

Created on
Mar 28, 2023 9:23 PM

Instance
ibm-q/open/main

Program
circuit-runner

# of shots
1024

# of circuits
1

Figure 2.18: The Details view

Finally, the **Result – histogram** view, illustrated in *Figure 2.19*, shows you the results of your experiment as rendered on a histogram.

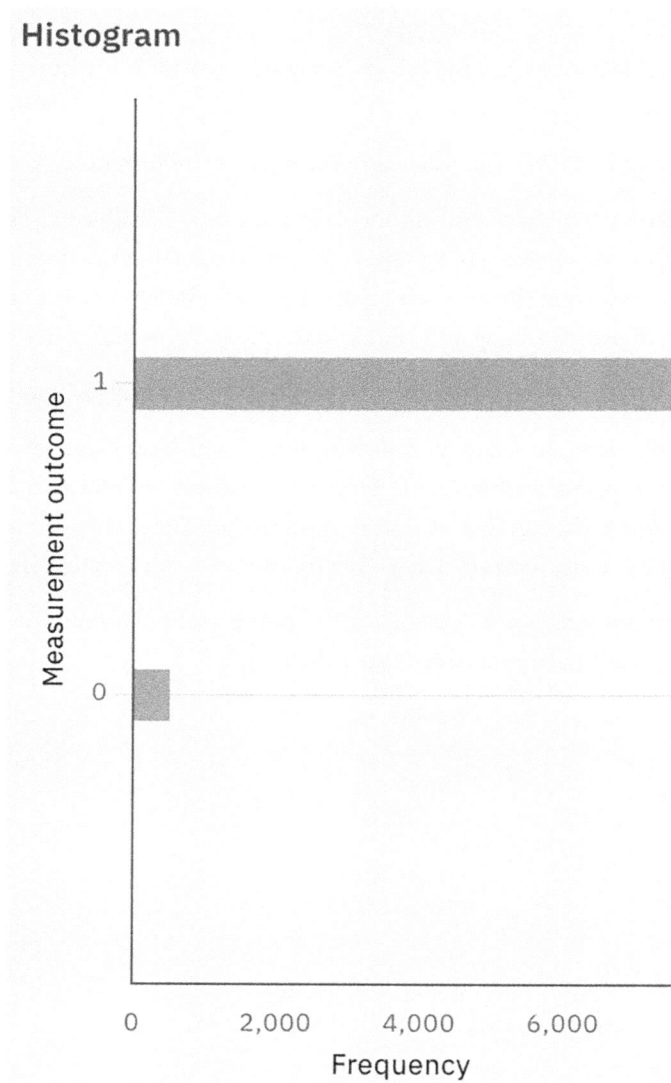

Figure 2.19: Job results – histogram view

In this view, the *x* axis represents the frequency of each state that resulted after each shot of your circuit. The *y* axis represents each state that had a result.

All these views can be seen on a separate page altogether by clicking the **See more details** button, located at the top right of the report. This will provide the same details regarding your experiment, plus it will include the transpiled circuit diagram. The transpiled diagram will show you the same circuit, only it will use the basis gates of the specified quantum system. We will cover what basis gates are and how they are transpiled into the circuit in a later chapter. For now, think of it as a circuit using gates that are specific to the quantum system, as illustrated in the following screenshot:

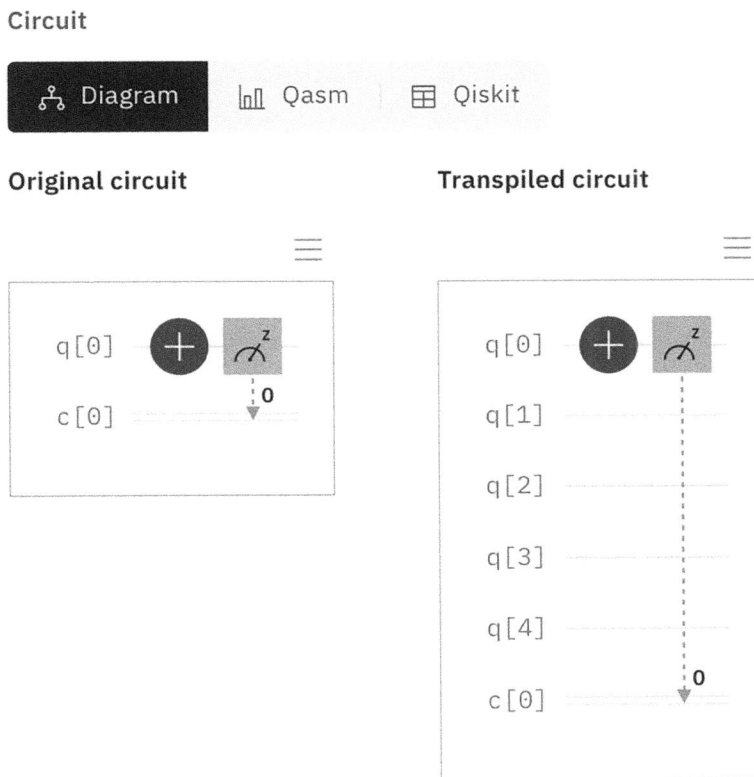

Figure 2.20: The Details view with the original circuit (left) and the transpiled circuit (right)

The diagram of the circuits is just one of the three representations of the circuit. The other two tabs will display the **Qasm** and **Qiskit** representations. Keep in mind that depending on the size of the device that you ran this on, you may see all qubits listed (which could range over 100 qubits). In this case I truncated the view so you only see a few qubits to save space.

Now that we have the results from running our first quantum circuit, let's take a closer look at our results and see what we got back.

Reviewing your results

The histogram result in *Figure 2.19* provides information about the outcome of our experiment. Some parts might seem straightforward, but let's review the details. It may seem trivial now, but later when we work on more elaborate quantum algorithms, understanding the results will prove invaluable.

There are two axes to the results. Along the y axis, we have all the possible states (or measurement outcomes) of our circuit. This is what the measurement operation observed when measuring the qubit. Recall that we measured the first qubit, so from the least significant bit (on the far right), q_0 is in the right-most position within each possible state result. Therefore, as we add more qubits, they are appended to the left of the previous qubit. For example, a three-qubit system would be set in the following order, q_2, q_{1s}, q_0. We know that our likely result of $|1\rangle$ is correct due to the fact that we placed a NOT gate on the first qubit, which changes its state from 0 to 1. If we were to add two more qubits, then the second and third qubit would simply take a measurement that equates to measuring the initial state, which we know to be 0, creating a likely result of $|001\rangle$.

The x axis provides the results for each of the possible states. Since we ran the experiment 8000 times, the results show that we a have very high chance of the first qubit resulting in the state of 1. The reason why the result is not 100% is due to noise from the quantum device. We will cover the topic of noise in later chapters, but for now we can be confident of a high probability, based on our results, that the NOT gate worked.

In this section, we simulated a simple NOT gate operation on a qubit and ran the circuit on a quantum device.

Summary

In this chapter, you learned about the IBM Quantum Composer and its many components. You created an experiment that simulated a classic NOT gate. You then viewed the results on a histogram, and read the probabilities based on the results.

This has provided you with the skills to experiment with other gates to see what effect each operation has on each qubit and what information might be determined or used based on the results of the operation. This will be helpful when we look at some of the quantum algorithms and how these operations are leveraged to solve certain problems.

In the next set of chapters, we will move away from the click-and-drag work of the UI and instead create experiments using Jupyter Notebook, as well as beginning to program quantum circuits using Python.

Questions

1. From the Composer, where would you find the time it took to run your circuit on a quantum computer?

2. How would you remove or add a qubit to your circuit on the Composer?

3. On which view would you specify which quantum system to run your circuit?

4. Which sphere would be ideal to view the quantum state of three qubits in a single sphere?

Join us on Discord

Join our community's Discord space for discussions with the author and other readers:

`https://packt.link/3FyN1`

3

Introducing and Installing Qiskit

In this chapter, you will learn about the **Quantum Information Science Kit (Qiskit)** and its advanced features to develop and implement various quantum algorithms, quantum application modules, and noise models. Qiskit (pronounced kiss-kit) is comprised of various features that help you build quantum circuits, algorithms, and applications easily, and it allows you to run them on both classical simulators and real quantum systems and visualize the results. In this chapter, you'll also see instructions on how to install Qiskit on your local machine to create quantum circuits and run them on a quantum computer.

This chapter will also discuss how to contribute to the open-source community and the development of future quantum applications, as well as how to connect to other like-minded developers and enthusiasts via the **Qiskit community**.

The following topics will be covered in this chapter:

- Understanding quantum and classical system interconnections
- Understanding Qiskit APIs
- Installing and configuring Qiskit on your local machine
- Getting support from the Qiskit community

Technical requirements

Knowledge of GitHub is recommended as we will review how to contribute to the Qiskit open-source project, which is hosted on GitHub. Having **Agile** and **open-source development** practices is also recommended, but not required. Here is the source code used throughout this book: https://github.com/PacktPublishing/Learning-Quantum-Computing-with-Python-and-IBM-Quantum-Second-Edition.

Understanding quantum and classical system interconnections

In this section, we'll review how quantum computational systems are integrated with classical systems. As quantum computers do not have ways to store the state of a qubit, there is a dependency on classical systems to provide persistent storage for information that is sent to or received from a quantum computer.

Since most data originates from classical sources, whether they are from data repositories or remote sensors, there is a need to prepare the data to be used in a quantum system. Likewise, the results from the quantum systems need to be returned not in a quantum state but in binary form so that they can be read back to a classical system for any post-processing that's required.

This hybrid or interconnectivity between classical systems and quantum systems is what we will be reviewing in this section so that you understand how both systems work together to provide you with the most optimal results. Qiskit Runtime, which is a new feature that was introduced in early 2022, has some good examples you can try. There are lots of papers that describe other forms of integrating classical and quantum resources, such as this paper, *A Serverless Cloud Integration For Quantum Computing*: `https://arxiv.org/abs/2107.02007`.

Reviewing the Qiskit library

If you worked on some of the previous chapters, then you would have noticed that we used Qiskit to create sample circuits, which we used to describe some quantum concepts. As Python developers, you would have also noticed that Qiskit is functionally no different from using any other Python libraries, such as **NumPy**, **scikit-learn**, and so on. How we use it within our Python notebooks is also the same as we would use any other package, where we can import the complete package or just a subset of classes and functions. By having the Qiskit modules available through Python, this allows us to integrate our classical algorithms and applications into a quantum system. Leveraging the libraries available in Qiskit to create quantum circuits that execute on quantum devices from a classical development environment such as Python makes integration with your existing classical applications very seamless and straightforward.

Qiskit, much like most other open-source projects, is easy to set up, both as a package with Python or as a branch or a fork if you're just acting as a contributor. It's very compact and does not require much with respect to resources to run on local machines.

Another advantage of creating it as a package for an existing platform such as Python is that there is no need to install a separate integrated development environment or set up complex build systems with confusing dependencies. For those of you who already have Python installed with the currently supported version, you can install Qiskit with a simple `pip` command:

```
pip install qiskit
```

But let's not get too ahead of ourselves. Now that we understand the purpose of Qiskit and its general functionality, we will work our way to installing Qiskit locally by first understanding how it is organized. Then, we'll cover how it interacts with your classic systems such as your laptop, server, or cloud application.

Understanding how to organize and interact with Qiskit

If you use Python for most of your development, which I assume you do, based on the title of this book, then you will understand that most packages are created in some form of hierarchy. At the top level, there are the application modules, while the lower levels refer to the components within each module.

Qiskit has components such as classes or objects, and under each of those components, you have functions and members. Qiskit is no different regarding how everything is organized from most other packages, which makes it very easy to find certain features.

At the base level you have hardware connectors; these are what connects Qiskit to the various quantum providers. In addition to hardware connectors are the classical simulators; in this book, we will be using the Qiskit Runtime service to run our circuits, which includes some locally installed Qiskit simulators. Of course, as these simulators run on classical systems, they are limited to the number of resources to simulate quantum circuits. As the quantum circuits become more complex, the cost in resources grows rather fast. This has been highlighted in various publications where certain complex quantum circuits can be simulated on classical systems; however, there are discrepancies in the accuracy across the various classical results. This is why having the hardware connectors available to run complex circuits is important, as it allows you to offload complex circuits from classical simulators to real quantum systems that run at utility scale. You might be asking yourself, *what makes a circuit complex?* Well, I can say that it does not have to do with relationship status. It's more about the width of the circuit, which correlates to the number of qubits, and the depth of the circuit, which correlates to the number of operations deep, particularly the number of multi-qubit gates that entangle two or more qubits together. We'll cover details about each of these in more detail as you progress through the book.

Above the connectors and simulators is the fundamental building block for researchers and developers, the Qiskit Runtime. We will go deeper into what the Qiskit Runtime is in later chapters, but for now just think of it as a runtime that provides you with a lot of features to create, run, and optimize your quantum circuits.

In the previous versions of Qiskit, the modules were set up such that the domain of each algorithm was spread out: by that, I mean the modules covered error correction, simulators, gate and circuit components, and applications. In this case, an algorithm developer would have to learn how to incorporate multiple modules together, therefore causing the developer to have to understand the various components and modules at the base level to incorporate them into their application. This has since changed after the introduction of the latest code changes to Qiskit.

First, we need to introduce the three development layers or segments, which allow developers to provide modules to each other to help create quantum applications. Having these three layers, which are not that much different from classical application development, allows classical developers to solely focus on their own layer, which eliminates the need to fully understand what is occurring at another layer. Let's take a quick look at the three development layers.

- A **kernel** developer is one who develops code at the lowest level of the three layers. They work mostly on creating quantum circuits, the composition of gates, hardware pulse level controls, and other features that are close to the hardware. Qiskit Terra is the module that the kernel developer would work with, which includes the circuit library that allows them to create new or use existing circuits.

- An **algorithm** developer is one who leverages the circuits created by the kernel developer to create quantum algorithms. These algorithms can provide ways to encode classical data into a quantum state. For example, the information of a pixel can be represented as a quantum state where the qubits would represent the location and color value of each pixel of an image. They can also create a quantum algorithm that would not need to encode any classical data at all. The algorithm developer could also include some of the latest Qiskit features that provide infrastructure optimizations, such as the Qiskit Runtime, so that the integration of classical and quantum systems is robust.

- A **model** developer is one who applies algorithms to create applications that solve real-world problems. These model developers can be domain or industry experts that understand the problems that may be intractable for classical systems and determine how to apply quantum algorithms to these problems. By creating models for certain problems, the model developer could provide a quantum application that could, for example, integrate as part of a large workflow or as a service provider, which classical applications could call upon as needed.

These three layers working together allow the developer to focus solely within their layer to develop components that could provide the others with the tools they need to enhance their applications. This also facilitates collaboration between each of the developers, as they can provide feedback to each other to further optimize their components.

The following diagram illustrates the layers and what Qiskit libraries or components would generally apply to each developer type.

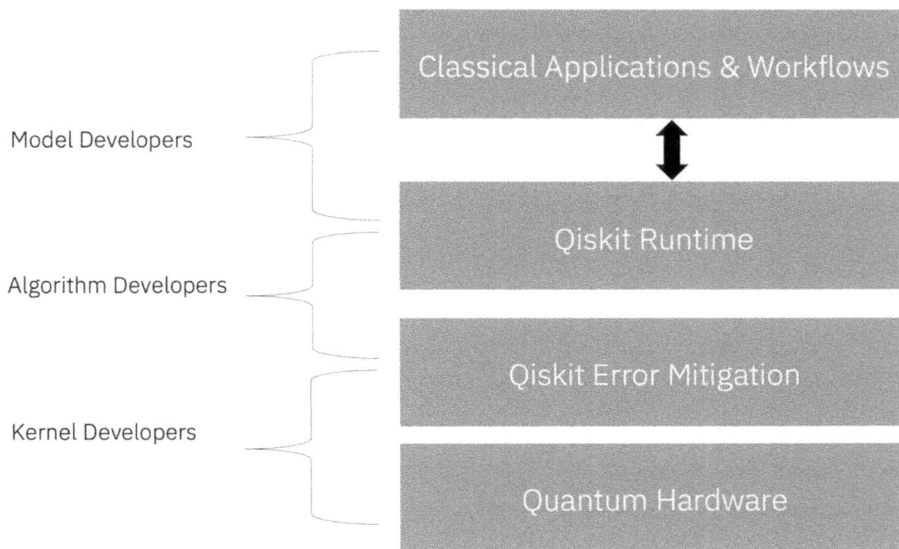

Figure 3.1: Kernel, Algorithm, and Model developer layers

Of course, the preceding information is based on the current version of Qiskit. In the future, like many projects, this may change. I highly recommend keeping up to date with the current **Application Programming Interface (API)** documentation to ensure that you are using the proper calls when writing your code. The API for this can be found on the Qiskit documentation page at `https://www.qiskit.org/documentation/`.

The documentation page provides the latest information on the four available modules, often referred to as elements due to their names, as explained at the beginning of this chapter.

So far, we have defined the three different development layers that help simplify developers jumping into programming quantum applications without too much of a learning curve. For example, a model developer might only need to understand how the quantum algorithms work to create a model for a classical application rather than having to also learn which gates the circuits used to create the algorithm.

The following section will describe the API references so that you understand how to leverage them in your code. The development specifics will be covered in future chapters, where we will talk about the functionality and operations that each can provide.

Understanding Qiskit APIs

Qiskit was built for anyone who wants to work with quantum computers at every level and domain. By this, we mean that if a quantum researcher wanted to work on how the pulses are scheduled on a quantum device, they could do so very easily. The same can be said about users who simply want to extend their applications to leverage a quantum computer to compute information.

In this section, we will learn about the various APIs that are available in Qiskit today. As mentioned earlier, Qiskit has various layers that can be leveraged by any domain expert to start using quantum computing in their applications.

Let's take, for example, chemistry researchers who wish to compute the energy state of two molecules but don't want to go through the hassle of learning about quantum gates and pulses. They just want to load their dataset, classically, to a quantum algorithm and obtain the results transparently. Qiskit was built as a full stack open-source software package to facilitate those and many more user-type scenarios using the application modules.

Quantum physicists can experiment at the hardware level by researching ways to schedule pulses to single and multi-qubits. Quantum researchers can work on developing quantum circuits that could minimize noise, which would optimize the results of your quantum circuits.

Algorithm researchers and developers usually work on creating quantum algorithms that can be used by various domains and industries either to solve problems faster or provide more accurate results.

Finally, domain researchers such as chemists, data scientists, economists, and many others can integrate their classic applications into a quantum system to compute complex problems more optimally or accurately using various features such as the Qiskit Runtime.

Qiskit, at the time of writing, has released its latest version, Qiskit 1.0. This new version provides you with a lot of great features that will take your development skills to the next level. Most particularly to the new era of quantum utility!

Let's start off by learning about the built-in simulators that are available in Qiskit. The simulators are great for getting started, but as your development skills and understanding of quantum increase, so to will your need to run more complex circuits where classical simulators, such as those described herein, could have some limitations.

Aer

Before getting into what Aer is, let's first make sure we install it, as Aer has moved to its own separate component and as it makes sense to run some simulations when starting, do install it onto your system as it is now a requirement if you plan to run local simulations on your classical system. Simply run `pip install qiskit-aer` from your command line, or Python environment, and that should be all you need. Aer provides a framework that can be used to develop debugging tools and create noise models. These tools help replicate a lot of the characteristics of a quantum system by simulating the noise that affects not just the qubit but also the environment and computations. There are generally five highly efficient compiled *simulator categories* available in Aer; they are:

- **AerProvider**, the main class that contains all the simulators
- **QasmSimulator**, a quantum simulator that allows for simulation methods and options
- **StatevectorSimulator**, an ideal quantum state vector simulator used to produce non-noisy results from your circuit
- **UnitarySimulator**, an ideal quantum unitary simulator
- **Pulse**, a simulator used to generate and schedule pulse operations

> Note, there is discussion over whether **Pulse** will be removed in the near future. It's included here for the sake of completeness, but it may not always be available. For that reason, we will not explore Pulse further in this chapter.

We will look at the differences between each simulator category in the upcoming sections and in *Chapter 9, Simulating Quantum Systems and Noise Models*, you will learn more about the specific simulators within each category, including those within Aer itself.

The Aer simulator

Aer itself is also a category that contains a list of its own types of simulators that are specific to obtaining specific information about the quantum circuit, such as the density matrix, matrix product state, and multiple stabilizer simulators. This simulator is the main simulator to reproduce how an actual backend system can behave and includes an `options` object, which can be used to provide parameters such as density matrices to reproduce noise typically found in a quantum system.

The Qasm simulator

The **Qasm** simulator allows us to run our circuits in both clean and noisy simulated environments. The difference between the two is the amount of noise that you wish to apply to the simulator. On the one hand, it could run as an error-free ideal system that you can use to confirm the computational results of your circuit. On the other hand, you could run your circuit through a simulator that includes noise models so that you can replicate the noise and understand how it affects your computations. We will learn more about noise and noise models in *Chapter 10, Understanding and Mitigating Quantum Noise*.

The Qasm simulator also has multi-functional capabilities and methods to simulate circuits, such as statevector, density_matrix, stabilizer, matrix_product_state, and many more. By allowing you the flexibility to configure the Qasm simulator using any of these methods, you can expect an ideal outcome from the measured circuits, along with any models that you wish to incorporate.

The Qasm simulator also provides a list of backend options you can use to execute your quantum circuit. These options include setting threshold values to truncate results or setting floating-point precision values and maximum value constraints for executing circuits. These features make Aer the ideal component for those who wish to develop an ideal or replicated noisy system. Typically, Aer is used by researchers who wish to develop noise mitigation or error correction techniques.

Statevector simulator

The **Statevector** simulator is, as its name suggests, a state vector simulator that provides the final state vector of the circuit without the measurement operation at the end.

Results from the Statevector simulator can be visualized by leveraging the various visualization tools of quantum states, such as **histograms** and **cityscape**. The **cityscape** option provides a nice 3D view of both the real and imaginary components of the density matrix (ρ). Other visualization plots include **Hinton** diagrams, **Pauli vector** plots, and **Bloch spheres**, to name a few. Some of these, such as the Bloch sphere and the qsphere and other visualization tools will be covered in future chapters, as they will help you visualize some of the effects that gates have on qubits.

The Unitary simulator

The **Unitary** simulator is quite simply just that — it provides the unitary matrix result of your circuit by computing the overall matrix of the circuit. The idea is that a circuit with only unitary operators/gates each operating on a subset of the qubits can be expressed as a single unitary operator. This can be accomplished by multiplying all the operator matrices in the circuit to arrive at a single overall matrix/operator.

This is very helpful if you want to confirm that the operations you applied to the qubits match your expected calculations.

You can imagine how helpful this will be when you start to work on multiple qubits with many operators. The Unitary simulator helps provide state information so that you can ensure that the results are what you expected.

Installing and configuring Qiskit on your local machine

In this section, we will walk you through the installation process of Qiskit. It is important to note that to complete the examples in this book, you will need to install Qiskit on your machine locally, as the IBM Quantum Platform no longer has a lab, nor does it have any simulators to run circuits on the cloud, only the actual quantum systems, which you will have limited access. The installation will include installing Anaconda, which is the tool used by many Qiskit developers to install Python, Jupyter Notebooks, Qiskit, and many other data science packages. It also serves as a simple way to manage packages and how they are installed on your local machine. In our case, it will help by installing the prepackaged dependencies we will need, such as Python, Jupyter Notebooks, `pip`, and many others.

Once installed, you can create an environment specific to quantum development with all the dependencies and features already installed. By having a local installation, you can run your circuits from the local system onto simulators on your local device.

Preparing the installation

Qiskit is an open-source project that is available for free to everyone. It is licensed under the **Apache 2.0** license (`https://apache.org/licenses/LICENSE-2.0`). A copy has also been included in each Qiskit module (for example, `https://www.github.com/Qiskit/qiskit/blob/master/LICENSE.txt`). This allows you to use the source code, along with all its rights and privileges, as defined in the license.

The installation of Qiskit is quite simple, particularly if you are already familiar with the package management application known as **pip**. To review the Qiskit metadata package information, such as its current stable version, build status, and other details, go to `https://pypi.org/project/qiskit`.

We have highlighted that you should install the full version as there have been issues with the mini version. You can, of course, try either, but if you get issues with the mini version, it is recommended that you install the full version.

Installing Anaconda

Anaconda (`https://www.anaconda.com/distribution`) is an open-source cross-platform distribution of Python. It allows the user to create separate environments so that they can install multiple versions of Python. This is very useful, particularly for those of you who are Python developers and already have a version of Python installed on your machine.

By creating a separate environment using Anaconda, you can eliminate issues that may come up due to installing a different version of Python that may affect your existing Python projects or applications. Having separate environments also provides you with the ability to have multiple versions of Qiskit. You need to have a working version of Qiskit up and running while you install an update on a separate environment so that you can test if your quantum applications currently support the latest releases without worrying about dependency issues.

It is recommended to follow the installation instructions on the Anaconda site. The installation steps of Anaconda also include versions of Jupyter Notebook, which comes in handy, as the Qiskit notebooks will not be available locally. However, since the Qiskit notebooks are built on Jupyter Notebooks, you shouldn't expect to see much of a difference between the two.

After installing Anaconda with the supported version of Python – at the time of this writing, the currently supported version is 3.9 – be sure to create an environment in your installation and switch to that environment before proceeding and installing Qiskit. Otherwise, it will install on your base environment. After successfully completing the installation and creating your Anaconda environment, you are now ready to install Qiskit!

Installing Qiskit

Before installing Qiskit, be sure to check the installation page (`https://docs.quantum.ibm.com/start/install`) for any updates on either the installation or configuration steps, as things might change. The following steps will lead you through the installation process:

1. We'll begin by ensuring that you are in the environment you created. The best way to determine this is to launch your command line and enter the following:

```
conda info --envs
```

The preceding code will list all the environments on your system. You will see one titled base and another with the name of the environment that you created. The current environment is identified by an asterisk, as illustrated in the following screenshot:

```
# conda environments:
#
base                      *  /Users/█████████████████/opt/anaconda3
```

Figure 3.2: Output of the current environment command

As shown in the preceding screenshot, another way to identify the environment is to look at the far left of the command line before the machine name. There, in parentheses, is the current environment. In the preceding screenshot, I created an environment called QiskitEnv. Now, let's activate the environment by running the following in the command line so we can enable it and start the installation process:

```
conda activate QiskitEnv
```

This will now activate the environment on your machine.

For details, I recommend reviewing the documentation on getting started with conda here: https://docs.conda.io/projects/conda/en/latest/user-guide/getting-started.html.

2. Once you are in the Qiskit environment after activating it in the previous step, you can now run the pip command to install Qiskit:

```
>pip install qiskit
```

Based on your machine and network speed, this may take a few moments.

3. Once completed, you can verify the installation by entering the following on the command line:

```
>pip list | grep qiskit
```

This will list the installed Qiskit packages and their respective versions, which you should see includes all the various Qiskit libraries. To see the most current list of optional packages, just visit the Qiskit metadata package information page at https://pypi.org/project/qiskit.

With that, you have installed and verified that Qiskit is installed on your local device. Now, you can launch a Jupyter Notebook and start using Qiskit!

Wait! Not so fast. There are just a couple of steps we should cover before we start coding and running circuits. We want to make sure your local machine is configured. The first thing you need to ensure is that you have your **token ID** saved on your local device. This way, when you are ready to run an experiment on a real device or on the simulator on the cloud, you can do so very easily.

Configuring your local Qiskit environment

Next, we'll need to install some new features to leverage the latest building blocks and visualization packages. The IBM Runtime package and optional visualization package will allow you to run circuits efficiently on a quantum system and visualize the results from your circuit, respectively. Subsequent steps include saving your account information onto your local machine, which will be used to connect and use the IBM Quantum systems.

The steps needed to get yourselves up and running are as follows. Note for **Mac** users that the strings in the brackets, in this case, visualization, need to be wrapped with single quotes (i.e., 'visualization') – otherwise, you will get an error:

1. Open your terminal and run each of the following:

    ```
    pip install qiskit-ibm-runtime
    pip install qiskit[visualization]
    ```

    Once the installations have been completed, you can move on to the next step, which is to set up your account information on your local machine by copying your account API token.

2. There are two places where you can obtain your API token; the first is from your dashboard on the IBM Quantum Platform page (https://quantum.ibm.com), as illustrated in the following figure:

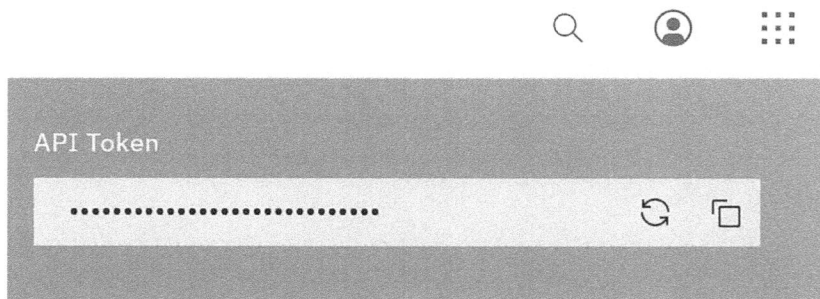

Figure 3.3: API token on the dashboard

3. The second way to obtain your API token is via the **Manage account** page. To get to your account page, just click on your avatar at the top right of the page and select **Manage account** from the drop-down list, as illustrated in the following screenshot:

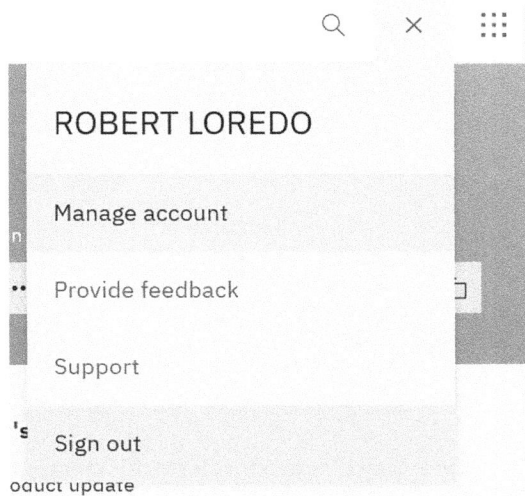

ROBERT LOREDO

Manage account

Provide feedback

Support

Sign out

Figure 3.4: API token on the Manage account page

4. After the account page opens, click the **Copy token** icon located to the right of the **API token** field, as highlighted in the following screenshot:

API token

You can also use the following API token to access IBM Quantum services from your local environment with Qiskit. Click here for instructions.

API token ⓘ

***********   Generate new token

Figure 3.5: Copy your account API token

Now that you have copied your **API token**, let's save it on your local machine.

5. Launch **Jupyter Notebook** by entering the following on the command line:

```
jupyter notebook
```

6. As we are launching this locally, we do not have the launcher here to create a new notebook, so we will have to create one ourselves. Let's do that now by clicking **New | Python 3** at the top right of Jupyter Notebook, as illustrated in the following figure:

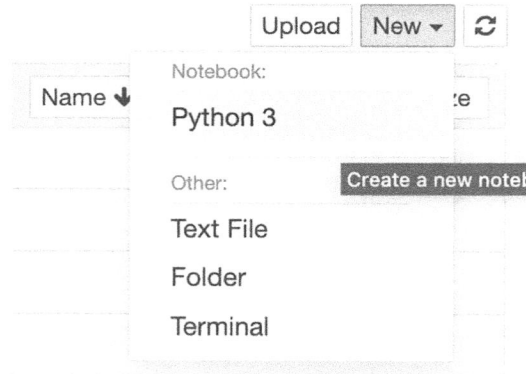

Figure 3.6: Creating a new Python 3 notebook

This will create a new Python 3 notebook. Note this created a blank notebook, so we also do not have the nice boilerplate cell that imported a lot of the commonly used classes and functions. We will have to either import them, as we need them, or you can just copy/paste in the boilerplate code from a previously created notebook that contains the boilerplate cell. In the following, we will just add the classes and functions as needed.

7. Once it has launched, enter the following into the first cell. You will also want to do this on the "setup_save_account.ipynb" file that is included in the code samples you have access to. This file will be imported and used in the early chapters for convenience, so please be sure you update the API token information there as well; otherwise, you will see errors when running the sample code:

```
from qiskit_ibm_runtime import QiskitRuntimeService

# Save your IBM Quantum account to allow you to use systems:
QiskitRuntimeService.save_account(channel="ibm_quantum",
token='PASTE-API-TOKEN-HERE', set_as_default=True)
```

Be sure to include the single quotes (' ') around your API token in the argument; otherwise, you may get an error.

Now that we have saved our API token locally, we won't have to save it to our local system again unless we delete or change the API token value. Remember to copy your token, as indicated in the preceding command.

> **Important note**
>
> Note that you only run this command once. If by chance, you forget and rerun the above function again, you may get a warning. You can find other account setting commands here in the Qiskit API documentation: `https://docs.quantum-computing.ibm.com/start/setup-channel#select-and-set-up-an-ibm-quantum-channel`.

Congratulations! You have successfully configured your local version of Qiskit!

You are now ready to run circuits locally on your system. Creating and executing circuits can now be done locally on a simulator for those times when you are unable to obtain network access. Of course, once you are back online, you can use your local version to execute circuits on real devices. This also allows you the freedom to integrate with your own applications or systems with ease. By having the ability to run your code locally, you can integrate new code into your own local applications easily.

In this section, you learned how to install Anaconda, which includes a lot of the dependencies necessary to install Qiskit; how to create a quantum circuit; how to execute the circuit on a simulator; and how to execute the circuit on a quantum computer. Now, we'll learn how to contribute, collaborate, and get support from the Qiskit global community.

Getting support from the Qiskit community

The Qiskit community is a global group of developers, researchers, and pretty much anyone who is curious about quantum computing that comes together, collaborates, and supports each other to help build knowledge across all community members. It is also used to keep everyone up to speed on the latest in quantum research, education, events, and updates: `https://www.ibm.com/quantum/events`. A recent add-on is the ability to get certified as a Qiskit developer via the **Qiskit Developer Certification** exam. There is currently an updated course based on the Qiskit 1.x version coming out in late 2024.

In this section, you will learn about the community, its many programs, and how you can contribute and become a **Qiskit advocate** (`https://www.ibm.com/quantum/community#advocates`). Qiskit advocates are members of the Qiskit community who have passed a rigorous exam, have made many contributions to the Qiskit community, and have helped many others along the way. Let's start by introducing you to the community itself.

Introducing the Qiskit community

Ever since Qiskit was first deployed as an open-source project, the open-source community has contributed so many features and enhancements that it has only improved over time. The development ecosystem itself has flourished so much that it is being used in universities, industry, and governments around the world, even in Antarctica!

Members of the Qiskit community, often referred to as **Qiskitters**, often work together as a solid diverse group to ensure everyone is supported. Whether they are newbies to quantum computing or veteran quantum researchers, they all share a passion for collaborating and connecting on various projects. The link to information on Qiskit and the community can be found at `https://www.ibm.com/quantum/qiskit`, where you will find various links at the top and bottom of the page to tutorials and where to join the Qiskit community and be a part of the largest quantum ecosystem in the world.

One of the early projects was to create resources for those new to quantum computing. These resources vary from generating enablement materials to **YouTube** video series. The topics included both hardware and software that described what happened on the backend and software that described new research that others were working on. Along with the resources, there are also events that are planned all over the world at any given time. This includes events such as workshops, where communities join either in person or virtually to learn the latest in quantum computing.

Other events also include **hackathons** and code camps, of which the largest is **Qiskit Camp**, which the IBM Quantum team hosts quarterly in different continents around the world. The 3-to-4-day camp usually includes accommodation in very exotic locations, meals, transportation to and from airports, and so on. Researchers from **IBM Research** also participate as lecturers, coaches, and judges. Teams are created and brainstorm ideas for projects that they work together on during the weekend, where they would compete and win prizes. This is very similar to hackathons.

Recently, the Qiskit community initiated the **Qiskit advocate program**. This program was created to provide support to individuals who have actively been involved with the Qiskit community and have contributed over time. To become a Qiskit advocate, you will need to apply online (`https://www.ibm.com/quantum/community#advocates`), where you will be given an exam to test your knowledge of Qiskit and specify at least three community contributions. These qualifications, of course, can change over time, so it is recommended that you check the site for any updates and application deadlines.

Once accepted into the Qiskit advocate program, you will have the opportunity to network with other experts and access core members of the Qiskit development team. You will also gain support and recognition from IBM through the Qiskit community, as well as receive invitations to special events such as Qiskit Summer School, seminars, and other major events where you can not only collaborate with others but also lead or mentor as well.

Contributing to the Qiskit community

Support across members is key, not just for Qiskit advocates but for all members. The Qiskit community has set up various channels to offer support to all the members of the community. They have a **Slack workspace** (`https://qisk.it/join-slack`) that is very active and has various channels so that members can ask questions, post event updates, or just chat about the latest quantum research that had been recently published. There are also other collaborative sources that Qiskit connects through. The current list of collaboration tools can be found on the main quantum community page: `https://www.ibm.com/quantum/community`.

Specializing your skill set in the Qiskit community

One of the most common questions asked about contributing to the Qiskit community, particularly those who are interested in becoming Qiskit advocates, is, *what are the various ways you can contribute?* There are many ways in which you can contribute to the Qiskit community. Ideally, you want to become familiar with the different forms of contributions, such as the following:

- **Code contributions**: Adding a new feature, optimizing the performance of a function, and bug fixes are some of the good ways to start if you are a developer. If you are new to coding, there is a label that the Qiskit development team has created for this called **good first issue**. This is an umbrella term for the issues that are ideal for those who are new to the code base.

- **Host a Qiskit event in your area or virtually**: You can host an event and invite a Qiskit advocate to run a workshop or talk to a group about the latest updates in Qiskit.

- **Help others**: You can help others by answering questions asked by other community members, reporting bugs, identifying features that may enhance the development of circuits, and so on.

Specializing in an area such as noise mitigation, error correction, or algorithm design is an advantage to the community. The **Qiskit Slack community** has several channels that focus on specific areas of quantum computing: quantum systems, the IBM Quantum Platform, Qiskit Runtime, quantum algorithms and applications, Qiskit on Raspberry Pi, and many more. If you specialize in any of these areas, you can join the Slack group and collaborate on many technologies and topics.

In this section, you learned about the open-source contribution process and how to find tasks for both beginners and experts so that everyone can contribute.

Summary

In this chapter, you learned about the general features and capabilities provided by Qiskit so that you can create highly efficient quantum algorithms. You then learned how to install Qiskit locally, as well as how to contribute and find support from the Qiskit community.

We've learned more about Qiskit and how it fits on the development stack, and we covered an overview of the application modules and simulators provided in the Qiskit libraries. This provided you with the general skills and functionality to create circuits, which you can then use to apply various operations to the qubits via gates and operators.

Then, we learned about Aer, which allows us to create better simulators and how to execute them locally and on the IBM Quantum platform.

You learned details on how you can install your own version of Qiskit on your platform using Anaconda. Finally, we learned about the Qiskit community and its advantages to all, particularly those who are new to quantum computing and need a little support to understand some of the challenging content or find someone to collaborate with and expand their horizons.

With that, you now have the skills to install and configure Qiskit on your local machine to create and execute quantum circuits in offline mode.

In the next chapter, we will start delving into understanding the fundamental basics of quantum computing so we can learn how to create and execute quantum circuits.

Questions

1. In your own words, describe the difference between a kernel developer and an application developer.

2. If you wanted to obtain the unitary matrix of a circuit, which simulator would provide the unitary matrix result?

3. Can you name and describe in your own words each of the five simulator categories that are provided by Aer?

4. Which module would you need to import to plot a histogram?

Join us on Discord

Join our community's Discord space for discussions with the author and other readers:

https://packt.link/3FyN1

4

Understanding Basic Quantum Computing Principles

Quantum computing, particularly its algorithms, leverages three quantum computing principles, namely, **superposition**, **entanglement**, and **interference**. In this chapter, we'll review each of these so that we can understand what each provides, the effect it has on each qubit, and how to represent them using the quantum gate sets provided to us. The quantum computers hosted on the **IBM Quantum Platform** leverage all these principles using the various quantum gates, some of which you used earlier in this book.

The following topics will be covered in this chapter:

- Introducing quantum computing
- Understanding superposition
- Understanding entanglement
- Understanding interference
- Exploring the Bell states

Technical requirements

In this chapter, some general knowledge of physics is recommended; however, my goal is for the explanations to help you understand the quantum principles without the need for you to register for a physics course. Here is the full source code used throughout this book: https://github. com/PacktPublishing/Learn-Quantum-Computing-with-Python-and-IBM-Quantum-Experience.

Introducing quantum computing

Quantum computing isn't a subject that is as common as learning algebra or reading some of the literary classics. However, for most scientists and engineers or people in any other field that includes studying physics, quantum computing is part of the curriculum. Those of us who don't quite recall our studies in physics, or have never studied it, need not worry, as this section aims to provide you with information that will either refresh your recollection of the topic or at least, perhaps, help you understand what each of the principles used in quantum computing means. Let's start with a general definition of quantum mechanics.

Quantum mechanics, as defined by most texts, is the study of nature at its smallest scale—in this case, the subatomic scale. The study of quantum mechanics is not new. Its growth began in the early 1900s thanks to the efforts of many physicists, whose names still chime in many of the current theories and experiments. The names of such physicists include Erwin Schrödinger, Max Planck, Werner Heisenberg, Max Born, Paul Dirac, and Albert Einstein, among others. As the years passed, many other scientists expanded on the foundations of quantum mechanics and began performing experiments that challenged many of the classical theories, theories such as the photoelectric effect as well as more modern approaches such as the wave function, which is used to provide various physical properties of a particle.

One of the more popular experiments that have come out of quantum mechanics is the **double-slit experiment**. Although this is found in classical mechanics, it is referenced in quantum computing to describe the behavior of a **quantum bit** (**qubit**). It is in this experiment that researchers were able to demonstrate that light (or photons) can be characterized as both waves and particles.

Many distinct experiments have been conducted over the years that illustrate this phenomenon, one of which was to fire photon particles through a double slit one at a time, where at the other side of the double slit, there was a screen that captured, as a point, the location where each particle would hit. When only one slit was open, all the particles would appear as a stack of points directly behind the slit, as shown in the following diagram:

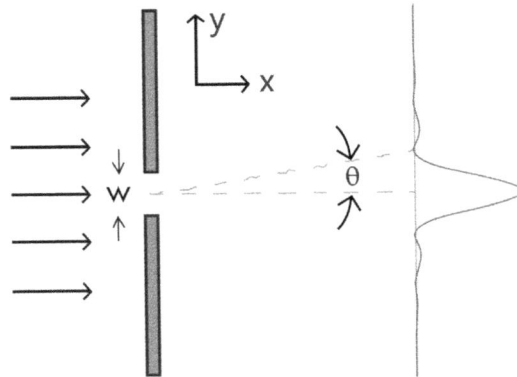

Figure 4.1: Single-slit experiment (image source: https://commons.wikimedia.org/wiki/File:S-ingleSlitDiffraction.GIF)

From the previous diagram, you can see that all the particles are captured in an area directly across the slit. Here, the angle theta θ indicates the angle from the center of the slit (pattern) to the first minimum intensity.

However, when the second slit was open, it was imagined that there would be an identical stack of points on the screen, therefore two stacks. But this was not the case, as what was captured appeared to be a formation altogether different than what would be expected from a particle. In fact, it had the characteristics of a wave in that the points on the screen seemed to display a diffraction pattern, as shown in the following diagram:

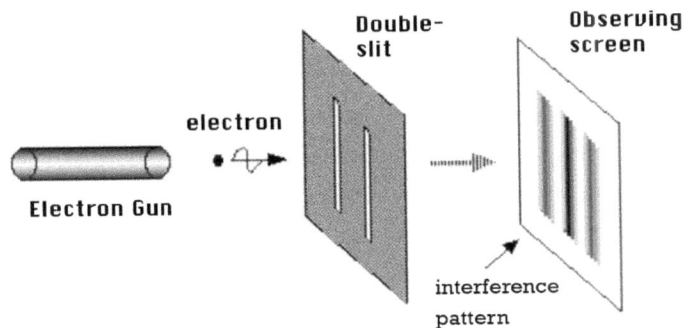

Figure 4.2: Double-slit experiment (image source: https://commons.wikimedia.org/wiki/File:Double-slit.PNG)

From the previous diagram, you can see that all the particles are spread out from the center with interference gaps.

This diffraction pattern is caused by the interference of the light waves passing through the slits. Here, there are more points at the center of the screen than there are toward the outer ends of the observing screen. This interference of individual particles is the basis for what is now known as **wave-particle duality**, which generally infers that photons of light can behave like both a wave and a particle. This property is used in quantum computing, particularly in algorithms such as Grover's and Shor's algorithms.

> This wave-particle phenomenon gave birth to lots of interesting research and development such as the **Copenhagen interpretation**, the **many-worlds interpretation**, and the **De Broglie-Bohm** theory.

What this illustrates is that the light appeared as bands of light in certain areas of the board with some probability. By observing the preceding diagram, you can see that there is a higher probability that the electron fired from the gun will land in the center band of the screen as opposed to the outer bands as illustrated by the darker shades of gray. Also, note that due to interference, the spaces in between the bands that capture the electrons have less probability (blank areas between bands).

It is these effects of wave interference and probabilities that we will cover in this chapter, but first, we will start with the electron itself to understand superposition.

Understanding superposition

Superposition is something we generally can't see with the naked eye. It's defined as a combination of two similar yet distinct phenomena occurring at once: for example, being able to whistle and hum at the same time. Both are the same in that they are audible waves but distinct in how they sound. You can whistle without humming, and vice versa; however, doing them both at the same time is placing them in a superposition as you are creating a combination of both distinct sounds at the same time.

In quantum mechanics, we are typically discussing the superposition of an electron. Since an electron is very small and there are so many of them, it is hard to distinguish one with even a powerful microscope. It is commonly referred to as an elementary particle. There are, however, some analogies in the classical world that we can use to illustrate what superposition is. For example, a spinning coin is what most texts use to describe superposition.

While it is spinning, we can say that it is in the state of both heads and tails. It isn't until the coin collapses that we see what the final state of the coin is. This explains superposition from a probability perspective; however, the formal definition is commonly found in any classical physics book when describing the spin of an electron. I will leave this for you to search for as there are lots of references and resources available online that go into detail.

In this chapter, we're going to use this spinning coin analogy just to help you understand the general principle of superposition. However, once we start working on our quantum circuits, you will see some of the differences between superposition and its probabilistic behavior in the classical world versus its behavior in the quantum world.

Let's start by reviewing the random effects we saw in the slit experiments in the classical world.

Learning about classical randomness

Previously, we discussed the randomness of a spinning coin as an example. However, the spinning coin and its results are not as random as we think. Just because we cannot guess the correct answer when a coin is spun on a table or flipped in the air does not make it random. What leads us to believe that it's random is the fact that we don't have all the information necessary to know or predict or, in fact, determine that the coin will land on either heads or tails.

All the relevant information, such as the weight of the coin, its shape, the amount of force required to spin the coin, the air resistance, the friction of the platform the coin is rolling on, and so on, as well as the information of the environment itself, is not known to us in order for us to determine what the outcome would be after spinning a coin. It's because of this lack of information that we assume the spinning of the coin is random. If we had some function that could calculate all this information, then we would always successfully determine the outcome of the spinning coin.

The same can be said about random number generators. As an example, when we trigger a computer to generate a random number, the computer uses a variety of information to calculate and generate a so-called random number. These parameters can include information such as the current daytime that the request was triggered, information about the user or the system itself, and so on.

These types of random number generators are often referred to as **pseudorandom number (PSRN) generators** or **deterministic random bit (DRB) generators**. They are only as random as the calculation or seed values provided that are allowed. For example, if we knew the parameters used and how they were used to generate this random number, then we would be able to determine the generated random number every time.

Now I don't want you to worry about anyone determining the calculations or cryptographic keys that you may have generated. We use these PSRN generators because of the precision and granularity that they encompass to generate this number, which is such that any deviation can drastically alter the results.

So, why bother reviewing the probabilistic and random nature of a spinning coin? One, it's to explain the difference between randomness, or what we believe is random, in the classical world versus randomness in the quantum world. Two, at some point we will need to leave any form of classical analogy and accept the fact that the quantum behavior is not obvious nor easily measured. If you wish to get a deeper understanding of these phenomena, which we cannot easily describe using classical physics or analogies, I recommend about reading the **Heisenberg uncertainty principle**.

In the classic world, we learned that if we had all the information available, we can more than likely determine an outcome. However, in the previous section, where we described the double-slit experiment, we saw that we couldn't determine where on the screen the electron was going to hit. We understood the probabilities of where it would land based on our experiment. But even then, we could not deterministically identify where precisely the electron was going to land on the screen. You'll see an example of this when we create our superposition circuit in the next section.

For those who wish to learn a little more about this photonic phenomenon, I would suggest reading the book by the famous physicist Richard Feynman titled *QED: The Strange Theory of Light and Matter*.

Preparing a qubit in a superposition state

In this section, we are going to create a circuit with a single qubit and set an operator on the qubit to set it in a superposition state. But before we do that, let's quickly define what a superposition state is.

We define the qubit as having two basis energy states, one of which is the ground (0) state and the second of which is the excited (1) state, as illustrated in *Figure 4.3*. The state value name of each basis state could be anything we choose, but since the results from our circuit will be fed back to a classic system, we will use binary values to define our states—in this case, the binary values 0 and 1. To say that the superposition of two states is *being in both 0 and 1 at the same time* is incorrect. The proper way to state that a qubit is in a superposition state is to say that it is *in a complex linear combination of states where, in this case, the states are 0 and 1.*

A simple analogy of this is to perhaps think of a bit as a standard light switch. In one position the light is on, in the other position the light is off. It's either one or the other. This is analogous to a bit, either *0* or *1* (Off or On, respectively). Now consider a light dimmer switch (technically, a rheostat) where the switch can be rotated to the On position and then rotated all the way down to the Off position. What you can also do with a dimmer is slide the switch to anyplace in between off and on, this in turn adjusts the intensity, or amplitude, of the amount of light emitted. Now, when you have the dimmer in between the On and Off position, you don't say the light is "On and Off at the same time" do you? Of course not. It is more of a combination of the two. Keep in mind of course, this is not the definition of a qubit, it's just a simple example of why saying something is two things at once is not entirely correct.

Visualizing the state of a qubit is generally difficult, particularly multi-qubit states, which involve more than one qubit and multiple quantum states. One of the earlier visualization models developed was the 2-state sphere that provided a geometrical representation of a 2-level quantum mechanical system called the **Bloch sphere**. The following figure is an example of a Bloch sphere, which represents a single qubit and its two orthogonal basis states, which are located on opposite poles. On the north pole, we have the basis state $|0\rangle$, while on the south pole, we have the basis state $|1\rangle$. The symbols surrounding the basis state values are the commonly used notations in most quantum computing text. This is called **Dirac notation**, which was named after the English theoretical physicist Paul Dirac, who first conceived the notation, which he called the **Bra-Ket notation**. Bra-Ket and Dirac notation are generally used interchangeably as they refer to the same thing, as we'll see later. Each has its unique form as follows, **Bra** has the following form, $\langle 0|$, and **Ket** has the following form, $|0\rangle$, where each denotes a mathematical *linear form* and *vector*, respectively.

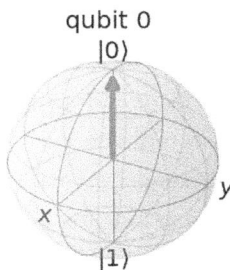

Figure 4.3: Two basis states of a qubit on a Bloch sphere

OK, so let's stop talking, and let's start coding. We're going to create a quantum circuit with a single qubit. We will then execute the circuit so that we can obtain the same result we can see in the preceding screenshot, which is the initial state of the qubit, state $|0\rangle$.

Before we get started, let's first import the helper file into your working directory. It contains a series of functions that will help us in two ways. First, it will provide a series of functions we can use to quickly get us started to execute circuits without having to cover any details just yet. But not to worry, you will learn the details as we progress throughout the book, and the dependency of the helper file will surely disappear. Second, this will also help keep the code base up to date as new features and changes happen, so that updates can be made to keep code running far beyond the current version. The location of the helper file is in the GitHub repo linked at the beginning of this chapter, titled helper_file_1.0.ipynb. Be aware that you may need to set up your account if you want to use a quantum system and not the local simulators on your device. If so, please open the setup_save_account.ipynb file and enter your API token in the specified attribute and run the file. Once you do, that will save your API on your local machine, so you won't have to set up each time.

Open a new Qiskit Notebook and enter the following code into the next empty cell:

```
# Load helper file
%run helper_file_1.0.ipynb

# Create a simple circuit
qc = QuantumCircuit(1,1)

# Get the state vector of the circuit
stateVectorResult = Statevector(qc)

# Display the state vector results onto a Bloch sphere
plot_bloch_multivector(stateVectorResult)
```

The first line will load the helper file into the working notebook. The file contains functions that we will use to import the functions and libraries we need to get started, such as those needed for executing circuits on simulators and backend systems and returning the results of our circuits. The next line creates a quantum circuit that includes 1 qubit and 1 classical bit, and in the next line we will pass the quantum circuit to the Statevector object, which will generate the state vector of the quantum circuit. This will return the resulting object, which will contain the state vector results. Finally, we display the results on a Bloch sphere, which should display what you saw in *Figure 4.3*.

Each qubit, as mentioned earlier, is made up of two basis states, which, in this example, reside on opposite poles of the Bloch sphere. These two basis states are what we would submit back to the classical system as our result—either one or the other. The vector representing these two points originates from the origin of the Bloch sphere, as you can see in the previous diagram or the result from your experiment. If we were to notate this as a vector, we would write the following:

$$|0\rangle = \begin{bmatrix} 1 \\ 0 \end{bmatrix}$$

Since the opposite would apply to the opposite pole, we would notate it as follows:

$$|1\rangle = \begin{bmatrix} 0 \\ 1 \end{bmatrix}$$

From observing the vector values, you can see that flipping the values of the vector is like a classical bit flip. Now that we understand the vector representation of a qubit, let's continue and set the qubit in a superposition state:

1. Insert a new cell at the bottom of the current notebook and enter the following code:

    ```
    # Place the qubit in a superposition state
    # by adding a Hadamard (H) gate
    qc.h(0)
    # Draw the circuit
    qc.draw(output='mpl')
    ```

*   The first line places a **Hadamard (H)** gate onto the first qubit, identified by the qubit's index value (0). It then calls the draw() function, which will draw the circuit diagram; note that the output parameter is added just to get a nicer output. If you would like to include these visualization features, be sure to install qiskit[visualization] from pip (pip install qiskit[visualization]). Otherwise, you can remove the parameter and get standard text visualization outputs.

    After running the previous cell, you should see the following circuit image, which represents adding the Hadamard gate to the qubit and the classical bit just below:

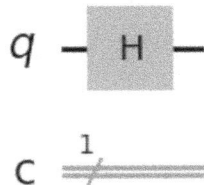

Figure 4.4: Circuit with a Hadamard (H) gate added to a qubit

The **Hadamard gate** (H gate) is a quantum gate that places the qubit in a superposition state, or, more specifically, a complex linear combination of the basis states, which means that when we measure the qubit, it will have an equal probability result of measuring a 0 or 1. Or in other words, it would collapse to one of the basis state values of $|0\rangle$ or $|1\rangle$.

Mathematically, the superposition state is obtained with the application of the Hadamard gate, and its results are represented in the following two superposition equations, which, as you can see, depends on which of the two basis states, $|0\rangle$ or $|1\rangle$, it was in prior to applying the Hadamard gate. The first superposition equation $|+\rangle$ is as follows and originates from the $|0\rangle$ state, which is often referred to as the positive $|+\rangle$ superposition state:

$$|+\rangle = \frac{|0\rangle + |1\rangle}{\sqrt{2}}$$

The second superposition equation $|-\rangle$, originating from the $|1\rangle$ state, is as follows, which is often referred to as the negative $|-\rangle$ superposition state:

$$|-\rangle = \frac{|0\rangle - |1\rangle}{\sqrt{2}}$$

Visually, on the Bloch sphere, this is equal to a $\pi/2$ rotation about the X and Z axes of the Bloch sphere. These rotations are Cartesian rotations, which rotate counterclockwise around the specified axis, in this case, the X and Z axes.

2. Now, let's get the state vector of our circuit, and see what the resulting quantum state will look like, and where the state vector lands on the Bloch sphere. In the following code, you will call the `Statevector` object and pass the quantum circuit into the `constructor` argument, the result of which will change the state of the qubit to a superposition state from the initial state, which you will see in the resulting Bloch sphere's output:

```
# Get the state vector of the circuit
stateVectorResult = Statevector(qc)

# Display the Bloch sphere
plot_bloch_multivector(stateVectorResult)
```

You should now see the results plotted on the Bloch sphere in a superposition of $|0\rangle$ and $|1\rangle$, as illustrated in the following figure:

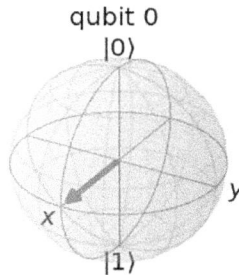

Figure 4.5: Superposition of a qubit after 90° rotation of the $|0\rangle$ basis state

As you can see in the preceding screenshot, this has placed the vector on the positive X axis, as described previously when adding an H gate from the $|0\rangle$ basis state. One thing to note is that visually, this could also have been done by rotating the Y axis by 90 degrees.

3. Now, let's clear the circuit by recreating the `QuantumCircuit` object with the same name. This time, we will initialize the qubit to the $|1\rangle$ state first and then apply a Hadamard gate to see what happens to the vector. Initialize the qubit to the $|0\rangle$ state and place it in a superposition. Clear the circuit and initialize the qubit to 1 before applying a Hadamard gate:

```
#Reset our quantum circuit
qc = QuantumCircuit(1)
#Rotate the qubit from 0 to 1 using the X (NOT) gate
qc.x(0)
#Add a Hadamard gate
qc.h(0)
#Draw the circuit
qc.draw(output='mpl')
```

You should now see the following circuit; in this case, we have omitted the classical bit when constructing our quantum circuit, which is why you do not see the classical bit in the following figure:

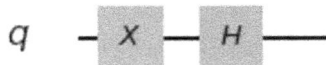

Figure 4.6: Applying an H gate superposition to the base state $|1\rangle$

4. Now, let's execute the circuit and plot the result on the Bloch sphere using the same code you used to execute the previous circuit:

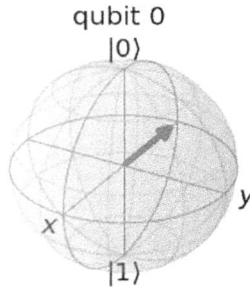

Figure 4.7: Superposition of a qubit after 90° rotation around the X and Z axes from the $|1\rangle$ state

Do you see the difference between adding an H gate to a qubit in the $|0\rangle$ state (Figure 4.5) and adding it to a qubit in the $|1\rangle$ state in the preceding figure?

Of course, the difference is where it lands on the X axis! Because the vector falls onto the positive X axis when applying a Hadamard gate to the $|0\rangle$ state, this is commonly notated as $|+\rangle$. This logically means that the vector falls onto the negative X axis when applying a Hadamard gate to the $|1\rangle$ state. This is commonly notated as $|-\rangle$.

Now, look at the right side of the superposition equations and pay close attention to the signs in between:

$$|+\rangle = \frac{|0\rangle + |1\rangle}{\sqrt{2}}$$

$$|-\rangle = \frac{|0\rangle - |1\rangle}{\sqrt{2}}$$

Notice that the signs match the direction of where the vector lands after the Hadamard gate is applied. From the $|0\rangle$ state, it moves toward the positive (+) direction of the X axis, and from the $|1\rangle$ state, it moves toward the negative (-) direction of the X axis.

This difference is referred to as a phase difference between the two results. This will be very important later in this and subsequent chapters, as phase difference plays an important role in many quantum algorithms and blends itself into the topic of interference, as we will learn shortly.

One last thing that we will discuss before moving on is to now look back to our earlier discussion on probabilities. Now that we've learned what superposition looks like in a circuit and on a Bloch sphere, let's execute and see what the probabilities are when we measure the qubit after it is in superposition. As you may recall from our first analogy of flipping or spinning a coin, we said that once the coin is spinning, it is in a superposition of heads or tails, or in this example, 0 or 1.

Once we observe the outcome, the result of the coin will be one or the other. However, classically, this is pseudorandom, as we learned. But in quantum computing, electron detection is truly random as there is no way to determine its outcome without disturbing it due to the **Heisenberg uncertainty principle**.

> The **Heisenberg uncertainty principle**, introduced by Werner Heisenberg in 1927, describes how it is not possible to predict the *momentum* of a particle from its initial conditions if the *position* is more precisely determined. The same is said for the reverse, where it is not possible to predict the position of a particle from its initial conditions if the momentum is more precisely determined.

This is the same as measuring a qubit; we are, in essence, measuring it, and therefore forcing it to collapse into one of two basis states.

5. Then, measure the qubit after it is in superposition and recreate the circuit. Let's start from the |0⟩ state and apply a Hadamard gate, as we did earlier:

```
# Recreate the circuit with a single qubit and classical bit
qc = QuantumCircuit(1,1)
# Add a Hadamard gate
qc.h(0)
```

6. Now, using our helper function, let's create a circuit that includes a measurement operator so that we can measure the qubit, which will collapse into one of two states, as follows:

```
# Create a measurement circuit with 1 qubit and 1 bit
measurement_circuit = create_circuit(1,True)
# Concatenate the circuits together
full_circuit = qc.compose(measurement_circuit)
# Draw the full circuit
full_circuit.draw(output='mpl')
```

In the previous code, we created a measurement circuit that includes a measurement operation that basically collapses the qubit from its current state to that of either 0 or 1. The second line of the code then concatenates the first circuit qc and this new measurement_circuit together, creating a new circuit called full_circuit which will be drawn as follows:

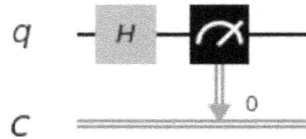

Figure 4.8: Full circuit with rotation and measurement from qubit (q) to classic bit (c)

The previous diagram illustrates our full circuit, which you can see now includes two new components, the first of which is the classic register below the quantum register. The second component is the measurement operator, which will extract the result of the qubit and pass it onto the classical bit. The result will collapse the state of the qubit to either 1 or 0.

7. Now, let's run this circuit to see what results we get back. We will add a few shots and see the results. Shots refer to running through the experiment a few times and aggregating its results. We'll use our helper file to help us run this circuit:

```
# Run the quantum circuit and obtain results
transpiled_QC, result, stateVectorResult = simulate_on_sampler(full_
circuit, None, None)

counts = result[0].data.c.get_counts()
print(counts)
```

The previous code will now use a different backend from our helper file, the BasicSimulator rather than the Statevector, which will allow us to obtain the measured results of the circuit. In this case, we will extract counts, which stores the number of times the measurement resulted in either a 0 or 1 out of 1024 shots.

The result of the previous code is as follows:

```
{'1': 478, '0': 546}
```

Notice that the results are almost 50%, which illustrates that you can have an equal probability of landing on either the 0 or 1 state for each shot!

Note that your actual value results might be different than what was shown previously, but the probability should be close to 50%. Retry running the code a few times and play around with the number of shots to see if you get any differences. The limitation for shots can be found in the max_shots value for each simulator and quantum system's properties.

The reason why we run so many shots of a circuit is to get enough measurements to obtain accurate statistics of a measurement operation on a superposition state that is probabilistic. The noise in the system contributes to the deviation from a perfect statistic of 50/50 in the counts, because the near-term quantum devices used these days are not fault-tolerant yet. Fault-tolerant devices are those that have logical qubits, which can comprise one or more physical qubits, and are used to minimize errors so that operations complete as specified by the quantum circuits. They exhibit very low error rates and large quantum volumes, which we will cover in *Chapter 9, Optimizing and Visualizing Circuits*. Current near-term devices need to run multiple shots to provide your quantum algorithm with good probabilistic results.

Building a coin-flipping experiment

If you've ever taken a course in probability and statistics, you might have seen the coin flip example. In this example, you are given an unbiased coin to flip multiple times and track the results of each flip (experiment) as either heads or tails. What this experiment illustrates is that with an unbiased coin and enough samples, you will see that the probability of either heads or tails starts to converge to about 50%.

This means that, after running enough experiments, the number of times the coin lands on heads becomes very closely equal to the number of times that it lands on tails.

Let's give this a try in the IBM Quantum Composer, to better visualize what's happening (note, backend systems might not be available or the same, so use any backend you see available. Like most of the backends throughout this book, we'll be using those that were available at the time of writing this:

1. Open the Composer Editor and create a new blank circuit.

2. For simplicity, let's remove all except one qubit. This will simplify our results.

3. Click and drag the Hadamard gate onto the first qubit.

4. Click and drag the measurement operation onto the first qubit after the H gate. This will indicate that you wish the value of this qubit to be measured, and assign its resulting value of either 1 or 0 to the corresponding classic bit; in this case, the bit at position 0, as shown in the following screenshot:

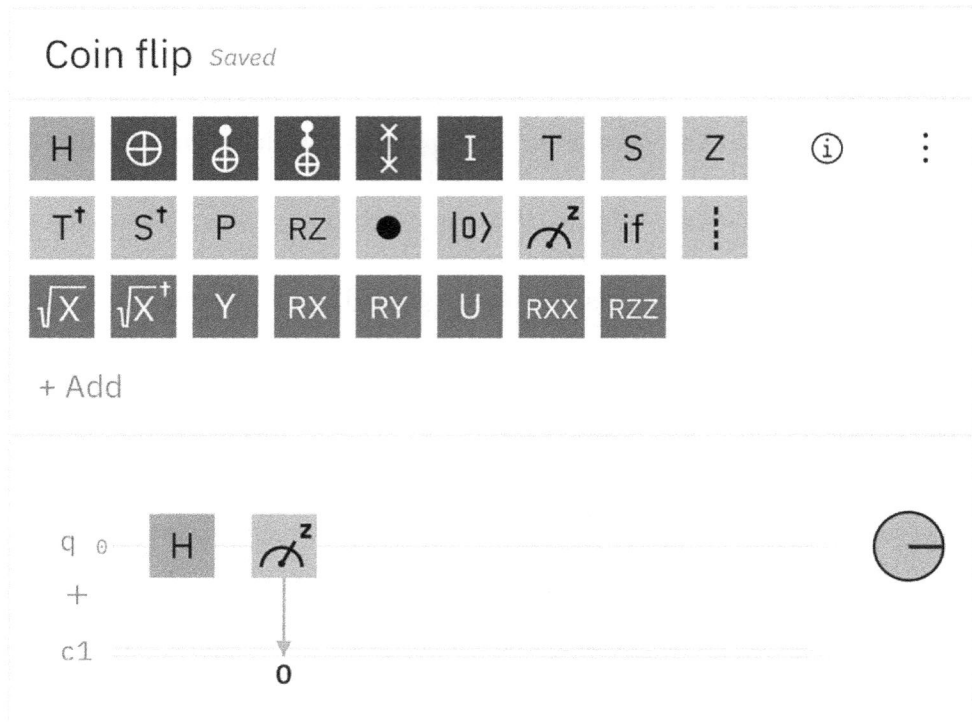

Figure 4.9: Coin flip experiment

5. Name your circuit Coin flip and save it.

6. Click **Setup and run** to expand the options.

7. Select a backend device and set the run count to 1024. This will run the experiment 1,024 times. Note at the time of this writing there are some changes occurring which might change how to run a circuit using Composer. If so, please refer to the instructions on the platform for any changes.

8. Click **Run on 'device selected'**.

9. Once completed, click on the completed experiment in the **Composer jobs** list.

The measurement outcome results will now show two different states. Remember that the Computational basis states are represented along the *X* axis, which you can see is either a 0 or 1:

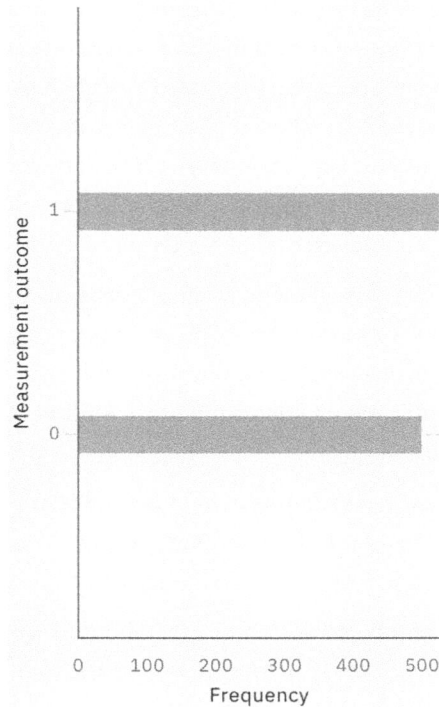

Figure 4.10: Coin flip results

Another thing to note is the Frequency (the X axis) of each of the two states. This will differ each time you run the experiment as it represents how many times the outcome was either 0 or 1 for each shot.

What you will notice from the preceding screenshot is that the results will fall close to 50% each time you run the experiment. Rerun the experiment a few more times and examine the results for yourself. The use of the Hadamard gate allows you to place a qubit on a circuit into a linear combination of the two basis states, 0 and 1. As mentioned earlier, this helps to leverage superposition.

Understanding entanglement

The second quantum computing principle used by quantum computers is **entanglement**. By entangling two or more qubits, we are, in essence, linking the value of one qubit and synchronizing it with one or more other qubits. By synchronizing it, we mean that if we measure (observe) the value of one of the entangled qubits, then we can be sure that the other qubit will have the same value, whether we measure it at the same time or sometime later.

Entanglement is probably one of the most interesting of the three quantum computing principles. This is mainly because it still baffles physicists to this day, with many taking different philosophical sides in the discussion. I won't bore you with the details, but I will aim to provide you with enough information for you to understand what entanglement is, but not to have a way to prove it to create quantum algorithms and applications. Yes, it sounds confusing, but believe me, the devil is in the detail and there just isn't enough space for us to formulate a comprehensive answer to how entanglement works. But enough of that—let's get to work!

Quantum entanglement, or just entanglement, is simply defined as a quantum mechanical phenomenon that occurs when two or more particles have correlated states. What this, in essence, means is that if you have two particles or, for our purposes, qubits, that are entangled, this means that when we measure one qubit, we can determine the result of the other qubit based on the measurement of the first qubit.

As you may recall from our previous example, if we put a qubit in a superposition and we measure that qubit, we have a 50/50 split as to whether that qubit would collapse to either of two states, $|0\rangle$ or $|1\rangle$.

Now, if that same qubit were entangled with another qubit and we were to measure one of the qubits, that qubit will be either $|0\rangle$ or $|1\rangle$. However, if we were to measure the second qubit, either at the exact same time or sometime later, it too will have the same value as the first qubit we measured!

One thing to note is that this can also be the opposite if you so choose it to be. For example, let's say you set the second qubit to the $|1\rangle$ state prior to entangling. You have now entangled opposite states. These combinations of entangled states will be covered in more detail when we discuss quantum algorithms in *Chapter 12, Applying Quantum Algorithms*.

You're probably thinking, *how can this be?* If we take two qubits and place them in superposition and we measure them separately, we will correctly see that each qubit will collapse to a value of 1 or 0, where each time we measure the qubits individually, it may not collapse to the same value at the same time. This means that if we run the experiment one shot at a time, we would see that, sometimes, the first qubit will measure 0, while the second qubit could measure 0 or 1.

Both are separate and do not know the value of each other either before, during, or after measurement. However, if we were to entangle the two qubits and repeat the same experiment, we would see that the qubits will measure the exact same values each time! Each will result in one of four different outcomes of either 00, 11, 01, or 10. Each of these four is based on what is known as the Bell states, which will be covered later in the chapter.

Impossible, you say? Well, it's a good thing for us that we now have a quantum computer that we can run and try this out!

Implementing the behavior of entangled qubits

In the following code, we will see that when qubits are not entangled, their results are such that we cannot infer what the result of one qubit would be based on the result of the other qubit. Since we are measuring two qubits, our results will be listed as two-bit values:

1. First, we'll create a new circuit with two qubits, place them each in superposition, and measure them:

```
#Create a circuit with 2 qubits and 2 classical bits
qc = QuantumCircuit(2,2)
#Add an H gate to each
qc.h(0)
qc.h(1)
#Measure the qubits to the classical bit
qc.measure([0,1],[0,1])
#Draw the circuit
qc.draw(output='mpl')
```

In the preceding code, we created a quantum circuit with two qubits, added an H gate to each of the qubits so that we can place each qubit into a superposition state, and finally, added a measurement from each qubit to its respective bit.

The result from the previous code should display the following circuit, where we can see that each qubit has an H gate that's measured to its respective classical bit register; that is, qubit 0 to bit 0 and qubit 1 to bit 1:

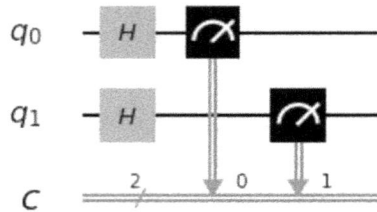

Figure 4.11: Two qubits in superposition and measured to their respective classic bits

2.   Then, we execute the circuit and display the results:

```
# Run the quantum circuit
transpiledQC, result, stateVectorResult = simulate_on_sampler(qc,
None, None)
#Obtain the results and display on a histogram
counts = result[0].data.c.get_counts()
plot_histogram(counts)
```

In the previous code, we created the backend to run on the simulator with `1000 shots` and plot the results in a histogram to review them.

Note from the following results that the outcomes are very random from each qubit, which is what we expected. One thing I would also like to mention regarding notation is the ordering of the qubits. When written, the order of the qubits is a little different than the bit order. In quantum notation, the first qubit is also listed on the left-hand side, while subsequent qubits are added toward the right-hand side. In binary notation, however, the first bit is on the right-hand side, while subsequent bits are added toward the left-hand side.

For example, if we want to represent the 3-qubit value of the number 5, we would do so using $|101\rangle$, which is the same as the bit representation of the same number. However, the qubit order here is different as the first qubit is listed in the left position (q[0]), the second qubit (q[1]) is listed in the middle position, and the last qubit (q[2]) is listed in the right position.

On the other hand, in binary notation, the first bit (b[0]) is in the right position and moves up in order to the left. When measuring, we link the results from the qubit to the bit (as shown in the preceding screenshot), which correctly maps the results of each qubit to its respective binary position so that our results are in the expected bit order.

The plotted histogram is shown in the following screenshot:

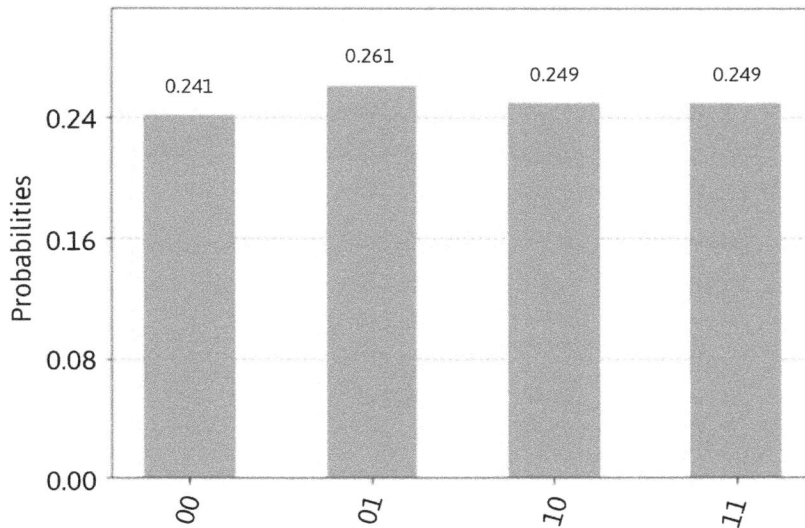

Figure 4.12: Random results of all combinations from both qubits

In the previous screenshot, each qubit has collapsed to a state of either 0 or 1, so since there are two qubits, we should expect to see all four random results, which are **00**, **01**, **10**, and **11**. Your probability results might differ a bit, but overall, they should all be close to 25% probability.

3. This is expected, so let's entangle the two qubits and see what happens then. For this, we will entangle the two qubits and rerun the experiment.

    Let's entangle the two qubits by adding a multi-qubit gate called a **Controlled NOT (CNOT)** gate. Let me explain what this gate is before we include it in our circuit.

    The CNOT gate is a multi-qubit gate that operates on one qubit based on the value of another. What this means is that the qubit gate has two connecting points—one called **control** and another called **target**. The target is generally an operator, such as a **NOT** (X) gate, which would flip the qubit from 0 to 1, or vice versa.

    However, the target operator can also be almost any operation, such as an H gate, a Y gate (which flips 180° around the Y axis), and so on. It could even be another control, but we will get into those fancy gates in *Chapter 6, Understanding Quantum Logic Gates*.

The CNOT gate acts in such a manner that when the qubit tied to the control is set to 0, the value of the target qubit does not change, meaning the target operator will not be enabled. However, if the value of the control qubit is 1, this will trigger the target operator. This would, therefore, in the case of a CNOT gate, enable a NOT operation on the target qubit, causing it to flip 180° around the *X* axis from its current position. This is illustrated in *Figure 4.13*, where qubit 0 is the control and qubit 1 is the target; in this case, the target is a NOT gate, hence making this a CNOT gate.

The following logic table represents the control and target value updates based on the value of the control for a CNOT gate, as well as the states before and after the CNOT gate:

Before CNOT		After CNOT	
Control	Target	Control	Target
$|0\rangle$	$|0\rangle$	$|0\rangle$	$|0\rangle$
$|0\rangle$	$|1\rangle$	$|0\rangle$	$|1\rangle$
$|1\rangle$	$|0\rangle$	$|1\rangle$	$|1\rangle$
$|1\rangle$	$|1\rangle$	$|1\rangle$	$|0\rangle$

Table 4.1: Two-qubit CNOT logic table

Now that we can see how the CNOT gate works on two qubits, we will update our circuit so that we can entangle the qubits together. In the following code, we will create a circuit with 2 qubits where we will apply a Hadamard gate to the first qubit and then entangle the first qubit with the second qubit using a CNOT gate:

```
# Create a circuit with 2 qubits and 2 classic bits
qc = QuantumCircuit(2,2)
# Add an H gate to just the first qubit
qc.h(0)
# Add the CNOT gate to entangle the two qubits,
# where the first qubit is the control, and the
# second qubit is the target.
qc.cx(0,1)
# Measure the qubits to the classical bit
qc.measure([0,1],[0,1])
# Draw the circuit
qc.draw(output='mpl')
```

The resulting diagram of the circuit should look as follows:

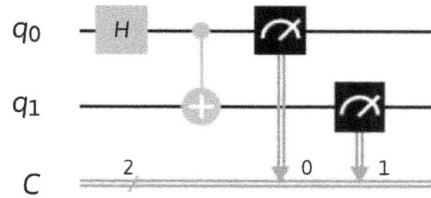

Figure 4.13: Entanglement of two qubits

The previous screenshot shows you that, this time, we are only placing a Hadamard gate on the first qubit and leaving the second qubit to be operated on only by the CNOT gate. Since qubit 1 (q_1) is set as the target, it will be dependent on the control qubit, which, in this case, is qubit 0 (q_0).

4. Now, we will run the experiment and plot the results. This is similar to the previous experiments we completed, where we will execute the circuit, extract the result counts, and plot them on a histogram to visualize the results:

```
# Run the quantum circuit
transpiledQC, result = run_qasm_circuit(qc, None, None)

counts = result.get_counts(qc)
plot_distribution(counts)
```

The results shown in the following screenshot show two quantum computing principles—the superposition of the qubits, 0 and 1, and the entanglement—where both qubits' (control and target) results are strongly correlated as either **00** or **11**:

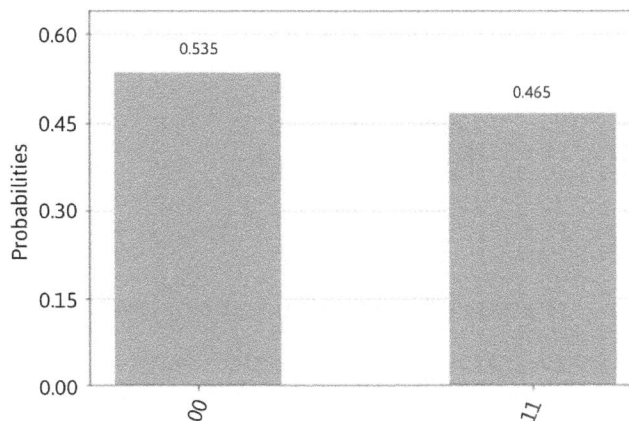

Figure 4.14: Results of two entangled qubits

Let's extend our coin-flipping example by adding another coin and entangling them together so that when we run our experiment, we can determine the value of one coin without having to measure the other.

Entangling two coins together

In the same way as our previous experiment, each qubit will represent a coin. In order to do this, we will use a CNOT gate, which connects two qubits where one is the source and the other the target.

Let's try entangling our coins (qubits) to see how this works:

1. Open the Composer and create a new blank circuit with 2 qubits. As a reminder, you can increase or decrease the number of qubits by selecting a qubit and clicking on either the + or trash icon to add or remove a qubit from the circuit, respectively.
2. Click and drag a Hadamard gate onto the first qubit, q_0.
3. Click and drag the CNOT gate (*round white gate with crosshairs on blue background*) onto the first qubit, q_1. This will assign the control qubit to the first qubit. When selecting the CNOT gate, the first qubit you drop it on will be set as the control. Visually, the source control of the CNOT gate is a solid dot on the qubit to which the gate was dragged on to (see *Figure 4.15*).

    By default, the target will set itself to the next qubit. In this case, it will drop to qubit 2. Visually, the target for a CNOT is a large dot with a cross in the middle, made to resemble a target.

4. Click and drag a measurement operator onto each of the two first qubits as shown in the following screenshot:

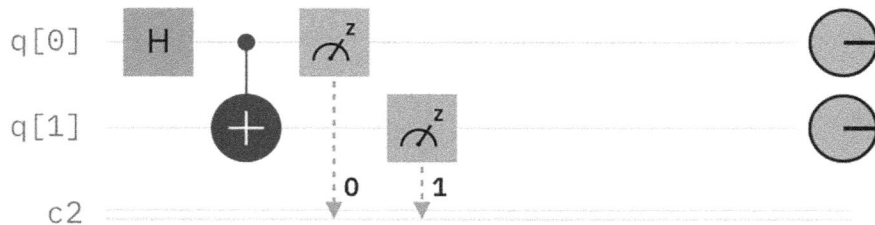

Figure 4.15: Entangled qubit circuit representing entangled coins

5. Name and save your experiment as `Entangled coins`.
6. Click **Setup and run** on the circuit to launch the **Setup and run** dialog.

7. Select any device from the backend selection as the backend device and select the `shots` value to `1024`. This will run the experiment 1,024 times, which is the default value that you can change if need be.

8. Click **Run on** and select whichever device you selected in the previous step.

9. Once completed, click the `Entangled coins` experiment from the `Completed jobs` list.

Now let's review the results and see what happens when we entangle two qubits:

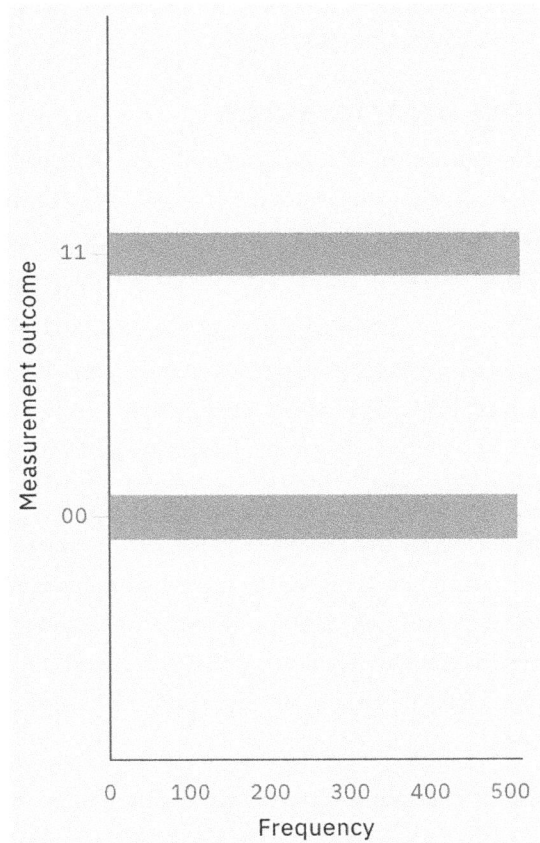

Figure 4.16: Entangled coins results

As you can see in the preceding screenshot, the results still have two states, as they did in the previous experiment. However, one thing to observe here is the results of the two qubits. Note that the state of both qubits is either 00 or 11.

What makes this experiment interesting is when we flipped one coin in the previous experiment, you saw that the results were 50% (0 or 1). However, now we are running the same experiment, but we are entangling another coin. In effect, this results in both coins becoming entangled together and thus their states will always be the same as each other. This means that if we flip both coins and we observe one of the coin values, then we know that the other entangled coin will be the same value.

Now that you are familiar with superposition and entanglement, let's move on to the last quantum computing principle, which is interference.

Understanding interference

One of the benefits of quantum computing is its ability to interleave these principles in such a way that usually, while explaining one, you can very easily describe the other. We did this earlier in this chapter with respect to interference. Let's review and see where we have come across this phenomenon and its usage so far.

First, recall that, at the beginning of this chapter, we described the double-slit experiment. There, we discussed how an electron can act as both a wave and a particle. When acting like a wave, we saw that the experiment illustrated how the electrons traveled and landed at certain spots on the observation screen. The pattern that it displayed was generally one that we recognize from classic physics as wave interference.

The pattern had probabilistic results along the backboard, as shown in the observing screen in *Figure 4.2*, where the center of the screen has the highest number of electrons and the blank areas along both sides had the least to none. This is due to the two types of interference of the particle waves, namely, **constructive** and **destructive**. Constructive interference occurs when the peaks of two waves are summed up where the resulting amplitude is equal to the total positive sum of the two individual waves.

Destructive interference occurs similarly to constructive interference except that the amplitudes of the waves are opposite in that when summing them together, the two waves cancel each other out.

The following diagram illustrates the constructive and destructive wave interference of two waves when they are added together:

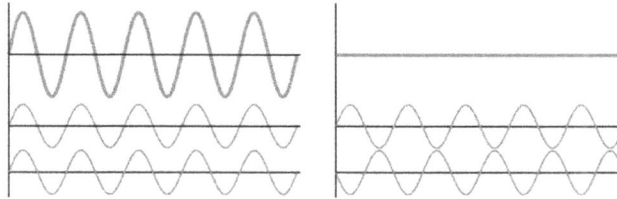

Figure 4.17: Constructive (left) and destructive (right) wave interferences (image source: https://commons.wikimedia.org/wiki/File:Interference_of_two_waves.svg)

The preceding diagram illustrates how two waves interfere with each other constructively and destructively. The two waves toward the bottom of the diagram represent the individual amplitudes of each wave, while the top line represents the added amplitude values, which represent the result of the interference between the two waves.

Now that you understand the difference between constructive and destructive interference, *how can we apply this to what we've learned so far?* Well, if you recall, earlier, when we placed a qubit in superposition, we had two distinct results.

One was from the basis state $|0\rangle$, while the other was from the basis state $|1\rangle$. Do you remember when we started at either of these two qubit basis states, where on the X axis of the qubit the Hadamard landed? From $|0\rangle$, it would land on the positive side of the X axis, but if we placed the qubit into superposition starting from the $|1\rangle$ state, it would land on the negative X axis.

Having the ability to place the qubit state vector on either the positive or negative X axis provides us with a way to place the qubit in either a positive or negative state. Very similar to the waves in the preceding diagram, which have positive (peaks) and negative (troughs) amplitudes, qubits can also represent similar states. Let's simplify this by re-introducing the two Dirac notation values, $|+\rangle$, and $|-\rangle$, where the $|+\rangle$ state represents the state vector on the positive X axis, and the $|-\rangle$ state represents the state vector on the negative X axis.

These new vector definitions, which represent the vector state of a qubit in superposition, will be used by some of the algorithms as a technique to identify certain values and react to them using interference—techniques such as **amplitude estimation** and search algorithms such as **Grover's algorithm.**

In this section, we reviewed the quantum computing principle of interference. This, along with the other two principles, superposition and entanglement, will come in handy as you learn about how these principles are used in quantum algorithms in ways that provide potential speed up over classical algorithms. To do so, we will review an example that we will use throughout this book, to understand the very foundation of all quantum algorithms, the **Bell states**.

Exploring the Bell states

For most of the examples in this book, you will notice that we reuse a simple two-qubit quantum circuit to run many of our experiments. This circuit contains two gates, a single-qubit gate, and a multi-qubit gate, a Hadamard and CNOT, respectively.

The reason for choosing this was not random. In fact, this circuit has a name, the Bell state. The Bell state, which was originally described in a theoretical paper by John Bell in 1964, describes how there are four maximally entangled quantum states between two qubits that are in a super-position state. These four states are commonly referred to as the **Bell states**.

At this point, you may be wondering why this is so important. Well, if we can prepare qubits to a particular state, in this case, the maximally entangled state, this can help streamline the creation of various quantum circuits and algorithms. To learn more about this, let's first prepare the four Bell states, and perhaps, along the way, you might see its importance and understand the signif-icance to some use cases such as quantum teleportation or super dense coding.

Preparing the Bell states

We'll begin by first preparing the Bell state that we will use throughout this book.

We'll label each of these states as we create them, this first one being labeled as $|\phi^+\rangle$. Preparing the Bell state entails three simple steps:

1. Prepare your two-qubit input values. For this first state, $|\phi^+\rangle$, we will use the initialized state of $|00\rangle$:

$$|\phi\rangle = |00\rangle$$

2. Next, add a Hadamard to the first qubit. This will place the first qubit in a superposition state:

$$|\phi^+\rangle = \frac{(|0\rangle + |1\rangle\,|0\rangle)}{\sqrt{2}}$$

3. Finally, add a CNOT gate, where the control is set to the qubit in superposition. In this case, the first qubit and the target are set to the second qubit. Doing so will ensure that when the first qubit is 1, this will trigger the target qubit to rotate about the *X* axis from the $|0\rangle$ state to the 1$\rangle$ state, or else it will remain in the $|0\rangle$ state. This gives us our final state:

$$|\phi^+\rangle = \frac{(|00\rangle + |11\rangle)}{\sqrt{2}}$$

This final state is the first Bell state, $|\phi^+\rangle$, which will result in an equal probability of either $|00\rangle$ or $|11\rangle$.

The only difference between preparing the first Bell state and the others is just in *step 1*, where you need to prepare your inputs. *Step 2* and *step 3* are the same for all. What this means is that for a two-qubit circuit, the remaining input states in *step 1* to prepare are $|01\rangle$, $|10\rangle$, and $|11\rangle$. Luckily for us, the following formula can be used to help us identify the remaining Bell states:

$$f(|q_1, q_0\rangle) = (\frac{|0, q_0\rangle + (-1)^{q_1}|1, \overline{q_0}\rangle}{\sqrt{2}})$$

By using this formula, we can calculate that all four Bell states are as follows:

- For the input state $|00\rangle$, we get the following equation:

$$|\phi^+\rangle = \frac{(|00\rangle + |11\rangle)}{\sqrt{2}}$$

- For the input state $|01\rangle$, we get the following equation:

$$|\phi^-\rangle = \frac{(|00\rangle - |11\rangle)}{\sqrt{2}}$$

- For the input state $|10\rangle$, we get the following equation:

$$|\Psi^+\rangle = \frac{(|01\rangle + |10\rangle)}{\sqrt{2}}$$

- For the input state $|11\rangle$, we get the following equation:

$$|\Psi^-\rangle = \frac{(|01\rangle - |10\rangle)}{\sqrt{2}}$$

Now, let's create these circuits by executing all the Bell states on both a simulator and a quantum computer.

Implementing the Bell states

In this section, we will create the first two initial states, $|00\rangle$ and $|10\rangle$, and leave you to create the remaining input states:

1. We'll begin by creating the first Bell state, $|00\rangle$. Let's create a two-qubit QuantumCircuit circuit, and prepare the input state, $|00\rangle$. Since all quantum circuits are initialized to the state $|00\rangle$, we do not need to do anything to the circuit. We'll add a barrier to indicate the separation between steps:

    ```
    # State 1: |/+>
    state1 = QuantumCircuit(2)
    # Initialize input to |0,0>
    state1.barrier()
    ```

2. Then, add a Hadamard gate to the first qubit:

    ```
    # Prepare the Bell state
    state1.h(0)
    ```

3. Add a CNOT gate where the control is the first qubit, and the target is the second qubit:

    ```
    state1.cx(0,1)
    ```

4. Finally, add measurements to all qubits and draw the circuit:

    ```
    state1.measure_all()
    state1.draw(output='mpl')
    ```

    This will render the final circuit for our first Bell state, $|00\rangle$, as follows:

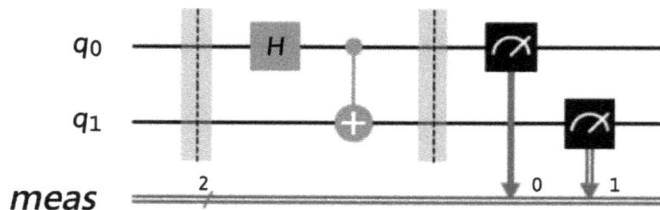

Figure 4.18: Prepared Bell state,$|\phi^+\rangle = |00\rangle$

5. Now let's execute this circuit with our helper function. Set the `simulator` argument to specify whether you want to execute it on a simulator or quantum system. To avoid any noise in our results, in this example, we will run the circuit on a quantum simulator to verify that our results are as expected:

```
# Execute the Bell state |/+>
transpiledQC, result, stateVectorResult = simulate_on_
sampler(state1, None, None)

# Obtain the results and display on a histogram
counts = result[0].data.meas.get_counts()
plot_histogram(counts)
```

The results of this experiment render the following familiar output, which confirms the first Bell state, OO:

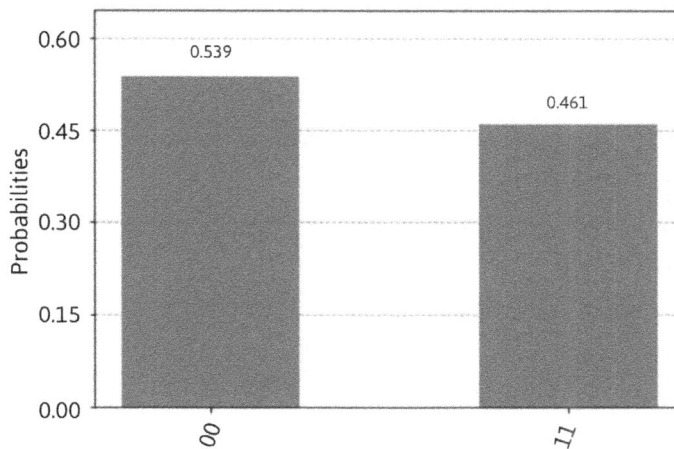

Figure 4.19: Results for the first state, $|\phi^+\rangle = |00\rangle$

6. We'll now continue to represent the next state, $|\Psi^+\rangle = |10\rangle$, and confirm the results as we did previously.

As mentioned earlier, the only difference between the four Bell states is in the first step, which is to prepare the input states. In this case, our input state is $|10\rangle$. We can follow the same steps as before after adding an X gate to the second qubit:

```
# State 2: |/+>
state2 = QuantumCircuit(2)
# Initialize input state to |1,0>
state2.x(1)
state2.barrier()
# Prepare the Bell state
state2.h(0)
state2.cx(0,1)
state2.measure_all()
state2.draw(output='mpl')
```

This will result in the following circuit, which is very similar to the first except for the added X gate in the preparation step:

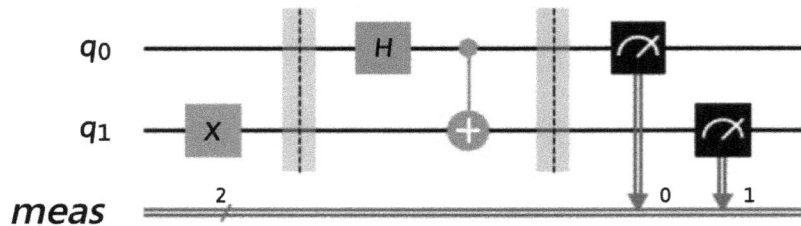

Figure 4.20: Prepared Bell state, $|\Psi^+\rangle = |10\rangle$

7. As with the first Bell state, let's execute this circuit and observe the results:

```
# Execute the Bell state |/+>
transpiledQC, result, stateVectorResult = simulate_on_
sampler(state1, None, None)

# Obtain the results and display on a histogram
counts = result[0].data.meas.get_counts()
plot_histogram(counts)
```

The results from executing the preceding circuit are as follows:

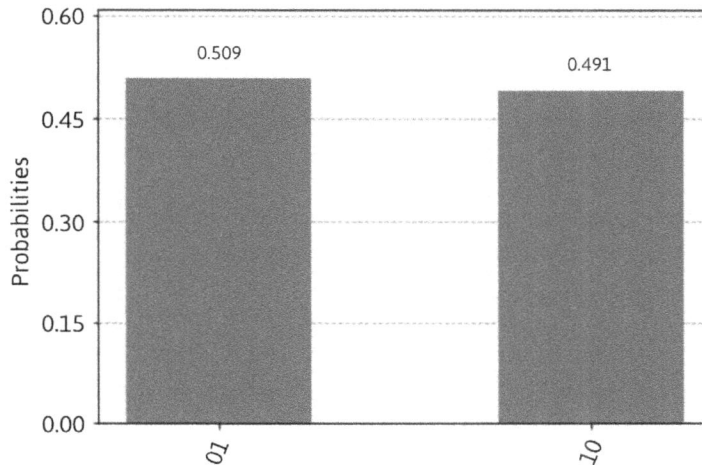

Figure 4.21: Results of the Bell state, $|\Psi^+\rangle = |10\rangle$

After reviewing both results, we should note a couple of things. The first is that we can see from the first Bell state that both qubits are equally entangled, in that if you were to measure one qubit, let's say the first one, then you would know that the second qubit should be in the same state. Hence, if you measure the first qubit and the result is 0, then without measuring, you know the state of the second qubit.

Whether you measure the second qubit at the same time or at a later juncture, the same can be said about the second Bell state; the only difference, in that case, is that if you measure one qubit, then you know that the other will result in the opposite basis state value. Hence, if the first qubit results in 0, then the second qubit will result in 1, or vice versa.

This correlation between two qubits is the basis for two famous quantum applications—**quantum teleportation** and **super dense coding**, where, in each, there are two qubits that are prepared in an entangled state. This preparation of the two qubits is represented by the Bell states, where the preparation can be in either of the four Bell states we have just described.

When reading about use cases that describe quantum teleportation, you will hear a similar example to this: *Eve prepares a pair of entangled qubits and sends one to Alice and the other to Bob*; you'll now know how Eve prepares the pair of entangled qubits.

Now that we understand the Bell states and how they can be applied in applications such as quantum teleportation and super dense coding, we'll continue our journey in later chapters to illustrate how quantum algorithms offer computational advantages over classical systems.

Summary

In this chapter, you learned about the three quantum computing principles used in quantum computing. You created a quantum circuit and placed a qubit in superposition and an entangled state between two qubits in a quantum circuit.

You also understood the two types of interference, constructive and destructive, and learned how they are notated and represented individually as qubits by placing them in superposition to create $|+\rangle$ and $|-\rangle$ simulations.

You also had a sneak peek at some Qiskit development skills by leveraging some quantum gates such as the Hadamard and CNOT gates, as well as operations such as measurements. This will prepare you for future chapters when you will create circuits where these gates and operations are commonly used in various algorithms. This makes sense as these gates and operations represent the core quantum computing principles that we have learned.

You also ran a couple of experiments: the first one was an experiment that simulated a coin toss in which a circuit was created using the Hadamard gate, which leveraged superposition. The second experiment also simulated a coin toss, only we had entangled each of the two coins together. This is an expansion of the second circuit, which included your first multi-gate, a CNOT gate. These allowed you to examine how both superposition and entanglement results map from your quantum circuit to the classical bit outputs. We also learned about the Bell states, which illustrate a great example of the use and advantage we get with quantum entanglement. These four special states that represent a linear combination of superposition states will be used when learning about quantum algorithms in later chapters of this book.

In the next chapter, we will learn about all the other gates, both single and multi, to understand the operations they perform on each qubit.

Questions

1. How would you create a circuit that entangles two qubits where each qubit is different (that is, 01, 10)?
2. Create a circuit with a multi-qubit gate, such as a Controlled-Hadamard gate.
3. Create all 4 Bell states in a circuit.
4. What are the three quantum computation principles?

Join us on Discord

Join our community's Discord space for discussions with the author and other readers:

`https://packt.link/3FyN1`

5

Understanding the Qubit

We are all very familiar with the classical bit, or just the bit, with respect to current computer hardware systems. It is the fundamental unit used to compute everything from simple mathematical problems, such as addition and multiplication, to more complex algorithms that involve a large collection of information.

Quantum computers have a similar fundamental unit called a **quantum bit,** or **qubit,** as it is commonly referred to. In this chapter, we will describe what a qubit is, both from a mathematical (computational) and a hardware perspective, to help you understand how they are used to calculate information. We will cover the differences between qubits and bits, particularly regarding how calculations are defined. This chapter will then transition from single to multi-qubit states and talk about the advantages of multi-qubit states.

We will also provide an overview of the hardware implementation of a qubit and how qubits are used to compute information. Since we will be using the Qiskit Runtime service to run our experiments, you will be using the superconducting qubit systems that are available to you. The descriptions and calculations are hardware independent; much of the information we will cover will apply to most of the other available quantum hardware systems.

Finally, we will discuss how quantum systems read, manipulate, and control the flow of information to and from a qubit from a classical system.

The following topics will be covered in this chapter:

- Comparing classical and quantum bits
- Visualizing the state vector of a qubit
- Visualizing the state vectors of multiple qubits
- Implementing qubits on a superconducting system

Technical requirements

In this chapter, some basic knowledge of computer architecture, basic linear algebra, and binary logic might come in handy. Knowledge of how bits are used to calculate will be useful but is not a hard requirement as the focus will be primarily on the qubit. Here is the source code used throughout this book: https://github.com/PacktPublishing/Learning-Quantum-Computing-with-Python-and-IBM-Quantum-Second-Edition.

Comparing classical and quantum bits

In this section, we will compare and review the building blocks of a classical bit and a few of the operations that are performed on them via classical gates. We will then learn about the fundamental unit of a quantum computer, the qubit, and how it is similar to the bit, yet due to its quantum computational principles, which we learned about in the previous chapter, has a larger computational space than the bit.

Reviewing the classical bit

Before we delve into what a quantum bit is and how it is used, let's take a brief moment to refresh our memories about the classical bit. Just as the quantum bit is the fundamental building block of quantum algorithms, the bit has the same role in classical computational systems.

In computational systems, the bit is used to define a logical state, often referenced as either on or off, true or false, or the most commonly used option, 1 or 0. The transition between states can be applied physically either after it's triggered by an operation, such as the result of an **AND gate**, or as a result of some input from an external entity, such as reading from an external data source. It is usually represented using transistors, which detect voltage differences and usually contain a threshold that determines whether the transistor is in a low (0) or high (1) state. The voltage thresholds, usually referred to as **Transistor-Transistor Logic** (**TTL**) voltage, are generally between 0 and 0.5 volts to indicate low and between 2 and 5 volts to indicate high.

The following diagram illustrates the simple process of a NOT operation being conducted on a bit. The bit is first initialized or set to a state, either 0 or 1. Then, an operation is performed on the bit and, depending on the result of the operation, the bit's state will either change or remain the same. The information is then available to be read and/or stored. In this example, the NOT operation would change the state from 0 to 1 or vice versa:

Initialized bit state   Bit operation   Resulting bit state

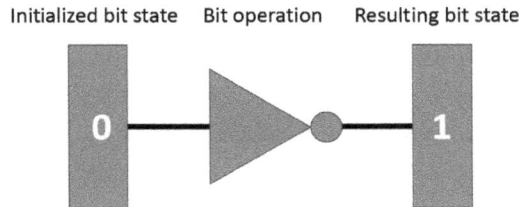

Figure 5.1: NOT operation of a bit

The implementation of a bit can be in various forms: flip flops, TTL, and so on. The information can be stored by writing the value to a persistent data repository to be read later. Calculations using bits are usually done using a **bitstring**, which is a set of individual bits combined to represent a string of 1s and 0s, usually noted as follows:

$$x = \{0,1\}^4$$

This indicates that x is a bitstring of 4 bits, where each bit can be either 1 or 0; for example, 0010 or 1101.

Calculations using bits are generally done using binary logic. For example, let's say we wanted to add two numbers; say, 2 and 3. We would simply assign the values 2 and 3 to a variable, which is stored in binary. Then, we would add the two numbers using binary addition and carry the values, which will result in 5, illustrated as follows. Please create a new notebook and enter the following:

```
%run helper_file_1.0.ipynb

#Adding two binary numbers
two = 0b010
three = 0b011
answer = two + three
print(bin(answer))
```

Running the preceding code snippet in a new notebook would result in the binary value of 5, which is 0b101. The code reads the binary values of 2 and 3 and returns the result as a binary called answer, which is printed as a binary using the bin() function. In order to obtain the results of adding two numbers together, classical systems use Modulo 2 arithmetic, which is the result of using logic gates, in this case, an **XOR** gate. When **XORing** two input bits, that is, $(1 + 0)\mod 2 = 1 \text{XOR} 0$, the input values can also be written as two binary numbers, x_1 and x_2; that is, $x1 \otimes x2$. Note that the result will work for the following input values of x_1 and x_2: 0+0, 0+1, and 1+0. However, when input values of x_1 and x_2 are 1+1, we will need a second qubit to carry the value, hence the result for 1+1 will be 10.

So, why did we go through such a simple example? The point was not to bore you with a simple binary calculation; the idea was to provide a refresher about the mechanics of what happens at the gate level when computing on a classical system. This way, when describing the quantum system, it will help you compare and contrast the differences regarding how information is created, calculated, and stored. With that, we'll move on to the next section and describe what a qubit is.

Understanding the qubit

Similar to the bit, which we described previously, the qubit is the fundamental unit in quantum information science. The qubit is similar to the bit in that it can represent the same two states, namely 0 and 1, although a qubit represents a quantum state. The value of the qubit can be read. By read, we mean we can measure the results, which we covered in *Chapter 4, Understanding Basic Quantum Computing Principles*.

They can also be manipulated to derive calculations based on operations performed on each qubit. Recall that the state of a bit can be represented by either a 0 or a 1. A qubit can also be represented as a complex linear combination of 0 and 1. In order to prevent confusion and to differentiate between a bit and a qubit, we will use **Dirac notation**, $|0\rangle$ and $|1\rangle$, to represent the quantum version of the aforementioned 0 and 1 states, respectively. Let's start by visualizing a few things to help us see the difference between the two states.

To begin, the state of a qubit is generally represented as an array or a vector that describes the computational basis states of the qubit, which, in a **Hilbert space**, is often denoted as $|\psi\rangle$.

> A Hilbert space is, in essence, a vector space of all possible real and complex numbers. Hilbert spaces are often applied in the context of infinite-dimensional vector spaces, whereas Euclidean space, for example, refers to a finite-dimensional linear space with an inner product.

The quantum state can be presented as two basis vectors that are orthogonal to each other, as follows:

$$|0\rangle = \begin{bmatrix} 1 \\ 0 \end{bmatrix}$$

The second vector is given as follows:

$$|1\rangle = \begin{bmatrix} 0 \\ 1 \end{bmatrix}$$

As we can see, bits and qubits are similar in that they can represent two basis states, in this case, 0 and 1. Where the qubits differ from classical bits is that a qubit is always in a linear combination of basis states, which is to say that they are always in a superposition of $|0\rangle$ and $|1\rangle$. More formally, this is represented in the following format:

$$| \psi \rangle = \alpha \mid 0 \rangle + \beta \mid 1 \rangle$$

From the previous equation, we can say that α and β are complex in that the sum of their magnitudes is equal to 1 and each squared coefficient represents the probability amplitude, which represents the probability of measuring a $|0\rangle$ or a $|1\rangle$, of the corresponding basis state:

$$|\alpha|^2 + |\beta|^2 = 1$$

Another thing to know about quantum mechanics is that we cannot obtain the values of α and β, even when measuring the qubit. Measuring a qubit requires a qubit to collapse into one of the basis states of 0 or 1.

α and β merely provide some probabilistic information as to whether the results would be one or the other, but this is not a certainty. This is one of the mysteries of quantum mechanics. For now, you can conceptualize measuring a qubit as similar to observing or collapsing a spinning coin to reveal whether it is heads or tails. Once it's been measured, or collapsed, you are not able to have the coin *continue* spinning without restarting the experiment, so all information is lost. You would have to repeat the full operation of spinning the coin again.

Visualizing the qubit states can be done using a simple two-dimensional plane, where the x axis is used to denote the $|0\rangle$ state and the y axis is used to denote the $|1\rangle$ state. Therefore, the vector can be used to represent the probability of each state, which should total 1.

In this section, we covered the differences between bits and qubits. In the next section, we will learn how to visualize qubits and their states using state vectors.

Visualizing the state vector of a qubit

Another visual representation of a qubit and its states is the **Bloch sphere**, named after the physicist Felix Bloch. The Bloch sphere is an ordinary three-dimensional sphere that's generally used as a geometrical representation of the qubit. By this, we mean the sphere can represent a qubit's state as a point anywhere on the surface of the Bloch sphere. As described in the previous chapter, the basis states are represented by the north and south poles.

Conventionally, the north pole of the Bloch sphere represents the $|0\rangle$ state, while the south pole represents the $|1\rangle$ state. Any point on the surface of the Bloch sphere can represent the linear combination of states as a unit vector from the center (origin) to the surface of the Bloch sphere.

Since we have the quantum mechanical constraint that the total probability of the vector must equal 1, we get the following formula:

$$|\psi\rangle|^2 = 1$$

The vector can then only rotate around the X (φ) and Z (θ) axes of the Bloch sphere by using the following representation:

$$|\psi\rangle = \cos(\theta/2)|0\rangle + (cos\emptyset + i\,sin\emptyset)\sin(\theta/2)|1\rangle$$

Here, θ (representing the amplitude of the qubit) and ϕ (representing the phase of the qubit) have the values (limits) $0 \le \theta \le 2\pi$ and $0 \le \phi < 2\pi$. What this illustrates is that any point on the sphere is unique as long as the values of θ and ϕ are themselves unique, where θ represents the colatitude to the z axis and ϕ represents the longitude from the x axis. The quantum state $|\Psi\rangle$ is set from the initial state $|0\rangle$ after the rotations of θ and ϕ have been applied, as illustrated in the following diagram:

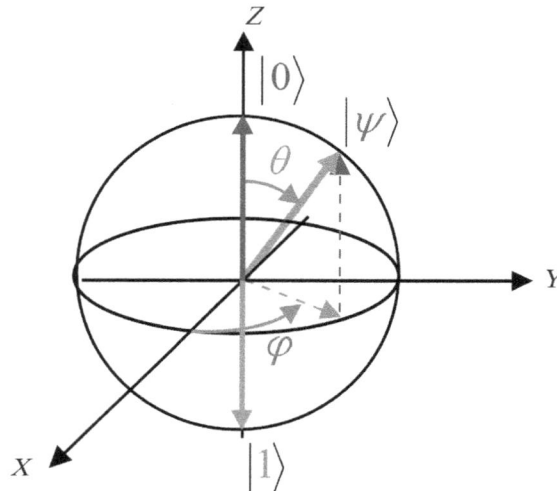

Figure 5.2: Qubit Bloch sphere

(image source: https://commons.wikimedia.org/wiki/File: Sphere_bloch.jpg)

To continue describing a qubit, we will use visuals to help illustrate some key concepts that can be seen on the Bloch sphere. This will also help provide further hands-on exercises for you.

Visualizing the representation of a qubit

In this section, we will visualize the representation of a qubit state using two visualization plotters, the **Bloch sphere** and the **qsphere**. We will begin by creating the Bloch sphere of a qubit in the initial state of $|0\rangle$ so that we can visualize the state vector and phase of a qubit:

1. Create a new notebook and we'll start as we would with all our notebooks by loading our helper file first. Note, of course, if you wish to reuse the notebook from earlier, you can do so and skip this step:

    ```
    # Load the helper file
    %run helper_file_1.0.ipynb
    ```

2. Next, we will create a simple circuit with just a single qubit and use the visualization tools we imported to visualize the qubit state. We'll import the first one in its initial state of $|0\rangle$.

    The following snippet will create the quantum circuit with a single qubit, and then we will get the state vector simulator from our backend. We will be using the state vector simulator to obtain the state information about the circuit once it has finished, whereas the **qasm** simulator returns count information. Finally, we will execute our circuit and get the state vector results:

    ```
    #Create a simple circuit with just one qubit
    qc = QuantumCircuit(1)
    ```

3. Next, we will run our circuit on the state vector simulator and view the results on the Bloch sphere by passing the `statevectorResult` object into the argument of the `plot_bloch_multivector` function:

    ```
    # Get the state vector result from the circuit
    stateVectorResult = Statevector(qc)
    print('state vector results', stateVectorResult)
    ```

    After the preceding cell has finished executing, you should have the state vector results printed out on your console as follows.

    ```
    state vector results:  Statevector([1.+0.j, 0.+0.j],
                dims=(2,))
    ```

Next, we will display first on a Bloch sphere using the Statevector objects draw function. This function is very similar to that of the visualization method we used before, except, in this case, we can include an argument describing which sphere to use to display the state vector information. In this example, we are using bloch to indicate a Bloch sphere; we'll be using this going forward to simplify when bouncing between Bloch sphere and qsphere. Note that we should expect to see our state vector in the initial state of $|0\rangle$ since we have not performed any operations on the qubit.

```
# Display the Bloch sphere
stateVectorResult.draw('bloch')
```

The output that you will see from the preceding function is the Bloch sphere with the qubit state pointed to the north pole or to the $|0\rangle$ state, illustrated as follows:

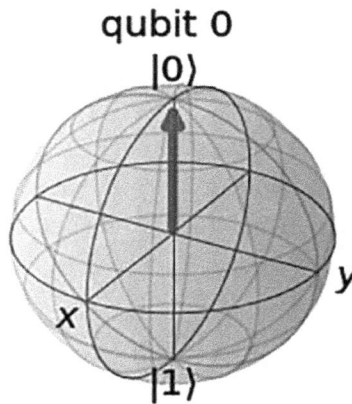

Figure 5.3: Qubit Bloch sphere state vector initialized to $|0\rangle$

4. Next, we will display the state vector results on the qsphere. In this visualization, you will see the state vector in the same state as the Bloch sphere shown in the preceding diagram:

```
stateVectorResult.draw('qsphere')
```

You will also see that it includes the phase of the state vector represented by the color-shaded sphere at the bottom right, as shown in the following output:

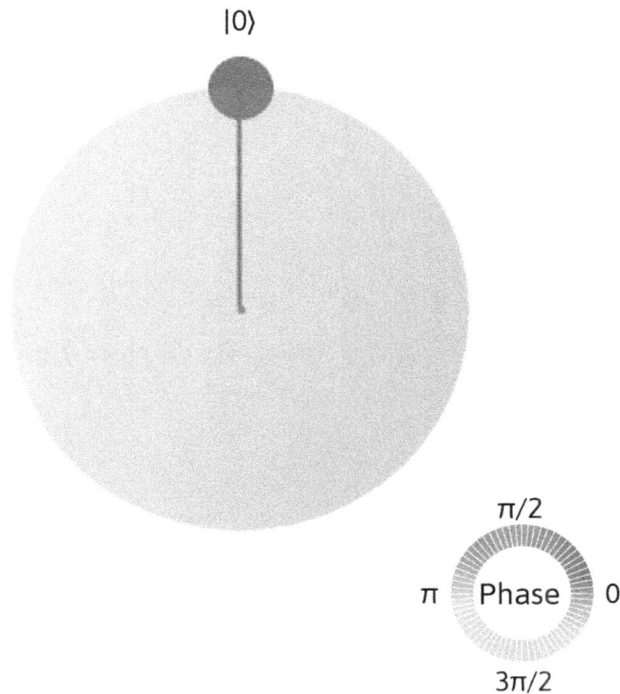

Figure 5.4: Qubit state vector initialized to |0⟩ with phase = 0

From the preceding diagram, note that the state vector at the surface of the qsphere is pointed toward the north pole, indicating it is in the state |0⟩. It is also shaded in blue to indicate the phase of the qubit; in this case, since we did not shift the phase, it is set to the default phase of *0* (blue, as described in the legend wheel at the bottom right of the qsphere).

Note that all images are available in color at the following address: [ADD COLOR IMAGE PACK URL]

This is to indicate the phase of the state vector. The color chart at the bottom right of the preceding diagram is a reference to the phase of the state vector, which is currently *0*.

5.   Now that we are familiar with the state vector of a qubit, let's take it out for a spin. We'll start by flipping the vector from the initial state of $|0\rangle$ to the state of $|1\rangle$ using the NOT gate and then rerun our state vector and plot the results:

```
qc = QuantumCircuit(1)
qc.x(0)
#Run circuit using state vector and display results
stateVectorResult = Statevector(qc)
stateVectorResult.draw('qsphere')
```

As you can see, we are now at the $|1\rangle$ state with the phase still at **0**, as illustrated in the following diagram:

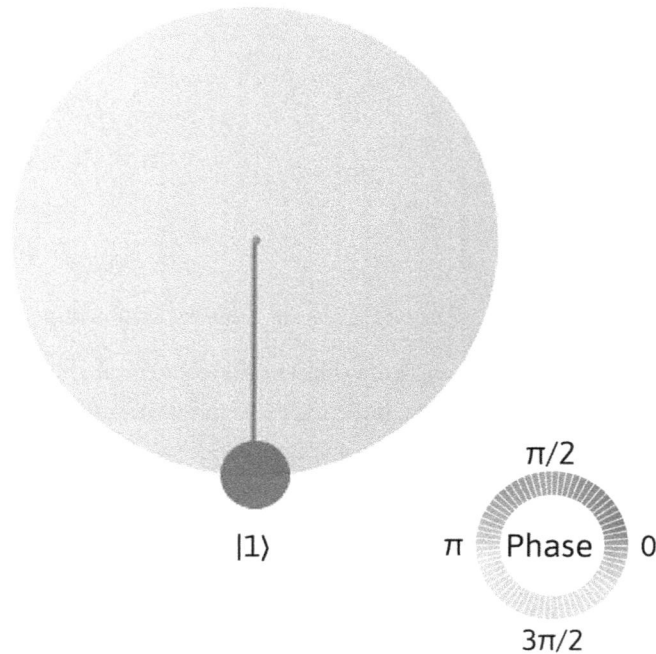

Figure 5.5: Qubit state vector set to $|1\rangle$ with phase = 0

6. Next, we will place the qubit into superposition by adding a Hadamard gate and executing the circuit again. We'll create a new circuit and include a Hadamard gate, as shown in the following code snippet, followed by executing the circuit and plotting the Bloch sphere of the state vector results, which indicates the position of the state vector. In this case, it is on the equator:

```
qc = QuantumCircuit(1)
qc.h(0)

#Run the circuit using the state vector and display results
stateVectorResult = Statevector(qc)
stateVectorResult.draw('bloch')
```

Note that the state vector is a precise linear combination of $|0\rangle$ and $|1\rangle$:

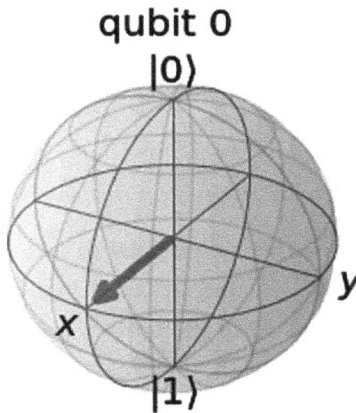

Figure 5.6: Bloch sphere superposition representation, a linear combination of $|0\rangle$ and $|1\rangle$

Let's see what this looks like on the qsphere by plotting the state vector results.

7. Plot the state vector results on the qsphere:

```
stateVectorResult.draw('qsphere')
```

You can see the output of the previous code snippet in the following diagram:

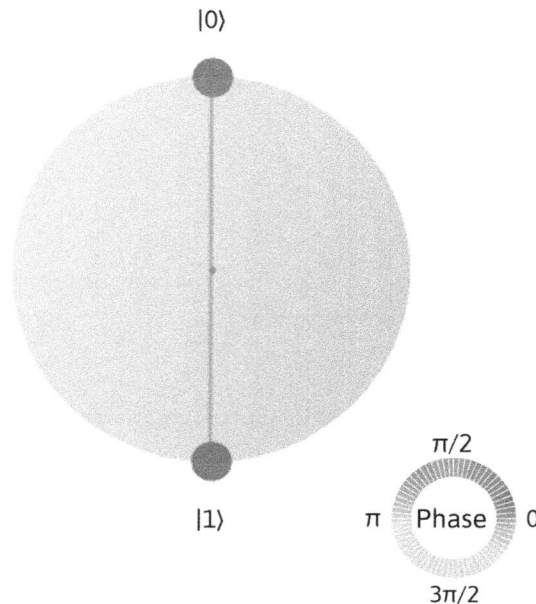

Figure 5.7: Qubit state vector set to a linear combination of |0⟩ and |1⟩, superposition

The results might seem a little confusing. You may be asking yourself why there are two vectors when we only have one qubit and why they are based on the Bloch sphere result. *Shouldn't we only see one?* Well, the difference is that the qsphere visualizes something that the Bloch sphere does not; that is, the visual representation of the amplitude of each possible state. If you look at the size of the ball on the surface of the previous outcome of the qsphere when we executed either the |0⟩ or |1⟩ state, the diameter of the ball was much larger than the two on the surface of the preceding diagram. This is because the amplitude is equal for both |0⟩ and |1⟩, so the size is split between the two, whereas in the previous examples, the amplitude was purely in one of the two states.

In this section, we learned that the qubit could represent itself as a bit by using the two basis states of 0 and 1. We also saw that it can be represented as a linear combination of the two basis states, that is, the amplitude (longitudinal) and phase (latitudinal).

It is by leveraging these features that quantum algorithms can provide the potential for optimizing computational solutions much more than using classical bits. We also saw how to visualize the state of a qubit using two Qiskit visualization functions, the Bloch sphere and the qsphere, which provide information such as amplitude and phase.

In the next section, we will look at how multiple qubits are presented and how to visualize and plot both their real and imaginary components.

Visualizing the state vectors of multiple qubits

So far, we've learned the various ways to represent a qubit, both as a vector $|\psi\rangle$ and visually on a Bloch sphere. We did something similar with the qsphere. In this section, we will learn how to represent multiple qubits and how to represent them in their general state. We will start by making a slight update to the notation. A single qubit is presented as the following vector:

$$|\psi\rangle = \alpha_0|0\rangle + \alpha_1|1\rangle = \begin{bmatrix} a_0 \\ a_1 \end{bmatrix}$$

We can therefore represent two qubits similarly, in the following form:

$$|\psi\rangle = \alpha_{00}|00\rangle + \alpha_{01}|01\rangle + \alpha_{10}|10\rangle + \alpha_{11}|11\rangle = \begin{bmatrix} a_{00} \\ a_{01} \\ a_{10} \\ a_{11} \end{bmatrix}$$

From the preceding equation, you can see that the state $|\psi\rangle$ is used to represent multiple qubits, versus $|\psi\rangle$ for single qubits. The difference is case sensitive: lowercase for single qubits and uppercase for multiple qubits. The probability amplitudes, along with the constraint by the normalization of 1, can therefore be represented as follows:

$$|\alpha_{00}|^2 + |\alpha_{01}|^2 + |\alpha_{10}|^2 + |\alpha_{11}|^2 = 1$$

Let's look at an example that comprises two qubits, the first one in the state $|\psi\rangle$, as follows:

$$|\psi\rangle = \alpha_0|0\rangle + \alpha_1|1\rangle$$

The other qubit, in the state $|\varphi\rangle$, is as follows:

$$|\phi\rangle = \beta_0|0\rangle + \beta_1|1\rangle$$

Combining the two entails taking the **tensor product**, which is used to describe systems of multiple subsystems, of the two qubit states illustrated with the symbol $\otimes$, as follows:

$$|\Psi\rangle = |\psi\rangle \otimes |\varphi\rangle = (\alpha_0|0\rangle + \alpha_1|1\rangle) \otimes (\beta_0|0\rangle + \beta_1|1\rangle)$$

Multiplying across, we will get the following:

$$|\phi\rangle = \alpha_0\beta_0|00\rangle + \alpha_0\beta_1|01\rangle + \alpha_1\beta_0|10\rangle + \alpha_1\beta_1|11\rangle$$

This results in the amplitude vectors, as follows:

$$|\phi\rangle = \begin{pmatrix} \alpha_0\beta_0 \\ \alpha_0\beta_1 \\ \alpha_1\beta_0 \\ \alpha_1\beta_1 \end{pmatrix}$$

Finally, another way to state multi-qubits by their tensor product is by representing them by their product state. Here, the product state of n qubits is a vector of size 2^n. We'll use the same two-vector example described previously. The first is the *00* state:

$$|00\rangle = \begin{pmatrix} 1 \\ 0 \end{pmatrix} \otimes \begin{pmatrix} 1 \\ 0 \end{pmatrix} = \begin{pmatrix} 1 \\ 0 \\ 0 \\ 0 \end{pmatrix}$$

The *01* state is as follows:

$$|01\rangle = \begin{pmatrix} 1 \\ 0 \end{pmatrix} \otimes \begin{pmatrix} 0 \\ 1 \end{pmatrix} = \begin{pmatrix} 0 \\ 1 \\ 0 \\ 0 \end{pmatrix}$$

The *10* state is as follows:

$$|10\rangle = \begin{pmatrix} 0 \\ 1 \end{pmatrix} \otimes \begin{pmatrix} 1 \\ 0 \end{pmatrix} = \begin{pmatrix} 0 \\ 0 \\ 1 \\ 0 \end{pmatrix}$$

Lastly, the *11* state is as follows:

$$|11\rangle = \begin{pmatrix} 0 \\ 1 \end{pmatrix} \otimes \begin{pmatrix} 0 \\ 1 \end{pmatrix} = \begin{pmatrix} 0 \\ 0 \\ 0 \\ 1 \end{pmatrix}$$

The main takeaway from the previous equations is that we can describe two qubits individually as two *2 x 1* column vectors. However, when we want to represent the joint state of the full system, we represent them as a tensor product, which produces the *4 x 1* column vector illustrated previously. This is the mathematical representation of the quantum state, also referred to as the computational basis state of a two-qubit system.

In the next section, we'll briefly discuss the implementation of qubits on the IQP systems and also discuss other technologies that are used to implement qubits.

Implementing qubits on a superconducting system

At the beginning of this chapter, we learned that classical bits can be implemented by various platforms that detect differences between voltages or the phase of a current, or by the state of a flip flop. Just as a bit has different platforms that are used for their implementation, so do qubits.

Some of the more common qubit platforms are **neutral atoms**, **Quantum dots**, **Nitrogen-vacancy** (**NV**) centers within diamond, **trapped ions**, and **superconducting qubits**. Out of these platforms, it is the superconducting qubits that are used on the quantum devices hosted on the IQP. So, in this section, we will cover this platform.

> If you want to learn more about the other platforms, you can review the book *Quantum Computation and Quantum Information* by Michael Nielsen and Isaac Chuang, which covers a lot of these in some detail.

A superconductor is a material made up of a combination of niobium and aluminum that has no electrical resistance, but this can only typically be achieved at very low temperatures, usually around 20 milli-Kelvin. The electrons along the superconductors are therefore used as the basic charge carriers that comprise a pair of electrons, more commonly referred to as **Cooper pairs**. This is different from other conductors, which generally use single electrons. Talking about the specifics of the quantum mechanics or superconducting behavior of the Cooper pairs is beyond the scope of this book. However, you can find various references in *Appendix A* if you are interested. For now, we can think of superconductors as one of the components of the superconducting circuit that makes up the qubit.

Now that we have covered how to visualize the state of a qubit using the state vector simulator and display it on both a Bloch sphere and a qsphere, we can move on to the next chapter, which describes all the qubit gate operators and what effects they have on each other.

Summary

In this chapter, you learned the difference between bits and qubits and how they are represented, both mathematically and visually. You also saw the difference between how single and multi-qubit systems are represented, including their mathematical representations, as well as how they are constructed and operated on. We also covered how to visualize the qubit as a Bloch sphere and a qsphere.

You now have the skills to represent the vector states of single and multiple qubits. You also understand the difference between representing multiple qubits as separate entities and as part of a complete system by using the tensor products of the qubits. This will help you to implement and operate the qubits on IBM Quantum systems.

In the next chapter, we will cover how to perform operations on single and multiple qubits and how those operations are triggered on the qubits of the real devices.

Questions

1. Which would provide visual information about the phase of a qubit—the Bloch sphere or the qsphere?

2. Can you visualize multiple qubits on the Bloch sphere? If not, then describe why you wouldn't.

3. Write out the tensor product of three qubit states in all their forms.

4. What is the probability amplitude of a three-qubit system?

Join us on Discord

Join our community's Discord space for discussions with the author and other readers:

`https://packt.link/3FyN1`

6

Understanding Quantum Logic Gates

Quantum logic gates are very similar to their classical counterparts in that they are used to perform operations by manipulating the qubits in such a way that the results serve to provide a solution. Of course, that's about as far as the comparison can go. Classical gates transition the state of a bit from one to the other by a single operation, in this case, flipping the bit value from 0 to 1, or vice versa. **Quantum gates**, sometimes referred to as **qubit gates**, are different in part because they perform linear transformations on one or more qubits in a complex vector space to transition them from one state to another.

The following topics will be covered in this chapter:

- Reviewing classical logic gates
- Understanding unitary operators
- Understanding single-qubit gates
- Understanding multi-qubit gates
- Understanding non-reversible operators

After reading this chapter, you will have gained knowledge about the fundamental operations that can be performed on both single and multiple qubits. But before we dive right in, let's discuss the format with which I'll try to explain each qubit gate. First, from a learning perspective, some people tend to learn quicker when content is presented purely with mathematics; others prefer visual aids such as graphs; others still prefer a more intuitive approach with analogies and examples.

With that in mind, I shall do my best to ensure that each gate is presented by combining as many of these learning styles as possible. This will be done by providing not only the mathematical representation of each qubit gate, but also a visual representation, and of course, the source code to run the qubit gate operation and its result.

Technical requirements

In this chapter, we will discuss linear transformations of matrices in the **Hilbert space**, so it is highly recommended that you should know the basics of linear algebra.

Knowledge of the qubit and how its states are represented on a Bloch sphere, **QSphere**, or mathematically, is recommended as this chapter will perform complex linear transitions of those qubit states. Knowledge of basic classical single-bit and multi-bit gates is also recommended, but not required, as there is a refresher if needed.

Here is the full source code used throughout this book: `https://github.com/PacktPublishing/Learning-Quantum-Computing-with-Python-and-IBM-Quantum-Second-Edition`.

Reviewing classical logic gates

This section will serve as a refresher for classical logic gates such as **AND, OR, NOR**, and so on. If you are familiar with this subject, you can either skim through it to refresh your memory or skip it entirely and jump to the next section. *Otherwise, let's get logical!*

Logic gates are defined as a device, electronic or otherwise, that implements a logical (usually Boolean) operation. Single-bit and two-bit gates have one or two inputs, respectively. Each input bit value is a state value of either 0 or 1. The operation carried out on the input varies by the type of gate. Each gate operation is usually described using logic truth tables, as illustrated in the following table:

Gate	Operation	Input A B	Output Y	Graphical Representation
Buffer	Outputs the same value as the input	0 1	0 1	
NOT	Reverses the input state	0 1	1 0	

AND	Outputs a 1 if and only if both inputs are 1, otherwise output is 0	0 0 0 1 1 0 1 1	0 0 0 1	
OR	Outputs a 0 if and only if none of the inputs is 1, otherwise output is 1	0 0 0 1 1 0 1 1	0 1 1 1	
XOR	Outputs a 1 if and only if both inputs are different, otherwise output is 0	0 0 0 1 1 0 1 1	0 1 1 0	
NAND	Outputs a 0 if and only if both inputs are 1, otherwise output is 1	0 0 0 1 1 0 1 1	1 1 1 0	
NOR	Outputs a 1 if and only if both inputs are 0, otherwise outputs a 0	0 0 0 1 1 0 1 1	1 0 0 0	
XNOR	Outputs a 1 if and only if inputs are both either 0 or 1, otherwise outputs 0	0 0 0 1 1 0 1 1	1 0 0 1	

Table 6.1: Classical logic gates

The preceding table lists some of the common classical gates, descriptions of the operation that each gate performs on the input state, the result (output) of the gate operation, and their graphical representations.

Let's consider some things of note regarding classical bits that will help you later understand the differences they have compared to **quantum bits (qubits)**. First is that there are only two single-bit gates, the buffer and the NOT gate. Among these two, only the NOT gate performs a Boolean operation on the classical bit by flipping the bit value of the input, so if the input to the NOT gate was a 0, then the output would be a 1. On the other hand, the buffer gate simply outputs the same value as the input. All the other gates operate on two input bit values that output a single value, which is determined by the gate's Boolean operation. For example, if both input values to an AND gate are 1, it will output a 1. Otherwise, the output will be 0.

One problem, however, particularly with regard to the two-bit gates, is that if you only have access to the output, then the information about the input is lost. For example, if you obtain the result from an AND bit and the value is 0, *could you tell what the input values were for A and B (the inputs)?* Unfortunately, the answer to this question is no. The input information is lost because the output does not include any information about the input value, which renders the gates irreversible. Likewise, with other two-bit gates, if I gave you just the output value of the gate, you could not tell me with 100% certainty what the input values were.

Reversibility is a unique property that qubit gates have, in that you can reverse the operation of the qubit gate to obtain the previous state. This is also because the second postulate of quantum mechanics states that transformations between quantum states must be unitary, therefore reversible. We see this when we apply a Hadamard gate to a single qubit in the ground state 0; if we apply another Hadamard gate after the first one, then the state of the qubit returns to the ground state 0.

And finally, to close our discussion on classical gates, we'll discuss **universal logic gates**. These gates are the type of gates used to create other logic gates. **NOR** and **NAND** gates are good examples of universal gates in that they can be used to create NOT and AND gates. Let's take a look at the following diagram that illustrates creating a NOT gate (inverter) by using a NAND gate:

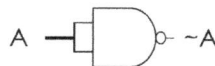

Figure 6.1: Using a NAND gate to create a NOT gate

As you can see, by wiring both inputs of the NAND gate together, forming a single input (**A**), this logically creates a NOT gate that flips the value of the input. Computational systems having universal gates is an important feature as it provides the ability to compose complex logical circuits to solve problems. This of course led to the creation of integrated circuits, which are specialized circuits used to compute problems or to perform specific operations such as an adder or a counter, respectively.

Now that we have reviewed the functionality of classical gates, we can continue to the next section where we will cover the basics of quantum logic gates. There, we will also see some similarities and some unique properties that they display with regard to the classical bit.

Understanding quantum unitary operators

Unitary operators are defined as a unitary transformation of a rigid body rotation of the Hilbert space. When these unitary operators are applied to the basis states of the Hilbert space, for example, the $|0\rangle$ and $|1\rangle$ state, the results transform the state vector position but it does not change its length. Let's see what this means for a qubit. The basis states of a qubit are mapped on the Hilbert space $\mathbb{C}$ as described in *Chapter 5, Understanding a Qubit*, $|V_0\rangle = \alpha|0\rangle + \beta|1\rangle$ and $|v_1\rangle = \gamma|0\rangle + \delta|1\rangle$, where α, β, γ, and $\delta \in \mathbb{C}$ are linear transformations that preserve orthogonality over unitary transformations. We'll wrap our heads around this definition a bit by looking at this mathematically first.

A linear transformation on a complex vector space can be described by a 2x2 matrix, **U**:

$$U = \begin{pmatrix} \alpha & \gamma \\ \beta & \delta \end{pmatrix}$$

Furthermore, if we obtain the complex transpose of the matrix U as $U^\dagger$, by transposing the matrix U and applying the complex conjugate, as illustrated:

$$U^\dagger = \begin{pmatrix} \alpha^\dagger & \beta^\dagger \\ \gamma^\dagger & \delta^\dagger \end{pmatrix}$$

Then we can say that the matrix U is unitary if $UU^\dagger = I$, where I represents the Identity matrix $\begin{pmatrix} 1 & 0 \\ 0 & 1 \end{pmatrix}$, as shown here:

$$UU^\dagger = U^\dagger U = \begin{pmatrix} \alpha & \gamma \\ \beta & \delta \end{pmatrix} \begin{pmatrix} \alpha^\dagger & \beta^\dagger \\ \gamma^\dagger & \delta^\dagger \end{pmatrix} = \begin{pmatrix} 1 & 0 \\ 0 & 1 \end{pmatrix} = I$$

An intuitive way to think of this is to just imagine unitary transformation simply as rotations of the complex vector space that preserve the length of the original vector. The rotation of the complex vector space further ensures that quantum transformations are not just unitary operations but are also **reversible operations** as they would rotate around a specified axis.

Reversibility of quantum gates is realized by unitary transformations. As seen in the previous unitary equation, if you have a unitary operator U applied to a qubit via a gate, then by applying the complex conjugate $U^\dagger$ of the unitary operator to the qubit via a second gate, the result would be equivalent to applying an Identity matrix to the original vector.

An example of this would be if you were to trigger an operation that would rotate the vector space around the x axis by an angle π, and you then apply the complex conjugate of that operation, then you'll return to the original position from which you started. This reversible functionality is something that is not possible with some classical-bit gates we mentioned earlier, such as an AND gate.

With quantum unitary transformations, there is no loss of information. Should you need to return to the previous state, you would merely have to use their conjugate transpose, in reverse order, and you'd get back to where you originally started. We will see some interesting examples of reversibility in all gates.

There is a special case operator that is not reversible, the **measurement** operator, which we will learn about in the *Understanding non-reversible operators* section.

Now that we understand unitary and reversible operators, we can get down to learning about quantum gates.

Understanding single-qubit gates

Before we start digging into the description of quantum gates, let's simplify the format so it's easy to both understand and reference. Intuitively, the easiest way to imagine the operation of each gate is by rotating the vector that ends on the surface of the Bloch sphere around a specified axis. Recall as well that the Bloch sphere always starts with the unit vector set to the initial state. The initial state is set when the quantum circuit is first created; in this case, it is initialized to the basis state $|0\rangle$ (the north pole of the Bloch sphere), as illustrated in the following diagram:

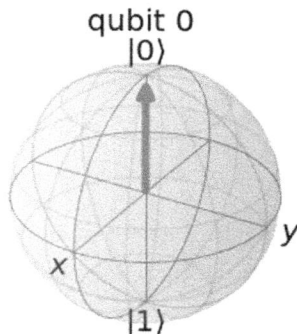

Figure 6.2: Bloch sphere representation of the basis state $|0\rangle$

One thing that will help us understand some of the labels we will see in the gate's truth table is to define the values of each axis, where each axis is referred to as **basis elements**. For example, we can see from the previous figure that the z axis has the north pole labeled as $|0\rangle$ and the south pole as $|1\rangle$. These two points form the computational basis elements for the basis state vectors $|0\rangle$ and $|1\rangle$. However, we do not yet have labels for the x or y axes. Let's define them now.

Each basis element (axis) has a positive and negative side that originates at the center of the Bloch sphere. Each basis has a name associated with each axis:

- **Computational** for the z axis
- **Hadamard** for the x axis
- **Circular** for the y axis

The x basis has a label defined as follows:

$$x = |+\rangle = 1/\sqrt{2} \ (|0\rangle + |1\rangle)$$

The -x basis has a label defined as follows:

$$-x = |-\rangle = 1/\sqrt{2} \ (|0\rangle - |1\rangle)$$

The y basis has a label defined as follows:

$$y = |i\rangle = 1/\sqrt{2} \ (|0\rangle + i|1\rangle)$$

The -y basis has a label defined as follows:

$$-y = |-i\rangle = 1/\sqrt{2} \ (|0\rangle - i|1\rangle)$$

The z basis has a label defined as follows:

$$z = |0\rangle$$

The -z basis has a label defined as follows:

$$-z = |1\rangle$$

The labels are also illustrated at the ends of each axis in the following Bloch sphere diagram, where the dotted line indicates the negative direction of the axis:

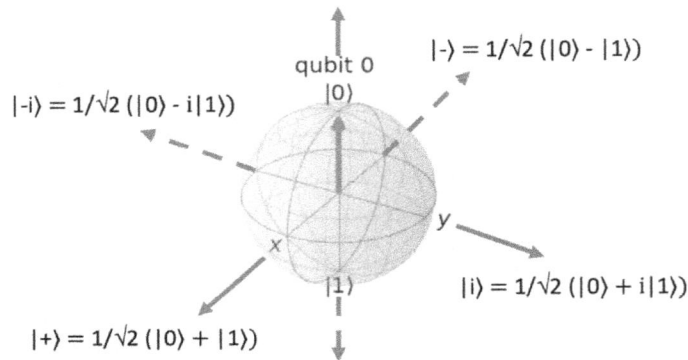

Figure 6.3: Basis state labels of each axis of a Bloch sphere

Each gate we apply in the code snippets will operate on the qubit starting from the initial $|0\rangle$ state. There are some gates you will see that we will have to prepare into a superposition state using an H gate to see the effects.

In this case, by transitioning the vector down onto the *x* axis, and then applying a Z gate rotation, you can then more clearly see the rotation take effect. Details on how this is done will be in the description of—yes, you guessed it—the Z gate. But for now, let's open the helper file and review one of the functions that will help us visualize the gates without having to write so much code, and handle some of the repetitive functions such as executing and visualizing the circuits. This way, we will just create the quantum circuits, add the gates, and execute the circuits using a function that will return the results and the images to visualize the results and the circuit diagrams. To start, let's review the function titled **execute_circuit_sv** from our helper file that will handle this:

```
# Will run the circuit on the state vector (sv) simulator
# Returns state vector results, circuit diagram, BlochSphere and QSphere
def execute_circuit_sv(quantum_circuit):
    #Get the state vector results
```

```
statevectorResults = run_sv_circuit(quantum_circuit)
#Draw the circuit diagram
circuit_diagram = quantum_circuit.draw(output="mpl")
#Draw the QSphere
q_sphere = statevectorResults.draw('qsphere')
#Draw the Bloch sphere
bloch_sphere = statevectorResults.draw('bloch')
#Return the results, circuit diagram, and QSphere
return statevectorResults, circuit_diagram, q_sphere, bloch_sphere
```

The preceding code will return the four components: state vector results, the circuit diagram, and both the QSphere and the Bloch sphere. We will use each of these to illustrate each state vector result, each gate on a circuit, and the visual representation.

Now we can focus on the quantum gates and their effect on the qubits, and not so much on executing the circuits or displaying the results.

Hadamard (H) gate

The **H** gate is one of the most commonly used quantum gates. It's not surprising as this is the gate that places the quantum state of the qubit into a complex linear superposition of the two basis states. This is what establishes the superposition of all qubits that are leveraged by most quantum algorithms. It is denoted as follows:

$$H = \frac{1}{\sqrt{2}} \begin{pmatrix} 1 & 1 \\ 1 & -1 \end{pmatrix}$$

The following truth table illustrates that the operation rotates the state vector of the qubit along the x axis and z axis by $\pi/2$ (90°), causing the state vector to be in a complex linear superposition of $|0\rangle$ and $|1\rangle$:

Input	Output
$|0\rangle$	$\dfrac{|0\rangle + |1\rangle}{\sqrt{2}}$
$|1\rangle$	$\dfrac{|0\rangle + |1\rangle}{\sqrt{2}}$

Table 6.2: Truth table of a Hadamard operation

Let's continue and create a new notebook and add a circuit using these steps:

1. First, we add an H gate to the qubit, and execute it on the backend, the same as we did in the previous example:

```
# Load helper file
%run helper_file_1.0.ipynb


#H-gate
#Create the single qubit circuit
qc = QuantumCircuit(1)
#Add an H gate to the qubit
qc.h(0)
#Execute the circuit and capture all the results
result, img, qsphere, bloch_sphere = execute_circuit_sv(qc)
```

2. Let's examine the state vector results by running the following cell:

```
result
```

This prints out the following state vector values of the qubit:

```
Statevector([0.70710678+0.j, 0.70710678+0.j], dims=(2,))
```

3. To draw the circuit diagram for the H gate, run the following in a cell:

```
img
```

This displays the circuit diagram with the **H** gate added to the qubit, as shown in the following diagram:

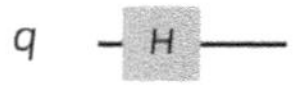

Figure 6.4: Circuit diagram with an H gate

4. Now to view the Bloch sphere representation, run the following in a cell:

```
bloch_sphere
```

5. The Bloch sphere representation has changed into a superposition state, which means it will have an equal probability result of $|0\rangle$ or $|1\rangle$.

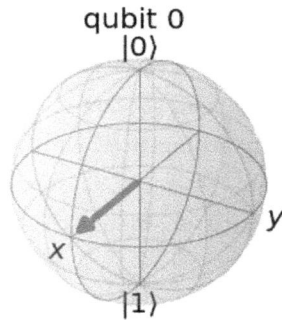

Figure 6.5: H gate Bloch sphere

6.   To view the QSphere representation, run the following in a cell:

```
qsphere
```

The QSphere, as you can see, has an equal probability of being either |0⟩ or |1⟩. The tip of the vectors, as you'll notice, have the same diameter, indicating visually that both have equal probability:

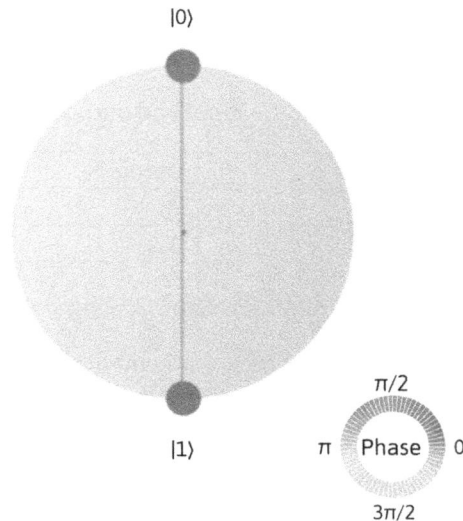

Figure 6.6: H gate QSphere representation

The Hadamard (H) gate is a unique gate. We will see this gate many more times in this chapter and future chapters—having the ability to negate a state vector, also referred to as a phase kick, is very useful in many quantum algorithms.

Pauli gates

The first group of single-qubit gates we will discuss are commonly referred to as **Pauli matrix** gates, named after the physicist Wolfgang Pauli. The complex matrix representation of the four gates, I, X, Y, and Z, are defined as *2 x 2* complex matrices, which are both Hermitian and unitary and are represented by the Greek letter sigma $(\sigma_0, \sigma_z, \sigma_y, \sigma_z)$, respectively. When the conjugate transpose of a complex N x N matrix is equal to itself, then such a matrix is known as a Hermitian matrix.

> Note that the Identity matrix is subscripted with a 0, and the *x, y, z* subscripts can also be represented as $(\sigma_1, \sigma_2, \sigma_3)$.

We'll start with the easiest of the gates, the Identity gate.

Identity (I) Pauli gate

The **I gate**, also known as the **Identity gate,** is a gate that does not perform any operation on the qubit. It does not change the state of the qubit. Mathematically, this is represented as an Identity matrix, hence the name of the gate. This equation is given as follows:

$$I = \sigma_0 = \begin{pmatrix} 1 & 0 \\ 0 & 1 \end{pmatrix}$$

The truth table for this gate shows that the input and output have the same state:

Input	Output
$|0\rangle$	$|0\rangle$
$|1\rangle$	$|1\rangle$

Table 6.3: Truth table of Identity gate

The idea of an Identity gate is generally used mathematically to illustrate certain properties of operations, as we did earlier in this chapter to prove that unitary operators are reversible. In that example, the Identity matrix was used to illustrate that multiplying a unitary operator with its complex conjugate would produce the same output as applying no operation, or an Identity matrix, to the qubit.

Let's move on to the next gate section.

NOT (X) Pauli gate

The **X gate** is also called the NOT gate because of the similar effect it has on the basis states as its classical-bit gate counterpart. One notable difference is that the X gate moves the state vector from one basis state to the other, as illustrated in *Table 6.4*. Visualizing this operation can be seen via the Bloch sphere result as a rotation of the vector from the initial state, $|0\rangle$. Because of its spherical presentation, we refer to operations as rotations around some axis, in this case, the X gate is a π (180°) rotation about the x axis, which is represented by the Pauli X-gate operator as follows:

$$X = \sigma_1 = \begin{pmatrix} 0 & 1 \\ 1 & 0 \end{pmatrix}$$

The following truth table illustrates that the operation rotates the input around the x axis by π (180), hence if the input is $|0\rangle$, then the output is $|1\rangle$, and vice versa:

Input	Output
$|0\rangle$	$|1\rangle$
$|1\rangle$	$|0\rangle$

Table 6.4: Truth table of X (NOT) gate

Let's now create a circuit by following the next steps to include in our notebook:

1. First, add an X gate to it, and execute it using our helper function to do the heavy lifting for us:

```
#X-gate
#Create the single qubit circuit
qc = QuantumCircuit(1)
#Add an X gate to the qubit
qc.x(0)
#Execute the circuit and capture all the results
result, img, qsphere, bloch_sphere = execute_circuit_sv(qc)
```

2. Let's examine the state vector results by running the following cell:

```
result
```

This prints out the state vector values of the qubit, which we expect should represent $|\psi\rangle = a|0\rangle + b|1\rangle$, where $a=0$ and $b=1$, as shown in the following result:

```
Statevector([0.+0.j, 1.+0.j], dims=(2,))
```

3. Then, to draw the circuit diagram for the X gate, run the following in a cell:

    ```
    img
    ```

    This displays the circuit diagram with the **X** gate added to the qubit, as shown in the following diagram:

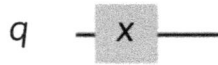

Figure 6.7: X gate

4. Now, to view the Bloch sphere representation, run the following in a cell:

    ```
    bloch_sphere
    ```

5. The Bloch sphere representation has changed the state of the qubit from $|0\rangle$ to $|1\rangle$:

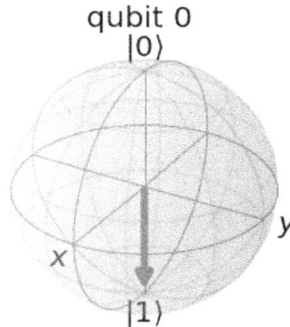

Figure 6.8: X gate Bloch sphere

6. Now, to view the QSphere representation, run the following in a cell:

    ```
    qsphere
    ```

    The QSphere represents the transition of the quantum state of the qubit from $|0\rangle$ to $|1\rangle$:

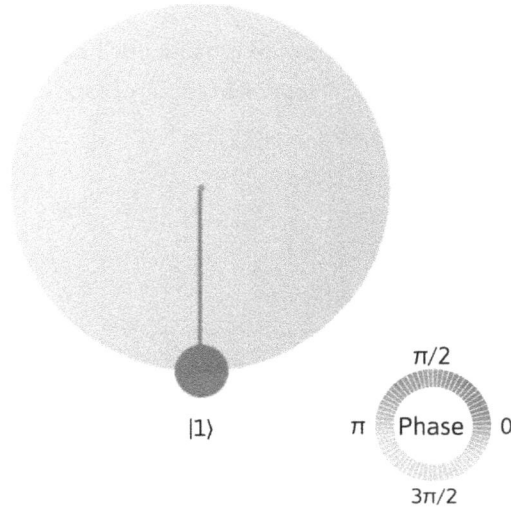

Figure 6.9: X gate QSphere

As we have seen, the X gate serves as a good example that quantum gates can also be used to perform the same operations as classical gates. One other thing you will notice from the QSphere result is the color wheel that represents the phase of the state vector, which in this case is blue to indicate it's in phase (0).

Y Pauli gate

The **Y gate** is a rotation around the y axis by π (180°), shown as follows:

$$Y = \sigma_2 = \begin{pmatrix} 0 & -i \\ i & 0 \end{pmatrix}$$

Here, the following truth table illustrates that the operation rotates the input around the y axis by π (180°), hence if the input to the gate is $|0\rangle$, then the output from the gate is $|1\rangle$ and vice versa; note the phase difference where $|0\rangle$ has the phase at i, and $|1\rangle$ has a phase shift, indicated by the $-i$:

Input	Output
$|0\rangle$	$-i\,|1\rangle$
$|1\rangle$	$-i\,|0\rangle$

Table 6.5: Truth table representing phase rotation of the y axis

Let's now create a circuit by using the following steps:

1. First, add a Y gate to it, and execute it using our helper function, which provides the quantum circuit and the visual representations of each circuit we execute:

    ```
    #Y-gate operation on a qubit
    #Create the single qubit circuit
    qc = QuantumCircuit(1)
    #Add a Y gate to the qubit
    qc.y(0)
    #Execute the circuit and capture all the results returned
    result, img, qsphere, bloch_sphere = execute_circuit_sv(qc)
    ```

2. Let's examine the state vector results by running the following cell:

    ```
    result
    ```

    This prints out the state vector values of the qubit:

    ```
    Statevector([0.-0.j, 0.+1.j], dims=(2,))
    ```

3. To draw the circuit diagram for the Y gate, run the following in a cell:

    ```
    img
    ```

    The preceding code displays the circuit diagram with the Y gate added to the qubit, as shown in the following diagram:

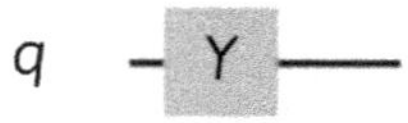

Figure 6.10: Y gate

4. Now, to view the Bloch sphere representation, run the following in a cell:

    ```
    bloch_sphere
    ```

5. The Bloch sphere representation has changed from $|0\rangle$ to $|1\rangle$; however, the rotation was done around the y axis as opposed to the x axis, and the result, in this case, is the same.

qubit 0
|0⟩

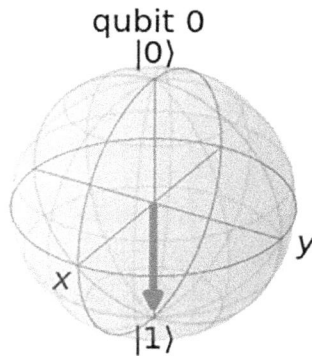

Figure 6.11: Y gate Bloch sphere

6. To view the QSphere representation, run the following in a cell. Of course, you can also use `bloch_sphere` to view the Bloch sphere:

```
qsphere
```

The QSphere, as you can see, has transitioned the state of the qubit from |0⟩ to |1⟩. Note that the colors indicating states might be different based on your system settings or as they could change over time in the code itself when visualized:

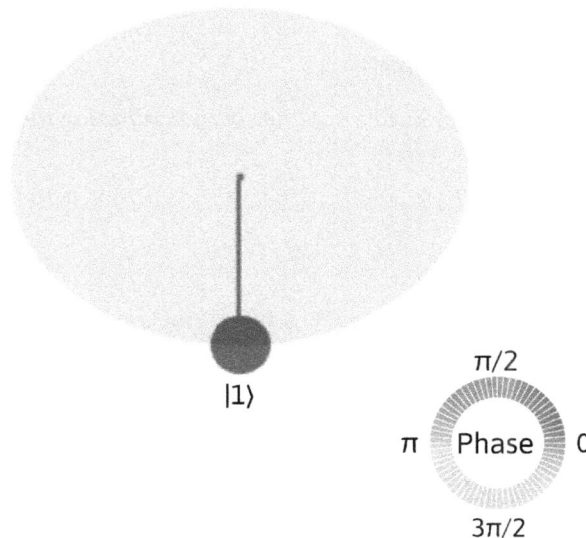

Figure 6.12: Y gate QSphere

The Y gate, as we can see from the results, operates very similarly to the X gate, at least when the origin of the state vector is the same.

Now, let's proceed to the final Pauli gate.

Z gate

The **Z gate** is also commonly referred to as a **phase gate**, mostly because rather than rotating along the vertical axis as the X and Y gates do, the Z gate rotates along the longitude of the Hilbert space, hence the phase of the Hilbert space. This is denoted as follows:

$$Z = \sigma_3 = \begin{pmatrix} 1 & 0 \\ 0 & -1 \end{pmatrix}$$

The following truth table illustrates that the operation rotates the input around the z axis by π (180°). If the rotation initializes from the $|0\rangle$ basis state, then the phase does not change; however, if the input initializes from the $|1\rangle$ state, then the output is a phase shift of p to $-|1\rangle$. This negation is a very important feature that you will see in many quantum algorithms:

Input	Output
$|0\rangle$	$|0\rangle$
$|1\rangle$	$-|1\rangle$

Table 6.6: Truth table of a phase shift around the x axis

Let's now create a circuit for the Z gate:

1. First, we place the qubit into a superposition state using the H gate, and then add a Z gate operator to it:

```
#Z-gate
#Create the single qubit circuit
qc = QuantumCircuit(1)
#Add an H gate to the qubit to set the qubit in #superposition
qc.h(0)
#Add a Z gate to the qubit to rotate out of phase by π/2
qc.z(0)
#Execute the circuit and capture all the results
result, img, qsphere, bloch_sphere = execute_circuit_sv(qc)
```

2. Let's examine the state vector results by running the following cell:

```
result
```

This prints out the state vector values of the qubit. Note that depending on how you have things set up, the very small values may be truncated to 0. If this is not set, you may see a very small value, such as 0.00000000e+00j:

```
Statevector([ 0.70710678+0.j, -0.70710678+0.j], dims=(2,))
```

3. To draw the circuit diagram for the Z gate, run the following in a cell:

```
img
```

This displays the circuit diagram with the H gate removed, so don't think you have to include the H gate in order to use the Z gate—as mentioned earlier, the H gate was just added to illustrate the operational effect of the gate:

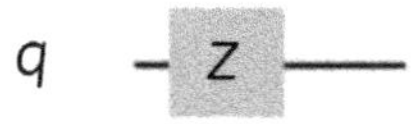

Figure 6.13: Circuit diagram with a Z gate

4. Now, to view the Bloch sphere representation, run the following in a cell:

```
bloch_sphere
```

5. The Bloch sphere representation has changed into a superposition state between $|0\rangle$ and $|1\rangle$; however, it is on the negative side of the x axis.

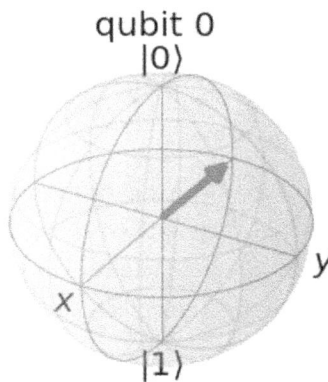

Figure 6.14: Z gate Bloch sphere

6. To view the QSphere representation, run the following in a cell:

    ```
    qsphere
    ```

    The QSphere, as you can see, has an equal probability of being $|0\rangle$ and $|1\rangle$; however, the $|1\rangle$ state you see is out of phase by π, as illustrated in the following output:

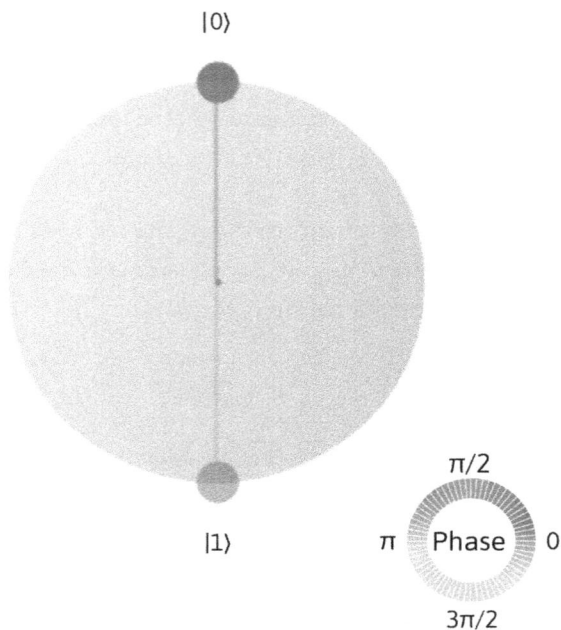

Figure 6.15: Z gate QSphere representation after first applying an H gate

As you can see in the preceding diagram, the Z gate provides a way to perform a phase shift on a qubit, causing the state of the qubit to change its sign from positive to negative. If you want to see this for yourself, then try the following.

Recall the code you ran earlier to execute an X gate. In that example, we started with the qubit initially at the basis state $|0\rangle$, and we then applied an X gate that resulted in the state $|1\rangle$. Now, add another line after adding the X gate and include the Z gate. You'll notice that the result is the same, $|1\rangle$, only now you'll notice that the state result is negative. I'll leave it to you to try it out for yourself and observe the difference.

Let's move on to the next section, where we will discuss **phase gates**.

Phase gates

Phase gates are what we use to map $|1\rangle$ to $e^{i\phi}|1\rangle$, where $e^{i\phi}$ is Euler's equation. This does not have an effect on the probability of measuring a $|0\rangle$ or a $|1\rangle$; however, it does affect the phase of the quantum state. This may not make sense just yet, but once you start learning about some advanced features that leverage phase shifts, it will be very clear. For now, let's learn about the gates that operate the various phase shifts on a qubit.

S gate

The **S gate** is like a Z gate; the only difference is the amount by which the state vector is rotating. For the S gate, that rotation is $\pi/2$. The matrix representation of the S gate is described here:

$$S = \begin{pmatrix} 1 & 0 \\ 0 & e^{i\frac{\pi}{\sqrt{2}}} \end{pmatrix}$$

The following truth table illustrates that the operation rotates the input around the z axis by $\pi/2$ (90°), hence if the input is $|1\rangle$, then the output is a phase shift of $e^{i\frac{\pi}{\sqrt{2}}}|1\rangle$:

Input	Output
$|0\rangle$	$|0\rangle$
$|1\rangle$	$e^{i\frac{\pi}{\sqrt{2}}}|1\rangle$

Table 6.7: Truth table representing phase rotation S

We will follow these steps to create a circuit with an S gate:

1. The truth table is best illustrated by placing the vector onto the x axis first; we will add an H gate first before appending the S gate:

```
#S-gate
#Create the single qubit circuit
qc = QuantumCircuit(1)
#Add an H gate to the qubit to drop the vector onto the #X-axis
qc.h(0)
#Add an S gate to the qubit
qc.s(0)
#Execute the circuit and capture all the results
result, img, qsphere, bloch_sphere = execute_circuit_sv(qc)
```

2.   Let's examine the state vector results by running the following cell:

```
result
```

This prints out the state vector values of the qubit:

```
Statevector([7.07106781e-01+0.j, 4.32978028e-17+0.70710678j],
dims=(2,))
```

3.   To draw the circuit diagram for the S gate, run the following in a cell:

```
img
```

This displays the circuit diagram where we added an H gate to induce superposition and then apply the **S** gate to the qubit, as shown in the following diagram:

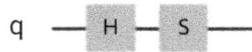

Figure 6.16: Circuit with an S gate

4.   Now, to view the Bloch sphere representation, run the following in a cell:

```
bloch_sphere
```

5.   The Bloch sphere representation has changed into a superposition state, which means it will have an equal probability result of $|0\rangle$ or $|1\rangle$ but with a phase shift of $\pi/2$:

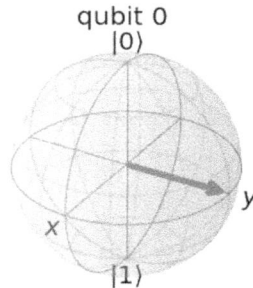

Figure 6.17: S gate Bloch sphere

6.   To view the QSphere representation, run the following in a cell:

```
qsphere
```

The QSphere, as you can see, has an equal probability of being $|0\rangle$ and $|1\rangle$ with a phase shift of $\pi/2$:

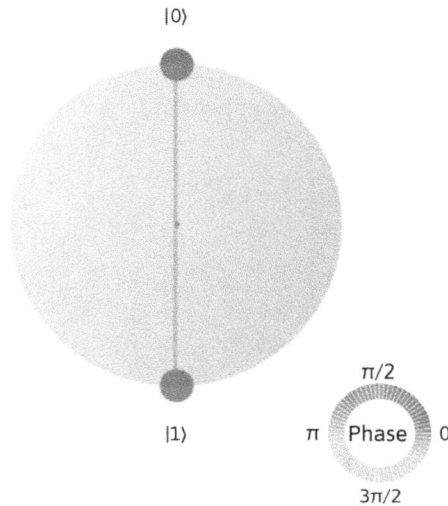

Figure 6.18: S gate, π/2 phase rotation on the QSphere

As the S gate transitions the state to the positive Z axis by $\pi/2$, we will now see how to transition the state to the negative Z axis by $\pi/2$.

S† (dagger) gate

The $S^\dagger$ gate is the same as the S gate, except it rotates in the opposite, or negative, direction. Hence the results are the same, but negated. The matrix representation illustrates this by including the negative in the phase shift:

$$S^\dagger = \begin{pmatrix} 1 & 0 \\ 0 & e^{-i\frac{\pi}{\sqrt{2}}} \end{pmatrix}$$

The following truth table illustrates that the operation rotates the input around the z axis by $-\pi/2$ (-90). As with the S gate, if the input is the $|0\rangle$ state, then the output is $|0\rangle$, but if the input is the $|1\rangle$ state, the output is a phase rotation in the negative direction:

Input	Output
$|0\rangle$	$|0\rangle$
$|1\rangle$	$e^{-i\frac{\pi}{\sqrt{2}}}|1\rangle$

Table 6.8: Truth table representation of phase gate $S^\dagger$

This is best illustrated by placing the qubit into a superposition first with an H gate. We then create a circuit diagram for $S^\dagger$ gate by using these steps:

1. We will add an H gate first before appending the $S^\dagger$ (sdg) gate:

```
#Sdg-gate
#Create the single qubit circuit
qc = QuantumCircuit(1)
#Add an H gate to the qubit to drop the vector onto the #X-axis
qc.h(0)
#Add an S† gate to the qubit
qc.sdg(0)
#Execute the circuit and capture all the results
result, img, qsphere, bloch_sphere = execute_circuit_sv(qc)
```

2. Let's examine the state vector results by running the following cell:

```
result
```

This prints out the state vector values of the qubit:

```
Statevector([0.70710678+0.j, 4.32978028e-17-0.70710678j], dims=(2,))
```

3. To draw the circuit diagram for the $S^\dagger$ gate, run the following in a cell:

```
img
```

This displays the circuit diagram with the $S^\dagger$ gate added to the qubit, as shown in the following diagram:

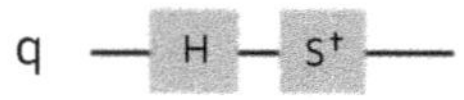

Figure 6.19: Circuit with an $S^\dagger$ gate

4. Now, to view the Bloch sphere representation, run the following in a cell:

```
bloch_sphere
```

5. The Bloch sphere representation has changed into a superposition state, which means it will have an equal probability result of $|0\rangle$ or $|1\rangle$ with a phase shift of $3\pi/2$ or $-\pi/2$.

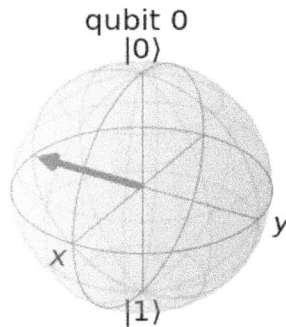

Figure 6.20: S† gate Bloch sphere

6. To view the QSphere representation, run the following in a cell:

```
qsphere
```

The QSphere, as you can see, has an equal probability of being $|0\rangle$ and $|0\rangle$ with a phase shift of $3\pi/2$ or $-\pi/2$:

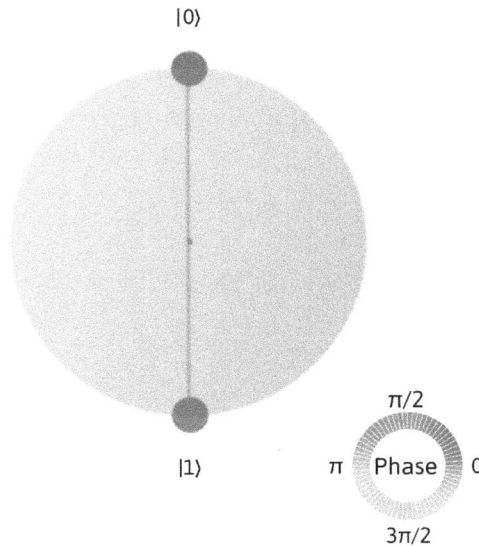

Figure 6.21: S† gate, $-\pi/2$ phase rotation on the QSphere

Now that we have created the circuit with an S† gate and can shift the phase of the qubit in opposite directions and are not limited to a single direction to apply phase shifts, we will move on to the next section, which will help us understand how to create a circuit with a T gate.

T gate

The **T gate** is the same as the S gate, only the rotation is $\pi/4$. The matrix representation of the gate is as follows:

$$T = \begin{pmatrix} 1 & 0 \\ 0 & e^{i\frac{\pi}{\sqrt{4}}} \end{pmatrix}$$

The following truth table illustrates that the operation rotates the input around the z axis by $\pi/4$ (45°), hence if the input is the $|0\rangle$ state, then the output will be the same. If the input is $|1\rangle$, however, then the output would be a phase rotation of $\pi/4$:

Input	Output
$|0\rangle$	$|0\rangle$
$|1\rangle$	$e^{i\frac{\pi}{\sqrt{4}}} |1\rangle$

Table 6.9: Truth table representation of phase gate T

As with all phase gates, it's best to begin in a superposition state, so we will start by including a Hadamard gate, then we will create a circuit using the T gate, as illustrated in the following steps:

1. First, we add an H gate before appending the T gate:

```
#T-gate
#Create the single qubit circuit
qc = QuantumCircuit(1)
#Add an H gate to the qubit to drop the vector onto the #X-axis
qc.h(0)
#Add a T gate to the qubit
qc.t(0)
#Execute the circuit and capture all the results
result, img, qsphere, bloch_sphere = execute_circuit_sv(qc)
```

2. We then examine the state vector results by running the following cell:

```
result
```

This prints out the state vector values of the qubit:

```
Statevector([0.70710678+0.j , 0.5+0.5j], dims=(2,))
```

3. To draw the circuit diagram for the T gate, run the following in a cell:

    ```
    img
    ```

    This displays the circuit diagram with the **T** gate added to the qubit, as shown in the following diagram:

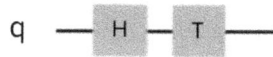

Figure 6.22: Circuit representation of the T gate

4. Now, to view the Bloch sphere representation, run the following in a cell:

    ```
    bloch_sphere
    ```

5. The Bloch sphere representation has changed into a superposition state, which means it will have an equal probability result of $|0\rangle$ or $|1\rangle$, and transitioned the phase of the state by $\pi/4$.

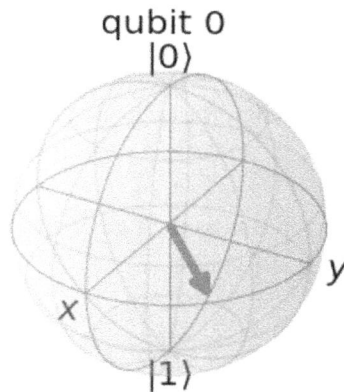

Figure 6.23: S† gate Bloch sphere

6. To view the QSphere representation, run the following in a cell:

    ```
    qsphere
    ```

The QSphere, as you can see, has transitioned the phase of the state by $\pi/4$:

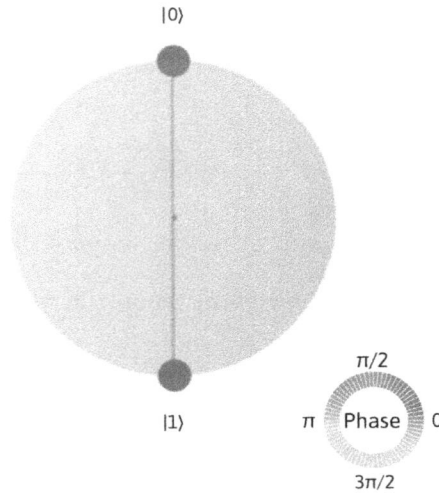

Figure 6.24: T gate, $\pi/4$ phase rotation on the QSphere

Similar to the S gate, we will want to rotate in all directions, so let's take a look at a phase gate that transitions the state of the qubit in the opposite direction.

T† (dagger) gate

The T† gate has the same phase rotation as the T gate, that is, $\pi/4$, only in the opposite direction. Its matrix representation is given as follows:

$$T^\dagger = \begin{pmatrix} 1 & 0 \\ 0 & e^{-i\frac{\pi}{\sqrt{4}}} \end{pmatrix}$$

The following truth table illustrates that the operation rotates the input around the z axis by $-\pi/4$ (-45 °), so if the input is $|0\rangle$, then the output is $|0\rangle$. If the input is $|1\rangle$, then the output is a negative rotation of $-\pi/4$:

Input	Output
$|0\rangle$	$|0\rangle$
$|1\rangle$	$e^{-i\frac{\pi}{\sqrt{4}}}|1\rangle$

Table 6.10: Truth table representation of phase gate T†

This too is best illustrated by placing the vector onto the *x* axis first, so we will create a circuit using the T† gate by following these steps:

1. First, we add an H gate before then appending the T† (tdg) gate:

```
#Tdg-gate
#Create the single qubit circuit
qc = QuantumCircuit(1)
#Add an H gate to the qubit to drop the vector onto the #X-axis
qc.h(0)
#Add a Tdg gate to the qubit
qc.tdg(0)
#Execute the circuit and capture all the results
result, img, qsphere, bloch_sphere = execute_circuit_sv(qc)
```

2. Next, we examine the state vector results by running the following cell:

```
result
```

This prints out the state vector values of the qubit, where you will notice that the imaginary number is now negative:

```
Statevector([0.70710678+0.j , 0.5 -0.5j], dims=(2,))
```

3. To draw the circuit diagram for the T† gate, run the following in a cell:

```
img
```

This displays the circuit diagram with the T† gate added to the qubit, as shown in the following diagram:

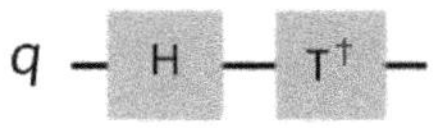

Figure 6.25: Circuit representation using a T† gate

4. Now, to view the Bloch sphere representation, run the following in a cell:

```
bloch_sphere
```

5. The Bloch sphere representation has changed into a superposition state, which means it will have an equal probability result of $|0\rangle$ or $|1\rangle$, and has transitioned the state of the qubit by $-\pi/4$.

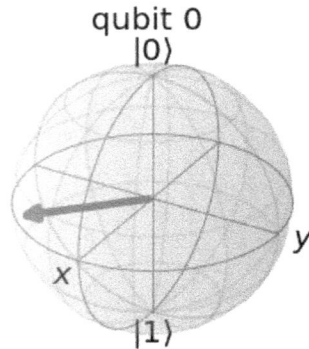

Figure 6.26: T† gate, $-\pi/4$ phase rotation on the Bloch sphere

6. To view the QSphere representation, run the following in a cell:

```
qsphere
```

The QSphere, as you can see, has transitioned the state of the qubit by $-\pi/4$:

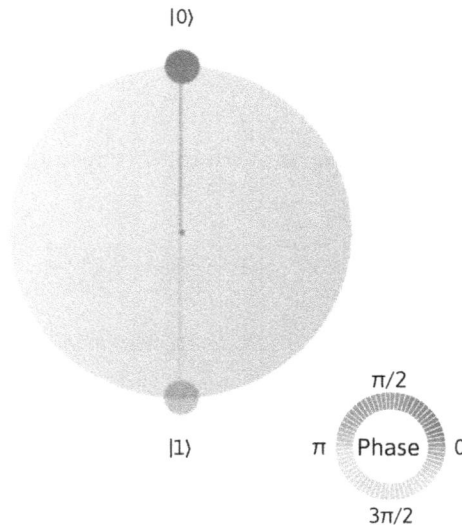

Figure 6.27: T† gate, $-\pi/4$ phase transition on the QSphere

The preceding gates, as you might have noticed, have predetermined rotation angles from the horizontal or vertical axis to help you set the state of the qubit. If you wish to specify the angle of rotation yourself, the following rotation gates allow you to specify the angle by which to rotate around a given axis. Like the other gates, these rotation gates are also reversible and unitary.

Rx gate

You can think of **Rx gates** as your custom rotation gates. Note that I used the term *rotate* and not *flip*. This is because visualizing the operation of the quantum gates is usually done via the QSphere.

Because of its spherical presentation, we refer to operations as rotations around the axis by $-\pi < \theta < \pi$ (we will see this clearly in the following code examples):

$$R_X(\theta) = \begin{pmatrix} \cos(\theta/2) & -i \cdot \sin(\theta/2) \\ -i \cdot \sin(\theta/2) & \cos(\theta/2) \end{pmatrix}$$

By applying a Y rotation, we get the following formula:

$$R_Y(\theta) = \begin{pmatrix} \cos(\theta/2) & -\sin(\theta/2) \\ \sin(\theta/2) & \cos(\theta/2) \end{pmatrix}$$

Finally, a Z rotation will yield the following formula:

$$R_Z(\theta) = \begin{pmatrix} e^{-i\theta} & 0 \\ 0 & e^{i\theta} \end{pmatrix}$$

We'll create a circuit using one of the rotation gates – let's go with the Rz gate:

1. First, we will rotate along the *z* axis by $\pi/6$. We'll be using the `math` library to `import pi`, and our friendly H gate will be applied to help illustrate the phase shift:

```
#Rz-gate
#Create the single qubit circuit
qc = QuantumCircuit(1)
#Import pi from the math library
from math import pi
#Add an H gate to help visualize phase rotation
qc.h(0)
#Add an RZ gate with an arbitrary angle theta of pi/6
qc.rz(pi/6, 0)
#Execute the circuit and capture all the results
result, img, qsphere, bloch_sphere = execute_circuit_sv(qc)
```

2. Next, we examine the state vector results by running the following cell:

```
result
```

This prints out the state vector values of the qubit:

```
Statevector([0.06830127-0.1830127j, 0.6830127+0.1830127j], dim=(2,))
```

3. To draw the circuit diagram for the Rz gate, run the following in a cell:

```
img
```

This displays the circuit diagram with the **Rz** gate added to the qubit, as shown in the following diagram:

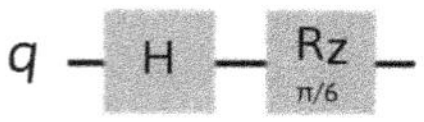

Figure 6.28: Circuit representation using an Rz gate

4. Now, to view the Bloch sphere representation, run the following in a cell:

```
bloch_sphere
```

5. The Bloch sphere representation has changed into a superposition state, which means it will have an equal probability result of $|0\rangle$ or $|1\rangle$ and has rotated the state by a phase of $\pi/6$.

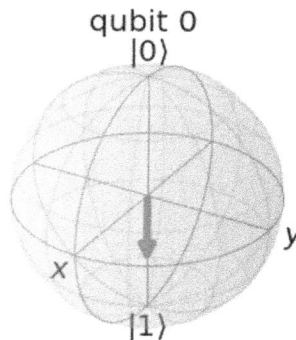

Figure 6.29: RZ gate Bloch sphere

6. To view the QSphere representation, run the following in a cell:

```
qsphere
```

The QSphere, as you can see, has transitioned the state by a phase of $\pi/6$:

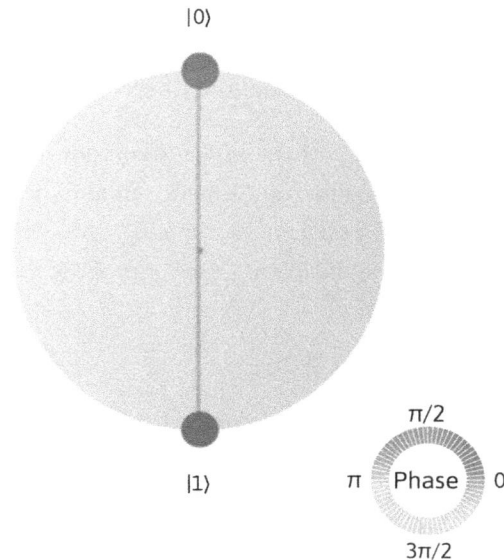

Figure 6.30: RZ gate QSphere transitioned phase of $\pi/6$

These rotation gates help us provide specific gate rotations around each axis.

There are other universal gates that imitate the function of a custom gate using a more general alternative, so let's review them next.

Universal U gate

The **U gate**, as mentioned earlier in the book, is used in order to define a universal quantum system where you would need to ensure that the quantum system adheres to certain criteria, the most popular of which are the **DiVincenzo criteria** one of which states that it should have a universal set of quantum gates.

We discussed how, in a classical system, both NOR and NAND gates are considered classical universal gates. In a quantum system, the **U** gate is defined as a universal gate, due to its ability to provide multiple degrees of freedom to rotate about the Hilbert space of a qubit. The U gate has parameter fields that determine how much the state vector should move along the given axis. Let's look at them individually first, and then we'll apply each gate to a qubit to examine the results.

The **U** gate has three parameters that are applied as rotations on all axes, that is, the x axis, y axis, and z axis, respectively. The matrix representation of the U gate is defined as follows:

$$U(\theta, \phi, \lambda) = \begin{pmatrix} \cos(\theta/2) & -e^{i\lambda}\sin(\theta/2) \\ e^{i\phi}\sin(\theta/2) & e^{i(\phi+\lambda)}\cos(\theta/2) \end{pmatrix}$$

In the preceding equation, θ, ϕ, and λ are the angles of rotation in radians as described in the preceding $U(\theta, \phi, \lambda)$ equation. Note that for the U gate to remain a unitary operation, that is, $U^{\dagger}U = I$, the angles must be confined to the range $0 \leq \theta \leq \pi$, and $0 \leq \phi \leq 2\pi$. We can also see these ranges in the U matrix, where these values lie in the arguments of the matrix, which leaves the phase l to also have a range of $0 \leq \lambda \leq 2\pi$.

Let's create a circuit that implements the U gate:

1. First, we will create a single-qubit circuit and apply the U gate to it with each angle set to $\pi/2$. We'll reuse our state vector helper function, execute_circuit_sv, so we can extract the state vector results, and the QSphere to visualize the state vector:

    ```
    #U-gate
    from math import pi
    #Create a single qubit circuit
    qc = QuantumCircuit(1)
    #Add a U gate and rotate all parameters by pi/2, and #apply it to
    the qubit
    qc.u(pi/2, pi/2, pi/2, 0)
    #Execute the circuit and capture all the results
    result, img, qsphere, bloch_sphere = execute_circuit_sv(qc)
    ```

    The result value we shall see is set to the following:

    ```
    Statevector([7.07106781e-01+0.j, 4.32978028e-17+0.70710678j],
    dims=(2,))
    ```

    Note that for convenience, I replaced the value `4.32978028e-17` from the results with a `0`, because the number is too small and insignificant.

2. The expected circuit diagram for **U** is as follows, with the parameters listed at the bottom:

Figure 6.31: The U gate set with all rotation parameters to $\pi/2$

3. Now, to view the Bloch sphere representation, run the following in a cell:

    ```
    bloch_sphere
    ```

    The Bloch sphere representation has changed so that the state is set after all parameters have applied the specified rotation.

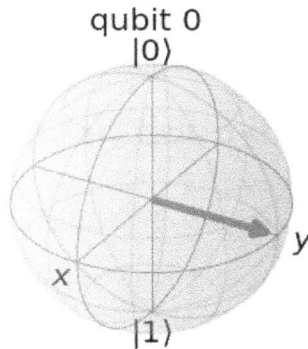

Figure 6.32: U gate, Bloch sphere representation with all parameters set to $\pi/2$

The QSphere representation, produced by executing the qsphere command, is shown as follows:

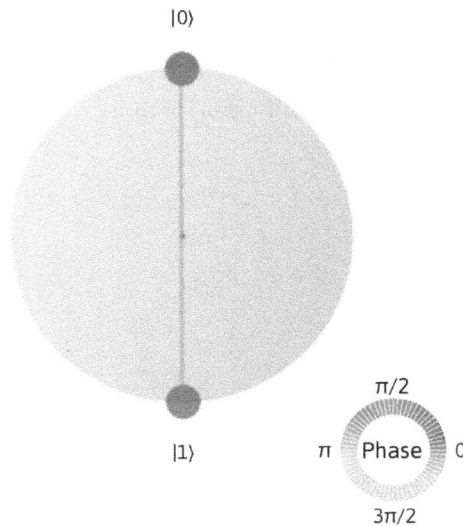

Figure 6.33: The QSphere representation of the U gate set with all parameters to $\pi/2$

As you can see, you can apply various angles to the U gate in order to set the state of the qubit into any point in the Hilbert space. This also allows you to initialize the state of a qubit using the U gate to set the state.

Now you know that single-qubit gates provide many ways to create a complex linear combination of their basis states, but manipulation of a single qubit alone is not enough to carry out the functionality that most quantum algorithms require. One such example is **quantum entanglement**. This is where multi-qubit gates come into play. Let's learn about those in the next section.

Understanding multi-qubit gates

As described in *Chapter 5, Understanding the Qubit*, two or more qubits can combine their states by their **tensor product**, sometimes referred to as the **Kronecker product**.

In this section, we will discuss the multi-qubit gates and how they operate on the qubits similarly to how single-qubit gates do, which includes them being unitary and reversible.

To keep the descriptions and examples uniform, the following descriptions of the multi-qubit gates will be presented the same way as the single-qubit gates. We will open the helper file again and review another function titled `execute_circuit_returns`. The helper function will have a few differences, the first of which will be the Qiskit primitive Sampler to run our circuits. We are using this for now so that you don't use up your quantum hardware allotted time on these simple circuits. Save the hardware for the fun work later in this book. Also, just like the previous helper function we used for single qubit gates, this will return multiple values including: total counts, circuit diagram, and histogram (or distribution) of results. Let's review the code:

```python
# Will execute the circuit on the Sampler primitive
# Returns results, circuit diagram, and histogram
def execute_circuit_returns(quantum_circuit):
    from qiskit.primitives import Sampler
    sampler = Sampler()

result = sampler.run(quantum_circuit, shots=1024).result()
    quasi_dists = result.quasi_dists

#Get the counts
counts = quasi_dists[0].binary_probabilities()

circuit_diagram = quantum_circuit.draw(output="mpl")
```

```
#Create a histogram of the results
histogram = plot_distribution(counts)
#Return the results, circuit diagram, and histogram
return counts, circuit_diagram, histogram
```

The purpose of switching over to the Sampler primitive is not that we can't use the state vector simulator; it's primarily so we can observe some of the interesting characteristics of our circuit and the gates. For those who wish to use the state vector simulator, do not worry. There will be some challenges in the *Questions* section at the end of this chapter that will allow you to use it.

Another difference you will see is that we are no longer using the Bloch sphere or QSphere to visualize the quantum states. Rather, we will replace them with a histogram plot of the quasi-distribution, which is a dict-like class for representing the quasi-probabilities. For each circuit we will be creating, we will include more than one qubit, as these multi-qubit gates all operate on two or more qubits.

Now that we have reviewed our helper function, let's move on to the next set of gates, the **multi-qubit gates, specifically 2-qubit gates**. These include the following:

- The **CNOT** gate
- The **Toffoli** gate
- The **Swap** gate

We will learn about these gates in the following sections.

CNOT two-qubit gate

The **CNOT gate**, often referred to as a **Control-NOT** gate, is similar to the **XOR** classical-bit gate in that if you provide two input states of either 0 or 1, the results will be the same as if the input states were run through an XOR gate. The CNOT gate is composed of two parts.

The first part is the **Control**, which is connected to one of the qubits, and is what triggers the CNOT gate to perform an operation on the other qubit connected to the other end of the CNOT gate, the **Target**.

The Target is an operation that will be performed on the other qubit; in this case, it's a **NOT** operation. Recall from the previous section on single-qubit gates that the NOT gate rotates the qubit about the x axis by π. The CNOT gate is one of the more commonly used multi-qubit gates as it is how qubits get entangled.

The CNOT gate is also described as a **Control-X (CX)** gate since the target is often coded as an X operation. You will see this CX gate convention when running the following example.

The matrix representation of a CNOT gate is a *4 x 4* matrix due to the tensor product of two qubits, as illustrated here:

$$CNOT = \begin{bmatrix} 1 & 0 & 0 & 0 \\ 0 & 1 & 0 & 0 \\ 0 & 0 & 0 & 1 \\ 0 & 0 & 1 & 0 \end{bmatrix}$$

Notice that the top-left *2 x 2* quadrant of the CNOT matrix represents an Identity matrix, I, and the bottom-right *2 x 2* quadrant represents the **X** matrix. This matrix describes the state when the first qubit, q_0, is the Target and the second qubit, q_1, is the Control.

The following truth table illustrates that when the Control qubit (the left side of the input vector) is 0, there is no change to the Target qubit (the right side of the input vector). When the Control qubit is set to 1, then the Target qubit operation is enabled and therefore rotates the Target qubit around the *x* axis by π (that is, 180°):

Input	Output
$|00\rangle$	$|00\rangle$
$|01\rangle$	$|01\rangle$
$|10\rangle$	$|11\rangle$
$|11\rangle$	$|10\rangle$

Table 6.11: Truth table representation of CNOT gate

Let's now create a circuit, add a CNOT gate, and execute it:

1. We'll begin by creating a two-qubit quantum circuit and applying a Hadamard gate on the first qubit, and a CNOT gate on the two qubits, where the Control is set to the first qubit and the Target is set to the second qubit:

```
#CNOT-gate
#Create a two-qubit circuit
qc = QuantumCircuit(2)
#Add an H gate to the qubit
qc.h(0)
#Add an CNOT gate where, control = first, target = second #qubit
qc.cx(0,1)
```

```
#Measure all qubits and send results to classical bits
qc.measure_all()
#Execute the circuit and capture all the results
counts, img, histogram = execute_circuit_returns(qc)
```

2. Then, we will review the result counts by running the following cell:

    ```
    counts
    ```

    This prints out the count results:

    ```
    {'11': 526, '00': 498}
    ```

3. To draw the circuit diagram for the CNOT gate, run the following in a cell:

    ```
    img
    ```

    The following circuit diagram illustrates the CNOT gate, where the Control is q_0 and the Target is q_1:

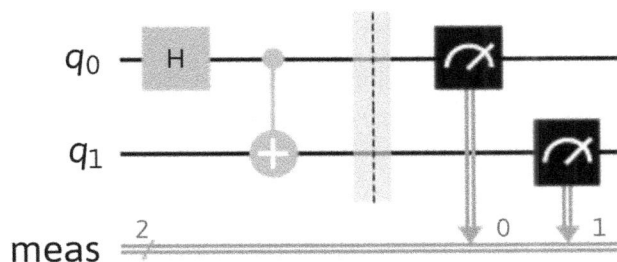

Figure 6.34: Circuit representation using a CNOT gate

4. To view the histogram results with the counts after executing the previous circuit, enter the following into a cell:

    ```
    histogram
    ```

The following illustrates the results including an H gate. The following graph shows the probabilities of the results being either 00 or 11:

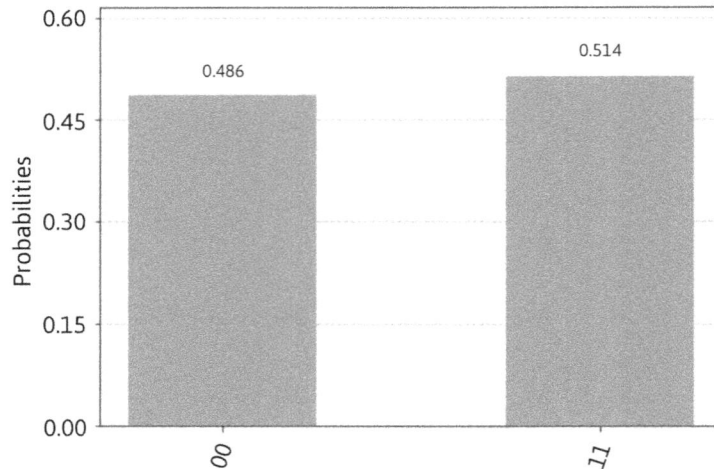

Figure 6.35: Histogram representation of CNOT results from circuit, where the y axis represents the quasi-probabilities of the result.

The results from the previous circuit illustrate how the CNOT gates can be used to entangle two qubits, where one qubit can control the operation of another qubit, in this case, applying a NOT gate to the target qubit.

In the following section, I will clarify what the entanglement of multiple qubits means. There are other Control gates that implement other operations, such as **Control-Y (CY)**, **Control-Z (CZ)**, **Control-H (CH)**, and more. These gates all share the same characteristics as the CNOT (**CX, Control-X**) gate in that they have a Source and Target. The main difference, as you can imagine, is the operation that the Target would follow. For the CNOT gate, the Target would operate with an X gate, and naturally, a Control-Y gate would operate a Y gate on the Target qubit. Try out a few for yourself and see how the results differ. Notice that the operations will be the same as if you run the single gate to the Target gate.

The last multi-qubit gate we will focus on, which is also used in a variety of quantum algorithms, is the **Toffoli** gate.

Toffoli multi-qubit gate

The **Toffoli** gate is named after Tommaso Toffoli, an Italian-American professor in computer and electrical engineering at Boston University. This gate is very similar to the multi-qubit Control gates mentioned earlier, only this gate has multiple Controls and a single Target, which in this case is a NOT gate. To simplify the description of multi-control gates, they are written out in the following format: **CCX**. This is to indicate it is a dual-controlled Control-Not gate, and a **CCCX** is a triple-controlled Control-Not gate.

The general matrix representation of a Toffoli gate is an *8 x 8* matrix because of the tensor product of three qubits, as illustrated in the following matrix. Notice that the first three diagonal *2 x 2* matrix blocks are the Identity matrix and the last *2 x 2* matrix (bottom right) is a NOT gate representation that flips the qubit. Note that the matrix for the Toffoli gate in Qiskit is slightly different as it increases the matrix size by 2^n, where *n* is the number of qubits onto which the gate is applied. In this case, we have 2^3 since we have a three-qubit gate:

$$\text{Toffoli} = \begin{bmatrix} 1 & 0 & 0 & 0 & 0 & 0 & 0 & 0 \\ 0 & 1 & 0 & 0 & 0 & 0 & 0 & 0 \\ 0 & 0 & 1 & 0 & 0 & 0 & 0 & 0 \\ 0 & 0 & 0 & 1 & 0 & 0 & 0 & 0 \\ 0 & 0 & 0 & 0 & 1 & 0 & 0 & 0 \\ 0 & 0 & 0 & 0 & 0 & 1 & 0 & 0 \\ 0 & 0 & 0 & 0 & 0 & 0 & 0 & 1 \\ 0 & 0 & 0 & 0 & 0 & 0 & 1 & 0 \end{bmatrix}$$

Let's run this gate to see the results of it on our quantum circuit:

1. We'll begin by creating a three-qubit quantum circuit and applying a CCX (Toffoli) gate, where the first two qubits are the control qubits, and the third qubit is the target qubit:

```
#Toffoli (CCX)-gate
#Create a three-qubit circuit
qc = QuantumCircuit(3)
#Enable the Control qubits, first two qubits, of the Toffoli gate
qc.x(range(2))
#Add the Toffoli gate (CCX)
qc.ccx(0,1,2)
#Execute the circuit and capture all the results
result, img, qsphere, bloch_sphere = execute_circuit_sv(qc)
```

The result of executing this circuit will be no surprise, and consists of 8 possible states since we are running everything on a three-qubit circuit, which means 2^3 basis states, where the last state, 111, is the only one set:

```
[0.+0.00000000e+00j 0.+0.00000000e+00j 0.+0.00000000e+00j
 0.+0.00000000e+00j 0.+0.00000000e+00j 0.+0.00000000e+00j
 0.+0.00000000e+00j 1.-3.05311332e-16j]
```

2. Let's visualize the Bloch sphere in a new cell:

    ```
    bloch_sphere
    ```

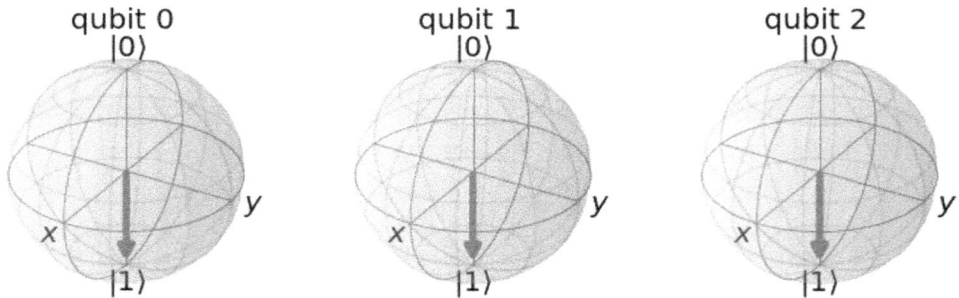

Figure 6.36: Bloch sphere representation from the Toffoli (CCX) gate circuit results

3. And now let's see our results on the QSphere with the qsphere command:

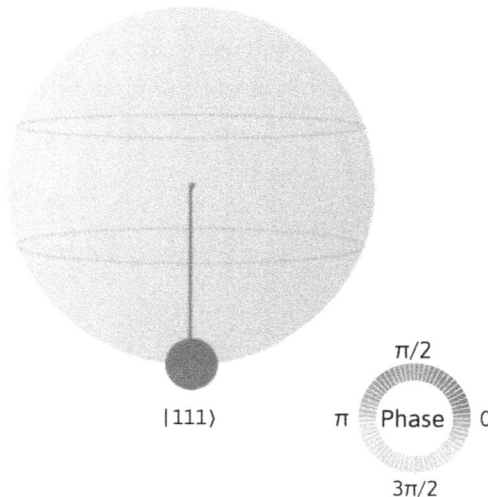

Figure 6.37: Qsphere representation from the Toffoli (CCX) gate circuit results

As we can see from the above results, the final state is $|111\rangle$, as expected, since the qubits all start in the $|000\rangle$ state, but as the control qubits are each set to $|1\rangle$, this sets the target qubit, a NOT gate, to enable and, therefore, change the state of the target qubit q_2 to the $|1\rangle$ state, therefore rendering the results $|111\rangle$.

The circuit diagram for the Toffoli gate is as follows:

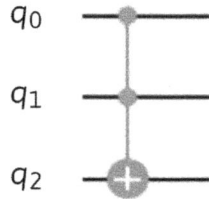

Figure 6.38: Circuit representation of a Toffoli (CCX) gate

4. Let's see how the base gates are used to create this three-qubit gate. In a new cell, run the decompose function of the quantum circuit:

    ```
    qc_decomposed = qc.decompose()
    qc_decomposed.draw(output="mpl")
    ```

    This will result in the following illustration of all the gates needed to create a single Toffoli gate. Note that this may be different as this was how it was displayed at the time of writing:

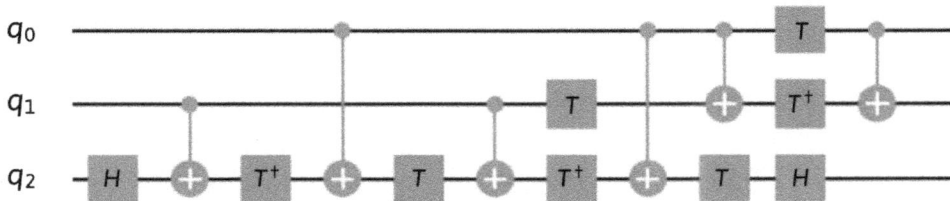

Figure 6.39: Gates necessary to create a Toffoli (CCX) gate

This looks very complicated. You can see that the use of the various single-qubit and multi-qubit gates used to represent this one gate are quite complex. In this example, you can see the use of H, CNOT, and $T^\dagger$ gates. There are other multi-qubit gates that leverage single and two-qubit gates in order to operate. The Toffoli gate allows us to operate on multiple qubits, which we shall see later on when we start to delve into quantum algorithms.

Let's look at a gate we would use to swap information between one qubit and another.

Swap gate

The **swap gate** is used to swap two qubit values. The matrix representation of the swap gate is defined as follows:

$$\text{SWAP} = \begin{bmatrix} 1 & 0 & 0 & 0 \\ 0 & 0 & 1 & 0 \\ 0 & 1 & 0 & 0 \\ 0 & 0 & 0 & 1 \end{bmatrix}$$

Let's create a circuit and implement this by swapping two qubits:

1. We will set the first qubit to the $|0\rangle$ state and the second qubit to the $|1\rangle$ state. Then, we will invoke a swap between the two using the swap gate and verify the results of each qubit:

    ```
    #Swap-gate
    from math import pi
    #Create a two-qubit circuit
    qc = QuantumCircuit(2)
    #Qubit 0 is initialized to |0> state
    #Prepare qubit 1 to the |1> state
    qc.x(1)
    #Now swap gates
    qc.swap(0,1)
    #Execute the circuit and capture all the results
    result, img, qsphere, bloch_sphere = execute_circuit_sv(qc)
    ```

    By viewing the resulting diagram of the circuit (img) you will see a circuit diagram of the swap gate as shown here, just after the X gate we included for comparison:

    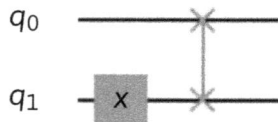

    Figure 6.40: Circuit diagram of an X gate followed by a Swap gate

2. Before viewing the Bloch sphere and QSphere result for each qubit, let's take a moment to review what we expect to see. Our two qubits are first initialized to the $|0\rangle$ state, and we then applied an X gate to the second qubit (q1) to change its state to $|1\rangle$. Finally, we added a Swap gate to swap the value of q_0 and q_1, which would result in $q_0 = |1\rangle$ and $q_1 = |0\rangle$. Let's see the results of both the Bloch sphere and QSphere:

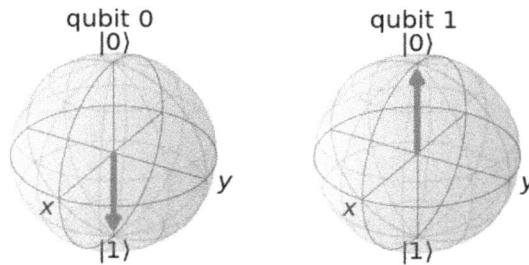

Figure 6.41: Bloch sphere representation of a Swap gate

3. Here, the results you see swap the value of one qubit with the other, which ends up with qubit 0 with the value we set or qubit 1, and vice versa. Let's now look at the QSphere results:

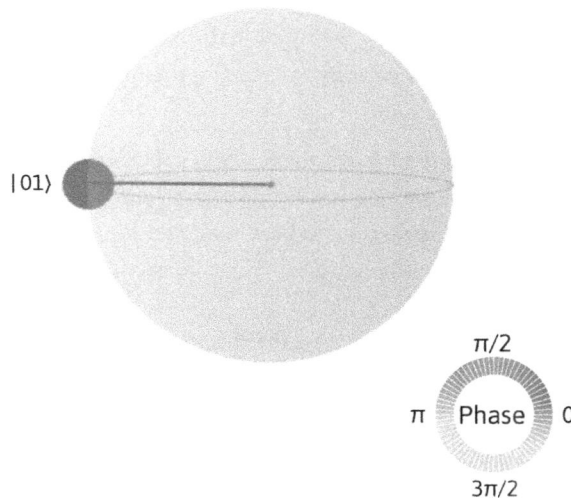

Figure 6.42: QSphere representation after applying the Swap gate

Excellent! The results, as we can see in the previous diagram, show that the state vectors for both qubits are set as expected, with $q_0 = |1\rangle$ and $q_1 = |0\rangle$.

This is a good opportunity to describe how the order of the qubit results is displayed in the Bra-Ket notation. Note from the values in the QSphere in the previous figure that the qubit at position 0 (the right-most value) is set to one and the qubit at position 1 is set to zero. This is the Bra-Ket qubit order. As more qubits are added, they are therefore appended to the left of the previous qubits, for example, $|q_1, q_0\rangle$

In this section, we have learned about multi-qubit gates, namely, CNOT and Toffoli gates. We also learned about an extra gate, that is, the Swap gate.

Now that we are familiar with single-qubit and multi-qubit gates, let's review the non-reversible measurement operators.

Understanding the measurement operator

A **non-reversible operator** is an operator that is applied on a qubit(s), and if applying the same operator again on the same qubits, then the results will not return the qubits to the same state that they had prior to applying the operator.

This section will cover the non-reversible operators, specifically the measurement operator, and the reasons why they are just as important as the other operators discussed previously.

Measurement is an operator that instructs the quantum system to measure the quantum state of the system. Before we dive into how we include the measurement instruction in our quantum circuits, let's first define what is meant by measuring the quantum state of the system.

Note that measurement outcomes are in general probabilistic. What we lose in information is the complex amplitude of each computational basis state, into which we can encode information. At best, we can rerun and measure the circuit multiple times to at least get statistics.

We know from quantum mechanics that the information about a quantum system is impossible to access, specifically the measurement of the qubit's complex amplitudes. For example, let's say that we have a qubit in a superposition state $|\psi\rangle$, where the complex amplitudes sum to 1:

$$\sum_{j=0}^{k-1} \alpha j \, |j\rangle = 1$$

A measurement of the preceding cannot provide the complex amplitude information in α. What the measurement of a qubit returns is the basis $|j\rangle$ with a probability $|\alpha j|^2$ of the state $|\psi\rangle$ in the standard basis.

We viewed an example of this earlier when describing the Hadamard gate. When we set the qubit in a complex linear combination of $a|0\rangle$ and $b|1\rangle$, where a and b are the complex amplitudes of the basis states, the measurement result was based on the probability $|\alpha|^2$ of measuring $|0\rangle$ and $|\beta|^2$ of measuring $|1\rangle$, which for a Hadamard gate results in 50%, or $|1/\sqrt{2}|^2$.

An important thing to note about measuring the state of a system is that once you measure it, the quantum information of the system is lost. What this means is that by measuring the qubit(s), the state will collapse into one of the two basis states, $|0\rangle$ or $|1\rangle$, based on the amplitude of the components, α and β, of the quantum state. After the measurement, you no longer have the information contained in a and b to do anything else.

If you were to try to measure the same qubit that you just measured, the result will be the same as the first measurement but will not set the qubit back to the quantum state in which it was prior to the measurement. Therefore, measurement is a non-reversible operator.

Once the measurement is completed, the result is then sent over to the classical bit, which will return the information back to the classical system. Now that we understand how the measurement works and what the results of the measurements are, let's run some code to see it at work!

In this example, we will create a Bell state circuit (we covered these in detail in *Chapter 4, Understanding Basic Quantum Computing Principles*), which contains a Hadamard followed by a CNOT gate:

1. First, we will add the measurement function, `measure_all()`, at the end of the circuit, which will automatically map the results of measuring the qubits to their respective classical bits. We will also add Hadamard and CNOT gates:

    ```
    #CNOT-gate
    #Create a two-qubit circuit
    qc = QuantumCircuit(2)
    #Add an H gate to the qubit
    qc.h(0)
    #Add a CNOT gate where, control = first, target = second
    #qubit
    qc.cx(0,1)
    #Measure qubits and map to classical bits
    qc.measure_all()
    #Execute the circuit and capture all the results
    result, img, histogram = execute_circuit_returns(qc)
    ```

2. Let's now view our results by entering the following in a new cell:

    ```
    Result
    ```

    Our results are as follows:

    ```
    {'11': 448, '00': 512}
    ```

3. Our helper function also included the `histogram` plot, which helps visualize the preceding results. To view the histogram, enter the following into the next cell:

    ```
    histogram
    ```

    The output is the following histogram plot:

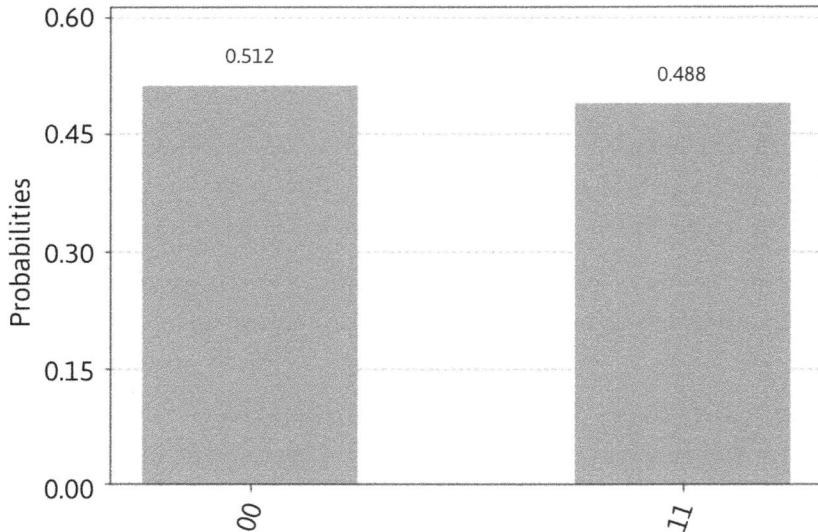

Figure 6.43: Histogram chart of measured results

4. Now let's see what the circuit looks like with the measurement operators added. Run the following in another cell:

    ```
    img
    ```

    At the end of the circuit illustrated in the following diagram, you will see that the measurement operators were added to all qubits. You'll see that the labels for the classical bits are titled **measure**, and the qubits are mapped to their respective bits labeled by the index numbers where the measurement terminates onto the classical bit:

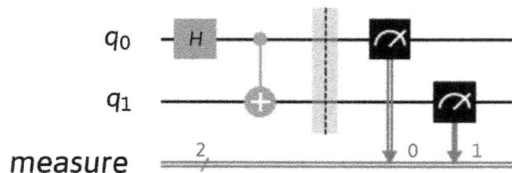

Figure 6.44: Measurement operators added to a quantum circuit

The barrier is added there just for convenience to visualize where the circuit operations end and where the measurement will commence.

5. The measure_all() function is a nice and convenient way to apply measurement operators to your quantum circuit. You can also apply a measurement operator to each qubit separately and at separate times, or you can arrange the mapping using a list if you wish to change the assignment of a qubit to a classical bit. Let's rewrite our function again, only this time we'll add the measurement operators individually for the first circuit (qc1) and then do the same with the second circuit (qc2) using a list. This way you can see the various ways in which you can apply measurement operators, either to all at once, or just to measure certain qubits:

```
#Measurement operator
#Create two separate two-qubit,
#and two classical bit circuits
qc1 = QuantumCircuit(2,2)
qc2 = QuantumCircuit(2,2)
#In the first circuit (qc1), measure qubits individually
qc1.measure(0,0)
qc1.measure(1,1)
#In the second circuit (qc2) measure using a list
qc2.measure([0,1],[0,1])
#Execute the circuit and capture all the results
result, img, histogram = execute_circuit_returns(qc1)
result2, img2, histogram2 = execute_circuit_returns(qc2)
```

After executing the code, display the two images (img and img2) in separate cells and notice that both circuits appear the same with respect to the measurement operators.

In this section, you learned about non-reversible operators. We also created a simple two-qubit circuit using a measurement operator.

Summary

In this chapter, you learned all the various ways you can operate on both single and multiple qubits. The operations provide various vector states that each qubit can rotate into. You also learned how to visualize the gates on a circuit and learned to decompose them down to universal gates so you can realize the information that is passed onto the quantum system.

You have now understood how these gates operate on qubits. You now have skills that will greatly help you understand how gates are used in many quantum algorithms to position the vectors in the Hilbert space of each qubit to help resolve various problems.

In the next chapter, we will learn about the **Quantum Information Science Kit (Qiskit)**, pronounced *kiss-kit* (depending on who you ask, it may also be pronounced *kwis-kit*). Qiskit provides, besides many of the objects and functions we have been using so far to manipulate qubits, other functionality that helps to create quantum algorithms, mitigate against noise found in near-term devices, and produce quantum algorithms for users to leverage without having to learn about them at the gate level.

Questions

1. For the multi-qubit gates, try flipping the Source and Target. Do you see a difference when you decompose the circuit?

2. Decompose all the gates for both single and multi-qubit circuits. What do you notice about how the universal gates are constructed?

3. Implement the Toffoli gate where the target is the center qubit of a three-qubit circuit.

4. Decompose the Toffoli gate. How many gates in total are used to construct it?

5. Apply the Toffoli gate along with a Hadamard gate to a state vector simulator and compare the results to that from the Sampler primitive. What differences do you see and why?

6. If you wanted to sort three qubits in the opposite direction, which gates would you use and in which order?

Join us on Discord

Join our community's Discord space for discussions with the author and other readers:

`https://packt.link/3FyN1`

7

Programming with Qiskit

Qiskit has various libraries that link between the core hardware of a quantum system and the tools necessary to create quantum circuits, both transcend upward through the code stack. It is, therefore, the foundation used to create quantum circuits, as well as generating and scheduling pulses from the circuits onto the hardware devices. Other features, such as optimizers and transpilers, are used to ensure the circuits are optimal to reduce decoherence and improve performance. In this chapter, we will explore all the key features available in Qiskit to help you create your own circuits, optimizers, and pulse schedules.

The following topics will be covered in this chapter:

- Understanding quantum circuits
- Generating pulse schedules on hardware
- Understanding the Job component

Qiskit has so many features and enhancements that it would take an entire book to write about them all. To cover as many of them as possible, we will create a quantum circuit and walk you through the various features. After reading this chapter, you will be able to understand how to create quantum circuits from basic to customized circuits with user-defined labels to help contextualize your circuit. You'll also get an understanding of the Job component, which is used to run your circuit on a quantum system.

We'll even delve into the hardware to schedule a pulse operation on a qubit to better understand how the circuit is translated from digital to analog signals to perform an operation on a qubit(s), followed by reading the information from the qubit and converting the signal back from analog to digital.

Sound exciting? Great! Let's get to it!

Technical requirements

In this chapter, it is expected that you are familiar with the basics of quantum circuits described in previous chapters, such as creating and executing quantum circuits, visualizing circuit diagrams, and knowledge of qubit logic gates.

Here is the source code used throughout this book: `https://github.com/PacktPublishing/Learning-Quantum-Computing-with-Python-and-IBM-Quantum-Second-Edition`.

Customizing and optimizing quantum circuits

In previous chapters, you had some exposure to quantum circuit operations to understand some of the basic quantum components. These basic operations included creating a quantum circuit, applying quantum gates to the circuit, and executing the circuit on a simulator.

We will now take a deeper look into quantum circuits to better understand what properties and functionalities are available to us to not just execute these circuits on a real device but to do so as optimally as possible. In this section, we will learn how to extract circuit properties, such as circuit depth, width, and size, and obtain the number of actual operators. Let's first start by reviewing the various forms of creating a quantum circuit.

Components of a quantum circuit

Qiskit provides various ways to create a quantum circuit, each depending on how much information you need throughout your circuit. Up to this point, we have been creating circuits using a single constructor that automatically creates the circuit registers needed. In this form, the arguments indicate the number of qubits and bits of both the quantum and classical registers, respectively:

```
# Load helper file
%run helper_file_1.0.ipynb

qc = QuantumCircuit(2,2)
```

In this section, we will describe other ways to create a circuit and discuss the advantage of using one form or the other.

Another way to construct a `QuantumCircuit` class is to create the quantum and classical registers independently of the quantum circuit constructor. Here, we will first create the quantum and classical registers, each with two qubits and two bits, respectively, and then draw the circuit. The constructor allows us to customize the label of our registers, which we were not able to do in the previous form:

```
# Import registers
from qiskit import QuantumRegister, ClassicalRegister

qr = QuantumRegister(2, 'my_QR')
cr = ClassicalRegister(2, 'my_CR')
qc = QuantumCircuit(qr,cr)
qc.draw(output='mpl')
```

From the preceding code, note that the second argument: that is, the name attribute: of the register constructors allows us to add a label to each register, as in the following screenshot:

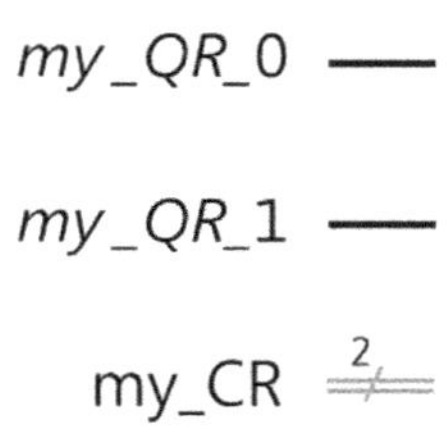

Figure 7.1: Customized quantum and classical register labels

Customizing the labels of our registers simplifies reading our circuits, particularly as the circuits become more complex when having multiple registers performing different processes. You may want to have one register created with a fixed number of qubits and another dynamic register where defining the number of qubits would vary based on some preprocessed step. You'll see the value of this when we create composites later in this chapter.

Of course, you can also combine creating the registers and the circuit constructor all in one line if needed:

```
qc = QuantumCircuit(QuantumRegister(2, 'my_QR'), ClassicalRegister(2, 'my_
CR'))
```

Let's assume now that you have two quantum circuits and you want to concatenate them together. The following example will illustrate how to concatenate two circuits into one without having to explicitly recreate one based on the two existing quantum circuits:

1. In the following code, we will create the first circuit and include labels on both the quantum and classical registers so that we can monitor that they are, in fact, combined:

    ```
    #Create the quantum and classical registers, each with
    #labels
    ```

```
qr1 = QuantumRegister(2, name='qr1')
cr1 = ClassicalRegister(2, name='cr1')
#Create the quantum circuit using the registers
qc1 = QuantumCircuit(qr1, cr1)
#Draw the circuit
qc1.draw(output='mpl')
```

The following screenshot shows what should be displayed after running the previous code:

$$qr1_0 \quad \text{—}$$

$$qr1_1 \quad \text{—}$$

$$cr1 \quad \overset{2}{=}$$

Figure 7.2: The first of the two quantum circuits we will join

2. Next, we will create a second circuit, which is very similar to the first one, only we will update the labels to identify it as the second:

```
#Create two Quantum and Classical registers
qr2 = QuantumRegister(2, name='qr2')
cr2 = ClassicalRegister(2, name='cr2')
#Create a second circuit using the registers created
#above
qc2 = QuantumCircuit(qr2, cr2)
#Draw the second quantum circuit
qc2.draw(output='mpl')
```

The results of the code should be no surprise: that it is the same as the first one only with the labels updated as expected:

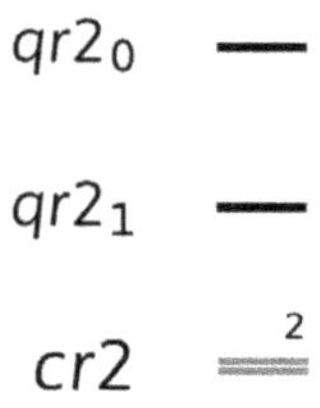

$$qr2_0 \quad \text{—}$$

$$qr2_1 \quad \text{—}$$

$$cr2 \quad \overset{2}{=}$$

Figure 7.3: The second of the two quantum circuits we will join

3. Now, let's finish up by combining one circuit with the other, which is to say we will widen the circuit from 2 to 4 qubits. To do this, we will use the **add_register** function, which combines the quantum and classical registers into a single circuit. Here, we will combine circuits **qc2** and **qc1** into a new circuit titled **qc_combined**, and then draw the results:

```
#Concatenate the two previous circuits to create a new #circuit
#Create an empty quantum circuit
qc_combined = QuantumCircuit()
#Add the two previous quantum and classical
#registers to the empty quantum circuit
qc_combined.add_register(qr1, qr2, cr1, cr2)
#Draw the concatenated circuit
qc_combined.draw(output='mpl')
```

As you can see in the following screenshot, the results are now a combination of the two previous quantum circuits into a new circuit, by combining the registers:

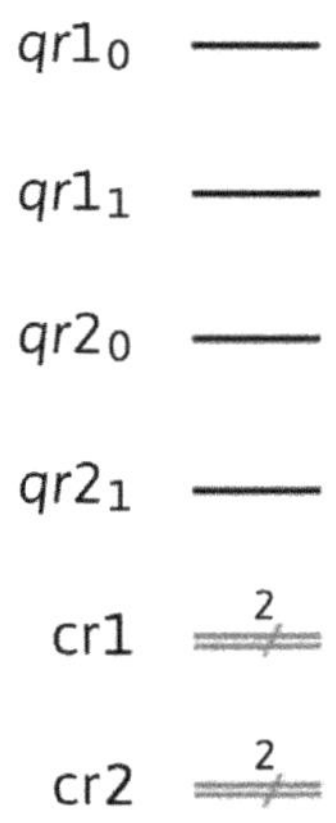

$$qr1_0 \text{ —— }$$

$$qr1_1 \text{ —— }$$

$$qr2_0 \text{ —— }$$

$$qr2_1 \text{ —— }$$

$$cr1 \text{ }\overset{2}{=\!\!\!/\!\!\!=}$$

$$cr2 \text{ }\overset{2}{=\!\!\!/\!\!\!=}$$

Figure 7.4: Concatenation of two quantum circuits

We originally created two individual quantum circuits, each with two quantum registers and two classical registers. We then concatenated them to create a quantum circuit with four quantum and classical circuits. The order of the quantum circuits is based on the order in which they were concatenated. As an extra exercise, repeat the previous concatenation code and switch the order to confirm or create more quantum circuits and add more circuits together.

One last circuit creation object I would like to share is the random circuit generator, which, as the name suggests, will generate a random circuit for you. Having the ability to create a random circuit could help you to create test circuits or examples given a set of parameters, such as circuit width and depth. As the following code block indicates, the random_circuit object requires two parameters. They are the number of qubits you want the random circuit to contain and the depth of the circuit, respectively: where depth indicates the number of standard gates, selected from the Qiskit circuit extensions listed in the API documentation, to add randomly per qubit. You can also indicate whether you want the circuit to include measurement operators:

```
#Import the random_circuit class
from qiskit.circuit.random import random_circuit
#Construct the random circuit with the number of qubits = 3
#with a depth = 2, and include the measurement operator for
#each qubit
qc = random_circuit(3, 2, measure=True)
#Draw the circuit
qc.draw(output='mpl')
```

The results from the random circuit will vary, of course, each time you execute it, as it should. What will not vary are the parameter options, particularly the number of qubits and the depth count. In this case, your results should have a circuit that contains three qubits and a depth of two operators. The following random circuit is the result of running the preceding code. Note that the measurement operator is not included in the depth count:

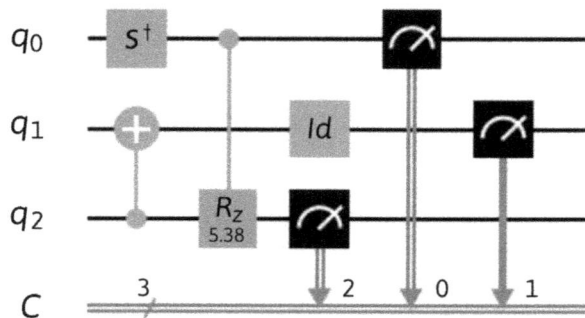

Figure 7.5: Random circuit generated with number of qubits = 3 and depth = 2

Now that you are familiar with the various ways to generate quantum circuits, we will continue and see what properties we can extract from the circuits created. These properties could be used to analyze the generated circuit and ensure it is optimized by leveraging some optimization features available to us in Qiskit.

Obtaining circuit properties and analysis

Constructing circuits could get very complex once you start building them out, particularly if you create composites of gates and combine them to form larger gates. You're going to want to get some information about your circuit along the way should you need to analyze your results.

The good thing for us is that Qiskit has taken care of some of this by making a lot of these properties available to us. Let's start with some basic properties. Let's say we want to know how many qubits we have in our circuit. As we learned in the previous section, we know that we can concatenate two or more circuits together. As we add more circuits together, it becomes difficult, or tedious, to determine the number of qubits and gates that our concatenated circuit will have. It's here that the width, depth, and operator count functions come in handy.

In the following code, we will create two two-qubit random circuits, each with different gate counts. We will then append one circuit to another and use our circuit property functions to help us get the total width, depth, and operator count. All circuits that we append will need to have the same number of qubits using this method:

```
#Import the random circuit class
from qiskit.circuit.random import random_circuit
#Create two random circuits, each with 2 qubit registers and
#random gate operator counts.
qc1 = random_circuit(2,2)
qc2 = random_circuit(2,4)
#Concatenate the two random circuits into one
qc = qc1.compose(qc2, [0,1])
#Draw the circuit
qc.draw(output='mpl')
```

The result should be a two-qubit circuit with a random set of gate operators with a total depth of 6. We know this because we created them and can see the values from the `random_circuit` constructor:

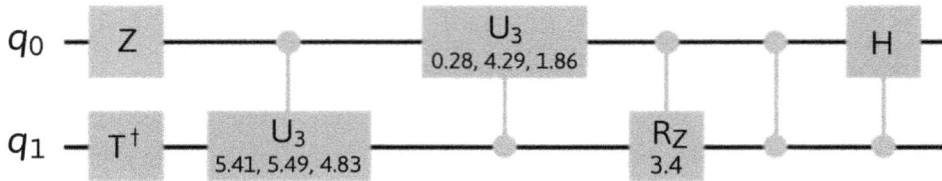

Figure 7.6: Randomly generated two-qubit circuits with a depth of 6

Now, let's use our circuit property functions to get the width, depth, size, and operator count of our circuit. To simplify this, we will create a helper function that will print out the circuit properties of the quantum circuit we will pass in as an argument:

```
#Define function to print circuit properties:
def print_circuit_props(qc):
    width = qc.width()
    depth = qc.depth()
    num_operators = qc.count_ops()
    circuit_size = qc.size()
    print('Width = ', width)
    print('Depth = ', depth)
    print('Circuit size = ', circuit_size)
    print('Number of operators = ', num_operators)
```

Now, we can run our circuit through our helper function, which will print out all the properties we need:

```
#Pass our quantum circuit to print out the circuit properties
print_circuit_props(qc)
```

Our results should have the same value for Width and Depth. However, since we are using random circuits, our circuit size and the number of operators will be different as they are based on the randomly chosen gates. However, by observing the circuit, you will see that the result values of size() and count_ops() are the same. The difference between the two is that the circuit size returns the total number of gates in the circuit, while the operator count lists the name of each gate type and the total number of each gate type in the circuit:

```
Width =   2
```

```
Depth =  6
Circuit size =  7
Number of operators =  OrderedDict([('cu3', 2), ('z', 1), ('tdg', 1),
('crz', 1), ('cz', 1), ('ch', 1)])
```

Now, let's try adding some classic registers, measurements, and barriers to see what we get back. We can use a shortcut to include measurement operators by using measure_all(), which will append a barrier, a measurement for each qubit, and the classical registers to match the number of qubits in the quantum register of our circuit:

```
#Use measure_all() to automatically add the barrier,
#measurement, and classical register to our existing circuit.
qc.measure_all()
#Draw the circuit
qc.draw(output='mpl')
```

The result now includes the classical components needed to measure and read out our qubits. These include the two-bit classical registers labeled as measure, a barrier separating the quantum gates from the measurement operators, and the measurement operators, as illustrated in the following screenshot:

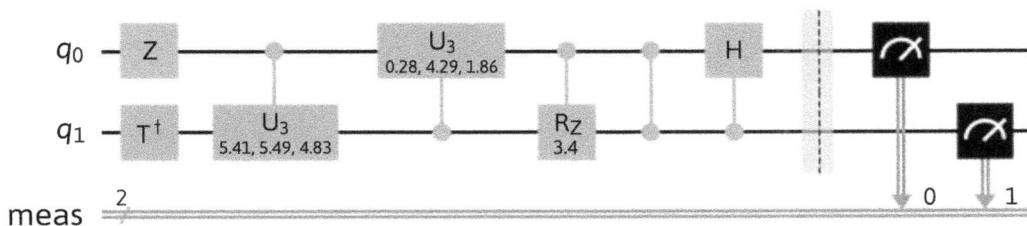

Figure 7.7: Random circuit with classical components added

Let's now print our circuit property functions to see an updated count:

```
#Print out the circuit properties
print_circuit_props(qc)
```

The results show what we generally would expect. The Width count increased by 2, due to the addition of the two-bit classical register. The Depth count increased by 1 due to the addition of the barrier. Note that the measurement operator is not included in the size or operator count, as follows:

```
Width =  4
```

```
Depth =  7
Circuit size =  9
Number of operators =  OrderedDict([('cu3', 2), ('measure', 2), ('z', 1),
('tdg', 1), ('crz', 1), ('cz', 1), ('ch', 1), ('barrier', 1)])
```

Before moving on to the next section, let's look at an interesting caveat to our circuit property functions. Most gates are created from basis gates that are specific to the quantum computers used. For most quantum systems, there are a set of basis gates used to create other gates.

However, some gates, such as the **Toffoli** and **Swap** gates, not only require more than a single qubit but are also composed of several basis gates. Let's look at the Toffoli gate as an example:

1. We will create a quantum circuit with 3 qubits and add only a Toffoli gate to it, as shown here:

    ```
    qc = QuantumCircuit(3)
    qc.ccx(0,1,2)
    qc.draw(output='mpl')
    ```

    Here, we see the Toffoli gate as expected, with the 0 and 1 source qubits entangled, with qubit 2 as the target:

    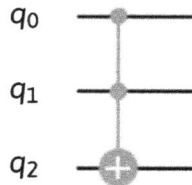

    Figure 7.8: The Toffoli gate on a quantum circuit

2. We print out our circuit properties of the quantum circuit with the Toffoli gate:

    ```
    #Print out the circuit properties
    print_circuit_props(qc)
    ```

    As we can see, the results are not surprising in that the values are not surprising either: a three-qubit gate with a width of 3 and a depth of 1:

    ```
    Width = 3
    Depth = 1
    Circuit size = 1
    Number of operators = OrderedDict([('ccx', 1)])
    ```

3. Now, let's print our circuit property, only this time, let's decompose our quantum circuit to see the results. As you will recall, when we invoke the decompose() function on our quantum circuit, we are requesting the circuit to be decomposed down to its basis gates used to create the gates in our circuit. In this case, we are referring to the basis gates that are used to create a Toffoli gate:

```
#Print out the circuit properties
print_circuit_props(qc.decompose())
```

Notice the difference? Quite surprising indeed! By observing the results, we see that the Toffoli gate requires 15 operators, which are made up of various gates, such as T, T⁺, H, and CNOT:

```
Width = 3
Depth = 11
Circuit size = 15
Number of operators = OrderedDict([('cx', 6), ('t', 4), ('tdg', 3),
('h', 2)])
```

The reason why I wanted to mention this was to make you aware that some of the gates used are not basis gates but are rather composites of basis gates used to generate the functionality of the desired gate. This is good to know when analyzing your circuit with respect to qubit noise or decoherence.

Try the same exercise, only this time try creating a two-qubit circuit with a Swap gate and see what results you get back.

Now that you are familiar with the various forms of creating quantum circuits, let's look at how we can reuse these circuits in a modular way that makes it easy to combine and comprehend them.

Customizing and parameterizing circuit libraries

There are times when you are going to want to reuse a circuit on multiple occasions. To simplify this, you can create a composite of operators and reuse them throughout your circuit. This not only simplifies creating the circuit from modules but also makes it very easy for others to understand what your circuit is doing in those composites. Qiskit creates these compositions based on the instruction sets or quantum circuits.

In the following steps, we are going to create a composite gate that is made up of multiple qubits and gates:

1. First, we create a two-qubit quantum circuit, give it a name, and convert it into a generic quantum instruction:

```
#Create a custom two-qubit composite gate
#Create the quantum register
qr = QuantumRegister(2, name='qr_c')
#Generate quantum circuit which will make up the
#composite gate
comp_qc = QuantumCircuit(qr, name='My-composite')
#Add any gates you wish to your composite gate
comp_qc.h(0)
comp_qc.cx(0, 1)
#Create the composite instructions by converting
#the QuantumCircuit to a list of Instructions
composite_inst = comp_qc.to_instruction()
#Draw the circuit which will represent the composite gate
comp_qc.draw(output='mpl')
```

The preceding code will create the following two-qubit circuit, which we will use as our composite gate:

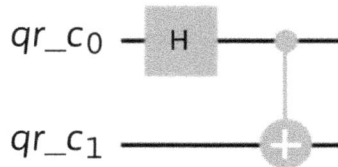

Figure 7.9: The quantum circuit that will represent the composite gate

2. Now, let's create a quantum circuit that will append the composite gate onto the circuit we created:

```
#Create your 2-qubit circuit to generate your composite gate
qr2 = QuantumRegister(3, 'qr')
#Create a quantum circuit using the quantum register
qc = QuantumCircuit(qr2)
#Add any arbitrary gates that would represent the function
#of the composite gate
```

```
qc.h(0)
qc.cx(0,1)
qc.cx(0,2)
#Draw the composite circuit
qc.draw(output='mpl')
```

The preceding code will create the circuit, which we prepopulated with some gates before including our composite gate:

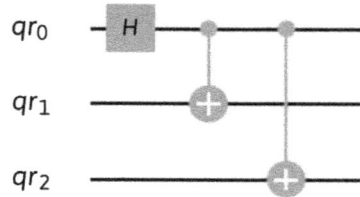

Figure 7.10: The quantum circuit that we will append to the composite gate

3. Since our composite gate is made up of two qubits, we will need to indicate which of the three qubits to append our two-qubit composite gate to. For this example, we will append it to the first two qubits:

```
#Append your composite gate to the specified qubits.
qc.append(composite_inst, [qr2[0], qr2[1]])
#Draw the complete circuit
qc.draw(output='mpl')
```

As we can see from the results, our composite gate was successfully appended to the first and second qubits. It also includes the name of the composite gate, which makes it simple for anyone, including yourself, to read the circuit and understand what the composite gate is doing within the circuit:

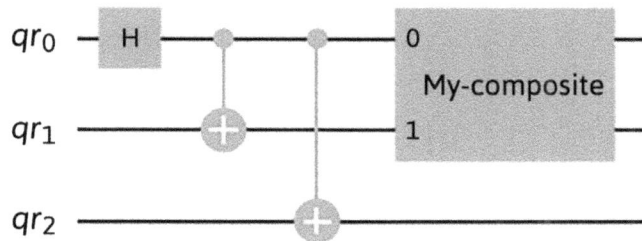

Figure 7.11: The quantum circuit with a composite gate representation of a pre-defined circuit

This makes reading your circuit much easier compared to how it would be if you were to just concatenate the two quantum circuits together.

Of course, this is ideal if you have a circuit that would run as is. However, there may be times when you wish to perhaps control the amount of rotation of some of the gates in the composite gate you generated. This is where the parameterization of composite gates comes in handy. We will now create another composite gate, only this one will include the ability to add parameters to your composite gate so that it is more dynamic. This is commonly referred to as a **Parameterized Quantum Circuit (PQC)**.

4. To parameterize a gate, we will need to create a `Parameter` class and set it to a rotation gate; in this example, we will apply the parameter to an R_z gate:

```
#Import the Parameter object
from qiskit.circuit import Parameter
#Construct the Parameter set to Theta
param_theta = Parameter('θ')
#Create a two-qubit quantum circuit and add some gates
qc = QuantumCircuit(2)
qc.h(0)
qc.cx(0, 1)
#Include a rotation gate which we wish to apply
#the Parameter value
qc.rz(param_theta, 0)
qc.rz(param_theta, 1)
#Draw the circuit
qc.draw(output='mpl')
```

Note that the parameter value is defined as θ, but is not set as an explicit value. It just reserves the `Parameter` value to later include a rotation value of θ:

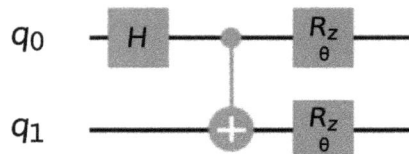

Figure 7.12: Set the parameter of the R_z gate to θ

5.   Let's bind the Parameter value of our gates to 2π and draw the circuit:

```
import numpy as np
#Bind the parameters with a value, in this case 2π
qc = qc.assign_parameters(parameters={param_theta: 2*np.pi})
#Draw the circuit with the set parameter values
qc.draw(output='mpl')
```

Note that our rotation gate has its theta value set to 2π as expected:

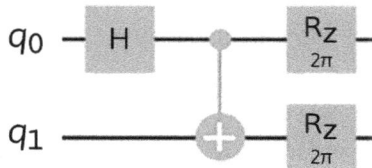

Figure 7.13: Rotation gates R_z now have the Parameter value θ set to 2π

Our circuit is now ready to run with the bound parameter values. By having this feature, we can iterate it over a loop and bind multiple values if need be, so that we can iterate over all of them without having to manually update the bound values. This greatly optimizes our ability to run and analyze the results of our circuit for each iteration.

In this section, we learned about various forms and ways to create quantum circuits using the classes and functions provided in Qiskit to help us analyze our circuit properties and construction. We also learned how to reuse the created circuits.

In the next section, we will dig even deeper into manipulating qubits, only this time not from basis gates, but to directly manipulate the qubits using the hardware itself!

Generating pulse schedules on hardware

So far, you have learned how to create quantum circuits, add gates that manipulate the qubits of the circuit, and execute the circuits. In this section, we'll go a little deeper to see how a quantum circuit is converted from digital instructions to pulse instructions that physically manipulate the qubits using microwave pulses as instructed by the quantum circuit. Microwave pulses are what manipulate the qubits on quantum devices. A signal is generated and tuned to a specific frequency of each qubit so that the signal only affects the qubit that the pulse is tuned to.

Much of this section will assume that you have some knowledge of signal processing, particularly that of transmon-like superconducting qubits and microwave pulses. For reference, this is a fantastic paper that goes into the details, https://arxiv.org/pdf/1904.06560.pdf, where sections *4.C* and *4.D* cover a basic overview of how microwave signals are used to manipulate qubits.

One thing you might be wondering by now is why you should have pulse access to manipulate the qubits. First, it is good to understand that superconducting qubits are manipulated by microwave pulses. These pulses send signals down to each qubit using the qubit's carrier frequency to ensure that the pulse operation will affect only the qubit that is tuned to that specific frequency. This way, if you are a kernel developer, for example, the ability to configure the pulses provides you with the ability to fine-tune the gate operations yourself rather than the default pulse shapes that are set up. These fine-tunings could be applied to not only single-gate operations but also two-qubit operations such as a CNOT gate.

We'll begin by illustrating how the hardware components are connected to the various pulse channels. IBM Quantum provides you with access to the machines in a way that is unique from most other quantum systems available on the cloud. Qiskit includes a `Pulse` library that allows you to control the pulses sent to the hardware that controls the device. Based on the `OpenPulse` documentation (https://arxiv.org/abs/1809.03452), it is tailored to provide the functionality to generate pulse signals used to control the qubits.

To understand how the pulse functionality works, we'll start by describing the four main components you will be using:

- Instructions
- Pulse libraries
- Channels
- Schedules

In the following sections, we will learn about the preceding components.

Before we proceed to the next section, we will use the following code, which will import everything we need to create, schedule, and trigger a pulse on a quantum device directly:

```
#Import pulse classes
from qiskit.pulse import Waveform, DriveChannel, Play, Schedule
```

Now that we have imported the files needed, we will move on to the next section, about instructions.

Learning about instructions

Pulse programs, or, as described in the Qiskit API documentation, **Schedules**, are a set of instructions used to describe the control of the electronic components of the quantum system. There are various instruction objects included within the `qiskit.pulse` library that have capabilities such as modulation of the frequency and phase of the pulse signal.

> `pulse`, in essence, provides you with the ability to specify the dynamics of each operation in a quantum circuit, so you can fine-tune each in a way to minimize as much noise as possible. `pulse` has various functionalities to give you access to the channels that send and receive information to and from each qubit, and includes libraries of pulses that you can use as a base and you can then modify each one accordingly.

You can also delay an instruction from triggering, similar to a `sleep()` function in most programming languages. Finally, it gives you the ability to trigger an operation and enable the acquire channel by playing and capturing the microwave pulse signals, respectively.

Understanding each of the following is dependent on understanding *why* you would want to use these functions. For example, setting the frequency is important as each qubit is tuned to a specific frequency, so any pulse operation should be sent at the carrier frequency of the specified qubit; otherwise, the operation will not work, or, worse, it might operate on a qubit that you do not want to update. Now, let's describe each instruction and its parameters:

- `SetFrequency(frequency, channel, name)`, where `frequency` is in Hz, `channel` indicates which channel the frequency will be applied to, and `name` is the name you can set for the instruction. The default *duration* of the `SetFrequency` instruction is 0. This very simply sets the frequency of the channel so that the pulses applied to the channel are tuned accordingly. If you do not specify a frequency when creating a pulse for a specific qubit, the default frequency for the qubit on the drive channel will be used.

- `ShiftPhase(phase, channel, name)`, where `phase` is the rotation angle in radians, `channel` indicates the channel that the frequency will be applied to, and the `name` parameter is the name you can set for the instruction. This instruction shifts the phase of the pulse by increasing its rotation angle by the provided amount in radians.

- Delay(duration, channel, name), where duration is the length of time in the delay (in the documentation, this is also referred to as *time step*, or dt), channel indicates which channel the delay will be applied to, and name indicates the name that you can set for the instruction. The Delay instruction is generally used to align pulses with respect to other pulse instructions. For example, if you wish to send two pulses and include a time gap between the pulses, you can specify the time gap by adding a Delay instruction with the desired time gap amount.

- Play(pulse, channel, name), where pulse is the pulse waveform you wish to apply, channel indicates which channel the pulse will be applied to, and name is the name you can set for the instruction. The Play instruction will apply the pulse output to the channel specified, where the pulse output was previously modulated using both the SetFrequency and SetPhase instructions.

- Acquire(duration, channel, mem_slot, reg_slot, kernel, discriminator, name), where duration is the number of time steps (dt) to acquire the data information, channel indicates which channel to acquire the data from, mem_slot is the classical memory slot in which to store each of the returned results, and reg_slot is the register slot used to store the classified and readout results. The kernel parameter is used to integrate the raw data for each slot, discriminator is used to classify kernelled IQ data into a 0 or 1 result, and name indicates the name you can set for the instruction.

Each instruction includes an operator that will be applied to the specified channels stated. The operators include pulse modulators, delays, and readouts from channels. Before we get into discussing channels, let's create some pulses using the Qiskit Pulse library.

Understanding pulses and Pulse libraries

Each microwave pulse is created by an **arbitrary waveform generator** (**AWG**), which specifies the frequency and phase of the pulse signal output. The frequency and phase are set by the SetFrequency and ShiftPhase instructions we learned about earlier, respectively.

> **Important Note**
>
> Qiskit Pulse provides a nice library of waveforms, which can simplify creating the pulses we need to operate on a qubit. The following are the types of available waveforms at the time of writing this chapter: Constant, Drag, Discrete, Gaussian, GaussianSquare, and Waveform. Each of these waveforms has a specific feature, for example, Drag is used to reduce leakage to the $|2\rangle$ state of the qubit and keeps it confined to the $|0\rangle$ and $|1\rangle$ states.

Each of the waveforms provided in the Pulse library has a specific feature. We'll cover a few of them below, but I would encourage you to read more in the Qiskit documentation, `https://docs.quantum.ibm.com/api/qiskit/pulse`, which includes a detailed description of each.

`Waveform` allows you to define your own pulse by providing an array of complex value samples as an argument. These samples each have a predefined time step, `dt`, which is the time period played for each and varies based on the specified backend. The following code is an example of a sample pulse for a simple sine waveform of 128 samples:

```python
#Import numpy and generate the sine sample values
import numpy as np
x = np.linspace(0,2*np.pi,64)
data = np.sin(x)
#Generate our Waveform
waveform = Waveform(data, name="sine_64_pulse")
#Draw the generated waveform
waveform.draw()
```

The following screenshot is the result of creating our sample pulse of a sine waveform:

Name: sine_64_pulse, Duration: 64.0 dt

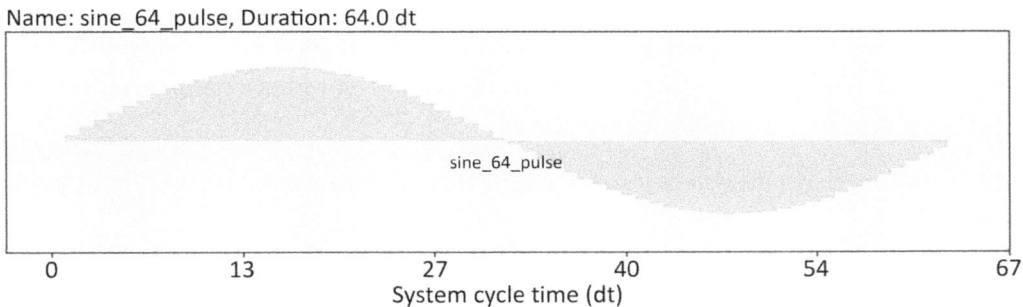

Figure 7.14: Sample pulse of a sine waveform

Let's now try generating one of the waveforms from the Pulse library.

The Pulse library has an array of different waveforms, such as `Gaussian`, `GaussianSquare`, `Constant`, and `Drag` (just to name a few). Each has its own distinct shape that we can leverage to fine-tune any pulse we wish.

Let's create a `GaussianSquare` pulse, which is simply a square pulse with Gaussian edges on both ends, rather than squared-off edges:

```python
#Import the Gaussian Square pulse from Pulse Library
```

```
from qiskit.pulse.library import GaussianSquare
#Create a Gaussian Square pulse
#Args: duration, amp, sigma, width, name
gaussian_square_pulse = GaussianSquare(128, 1, 2, 112, name="gaussian
square")
gaussian_square_pulse.draw()
```

The preceding code will result in the following pulse, where the duration (dt) is 128, the amplification max is at 1, sigma is set to 2, and the width of the pulse peak is 112 (dt):

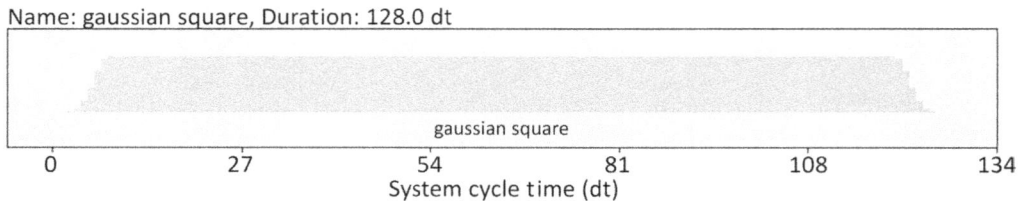

Figure 7.15: Gaussian square pulse

As you can see, the parameters available to us allow adjustments to the waveform in multiple ways. In the Gaussian Square waveform sample, we were able to adjust the amplitude, width, and its sigma, which therefore provides us with more control over the creation of the pulse, which could potentially reduce noise or any other affects that could come from a standard pulse that is created based on the quantum circuit instructions.

Now that we can create pulses, let's learn about the channels that we will transmit these pulses through.

Leveraging channels to transmit and receive instructions

There are two types of channels in Qiskit Pulse:

- The first type is the **Pulse channel**, which transmits the generated pulses to the quantum device. These include the **Drive channel**, **Control channel**, and the **Measure channel**.

- The other type of channel is the **Acquisition channel**. Currently, this type only includes the **Acquire channel**, which is the channel that receives pulses from the quantum device.

All channels only have one parameter, the index, which is used to assign the channel. The following list describes all the channels:

- The Drive channel is the channel used to transmit the pulse signal down to the qubit to execute the gate operation. When displayed, it has the prefix **D**.

- The Control channel is commonly used on multi-qubit gate operations such as Control-Not, Control-Phase, and more. They generally provide auxiliary control over the qubit via the drive channel. When displayed, it has the prefix **U**.

- The Measure channel transmits a measurement stimulus pulse to the qubit for a readout from the qubit. When displayed, it has the prefix **M**.

- The Acquire channel is the only channel that is used to receive information from the device. It is used to collect data from the quantum device. When displayed, it has the prefix **A**.

So far, we have learned that pulse programs are instructions that are made up of waveform pulses that are constructed to perform gate operations on quantum devices. We also covered the different channels available to transmit and receive information to and from quantum devices. With this information, we can now look at how to schedule these instructions to be executed on a real device.

Generating and executing schedules

Pulse schedules are a set of instructions sent through specified channels to be executed on a quantum device. The Schedule class can be made up of instructions or a combination of other schedules. That means you can create a schedule with one of the instructions we learned about earlier, or you can combine or append schedules to existing schedules. We will do all this in this section.

We will use what we have learned so far in this chapter to build a schedule. First, we will construct a schedule and insert a pulse from the Pulse library into it that will be triggered at time = 0. Then, we will create another schedule and insert a different pulse from the Pulse library into it. The second one will be appended to the first schedule and then shifted, so it is triggered at some time after the first pulse has completed. We'll then execute the schedule on a quantum device and get back its result:

1. Let's continue using the notebook we have been using so far to create our first schedule, and name it schedule_1. We'll also use the Play instruction to insert the Gaussian square pulse we generated earlier and assign the schedule to drive channel 0:

```
#Create the first schedule with our Gaussian Square pulse
schedule_1 = Schedule(name='Schedule 1')
schedule_1 = schedule_1.insert(0,
        Play(gaussian_square_pulse, DriveChannel(0)))
#Draw the schedule
schedule_1.draw()
```

The result we see is that our Gaussian square pulse was added to the schedule starting at time = 0, as follows:

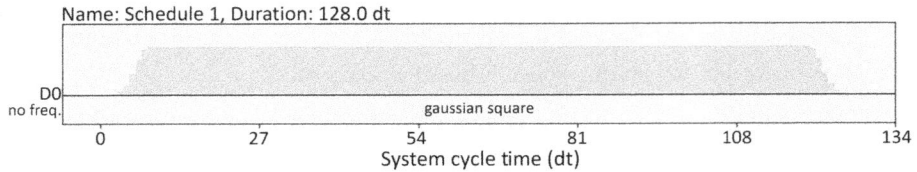

Name: Schedule 1, Duration: 128.0 dt

Figure 7.16: Schedule 1: Gaussian square pulse

2. Now, let's continue and create the second schedule, schedule_2, with the sample pulse we generated earlier:

```
#Create a second schedule with our sample pulse
schedule_2 = Schedule(name='Schedule 2')
schedule_2 = schedule_2.insert(0, Play(waveform, DriveChannel(0)))
#Draw the schedule
schedule_2.draw()
```

This results in the following schedule: note the duration of our sample pulse is 64, whereas the Gaussian square pulse has a duration of 128:

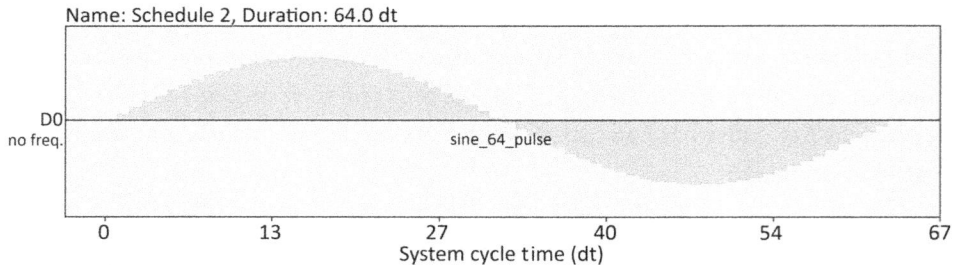

Name: Schedule 2, Duration: 64.0 dt

Figure 7.17: Schedule 2: sample (sine waveform) pulse

3. Next, we will create a third schedule, schedule_3, and we will construct it by inserting both schedule_1 and schedule_2 together with a gap of 5 time steps (dt) in between the two:

```
#Let's create a third schedule, where we add the first
#schedule and second schedules and shift the second
# to the right by a time of 5 after the first
schedule_3 = schedule_1.insert(schedule_1.duration+5, schedule_2)
schedule_3.draw()
```

The result is a combination of schedule_1 starting at time = 0 and then we insert schedule_2 starting at 5 time units after the first schedule. Note the use of the duration variable to ensure that the pulse does not overlap with the first. Schedule 3, therefore, has a total time of the two pulses plus the 5 time units in between the two, totaling 197, as the following figure illustrates:

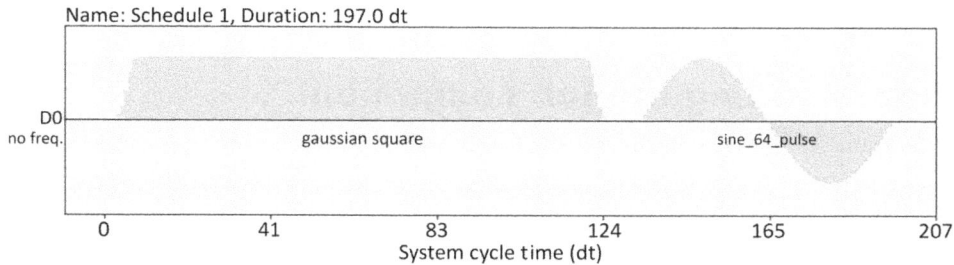

Name: Schedule 1, Duration: 197.0 dt

gaussian square   sine_64_pulse

DO
no freq.

0   41   83   124   165   207
System cycle time (dt)

Figure 7.18: Schedule 3, combining schedules 1 and 2 with a 5 time unit difference in between

4.   Of course, there are other ways to combine pulses. If you want to combine the two schedules without a gap in between, then you can simply use the append function to combine them:

```
#We could have also combined the two using the append operator
#The two schedules are appended immediately after one #another
schedule_3_append = schedule_1.append(schedule_2)
schedule_3_append.draw()
```

The preceding code results in the following output. Note how the total time units are equal to the total time units of both pulses, without the additional 5 time units in between the two pulses:

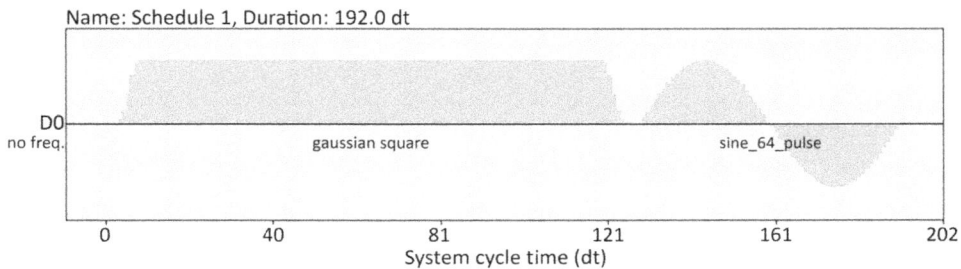

Name: Schedule 1, Duration: 192.0 dt

gaussian square   sine_64_pulse

DO
no freq.

0   40   81   121   161   202
System cycle time (dt)

Figure 7.19: Schedule 3, appending two schedules without a time gap in between

Up to this point, we were able to generate a pulse, apply it to an instruction, and schedule it to run on a specified channel to manipulate the qubit. Generating a set of pulses allows you to get an understanding of how we can schedule two separate gate operations to a single qubit sequentially on the specified channel.

In the next section, we'll see how we can find the status of our quantum circuits once they have been submitted.

Understanding the Job component

The last component we will cover is the Job component. The Job component is basically an instance of the circuit that has been executed on the backend and contains information from the executed circuit(s), such as results, which backend, duration, etc. What that means is that once you send the circuit to the backend to get executed, the backend will generate the Job instance and append information about the job: information such as status, result, job identifier, and so on. The following is a list of the available Job functions:

- `backend()` provides the backend that the job is running on.
- `status()` provides the status of the job.
- `result()` provides the job result after execution is completed on the backend.
- `cancel()` provides the ability to cancel the job.
- `job_id()` provides the alphanumeric job identifier.

We'll reuse the circuit we created earlier, `transpiled_qc`, for simplicity so we can review the Job object and its functions. Let's start by importing the `job_monitor` class and launching the Qiskit job watcher, followed by running the circuit on a backend and running the job monitor to see the status of the job in the output:

```
#Run the simple quantum circuit on local Sampler
from qiskit.primitives import Sampler
sampler = Sampler()

#Let's create a simple circuit
qc = QuantumCircuit(1,1)
qc.h(0)
qc.measure([0],[0])

#Let's run a circuit with the Sampler primitive
```

```
job = sampler.run(qc, shots=1024)
print(job.status())
```

The preceding code will execute a circuit and the following will display the details of the Job object; for example, it will indicate whether the job is in a queue, running, or completed successfully. In this case, the result of the status is that the job has successfully run:

Job Status: JobStatus.DONE

Other information can also be pulled from the Job object. The **Job ID** is the unique identifier of the job that is being run. This ID can be very useful for various reasons, such as tracking the results, and should you have an issue with a job running on the backend, you can reference the job ID when speaking to the support team, which will help the team find the job. The status and results can be called explicitly using the functions **status()** and **result()**, respectively. The result object provides all the information resulting from running the job on the backend. Let's run these functions to review the results of the job we just ran:

```
#From the previous output of executed jobs, obtain its job id
#and print out information about the Job.
print('Print Job ID: ', job.job_id())
print('Print Job Status: ', job.status())
print('Print Job Result: ', job.result())
```

The results of each of the functions in the code snippet are as follows:

```
Print Job ID:  dc25c6bd-2ce6-41d5-9caf-f1326f70b90d
Print Job Status:  JobStatus.DONE
Print Job Result:  SamplerResult(quasi_dists=[{0: 0.5107421875, 1:
0.4892578125}], metadata=[{'shots': 1024}])
```

This is where we can pull specific result information that we can use to visualize the status of the Job. For example, the following code will extract the counts from the results and display the counts in a histogram:

```
job_result = job.result()
quasi_dists = job_result.quasi_dists
# Get result counts
counts = quasi_dists[0].binary_probabilities()
#Print and plot results
print(counts)
plot_distribution(counts)
```

The results will produce the following histogram which pertains to the results from each shot as a total of probabilities. (quasi-probabilities) as follows:

```
{'0': 547, '1': 477}
```

The histogram will then display as follows:

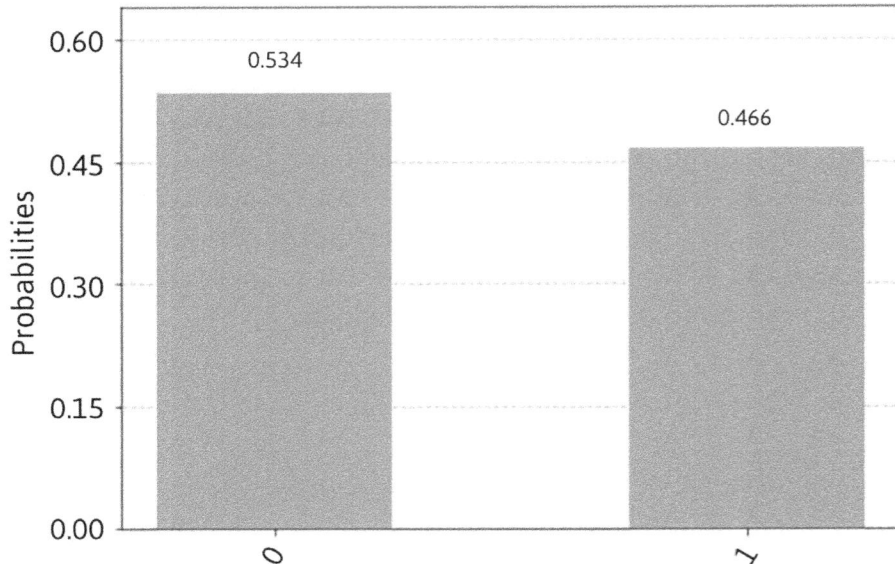

Figure 7.20: The probability results as a histogram

The job object helps us get details regarding the circuit that we have sent to run on a quantum system. This information can be used to provide the results back to our application and visualize the results accordingly. It also provides the status and other information that we can use to keep track of the job and share details about the results with others, such as support teams, so they can easily identify jobs on the backend.

Summary

In this chapter, we covered just some of the many features included in the Qiskit library. We reviewed creating quantum circuits, as well as executing them on the simulator and real quantum devices. We also reviewed how to concatenate circuits so as to enable you to combine and create composite circuits, which included binding parameters to enable adjustments to various gates.

We covered how the circuits are converted into pulses using Qiskit's Pulse library and created schedules, which are programs that send pulse information via various channels down to the hardware, and looked at how to obtain the details of the job that was running on the backend.

In the next chapter, we will cover techniques to optimize your quantum circuits by reviewing the features available via pass managers and optimizers. We'll also learn various ways to visualize your quantum circuits and monitor your jobs as they are executed on the quantum backend systems.

Questions

1. Construct a random quantum circuit with a width of 4 and a depth of 9.
2. Create another random quantum circuit with the same width as the circuit you created in *Question 1* and concatenate it so that it is added before the random quantum circuit you created.
3. Print the circuit properties of the concatenated quantum circuit from *Question 3* and specify the total number of operators, not including any measurement operators.
4. Create a circuit with a parameterized R_Y gate that would rotate by an angle of $\pi/2$.

Join us on Discord

Join our community's Discord space for discussions with the author and other readers:

`https://packt.link/3FyN1`

8

Optimizing and Visualizing Quantum Circuits

In the previous chapter, you learned how to program with **Qiskit**, using both circuits and pulse schedules. We'll continue with the topic of circuits in this chapter, specifically some new features that optimize and speed up the end-to-end process by reducing the overhead between the classical and quantum systems during heavy computation cycles.

Luckily, Qiskit provides plenty of features to allow us to do this with ease. Additionally, Qiskit provides a set of classes and features to optimize and enhance the visualizations of your circuits. Learning about these features will help optimize your circuit results and allow you to render the circuits in various styles and representations, such as a **directed acyclic graph (DAG)**.

We will cover the following topics in this chapter:

- Optimizing circuits using Preset Passmanager
- Visualizing and enhancing circuit graphs

After reading this chapter, you will be able to optimize your circuits by using various visual and programmatic representations of the backend systems and visualization tools. You'll also have some insights into the various transpiler features available that help optimize the transpilation of your circuit for a given quantum backend system. You'll have learned about **Preset Passmanagers** and how they can be leveraged to generate custom pass managers used to execute the circuit transformations inside the transpiler at varying optimization levels.

Technical requirements

In this chapter, it is expected that you are familiar with creating and executing quantum circuits on both a simulator and a quantum computer. Knowledge of quantum hardware, such as qubits and connectivity between qubits, is also recommended. You may also need to install **Graphviz**, **LaTeX**, and perhaps other dependencies in your Python development environment if indicated while running some cells.

Here is the full source code used throughout this book: `https://github.com/PacktPublishing/Learning-Quantum-Computing-with-Python-and-IBM-Quantum-Second-Edition`.

Optimizing circuits using Preset Passmanager

We need to ensure that when a quantum circuit is mapped to the quantum system (transpiled), it is done in the most efficient and effective way. This includes things such as mapping each qubit to those on the quantum system with the least amount of noise affected by decoherence or any other noise source that could introduce errors to your results. To accomplish this, we will learn about the **Preset Passmanager**, its usage, and the various features it makes available for us to create and execute optimal circuits. By optimizing the execution of the circuit to match the topology of the quantum device, we reduce the noise and its effect on our results.

In this section, we will learn about transforming a quantum circuit so that it is best matched to the quantum device. We will also learn how to optimize the circuit by using the layout optimizer. We will then learn about the backend configuration and its optimization, along with the pass manager and passes.

Transpiling a quantum circuit

When you create a circuit and run it on a quantum device, there are many things that occur between the time you send the circuit to be executed on the quantum device and the time the results are returned. We looked at a few of those steps when we discussed Qiskit Runtime in *Chapter 7, Programming with Qiskit*. In this chapter, we will look at the various features included in Qiskit Runtime, including those introduced in the latest version of Qiskit 1.0. First, let's look at a basic overview of just a few of the processes that occur when transpiling a circuit.

The following flowchart illustrates the general process in which the circuit is transpiled so that it can run on the specified backend and be optimized as per the provided settings:

Initial circuit

```
q_0: ─┤ U2(0,pi) ├──■────■────■──
      └──────────┘ ┌─┴─┐  │    │
q_1: ──────────────┤ X ├──┼────┼──
                   └───┘ ┌─┴─┐  │
q_2: ────────────────────┤ X ├──┼──
                         └───┘ ┌─┴─┐
q_3: ──────────────────────────┤ X ├─
                               └───┘
```

Unroll Basis Gates

Set Layout

Set Topology Map

Optimize Gates

```
q_0 -> 0 ─┤ U2(0,pi) ├──■────■────X────■──────────────────────────────
          └──────────┘┌─┴─┐┌─┴─┐ │  ┌─┴─┐                          ┌───┐
q_1 -> 1 ─────────────┤ X ├┤ X ├─■──┤ X ├──■──────────────────────┤ ■ ├─
                      └───┘└───┘    └───┘┌─┴─┐    ┌───┐    ┌───┐  ┌─┴─┐
q_2 -> 2 ────────────────────────────────┤ X ├─■──┤ X ├─■──┤ X ├─
                                         └───┘┌─┴─┐└───┘┌─┴─┐└───┘
q_3 -> 3 ─────────────────────────────────────┤ X ├─■──┤ X ├──────
                                              └───┘    └───┘
```

Final circuit

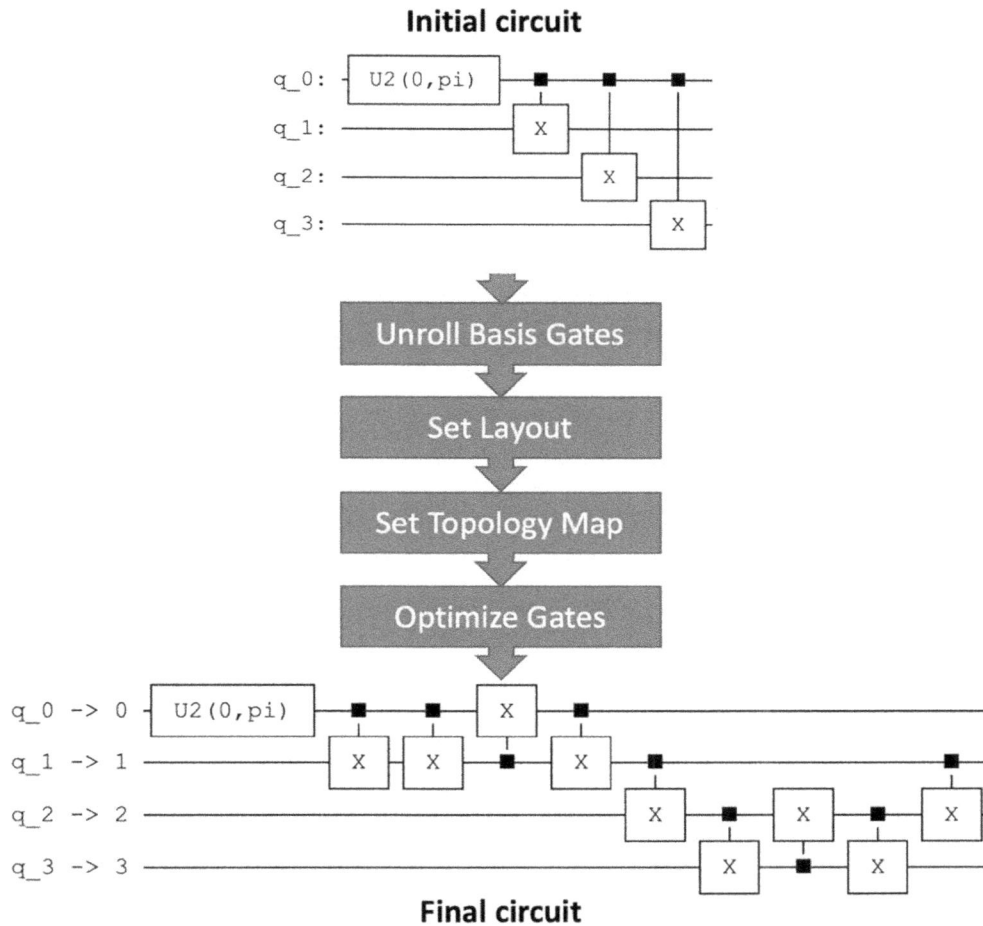

Figure 8.1: The transpiler process of a circuit from the initial circuit, with passes

We'll begin by introducing the general steps taken, as shown in the preceding flowchart, during the execution process:

1. First, the transpiler will unroll the gates in the circuit down to the basis gates of the specified backend system.

2. Next, it will set the layout of the circuit to the device. One example of a layout is the *trivial layout* in which the circuit maps the qubits on your circuit to the same physical qubits on the quantum device. For example, qubit 0 on your circuit is mapped to the same qubit index, in this case, qubit 0 on the physical device.

3. Next, it will map the circuit to the hardware topology. This is to ensure that the logic of your circuit is mapped onto the quantum hardware. For example, let's say you have a CNOT that connects the control qubit to the target qubit. However, if there is not a direct connection between the control and target qubits, then the transpiler will add some SWAP gates to ensure that the connection between the two qubits is made by swapping information between qubits in between the control and target qubits.

4. Finally, the circuit mapping will be optimized to ensure that the circuit depth is contained to a minimum for the given quantum system. Steps 2 and 3 can be mapped to any combination of qubits on the physical device; as you can imagine, finding the right combination of qubits to use that reduces the depth of the circuit is very difficult. Thankfully, the transpiler handles this for us.

The transpiler is made up of two primary components – that is, the **pass** and the **pass manager**:

- A transpiler **pass** is the component that transforms the circuit from its current state into a new state. For example, some passes mentioned in the previous steps are focused on layout selection, routing, optimizations, circuit analysis, and many others. To see an exhaustive list of available passes, you can run the following:

```
# Load helper file
%run helper_file_1.0.ipynb

# Import the transpiler passes object
from qiskit.transpiler import passes

# List out all the passes available
print(dir(passes))
```

The preceding code will list all the passes available. For a detailed description of Pass Manager, I recommend reviewing the API documentation under `qiskit.transpiler.PassManager`. To ensure you have the latest code information, check the main API documentation page found here: `https://docs.quantum.ibm.com/api/qiskit/transpiler`.

Additional examples can also be found in the guide here: `https://docs.quantum.ibm.com/guides/transpile`.

- The **pass manager** is the component that is available to you to specify which passes you wish to use. The pass manager also allows the passes themselves to communicate with other passes. This is ideal for scenarios where one pass would provide or obtain information from other passes to ensure the final circuit adheres to any configuration or optimization requirements. The pass manager also has some preset passes that it makes available to simplify the optimization of a circuit.

Generating preset passmanagers

To ease the use of these passes and passmanagers, Qiskit comes with a few pre-built transpilation pipelines (four at the time of this writing). Each can be found in the qiskit.transpiler.preset_passmanagers module. These pre-built preset pass managers are based on the optimization level selected. These four are currently numbered from 0 to 3. Generating these is also simplified by using the generate_preset_pass_manager() function. The preset pass managers are the default pass managers used by the transpile() function, which constructs a standalone passmanager that mirrors the transpile() function.

In the following section, we will create a simple circuit and transpile it by using the preset passmanager generator, which leverages existing preset pass manager pipelines. We'll also run the same circuit with two different optimization levels to see how the resulting circuit differentiates between the two. Finally, we will create a custom topology to transpile the circuit and compare the results of that to a circuit created via the preset optimizer. This will illustrate the consequences of selecting a layout that has not been optimized.

Comparing circuit mappings on different backend devices

To visualize information on the backend, we learned earlier that we can call the configuration and properties functions to output all the information. That can be handy if we want to extract specific data from the results; however, it is quite difficult to read. This is where the visualization tool comes in very handy. Let's first pick two backend systems to compare. In this example, I'll choose ibm_brisbane, and ibm_nazca, but you can select whichever quantum device you have available by running the service.backends() to get a list of available devices:

```
# Get a list of all available backend devices
service.backends()


# From the list of backends, select two.
# Get the backend device: ibm_brisbane
```

```
backend_brisbane = service.get_backend('ibm_brisbane')
# Get the backend device: ibm_nazca
backend_nazca = service.get_backend('ibm_nazca')
```

Now that we have selected both backend views, let's look at a visual representation of the gates and how they are physically connected using the coupling map. You can see the coupling map by calling the plot_gate_map visualization function as illustrated in the following code snippet:

```
# Visualize the coupling directional map between the qubits
plot_gate_map(backend_brisbane, plot_directed=True)
```

This will print out the full connection map of all the qubits for the specified backend, as shown in the following figure:

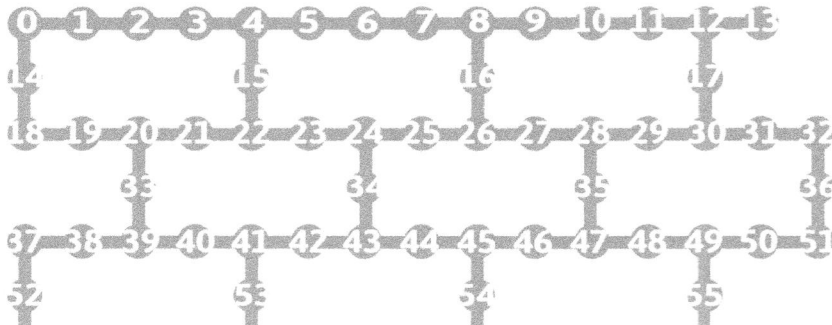

Figure 8.2: Cropped view of the ibm_brisbane connection map

In *Figure 8.2*, with ibm_brisbane (we'll refer to this backend device as Brisbane moving forward for simplicity), we can see that not only is it a 127-qubit device (cropped so it is easier to read), but also the qubits are connected in a heavy-hex formation. You can find details about this here: https://www.ibm.com/quantum/blog/heavy-hex-lattice. Due to the size of the processor, some of the qubit numbers are not clear, so you may need to zoom in to view these up close. Also, note that signals can travel in both directions between each qubit via the connections.

Let's now visualize the coupling directional map of ibm_nazca, hereafter referred to as just Nazca. Run the following cell:

```
# Visualize the coupling directional map between the qubits
plot_gate_map(backend_nazca, plot_directed=True)
```

Now, we can see the gate map with the coupling directional mapping between each qubit, as illustrated here:

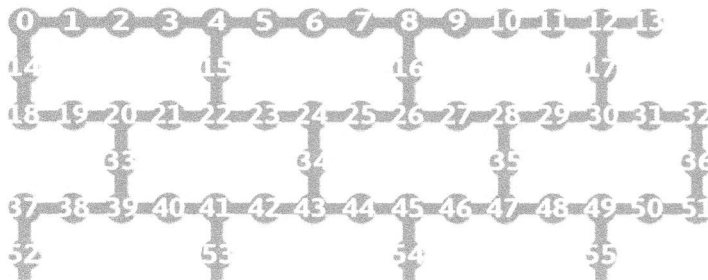

Figure 8.3: Qubit plot view with the coupling directional map enabled (ibm_nazca)

You may notice that the coupling maps have some similarities between the two systems.

Because of the different configurations of the qubits, the layout of the qubits from the quantum circuit we created might not be defined in the most optimal way when mapping the qubits on the quantum circuit to the qubits on the hardware device. Luckily for us, we have transpilation features, which include a parameter setting that allows us to set the level of optimization of the circuit layout. The next section will cover the various passes available, and the pass manager used to manage their usage.

Understanding passes and pass managers

Passes are generally used to transform circuits so that they are set up to perform as optimally as desired. There are five general types of passes that transform circuits:

- **Layout selection** determines how the qubit layout mapping will align with the selected backend configuration.
- **Routing** maps the placement of SWAP gates onto the circuit based on the selected swap mapping type, which can be set by providing a coupling map or backend topology, or by using stochastic methods, where the system will not assume the input state to the circuit is the ground/zero state to simplify the circuit.
- **Basis change** offers various ways to decompose, or unroll, the gates down to the basis gates of the backend or using the circuit's decomposition rules.
- **Optimizations** optimize the circuits themselves by removing redundant gates, such as having two of the same reversible gates, such as a Hadamard gate, back to back, which reverts the qubit to the original state.

- **Circuit analysis** provides circuit information, such as the depth, width, number of operations, and other details about the circuit.

- **Additional passes** are those that offer some other form of optimization, such as the various **check maps**, which check whether the layout of the CNOT gates is in the direction stated in the coupling maps and rearrange the directions if needed.

We covered most of the **circuit analysis** information in *Chapter 7, Programming with Qiskit*, to detect the size, width, and number of operations in a circuit. Let's look at the first pass type, Layout Selection, to see how we can leverage the provided layouts and learn the difference between the various optimization levels.

Learning about the Layout Selection type

Let's dig down into one of these types of passes to get a little more detail. Since we must map the qubits from the circuit to the specified hardware each time, and we want to execute our circuit on a quantum system, we'll view the layout pass. There are various layout passes to choose from when you want to map the qubits to the physical device. Reasons for this could include wanting your qubits to be as close as possible to avoid having multiple SWAP gates, or if you are working on error correction or mitigation, then you may want to map your gates exactly to the physical qubits to ensure your experiments are consistent. Let's look at a few of the basic layout options:

- TrivialLayout: This layout assigns the circuit qubits to the physical device's qubits in the same order as stated in the original quantum circuit. So, qubit 0 is mapped directly to qubit 0 on the physical device.

- DenseLayout: This layout selects the layout that has the most connected subset of qubits. If there is a need for many entangled qubits, this layout will find a subset in which qubits are closely connected to each other so as to avoid long distances and swaps.

- Sabre: This layout leverages a qubit mapping technique that looks at the reversibility of the quantum circuit where it will try to interpret the global circuit information to choose the optimal initial layout.

For each of the passes described above, there is a different default setting for the optimization level of the transpiler. The optimization level is comprised of 4 levels that range from 0 to 3, which specifies whether to not optimize the circuit at all (level 0) up to full optimization (level 3). The higher the optimization level, the more optimized the resulting circuit will be; however, it will of course require a bit more time to run.

In this section, you will learn how to apply and differentiate between each level.

Applying default layouts

Let's start with the default layouts. We'll set the various optimization levels in the transpiler function parameter and apply it to the two backend devices, Brisbane and Nazca, in the following steps. One thing to keep in mind is that at the time of writing, all systems available have the same connectivity between qubits and very similar properties. However, by the time this book is published, there will be varying systems with varying properties, so even though the results here might look the same, the results you see (if the systems you are comparing are different) will vary:

1. We'll reuse the same four-qubit quantum circuit we created earlier. I'll include it again here for your convenience:

    ```
    # Quantum circuit with a single and multi-qubit gates
    qc = QuantumCircuit(4)
    qc.h(0)
    qc.cx(0,1)
    qc.cx(0,2)
    qc.cx(0,3)
    circuit_drawer(qc)
    ```

    This will result in our basic circuit where each of the 4 qubits is entangled via the CX gates to the first qubit, q_0.

    We'll start with Brisbane and set the optimization level to 0, which is to say we will not use any optimization techniques on the circuit. What this will result in is the qubit on our quantum circuit [0,1,2,3], which will map to the same qubit index values on the backend device, Brisbane [0,1,2,…,126].

2. In the following code, we will leverage the qc circuit and use it to test the various optimization levels. We'll then print out the transpiled circuit depth and visualize the layout with the mapped qubits drawn as an overlay over the backend device. This will illustrate how the different methods are applied to the backend device:

    > Note that your results might be different due to the stochastic parts of the transpiler. So, whatever result you get is the optimal result at the time of execution. To ensure you get the same results, you will need to set the seed_transpiler parameter of the transpiler() function to a random integer value.

```
# Generate a preset pass manager for Brisbane
pass_manager = generate_preset_pass_manager(backend=backend_
brisbane, optimization_level = 0)


# Transpile the circuit with an optimization level = 0
qc_brisbane_0 = pass_manager.run(qc)


# Print out the depth of the circuit
print('Depth:', qc_brisbane_0.depth())
# Plot the resulting layout of the quantum circuit after # Layout
plot_circuit_layout(qc_brisbane_0, backend_brisbane)
```

The result, as follows, is as expected, where the qubits are mapped with no layout optimization at all, and there is the direct mapping of qubits from the quantum circuit to the hardware device. Note also that the depth is 6464:

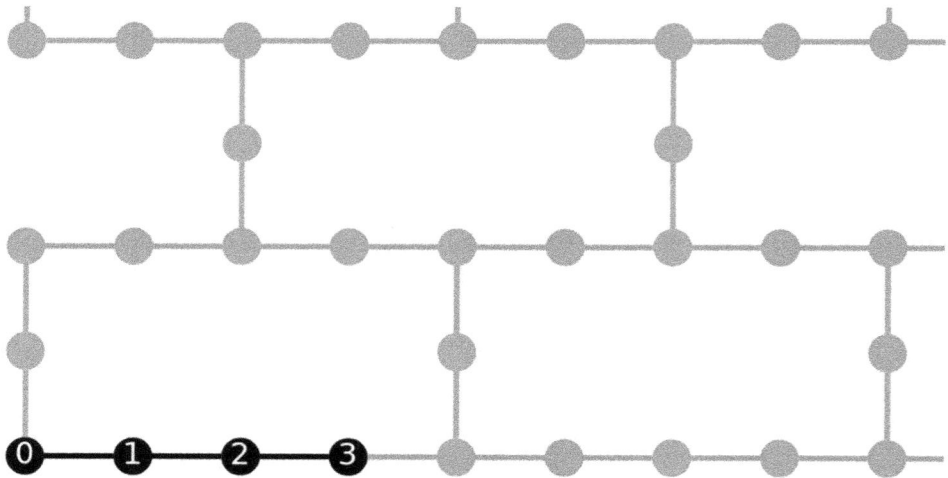

Figure 8.4: Transpiled quantum circuit on Brisbane with optimization = 0; direct qubit mapping with no changes

3. Now, let's draw the transpiled circuit on `Brisbane`:

```
# Draw the transpiled circuit pertaining to Brisbane
circuit_drawer(qc_brisbane_0, idle_wires=False, output='mpl')
```

This will render the transpiled circuit using the basis gates available on `Brisbane`; it has been truncated in the following figure to save space.

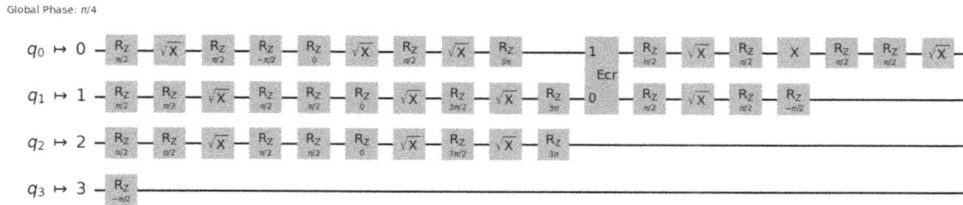

Figure 8.5: Transpiled circuit of basis gates on Brisbane

Please note that the unused qubits are not visible due to our use of the `idle_wires=False` parameter when calling the `circuit_drawer()` function. If we remove this parameter, you will see all qubits, even those that are not in use. Also note that the qubit mappings are depicted on the left side of the circuit diagram where the circuit mapping is pointing to the physical device's qubit. In the previous figure, we can see that from the circuit, q_0 maps to the 0th qubit on the physical device (as shown by the indicator q_0 -> 0).

4. Now, let's run the same thing on `Nazca` with the same level of optimization set to 0. We should see the same results, in that the transpiled circuit is mapped to the same qubits as our quantum circuit:

```
# Generate a preset pass manager for Brisbane
pass_manager = generate_preset_pass_manager(backend=backend_
brisbane, optimization_level = 0)

# Transpile the circuit with an optimization level = 0
qc_brisbane_0 = pass_manager.run(qc)
print('Depth:', qc_nazca_0.depth())
plot_circuit_layout(qc_nazca_0, backend_nazca)
```

The preceding code will result in the following depth information:

```
Depth: 4040
```

The resulting layout mapping, as follows, is also displayed:

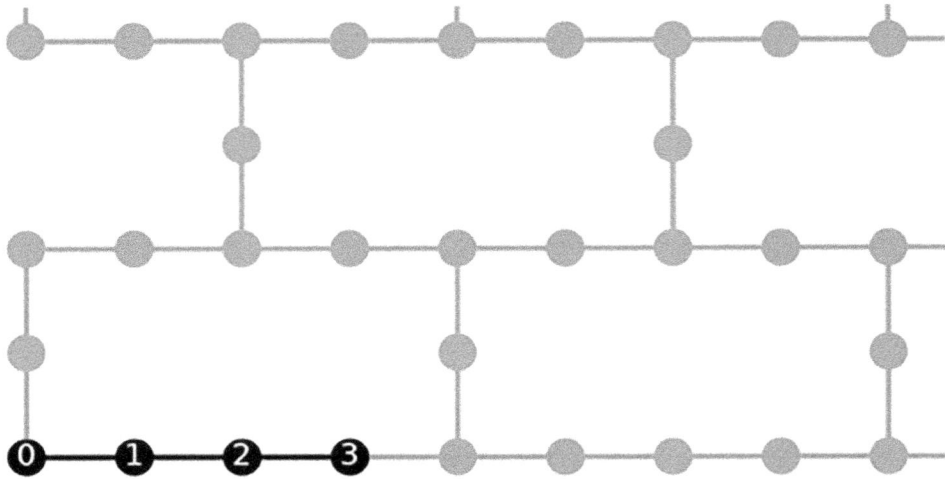

Figure 8.6: Transpiled circuit on Nazca

Let's now look at the transpiled circuit for the `Nazca` quantum device.

5. We'll now draw the transpiled circuit using the following code:

```
# Draw the transpiled circuit pertaining to Nazca
circuit_drawer(qc_nazca_0, idle_wires=False, output='mpl')
```

The preceding code will display the following circuit:

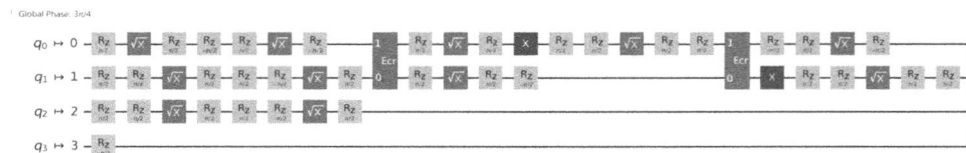

Figure 8.7: Transpiled circuit on Nazca

One thing to note is the set of multi-qubit gates between q_0 and q_1 after the first set of single-qubit gates. These multi-qubit gates can be used to create a CNOT, SWAP, or ROTX gate, represented by the red block labeled **Ecr**. This routing of information between qubits is the result of the routing pass, which looks for the most optimal connection between qubits. The following figure shows the decomposed SWAP gate.

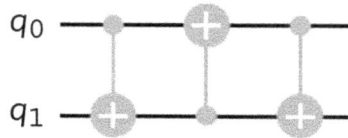

Figure 8.8: SWAP gate decomposed

6. Let's now maximize the optimization level to 3, which performs the highest optimization of the quantum circuit:

```
# Generate a preset pass manager for Brisbane:
pass_manager = generate_preset_pass_manager(backend=backend_
brisbane, optimization_level=3)

# Transpile the circuit with the optimization level = 3
qc_transpiled_brisbane= pass_manager.run(qc)
# Print the depth of the transpiled circuit
print('Depth:', qc_transpiled_brisbane.depth())
# Print the number of operations of the transpiled # circuit
print('Ops count: ', qc_transpiled_brisbane.count_ops())
# Plot the layout mapping of the transpiled circuit
plot_circuit_layout(qc_transpiled_brisbane, backend_brisbane)
```

The preceding code will print out the total circuit depth and the total number of operators (Ops count) in the transpiled circuit, along with the rendering of the transpiled mapping of the qubits onto Brisbane.

```
Depth: 133
Ops count:  OrderedDict([('rz',14), ('sx', 7), ('ecr', 3), ('x',
1)])
```

Here, you'll notice some gates you might not have seen before; you can find details about each gate in the circuit library on the Qiskit API documentation page here: `https://docs.quantum-computing.ibm.com/api/qiskit/circuit_library`.

The following diagram shows the rendering of the transpiled mapping of the qubits, as mentioned earlier:

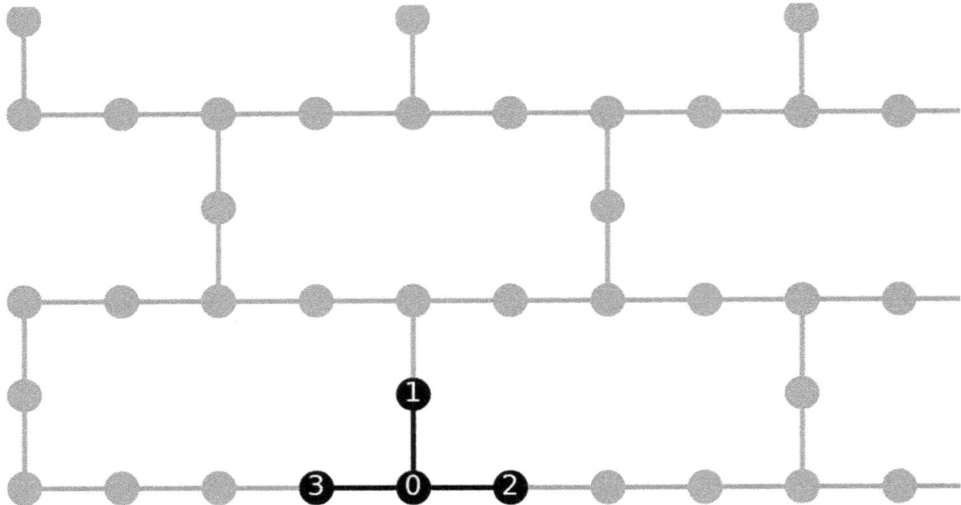

Figure 8.9: Transpiled circuit with the optimization level set to 3 for Brisbane

As you can see in the preceding diagram, to optimize the quantum circuit, the qubit order is adjusted from the previous example on `Brisbane`. This is due to the `optimization_level` parameter being set to 3 (highest), which includes mapping to the most optimal qubits. This also highlights the difference in circuit depth between the two.

7. Let's now draw the transpiled circuit to review the circuit layout to the backend:

```
# Redraw the transpiled circuit at new level
circuit_drawer(qc_transpiled_brisbane, idle_wires=False,
output='mpl')
```

The result, as follows, is the same circuit that is now mapped to different qubits compared to the circuit in *Figure 8.6*. The difference between this circuit and the previous one is simply that the transpiler has the maximum optimization level set, so it will map the qubit operators to the most optimal qubits. For example, here we see qubit 0 is mapped to qubit 4, as follows:

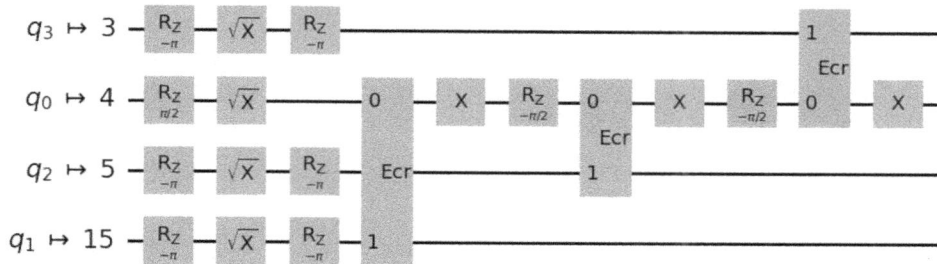

Figure 8.10: Transpiled circuit with the optimization level set to 3

8. We'll set the same optimization level on `Nazca` to 3 and then transpile the circuit:

```
# Generate a preset pass manager for Nazca:
pass_manager = generate_preset_pass_manager(backend=backend_nazca,
optimization_level=3)


# Transpile the circuit with the optimization level = 3
qc_transpiled_nazca= pass_manager.run(qc)


# Get the depth and operation count of the transpiled
# circuit.
print('Depth:', qc_transpiled_nazca.depth())
print('Ops count: ', qc_transpiled_nazca.count_ops())
# Print the circuit layout
plot_circuit_layout(qc_transpiled_nazca, backend_nazca)
```

Here, the total depth is the same, as is the number and type of operators:

```
Depth: 1919
Ops count:  OrderedDict([('rz', 23), ('sx', 13), ('ecr', 3)])
```

However, note that the layout is not necessarily linear; it seems *T-shaped*, where qubit 0 is connected to 3 qubits, like that of Brisbane:

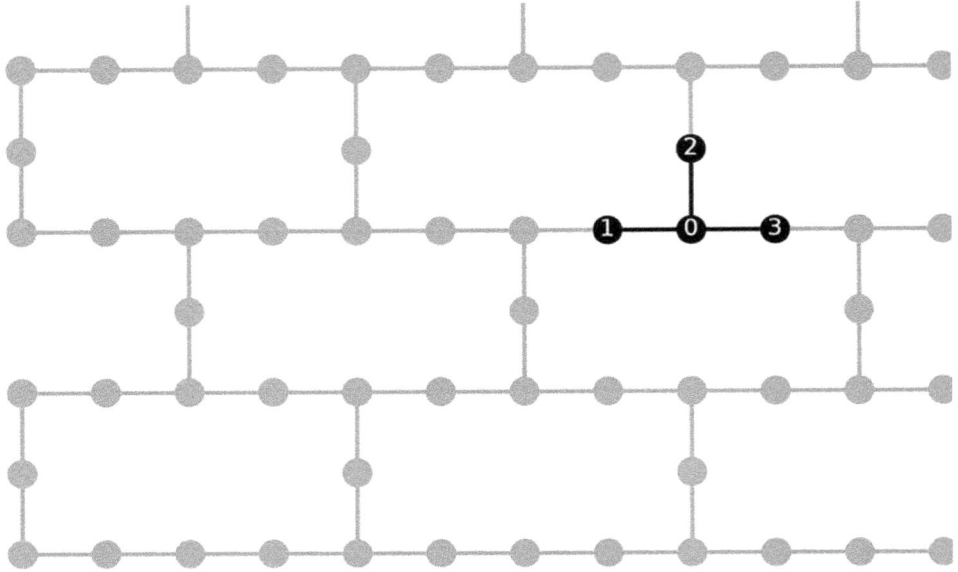

Figure 8.11: Transpiled circuit with the optimization level set to 3

As you can see, to optimize the circuit depth and reduce noise, the qubit order is reversed from the previous example run on Nazca.

9. Let's draw the circuit using the transpiled circuit and see how this mapping looks compared to the previous circuit mapping:

```
# Draw the transpiled circuit
circuit_drawer(qc_transpiled_nazca, idle_wires=False, output='mpl')
```

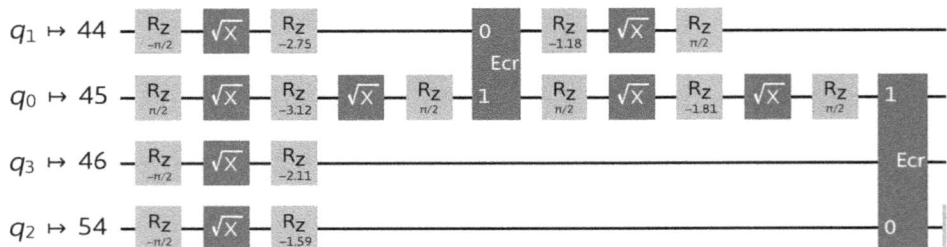

Figure 8.12: Transpiled circuit with the optimization level set to 3

Note the use of qubit **0**, now qubit **44** on the hardware, which was mapped as the qubit on which to base the connections to the other qubits, **0**, **3**, and **2** in the ECR at the end of the circuit. This is a good example, where the optimizer mapped the ECR gates to the physical qubits, for example, qubit **45** to qubits **44, 46**, and **54** on the device, to optimize based on other passes used besides the routing pass. One reason for this case could be that one of the passes considered the coherence time (relaxation time, T1) of the qubits, which is the time a qubit can maintain its quantum state, where the qubit with the longest coherence time, at the time the circuit was transpiled, is qubit 1.

Applying custom layouts

Finally, let's now create our own custom mapping, or **topology**, as it is often referred to:

1. Let's begin by reviewing the coupling map of an existing device; in this case, let's continue using brisbane, which has 127 qubits. We'll review the configuration of the backend first:

```
# Set the ibm_brisbane backend device to obtain #configuration
backend = service.get_backend('ibm_brisbane')
backend
```

The preceding code sets the backend so we can obtain the configuration and property values of the quantum device.

2. Let's examine the coupling map for ibm_brisbane by calling the backend configuration's coupling_map field:

```
# View the backend coupling map, displayed as CNOTs
# (Control-Target)
# Extract the coupling map from the backend
ibm_brisbane_coupling_map = backend.configuration().coupling_map
# List out the extracted coupling map
ibm_brisbane_coupling_map
```

The preceding code will result in displaying an array of the coupling layout of ibm_brisbane. You can verify this by comparing it to the backend view:

```
[[1, 0],
 [2, 1],
 [3, 2],
 [4, 3],
 ...
 [125.126]]
```

3. Next, we will draw the coupling map to see how efficient our circuit is with the default map:

```
# Generate a preset pass manager for Brisbane
# Set the backend to None so it will force using the coupling map
provided:
pass_manager = generate_preset_pass_manager(backend=None,
optimization_level=3,
coupling_map=ibm_brisbane_coupling_map)

# Transpile the circuit with the pass manager
qc_custom = pass_manager.run(qc)

# Draw the resulting custom topology circuit.
circuit_drawer(qc_custom, idle_wires=False, output='mpl')
```

Our circuit, using this topology, is now different from what we saw in brisbane in *Figure 8.10*. Here, we see that the same circuit is now transpiled based on earlier results of the brisbane topology, as follows (note that this can vary depending on the calibration of the system):

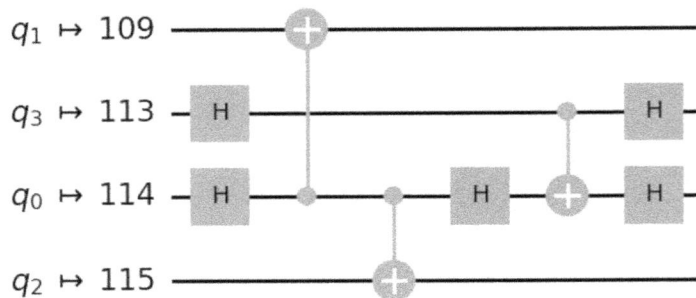

Figure 8.13: The custom circuit using the topology provided by the ibm_brisbane coupling map

4. Up to now, you have extracted the coupling map from existing backend systems, in this case, ibm_brisbane.

5. Now, let's create our own custom topology. For simplicity, we will create a simple linear topology, where the qubits are joined together in a line, as follows:

```
# Create our own coupling map (custom topology)
custom_linear_topology = [[0,1],[1,2],[2,3],[3,4]]
```

```
# Generate a preset pass manager
# Set the backend to None so it will force using the coupling map
provided:
pass_manager = generate_preset_pass_manager(backend=None,
optimization_level=3,
coupling_map=custom_linear_topology)

# Transpile the circuit with the pass manager
qc_custom = pass_manager.run(qc)

# Draw the resulting custom topology circuit.
circuit_drawer(qc_custom, idle_wires=False, output='mpl')
```

The result from the preceding circuit code is clearly not ideal:

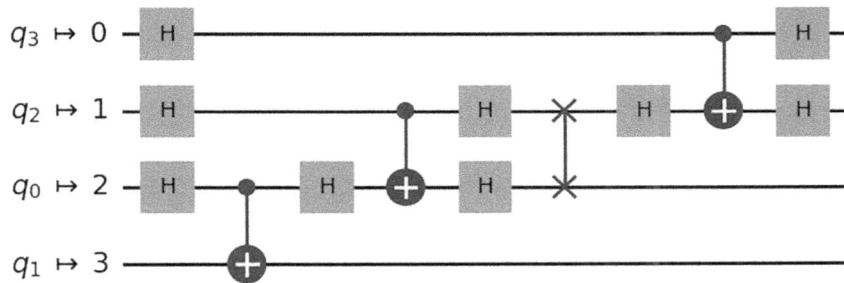

Figure 8.14: Custom linear topology of our circuit

The circuit requires many gates and is quite deep, which increases the risk of having noisy results. This is a good illustration of the importance of optimizers, which handle many of these potential issues. It's no surprise that there is so much research in identifying better ways to optimize circuits to avoid inefficient and noisy circuits. However, having the ability to customize your own topology allows you to create optimal passes that could find unique and effective ways to optimize the mapping of circuits for testing and experimental purposes.

There are many passes that optimize the circuit (we've just covered the layouts as it is easy to see the differences). If you were to look at the full list of passes, you would see that if you change the order of the passes, it will change the results of the circuit when mapped to the physical device. To account for this, we need to look at the pass manager.

Leveraging the pass manager

The pass manager is what allows the passes to communicate with each other, schedules which passes should execute first, and allows for custom passes to be included in the list of passes. This is not as simple as it sounds, as there may be a significant difference if one pass is used before another or perhaps is unable to communicate with another pass. We'll conclude this section with a simple example of the pass manager, using the following steps to create it:

1. We'll first append `TrivialLayout` to `PassManager` and execute the circuit:

    ```
    # Import the PassManager and a few Passes
    from qiskit.transpiler import PassManager, CouplingMap
    from qiskit.transpiler.passes import TrivialLayout, BasicSwap
    pm = PassManager()
    # Create a TrivialLayout based on the ibm_brisbane coupling map
    trivial = TrivialLayout(CouplingMap(ibm_brisbane_coupling_map))
    # Append the TrivialLayout to the PassManager
    pm.append(trivial)
    # Run the PassManager and draw the resulting circuit
    tv_qc = pm.run(qc)
    circuit_drawer(tv_qc, idle_wires=False, output='mpl')
    ```

    The resulting circuit is as follows. Note the specifics of this circuit as we will be comparing the differences between the layouts of this circuit and the upcoming circuit (in *Figure 8.16*):

    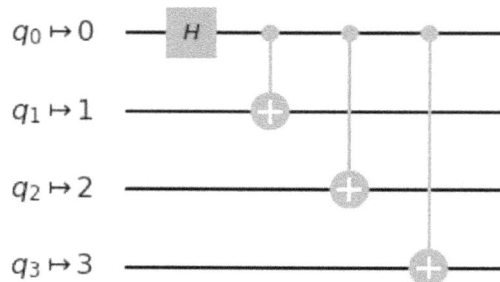

    Figure 8.15: PassManager with the appended TrivialLayout Pass circuit

2. Soon we will explore the functionality of the pass manager using the routing pass type. We saw a little bit of this when the SWAP gates were added to connect qubits when they are not directly connected on the physical device. In the following steps, we will look at passes that optimize the routing of these SWAP gates.

3. In the following code, we will create a `BasicSwap` pass, rerun `PassManager` on the circuit, and compare the results to the previous circuit:

```
# Create a BasicSwap based on the ibm_brisbane coupling
# map we used earlier
basic_swap = BasicSwap(CouplingMap(ibm_brisbane_coupling_map))
#Add the BasicSwap to the PassManager
pm = PassManager(basic_swap)
# Run the PassManager and draw the results
new_qc = pm.run(qc)
circuit_drawer(new_qc, idle_wires=False, output='mpl')
```

The previous code will create a `BasicSwap` router and add it to `PassManager` upon construction. The executed circuit result is as follows:

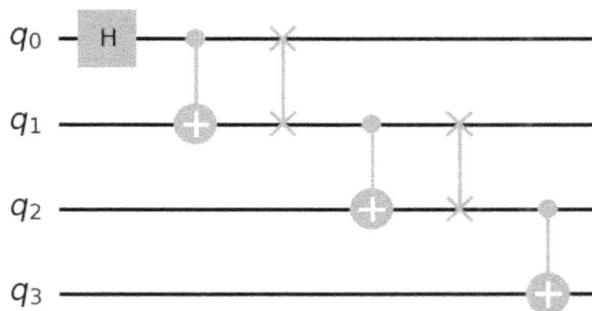

Figure 8.16: PassManager with a BasicSwap router pass circuit

As you can see, the circuit will adapt to each of the passes called from `PassManager` – in this case, we added the `BasicSwap` pass to the PassManager in the code, which then rendered the circuit mapping in one form, whereas the `TrivialLayout` pass rendered in a different form. Doing this gives you the ability to order how the various passes are run during the optimization process of the PassManager. Having this ability provides you with options to test out, should you be researching ways to optimize how your circuit is mapped and run on a backend device.

Let's take a moment to digest what we've learned so far. When using the `optimization_level` option to execute our circuit on a backend, the PassManager uses the preset passes based on the specific level selected (i.e., 0, 1, 2, or 3). What we managed to do here is customize which passes to use and in what order, as we did when we added the BasicSwap pass to the previous code. Having this ability not only provides you with the flexibility to experiment with various sequences of passes, but you can also create your own pass and compare it with those existing passes.

Now that you are familiar with pass managers, you can see that they can be very helpful if you want to use a combination of passes in a way that, when leveraged one after the other, improves the optimization of the circuit as it is modified along the way.

In this section, we also learned about the transpiler and how it provides ways to optimize circuits. We also learned about transforming and optimizing the circuit using the layout optimizer.

The next section of this chapter is a bit more visual, by rendering the circuits in different styles and operational flows such as **DAGs**. These features provide a way to view the circuits and their functionality in a different form rather than the default view of the circuits, which is how we have seen them so far.

Visualizing and enhancing circuit graphs

This section will focus on the various visualizations available in Qiskit. The graphs we have been using so far were from the default visualization library in Qiskit. However, we can specify other drawing tools that may be better suited for your documentation purposes. Say, for example, that you are authoring a research paper with **LaTeX** and you want to use the LaTeX content.

By simply adding style parameters from the Qiskit visualization library, you can then leverage the many features included with the visualization library. We'll cover a few of those now to get you started.

Learning about customized visual circuits

When rendering a circuit, it is often necessary or convenient to have the results in a format that suits the format of your document. It's here where the Qiskit `circuit_drawer` comes in handy with various features. Let's begin with a simple quantum circuit to illustrate the various visual rendering examples:

1. First, let's create a quantum circuit with various operators to get a good representation of all the visual components in the various formats:

```
# Sample quantum circuit
qc = QuantumCircuit(4)
qc.h(0)
qc.cx(0,1)
qc.barrier()
qc.cx(0,2)
```

```
qc.cx(0,3)
qc.barrier()
qc.cz(3,0)
qc.h(0)
qc.measure_all()
# Draw the circuit using the default renderer
circuit_drawer(qc, output='mpl')
```

This will render the following circuit drawing, which is just a random representation of gates. This circuit does not do anything special; it's just used to represent various components. As an option, you can use the random_circuit method to create a random circuit:

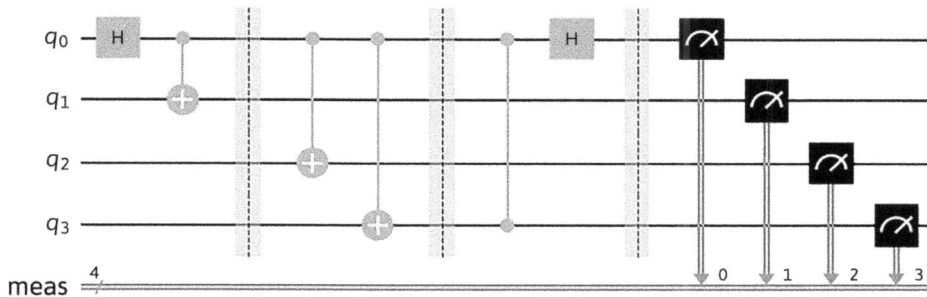

Figure 8.17: Circuit rendering using the default library

2. Next, we will render the preceding circuit using latex:

```
circuit_drawer(qc, output='latex')
```

This will render the latex version of the circuit:

> If you're running this on your local machine and not on the platform, you may have some warnings or errors indicating you need to install some file dependencies, such as installing pylatexenc. To install this library you will need to run pip install pylatexenc in a cell first, and then restart the kernel.

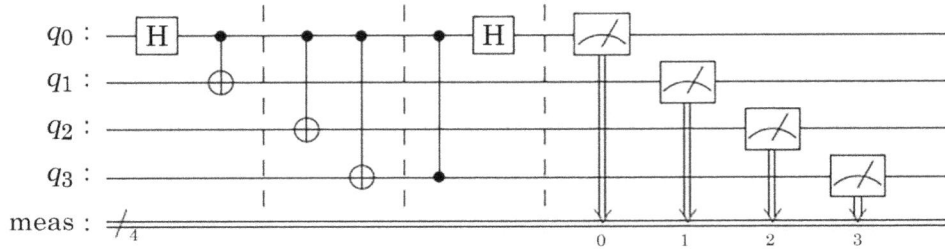

Figure 8.18: Circuit rendering using the latex library

3. If you are planning to post your circuit onto a website, blog, or social media and would like to include some styles on the image, you can do that as well by passing in the style contents as a parameter, such as backgroundcolor, gatetextcolor, and fontsize, just to name a few:

```
# Define the style to render the circuit and components
style = {'backgroundcolor': 'lightblue','gatefacecolor':
'white', 'gatetextcolor': 'black', 'fontsize': 9}
# Draw the mpl with the specified style
circuit_drawer(qc, style=style, output='mpl')
```

The preceding code results in adjusting the background, gate color schemes, and font size, as illustrated here:

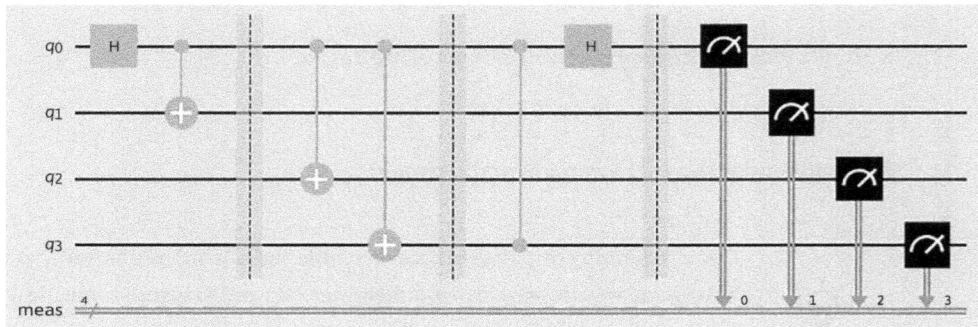

Figure 8.19: Rendered circuit with the custom style dictionary on matplotlib

To use the style setting, you must use the output `matplotlib` as this is the only library that supports the styles.

> Details on the available list of styles can be found in the *Style Dict Details* section of the Qiskit API documentation (`https://docs.quantum-computing.ibm.com/api/qiskit/qiskit.visualization.circuit_drawer`).

Finally, we will cover a full view of the circuit as a DAG, which will be helpful to see the circuit as a graph to understand how it flows.

Drawing the directed acyclic graph of a circuit

As circuits get larger, they will naturally get more complex, and even visualizing a circuit can get complicated. Imagine a circuit with thousands of qubits and with a depth of over 1,000. This would be difficult to render and almost impossible to read. This is where DAGs may help. Let's create one based on the circuit that we previously created to illustrate rendering and see how the DAG of that circuit looks.

In the following code, you will need two components; the first is the circuit-to-DAG converter. This will convert the circuit into a DAG. The second component is the DAG drawer, which will draw out the DAG where the nodes are represented as quantum registers, classical registers, quantum gates, barriers, and measurement operators. The edges are directional, which illustrates the flow of the circuit:

```
# Import the Circuit to DAG converter
from qiskit.converters import circuit_to_dag
# Import the DAG drawer
from qiskit.visualization import dag_drawer
# Convert the circuit into a DAG
dag = circuit_to_dag(qc)
# Draw the DAG of the circuit
dag_drawer(dag)
```

This results in the following rendering of the DAG:

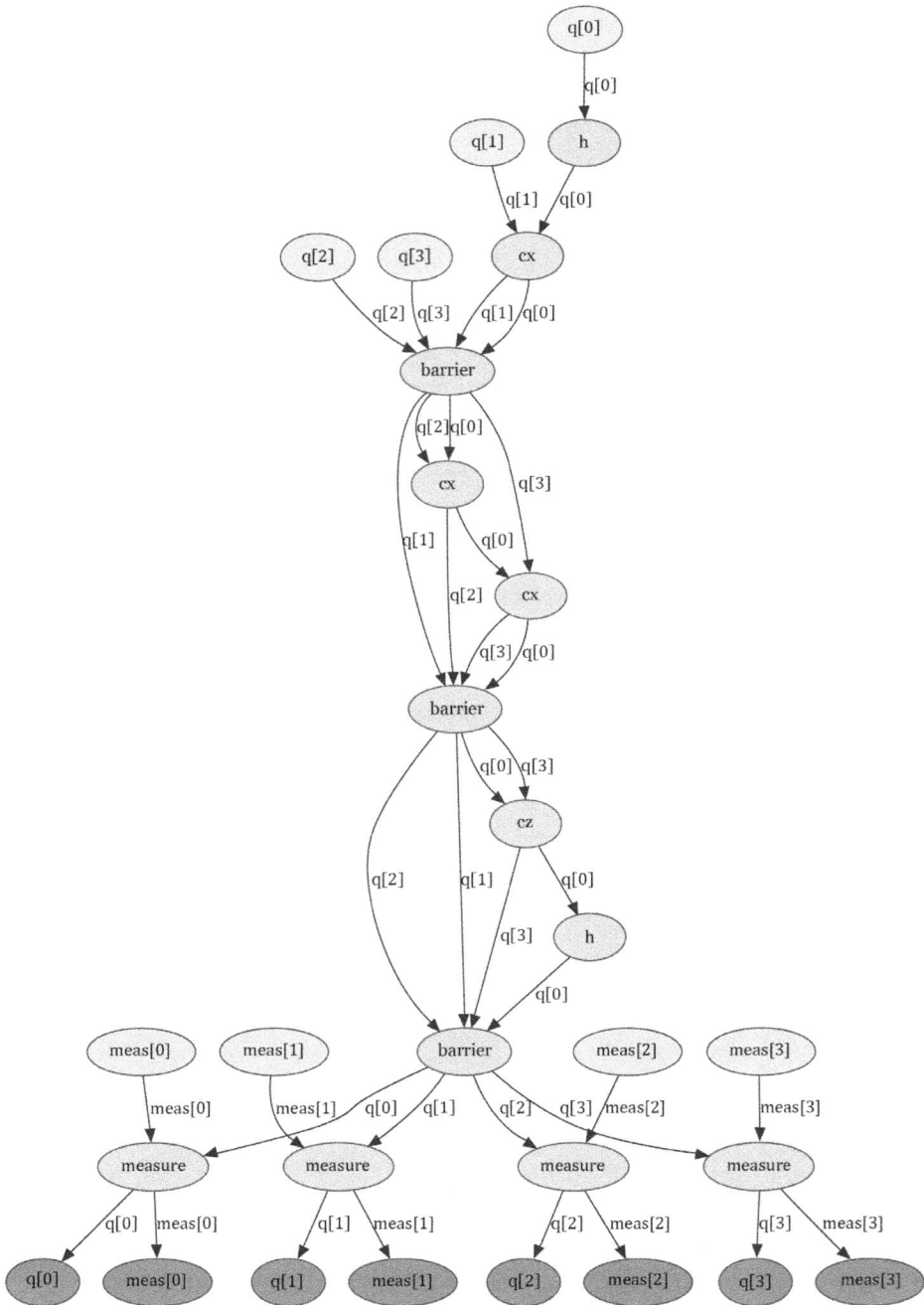

Figure 8.20: The DAG rendering of a quantum circuit

The DAG can help illustrate the flow and expected paths of the circuit in order from top to bottom, where the top level is the first operation, and each operation is appended as you traverse down the graph. For example, the preceding graph starts at the top with the qubits in green, then following the graph, we see that each qubit (represented by the edge labels between the nodes) is operated upon by a specified operation (represented by the nodes). The graph terminates at the end in red, where the measurement applied on the qubit is mapped to the specified classical bit, represented by the parameter values.

In this section, we learned about visualizing circuit graphs with the help of customized visual circuits. We also learned how to use DAGs to enhance our circuit graphs and visualize the path of our circuit.

Summary

In this chapter, you learned various ways to optimize your circuits when they are running on one of the many quantum computers that currently exist. You also learned about the different passes available to optimize the execution of your circuit on a specified quantum device. This includes generating a pass manager, which allows you to customize which passes to leverage based on the selected optimization level and allows you to choose their order.

We then covered topology and coupling maps, which helped you understand the importance of knowing the device configurations should you want to create your own passes. By visualizing the circuits in various formats, you now have the skills to customize the rendering of images, particularly if you are documenting your work and would like to keep a certain look and feel. Finally, we covered alternative rendering of the circuit operation flow by using DAGs.

In the next chapter, we will learn about various noises associated with quantum systems to understand how we can create noise models that we can use to simulate and identify ways to mitigate and run more efficient algorithms.

Questions

1. Can you name the two components of the transpiler?
2. Which component allows you to specify the passes to use?
3. What is the default optimization_level value when running the transpile() function?
4. Name the three Layout Selection Passes.

Join us on Discord

Join our community's Discord space for discussions with the author and other readers:

```
https://packt.link/3FyN1
```

9

Simulating Quantum Systems and Noise Models

Qiskit is a provider of high-performance backends that can be used to execute quantum circuits. The various backend simulators available can be used in unique ways where each can provide different information pertaining to your circuit. Qiskit also provides a variety of tools that can be leveraged to construct noise models to simulate various errors that occur on real quantum devices. These tools are very helpful should you need to compare the difference between your results from an ideal simulator and that which replicates the effects of noise from a quantum device.

Both the simulators and tools such as the **noise model** will help you understand the reasons for some of the effects on your results, as well as provide insights should you later want to mitigate those errors yourself.

The following topics will be covered in this chapter:

- Understanding the differences between simulators
- Generating noise models
- Building your own noise model
- Executing quantum circuits with custom noise models

In this chapter, we will review the Qiskit simulators and understand the differences between each of them and what unique functionality each one provides. We will also delve into the Qiskit noise models that we can generate based on the specified backend devices to allow us to simulate noise on our ideal Qiskit simulators.

After reading this chapter, you will be able to reproduce similar noise effects on the simulator. This will allow you to observe how the noise affects our results, which would allow us to simulate a real quantum device. Finally, we will cover how you can create your own noise models and apply them to your circuits.

Technical requirements

In this chapter, it is expected that you are familiar with the basics of quantum circuits described in previous chapters, such as creating and executing quantum circuits, obtaining backend properties and configurations, and customizing and visualizing circuit diagrams, and you should have knowledge of qubit logic gate operators and states. Also, some familiarity with noise effects such as decoherence time would be ideal; however, we will cover some of the basics in this chapter as a refresher. You will need to install the latest version of **qiskit-aer** to run the notebooks in this chapter; details can be found in the Qiskit documentation: `https://qiskit.github.io/qiskit-aer/getting_started.html`.

Here is the full source code used throughout this book: `https://github.com/PacktPublishing/Learning-Quantum-Computing-with-Python-and-IBM-Quantum-Second-Edition`.

Understanding the differences between simulators

In this section, you will learn about the various simulator backends that are included in Qiskit Aer, including the differences between them and their distinct features. Note that you will need to install **qiskit-aer** separately as it is not part of the base Qiskit install.

These features include generating noise models and configuring the simulator backends that allow you to take advantage of modifying their behavior and characteristics to suit your needs.

We will learn about the following simulators and their key features:

- The Aer simulator, which executes a quantum circuit with multiple shots to simulate a noisy backend quantum system
- The Statevector simulator, which provides the state vector of the quantum circuit
- The Unitary simulator, which provides the unitary matrix of the quantum circuit being executed

Let's move on and look at the quantum systems, herein referred to as simply backends.

Viewing all available backends

If you have read the previous chapters of this book, then you are aware of some of the simulators we have used. Let's start off by displaying every simulator available from the various sources.

We will create a new **notebook** on IQP and run the autogenerated cell to ensure you have loaded some base classes and methods and loaded your account information so we can access IQP:

1. We'll begin by importing some useful classes and functions including, those in the helper file:

    ```
    # Load helper file and import functions:
    %run helper_file_1.0.ipynb

    from qiskit import QuantumCircuit, transpile
    from qiskit_aer import AerProvider, AerSimulator, QasmSimulator,
    StatevectorSimulator, UnitarySimulator
    from qiskit.visualization import *
    from qiskit_ibm_runtime import QiskitRuntimeService, Sampler,
    Estimator, Session, Options

    # Load your IBM Quantum account(s)
    service = QiskitRuntimeService(channel="ibm_quantum")
    ```

2. Next, we'll display all the available simulators in the Qiskit Aer library by using the following code:

    ```
    # View all available backends
    provider = AerProvider()
    provider.backends()
    ```

    This will display a list of all the available simulators:

    ```
    [AerSimulator('aer_simulator'),
     AerSimulator('aer_simulator_statevector'),
     AerSimulator('aer_simulator_density_matrix'),
     AerSimulator('aer_simulator_stabilizer'),
     AerSimulator('aer_simulator_matrix_product_state'),
     AerSimulator('aer_simulator_extended_stabilizer'),
     AerSimulator('aer_simulator_unitary'),
     AerSimulator('aer_simulator_superop'),
    ```

```
QasmSimulator('qasm_simulator'),
StatevectorSimulator('statevector_simulator'),
UnitarySimulator('unitary_simulator')])]
```

3. The following code will list out the simulators that are part of the `Qiskit-Aer` library. These are also available as Python built-in simulators, should you not want to install Aer and just use Qiskit. For simplicity and performance considerations, we will be using the Qiskit simulators throughout this book. However, you can certainly interchange the Aer simulators with those actual quantum systems listed in `service` as needed. But since we want to conserve usage time, let's stick with the simulator for these basic circuits and learning concepts.

4. And finally, we can list all the quantum systems available from the Qiskit Runtime Service:

```
# View all available IBM Quantum backends
service.backends()
```

This will not only list the simulator but also list the real quantum devices available to you based on your account. Those listed will vary based on available devices and upgrades since this writing:

```
[<IBMBackend('ibm_brisbane')>,
 <IBMBackend('ibm_kyiv')>,
 <IBMBackend('ibm_nazca')>,
 <IBMBackend('ibm_sherbrooke')>,
 <IBMBackend('ibm_kyoto')>,
]
```

As this chapter is focused on simulators, we will learn about the local simulators that are installed from the Qiskit library going forward. We'll start with the Aer simulators, which we can use to execute small circuits.

Running circuits on the Aer simulator

The **Aer simulator** is not only used to execute quantum circuits but is also very versatile because of its ability to apply various simulation methods and configuration options.

A few of the available simulation methods are described as follows:

- statevector: This is a statevector simulation within the Aer library that allows ideal circuit measurements at the end of the quantum circuit. In addition, each shot that executes the circuit can sample random noise from noise models to provide noisy simulations.

- density_matrix: This method provides a density matrix simulation that like the statevector, samples the quantum circuits with measurements given at the end of each circuit.

- matrix_product_state: This is a tensor-network statevector simulator that leverages a Matrix Product State as the representation of the state.

- automatic: If no method is set, then this method will select one automatically based on the number of qubits, the quantum circuit, and the noise model.

There are many backend options available; below is a subset of the available backend_options:

- device: This sets the simulation device where CPU is set by default. However, the statevector, unitary, and density_matrix simulators can also run on systems equipped with an Nvidia **Graphical Processing Unit** (**GPU**). To configure the simulator to a GPU, simply set the options parameter, device='GPU'.

- precision: This sets the floating point to either single or double precision; the default is double. Setting the precision to single will halve the required memory of the backend, which could provide some performance improvement on certain systems.

- zero_threshold: This truncates small values to 0 and will truncate very small values. The default truncation value is set to 1e-10, but this can be adjusted to suit the needs of the developer.

- validation_threshold: This threshold is used to verify if the initial statevector of the quantum circuit is valid, with the default value set to 1×10^{-8}.

- max_parallel_threads: Setting this parameter to (the default value) 0 enables the simulator to run on all available cores.

- max_parallel_experiments: The maximum number of **qobj** (**QASM object**), which represents a single payload of a Qiskit provider to run circuits in parallel. The max value cannot exceed the max_parallel_threads value. If the max is set to 0, it will be set to the max_parallel_threads value.

- max_parallel_threads: This sets the maximum number of CPU cores for parallelization. The default value is set to 0, which means it will set it to the maximum number of CPU cores.

- max_memory_mb: Setting this parameter to 0 enables the simulators to maximize the size of system memory to store a state vector; the default value is set to 0. If more memory is needed, an error will be thrown. As a reference, a state vector of n-qubits uses 2^n complex values of approximately 16 bytes.

Now that you have knowledge of the simulation methods and backend options, we'll create a simple circuit and execute it using Aer's `QasmSimulator` class. For this example, we will create the same circuit example we have been using so far, consisting of Hadamard and CX gates, which places the quantum circuit in a superposition and entangles both qubits together:

> Here, we are creating a 2-qubit and 2-bit circuit; when using the `measure_all()` function, we will need to set the `add_bits` parameter to `False` so that it does not add the classical bits since we have already added them in the `QuantumCircuit` constructor.

```python
# Create a quantum circuit
qc = QuantumCircuit(2, 2)
qc.h(0)
qc.cx(0, 1)
qc.measure_all(add_bits=False)
```

Now, let's create the Aer simulator using the get_backend() function:

```python
# Instantiate the QASM simulator from the Aer provider
backend_simulator = QasmSimulator()
# Transpile the circuit
transpiled_qc = transpile(qc, backend_simulator)
# Run the circuit using the transpiled circuit
job = backend_simulator.run(transpiled_qc)
# Print out the result counts
result = job.result()
counts = result.get_counts(qc)
print(counts)
```

This will print out the results from executing the quantum circuit on the Aer simulator, with the method set to a state vector, obtaining the result counts.

As you can see, this runs the same results as if you ran `aer_simulator` as follows:

```python
# Get the Aer simulator and set the backend options
aer_simulator = AerSimulator(method='statevector')
# Transpile the circuit
transpiled_qc = transpile(qc, aer_simulator)
# Run the circuit with the Aer simulator
```

```
job = aer_simulator.run(transpiled_qc)
print(job.result().get_counts(qc))
```

Both forms execute the circuit in the same manner, with varying values in the results, of course. Here, you can see the results, which both ran a total, 1024 shots, as this is set by default:

```
{'00': 501, '11': 523}
```

We'll continue by extending the backend options to include other parameters that we might find useful, such as shots and memory, in the next section.

Adding parameters to the backend options

We may already be familiar with the shots parameter, which specifies how many times to execute the circuit on the backend. However, as illustrated in the previous example, the counts returned are the total values of all the shots, but not in the order in which each result was returned. There may be situations when you would like to examine the results of each shot in chronological order.

To examine the measured results that are stored in the individual memory slots, you will need to set the memory parameter in the backend options. Let's rerun the previous circuit; however, this time we will set the memory flag to True and display the results. We'll run just 10 shots this time to avoid a very large output string:

```
# Run the circuit on the simulator and set the memory to True
# Run the transpiled circuit using the backend options created
job = backend_simulator.run(transpiled_qc, shots=10, memory=True)
result = job.result()
# Pull the memory slots from the results
memory = result.get_memory(transpiled_qc)
# Print the results from the memory slots
print('Memory results: ', memory)
```

This will output the 10 memory slot entry results from the execution of the circuit. Notice that the results are varying combinations of 00 and 11, as expected for the circuit:

```
Memory results: ['00', '11', '11', '11', '00', '00', '00', '11', '00',
'11']
```

Having the memory feature built into the Aer simulator gives you the ability to visualize each result of your circuit count. The next section will illustrate how to initialize and set up all, or just a subset, of the qubits.

Initializing the qubits on a circuit

As we learned early on, each qubit is initialized to the ground state, or the $|0\rangle$ state. However, there may be times when we would like to set a different initial state. Luckily for us, the Aer simulator allows us to initialize the state of the circuit to some other state, $|\psi\rangle$, in lieu of all $|0\rangle$ states.

We will follow the next steps to initialize the qubits:

1. In the previous example, we created a circuit that contained a Hadamard and Control-Not gate to obtain the entangled state results of $|00\rangle$ or $|11\rangle$. In this example, we will initialize our circuit so that the results are the same without needing to add any gates:

```python
# Construct a 2 qubit quantum circuit
qc_init = QuantumCircuit(2, 2)
# Import numpy to simplify some math for us
import numpy as np
# Select the qubits by their index which you wish to initialize
init_qubits = [0, 1]
# Inititialize qubit states
qc_init.initialize([1, 0, 0, 1] / np.sqrt(2), init_qubits)
# Add measurements and draw the initialized circuit
qc_init.measure(range(2), range(2))
qc_init.decompose()
qc_init.draw(output="mpl")
```

This results in the following circuit diagram:

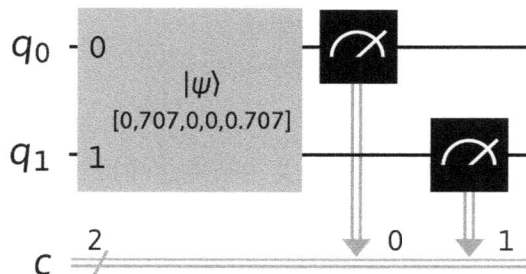

Figure 9.1: Initialized qubits to an initial state other than the zero state

Notice that the qubits are collectively initialized into the state of $[\frac{1}{\sqrt{2}}, 0, 0, \frac{1}{\sqrt{2}}]^T$. This circuit now has an initialized state that can be applied to any circuit should you wish a circuit to begin in a state other than the ground/zero state. Initializing a state can be needed when using a variational quantum algorithm that needs to be updated each time it is run to optimize its results.

2. Now, let's execute this circuit and observe each result:

```
# Set the memory to True so we can observe each result
result = backend_simulator.run(qc_init, shots=10,
    memory=True).result()
# Retrieve the individual results from the memory slots
memory = result.get_memory(qc_init)
# Print the memory slots
print(memory)
```

This prints out the following results:

```
['11', '11', '00', '11', '11', '00', '00', '00', '11', '00']
```

As you can observe from the results, we get only the two initialized state results of either $|00\rangle$ or $|11\rangle$, as expected.

3. Now, you don't have to initialize all qubits in a circuit; you can also specify a group of qubits to initialize, as illustrated in the following code:

```
# Create a 4 qubit circuit
qc_init2 = QuantumCircuit(4, 4)
# Initialize only the last 3 qubits
initialized_qubits = [1, 2, 3]
# Set the initial state, remember that the sum of
# amplitudes-squared must equal 1
qc_init2.initialize([0, 1, 0, 1, 0, 1, 0, 1] / np.sqrt(4),
                    initialized_qubits)
# Add a barrier so it is easier to read
qc_init2.barrier(range(4))
# Measure qubits, decompose and draw circuit
qc_init2.measure(range(4), range(4))
qc_init2.decompose()
qc_init2.draw(output='mpl')
```

This results in the following circuit, which initializes the state of the q_1 to q_3 qubits, while all the other qubits that are initialized remain in the ground/zero state:

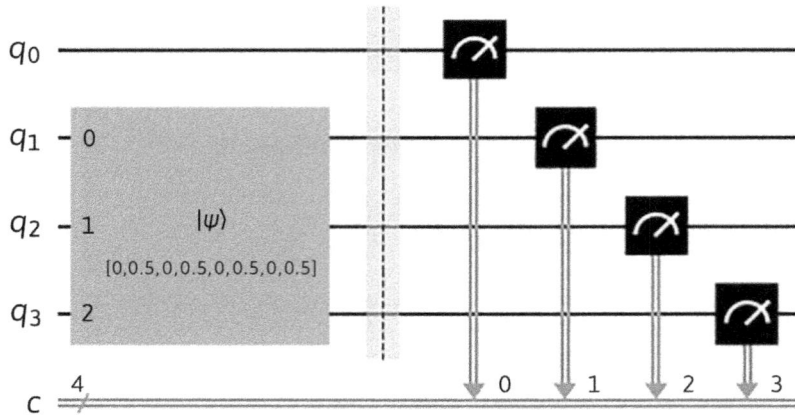

Figure 9.2: Initialization of the last three qubits

Here, our 3-qubit initialized state is set to $|001\rangle$, $|011\rangle$, $|101\rangle$, $|111\rangle$. However, since we are executing a 4-qubit circuit, and we have initialized the last 3 qubits, our results should include the fourth qubit (q_0), which would append a 0 to the least significant bit.

4. Let's run the experiment and see whether the initial state of the partial qubits is successful:

```
# Execute the circuit and print results and histogram
result = backend_simulator.run(qc_init2).result()
counts = result.get_counts(qc_init2)
print(counts)
plot_distribution(counts)
```

As expected, our results are as follows (note that due to the randomness of the circuit, actual results could vary):

```
{'0010': 275, '1010': 250, '0110': 255, '1110': 244}
```

We also get the following output graph:

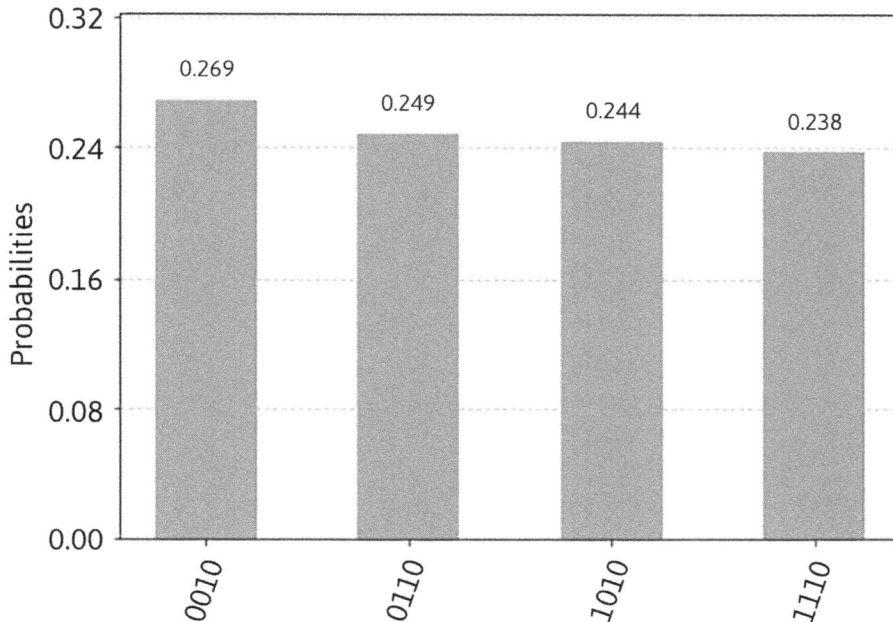

Figure 9.3: Results of initialized quantum circuit

As you can see, the results are exactly as we expected them to be. Notice that the least significant bit (the bit on the far right) is always set to 0 as it was not one of the initialized qubits. The other thing to take note of is that the other bits are exactly as we expected, $|0010\rangle$, $|0110\rangle$, $|1010\rangle$, $|1110\rangle$, where the bold indicates the initialized bits, and if you combine them all together, they will provide the results displayed.

5. Now that we have initialized a circuit, we can apply any gate as needed. The only difference is that the gates applied to the circuit after initialization will then be applied to the initialized state of each qubit, rather than the default initialized state $|0\rangle$. Let's test this out by adding a NOT (X) gate to all the qubits. This should result in all the values being flipped:

```
# Create a 4-qubit circuit
qc_init_x = QuantumCircuit(4, 4)
# Import numpy
import numpy as np
# Initialize the last 3 qubits, same as before
```

```
initialized_qubits = [1, 2, 3]
  qc_init_x.initialize([0, 1, 0, 1, 0, 1, 0, 1] /
np.sqrt(4), initialized_qubits)
# Add a barrier so it is easier to read
qc_init_x.barrier(range(4))
# Include an X gate on all qubits
for idx in range(4):
    qc_init_x.x(idx)
# Measure and draw the circuit
qc_init_x.measure(range(4), range(4))
# Decompose the circuit down a level
qc_init_x.decompose()
# Draw the completed circuit
qc_init_x.draw(output='mpl')
```

This results in the following circuit:

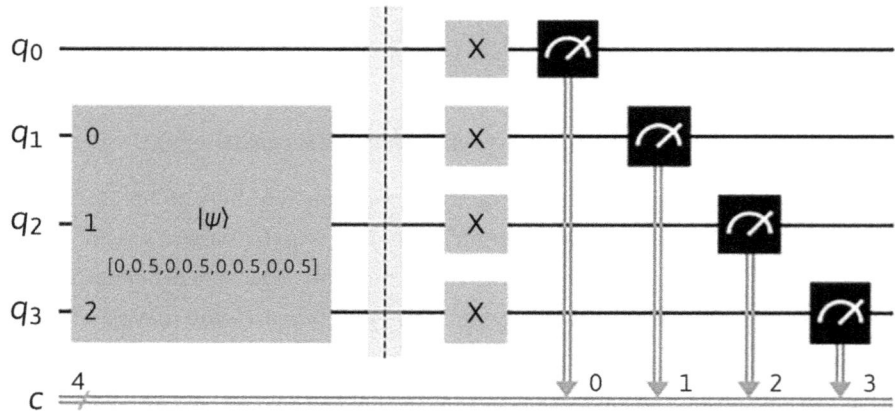

Figure 9.4: Initialized quantum circuit with X gates applied to all qubits before measuring

Notice the initialized qubits are as before, only after the X gates on all qubits that we have added just before measuring. This should result in all bits flipping from 0 to 1, and vice versa.

6. Let's execute the circuit and display the results using the following code:

```
# Execute and get counts
result = backend_simulator.run(qc_init_x).result()
```

```
counts = result.get_counts(qc_init_x)
print(counts)
plot_distribution(counts)
```

This results exactly as expected; the results are based on the initialized state, followed by the NOT gates being applied on all qubits:

```
{'0101': 256, '0001': 268, '1101': 232, '1001': 244}
```

We also get to see the following graph:

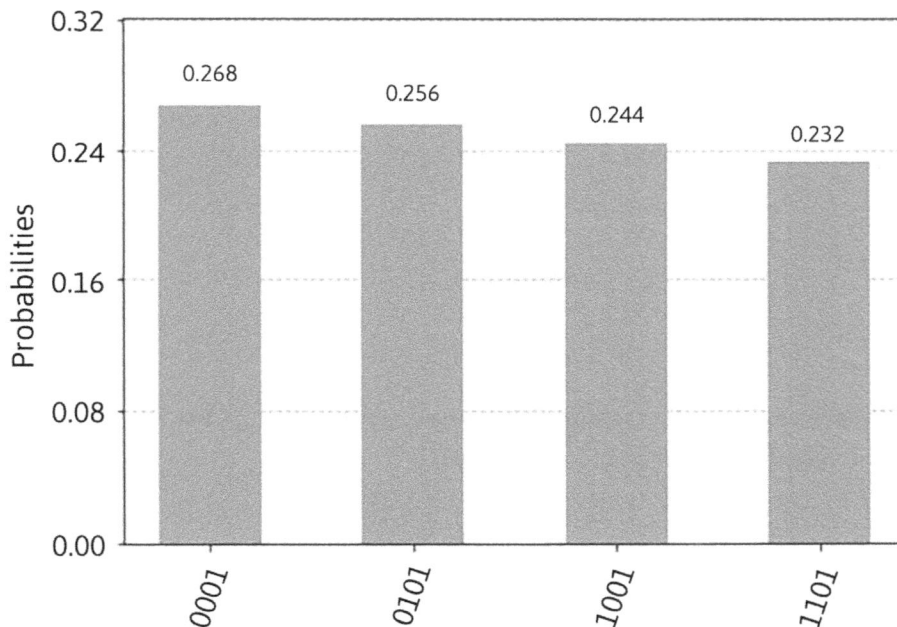

Figure 9.5: Results of the initialized circuit with X gate applied to all qubits

The Aer simulator's ability to be very flexible and configurable means that creating custom circuits with the ability to initialize qubit states is quite an advantage. We will see this in more detail in *Chapter 12, Understanding Quantum Algorithms*, where we will see how this is applied to variational or other hybrid quantum algorithms.

Now that we are familiar with the Aer simulator, let's move on to the statevector simulator and see what unique features we have available.

Running circuits on the statevector simulator

The **statevector simulator**, like the Aer simulator, allows you to initialize and execute a quantum circuit. There are of course some distinct differences, one of which is that it returns the state vector of the quantum circuit by executing a single shot. This allows you to capture a snapshot of the state vector so you can, in some sense, calculate or observe the expected results on the qubits. Because the statevector simulator simulates the ideal execution of a quantum circuit and results in the final quantum state vector of the device at the end of a simulation, this result can then be used for debugging or educational purposes.

We will also leverage some of the Aer visualization tools to help display the state information of the qubits and the quantum circuit. We will follow the next steps to do so:

1. To begin, let's create a simple 1-qubit circuit and add a Hadamard gate to it so we have a qubit in a superposition:

    ```
    # Construct quantum circuit
    qc = QuantumCircuit(1)
    # Place qubit in superposition
    qc.h(0)
    qc.draw(output='mpl')
    ```

    The result of this is as follows, where we have a single qubit in a superposition, that is, a complex linear combination of $|0\rangle$ and $|1\rangle$:

    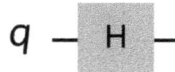

    Figure 9.6: Single qubit circuit with a Hadamard gate

2. Next, we want to see the state vector representation of the circuit. Before coding it, let's review the mathematics around it. We know that each basis state is represented by state vectors, such as the following for the $|0\rangle$ state:

    $$|0\rangle = \begin{bmatrix} 1 \\ 0 \end{bmatrix}$$

    Similarly, the $|1\rangle$ state can be represented by a state vector as follows:

    $$|1\rangle = \begin{bmatrix} 0 \\ 1 \end{bmatrix}$$

3. The initial state of a qubit is $|0\rangle$. The Hadamard gate generally applies the Hadamard matrix to the current state of the qubit, which places the qubit into a superposition state. Therefore, if a Hadamard gate is applied to a qubit in the state $|0\rangle$ the operation would be as follows:

$$H|0\rangle = \frac{1}{\sqrt{2}}\begin{bmatrix} 1 & 1 \\ 1 & -1 \end{bmatrix}\begin{bmatrix} 1 \\ 0 \end{bmatrix} = \begin{bmatrix} \frac{1}{\sqrt{2}} & \frac{1}{\sqrt{2}} \\ \frac{1}{\sqrt{2}} & -\frac{1}{\sqrt{2}} \end{bmatrix}\begin{bmatrix} 1 \\ 0 \end{bmatrix}$$

Multiplying the matrix by the vector results in the following:

$$H|0\rangle = \begin{bmatrix} \frac{1}{\sqrt{2}} \\ \frac{1}{\sqrt{2}} \end{bmatrix} = \begin{bmatrix} 0.707 \\ 0.707 \end{bmatrix}$$

4. Now, let's execute our circuit using the state vector simulator and output the state vector values:

```
# Select the Statevector simulator from the Aer provider
simulator = StatevectorSimulator()
# Transpile the circuit
transpiled_qc = transpile(qc, simulator)
# Run the transpiled circuit
result = simulator.run(transpiled_qc).result()
# Get the state vector and display the results
statevector = result.get_statevector(transpiled_qc)
statevector
```

From the results, we can obtain the state vector of the quantum circuit by simply extracting it from the Job object, in this case, `result.get_statevector()`.

This should result in the following output that correctly matches our expected results, which include the state vector matrix dimension information, and where the amplitude values in the results are exactly $\frac{1}{\sqrt{2}}$. Furthermore, if we square the amplitudes, the results will provide us with the probability of obtaining a 0 or a 1. The statevector results represent the expected results when applying a Hadamard to an initial state vector $H|0\rangle$ as we described in step 3:

```
Statevector([0.70710678+0.j, 0.70710678+0.j], dims=(2,))
```

5.   Let's extend this by adding another qubit in superposition:

```
# Construct quantum circuit
qc = QuantumCircuit(2)
# Place both qubits in superposition
qc.h(0)
qc.h(1)
qc.draw()
```

The result of this circuit is similar to the previous, just with an addition of an added qubit:

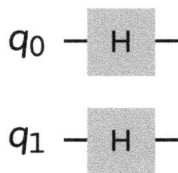

Figure 9.7: Two qubits in superposition

6.   Let's run this circuit using the state vector simulator and print out the results of our state vector:

```
# Transpile the circuit
transpiled_qc = transpile(qc, simulator)
# Run the circuit using the state vector simulator
result = simulator.run(transpiled_qc).result()
# Extract the state vector of the circuit from the # results
statevector = result.get_statevector(transpiled_qc)
# Output the state vector values
statevector
```

This results in the following output, which represents equal amplitudes for all 4 possible states, $|00\rangle$, $|01\rangle$, $|10\rangle$, and $|11\rangle$:

```
Statevector([0.5+0.j, 0.5+0.j, 0.5+0.j, 0.5+0.j], dims=(2,2))
```

Here, if we square each of the values to obtain the probability measurements, we will see that each has a 25% probability of being correct. Recall that all probabilities must add up to 1.

7. Finally, let's entangle the qubits and see what the state vector results would be when applying a Hadamard gate to the first qubit:

```python
# Construct quantum circuit
qc = QuantumCircuit(2)
# Place the first qubit in superposition
qc.h(0)
# Entangle the two qubits together using a CNOT gate,
# where the first is the control and the second qubit is
# the target
qc.cx(0, 1)
# Transpile the circuit
transpiled_qc = transpile(qc, simulator)
# Run the circuit on the state vector simulator
result = simulator.run(transpiled_qc).result()
# Obtain the state vector of the circuit
statevector = result.get_statevector(transpiled_qc)
# Output the state vector values
statevector
```

The state vector results are as expected, with equal amplitude values of $1/\sqrt{2}$ (0.707...) for 00 and 11, and no values $(0. + 0.j)$ for the states 01 and 10:

```python
Statevector([0.70710678+0.j, 0.+0.j, 0.+0.j, 0.70710678+0.j],
dims=(2,2))
```

8. We can also seek the aid of the visualization tools to help illustrate the state vector results for the circuit we just executed. We will add the `plot_state_city` vector function:

```python
# Display state vector
plot_state_city(statevector)
```

The results are the same values we saw earlier, only here we can see the amplitudes of both the real (left) and imaginary (right) components. When we square the amplitudes of our result, we will get a 50% probability for the 00 and 11 states, which is what we see in the following state vector plot. A state city plot is a term used to describe a view of a 3D bar graph (typically two-dimensional). The term is taken as the bar graphs on the 2D plot look like buildings in a city. In this case, we have two: one to represent the real values and another to represent the imaginary values of our state vectors.

Note that in our results, we did not have any value in any of the imaginary components of our state vector `1.+0.j`:

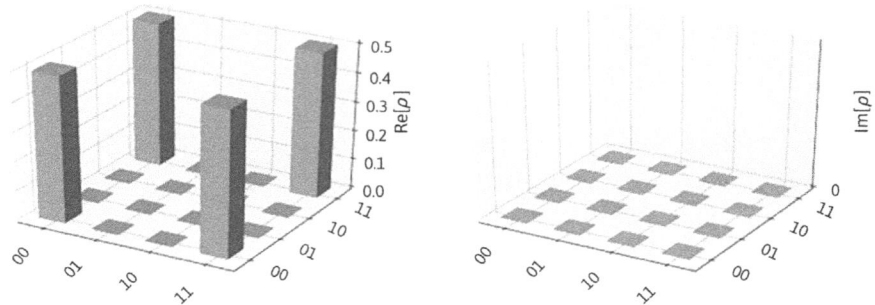

Figure 9.8: State vector plot with real (left) and imaginary (right) components

The state vector plot helps visualize the density matrix of 2-qubits, which itself has 16 complex qubit amplitudes. The topic of density matrices is outside the scope of this book but in short, it is generally an alternative to express all the quantum states such as $|00\rangle\langle11|$ and $|11\rangle\langle00|$, where this is the same with respect to the expected measurement outcome but allows us to describe these mathematically using the density matrix.

> Details describing the density matrix and how it is used can be found in the documentation here: `https://docs.quantum.ibm.com/api/qiskit/qiskit.quantum_info.DensityMatrix`.

The state vector plot isn't the only visualization tool we have available. Another great tool available is the **Qiskit qsphere**. This plots the state vector onto a two-dimensional graph and includes unique visualization features that allow you to see the probabilistic results and the phase when squaring the amplitudes of the state vector.

9. Let's plot the probabilistic results from the same state vector on a qsphere:

```
# Import the plot_state_qsphere class
from qiskit.visualization import plot_state_qsphere
%matplotlib inline
# Create quantum circuit
qc = QuantumCircuit(1)
# Place the qubit in a superposition state
qc.h(0)
```

```
# Execute the circuit on the statevector simulator
backend = StatevectorSimulator()
# Tanspile and run the circuit on the statevector simulator
transpiled_qc = transpile(qc, backend)
result = backend.run(transpiled_qc).result()
# Display the QSphere with results from the previous cell
plot_state_qsphere(transpiled_qc)
```

Let's review the results and how they are displayed in the qsphere:

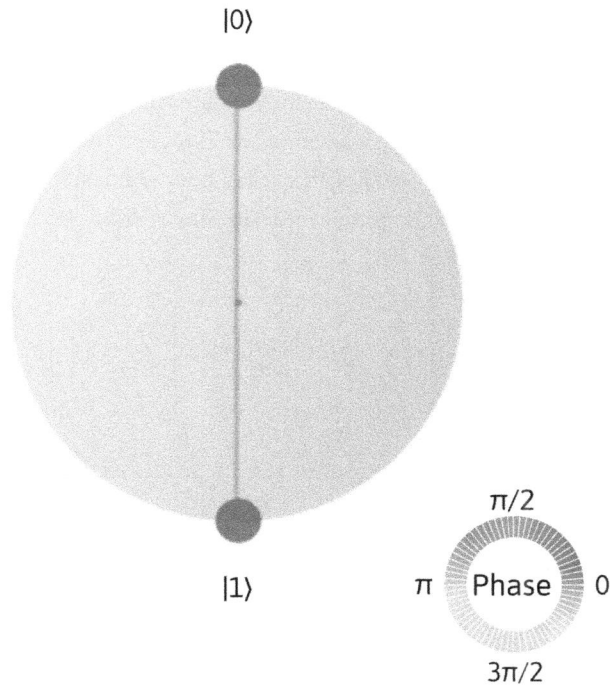

Figure 9.9: Qsphere representation of the results after squaring the state vector results

First, notice the vectors point to the north $|0\rangle$ state and south $|1\rangle$ state with the spheres at the end of each vector having equal diameters. This is to illustrate that there is an equal probability that the result will either be a 0 or 1, hence they are in superposition, as expected.

Next, the color of each sphere matches the color corresponding to the phase of the state as described in the phase wheel located at the bottom right of the qsphere. This indicates that each vector is in phase (0°), which corresponds to a blue color. The results here match the expected equation we derived earlier, where we are placing the qubit in a superposition state; however, we have not applied any phase rotations, which are rotations around the Z-axis in this case:

$$H|0\rangle = \frac{1}{\sqrt{2}}(|0\rangle + |1\rangle)$$

Let's do something interesting by introducing a phase shift. As we saw in the preceding screenshot, the vector moves from $|0\rangle$ to $|+\rangle$ in phase (0°) when we apply the Hadamard gate. We'll now include a Z gate, also known as a phase gate, which rotates the vector by an angle of π around the z axis. As before, we'll review the mathematics first to confirm what we should expect to see. Recall earlier how we described the effects of applying the Hadamard gate when the state vector originates from $|0ñ$. The following applies the Hadamard gate to the $|1ñ$ state:

$$H|1\rangle = \frac{1}{\sqrt{2}}\begin{bmatrix} 1 & 1 \\ 1 & -1 \end{bmatrix}\begin{bmatrix} 0 \\ 1 \end{bmatrix} = \begin{bmatrix} \frac{1}{\sqrt{2}} & \frac{1}{\sqrt{2}} \\ \frac{1}{\sqrt{2}} & -\frac{1}{\sqrt{2}} \end{bmatrix}\begin{bmatrix} 0 \\ 1 \end{bmatrix}$$

Multiplying the matrix with the vector results produces the following:

$$H|1\rangle = \begin{bmatrix} \frac{1}{\sqrt{2}} \\ -\frac{1}{\sqrt{2}} \end{bmatrix} = \begin{bmatrix} 0.707 \\ -0.707 \end{bmatrix}$$

1. We will create a circuit originating from the $|1\rangle$ state and apply the H gate to it to confirm the preceding vector results:

```
# Create a quantum circuit
qc = QuantumCircuit(1)
# Rotate the state from |0> to |1> by applying an X gate
qc.x(0)
# Place qubit in a superposition from the |1> state
qc.h(0)
# Transpile the circuit
transpiled_qc = transpile(qc, backend)
```

```
# Run the circuit
result = backend.run(transpiled_qc).result()
# Extract the state vector results and plot them onto the
# QSphere
plot_state_qsphere(result.get_statevector(transpiled_qc))
```

The resulting qsphere now has the same probability as before; however, since the rotation originated from the $|1\rangle$ state, it is now at the $|-\rangle$ side, therefore out of phase by π, which we can confirm by observing the following phase color chart (note that the color representations might change over time. Just compare the color to the color phase wheel for value to color mapping):

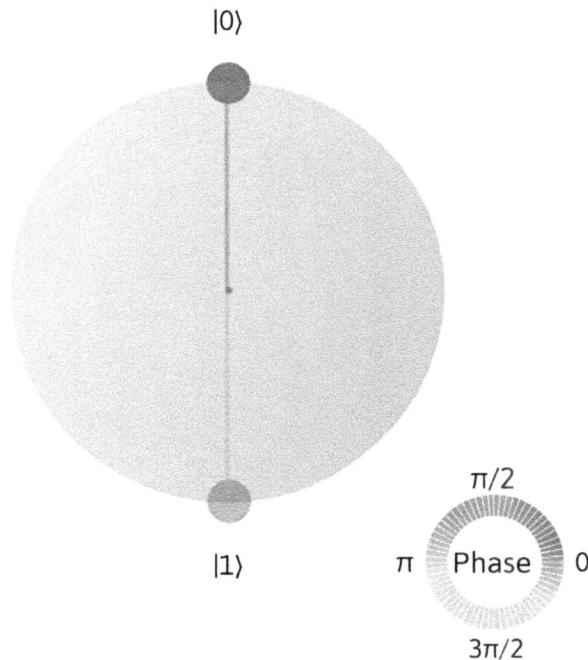

Figure 9.10: A superposition state that is also out of phase by an angle of π

2. Now, let's try the same thing, this time originating from the $|0\rangle$ state:

```
# Create a quantum circuit
qc = QuantumCircuit(1)
# Place qubit in a superposition from the |0> state
qc.h(0)
```

```
# Apply a Z (phase) gate, to rotate it by
# an angle π around the Z axis
qc.z(0)
# Transpile the circuit
transpiled_qc = transpile(qc, backend)
# Run the circuit
result = backend.run(transpiled_qc).result()
# Extract the state vector results and plot them onto the
# QSphere
plot_state_qsphere(result.get_statevector(transpiled_qc))
```

The results, as we can see, are the same – there is a relative phase difference of π between the two states, $|0\rangle$ and $|1\rangle$:

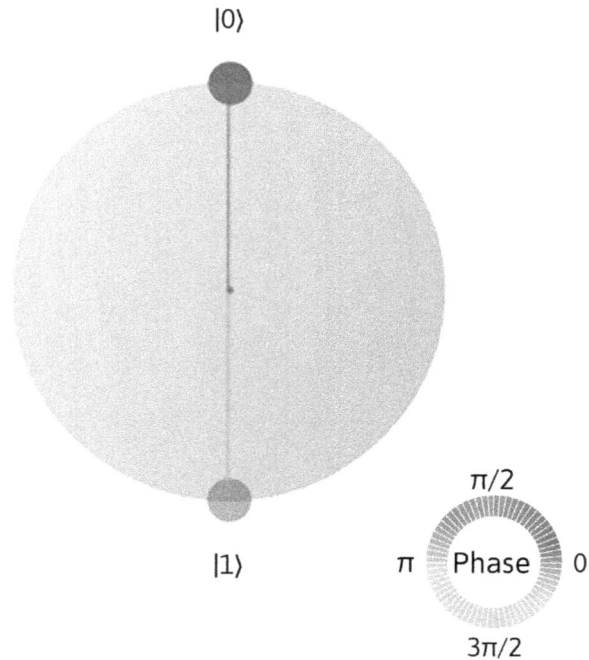

Figure 9.11: A state vector in superposition and out of phase by π

We can see that the state vector representation illustrates what we see mathematically, which is the following in this case:

$$H|1\rangle = \frac{1}{\sqrt{2}}(|0\rangle - |1\rangle)$$

From the preceding equation, the negative value represents the out-of-phase component. We will see later on how various quantum algorithms leverage this in order to take advantage of the effects of interference in *Chapter 12, Understanding Quantum Algorithms*.

So far, we have seen that we can obtain and visualize the quantum state information from our quantum circuits using the state vector simulator. This allows us to determine whether the state of our circuit is what we are expecting, which helps when we are trying to debug the results of our circuit. We can also visually inspect our quantum circuits using various graphs to review information such as the density matrix and the probabilistic results based on the results from our state vector. Next, we will look at how we can obtain the unitary matrix of our circuit by leveraging the unitary simulator.

Running circuits on the unitary simulator

The **unitary simulator** provides the construction of the unitary matrix, **U**, of the circuit. The unitary matrix is the operator representation of your quantum circuit, which allows you to determine whether the circuit represents an operator you are either trying to replicate or create. The unitary simulator builds out the unitary matrix by stepping through the circuit and applying each gate to the initial state of the circuit. As described in the API documentation (`https://qiskit.github.io/qiskit-aer/stubs/qiskit_aer.UnitarySimulator.html`), the semantic validations will verify the constraints of the **qobj** and backend options, which are as described as follows:

- The number of shots is set to 1, so only a single shot will be run to calculate the unitary matrix.

- The circuit cannot contain any resets or measurements. Since the unitary simulator's job is to just calculate the unitary matrix, there is no need to determine the measurement of the circuit.

- No noise models can be applied as it would require working with non-unitaries.

- If the circuit goes beyond any of the preceding constraints, it will raise an `AerError`.

We will leverage the same circuit we created earlier for the state vector example to run through our unitary simulator so we can compare and contrast the results:

1. First, let's validate what we should expect to see mathematically. As we will be applying a single Hadamard gate, it should be fairly simple to determine the unitary matrix. Starting from the initial state, we will apply an H gate to the circuit:

$$H = \frac{1}{\sqrt{2}}\begin{bmatrix} 1 & 1 \\ 1 & -1 \end{bmatrix} = \begin{bmatrix} \frac{1}{\sqrt{2}} & \frac{1}{\sqrt{2}} \\ \frac{1}{\sqrt{2}} & -\frac{1}{\sqrt{2}} \end{bmatrix} = \begin{bmatrix} 0.707 & 0.707 \\ 0.707 & -0.707 \end{bmatrix}$$

2. Now, we will run our circuit on the unitary simulator, where we will create a quantum circuit and add a Hadamard gate, then set the simulator to the unitary simulator provided by Aer. We should expect to see the same result:

```
# Create a quantum circuit and add a Hadamard gate
qc = QuantumCircuit(1)
qc.h(0)
# Set the simulator to the UnitarySimulator from the Aer
# provider
simulator = UnitarySimulator()
# Transpile the circuit
transpiled_qc = transpile(qc, simulator)
# Run the circuit on the unitary simulator
result = simulator.run(transpiled_qc).result()
# Extract the unitary matrix from the results
unitary = result.get_unitary(transpiled_qc)
# Print out the unitary matrix representation of the circuit
print("Unitary of the circuit:\n", unitary)
```

Your unitary results should match the results we calculated mathematically; you can ignore the significantly small numbers in the imaginary component:

```
Unitary of the circuit:
[[ 0.70710678+0.00000000e+00j 0.70710678-8.65956056e-17j]
 [ 0.70710678+0.00000000e+00j -0.70710678+8.65956056e-17j]]
```

3. Now, let's create another circuit, only this time, let's apply a phase shift after placing our circuit into a superposition. Let's do this by adding a Z phase gate after the H gate:

```
# Create a new circuit, adding an H gate followed by a Z gate
qc = QuantumCircuit(1)
qc.h(0)
qc.z(0)
# Transpile the circuit
transpiled_qc = transpile(qc, simulator)
# Run the circuit on the unitary simulator
result = simulator.run(transpiled_qc).result()
# Retrieve the unitary matrix from the results
unitary = result.get_unitary(transpiled_qc)
# Print the unitary matrix representation of the circuit
print("Unitary of the circuit:\n", unitary)
qc.draw(output='mpl')
```

This will produce the following unitary matrix representation of the quantum circuit we created. Note the difference in the signs:

```
Unitary of the circuit:
[[ 0.70710678+0.00000000e+00j 0.70710678-8.65956056e- 17j]
 [-0.70710678+0.00000000e+00j 0.70710678-8.65956056e- 17j]]
```

This will also give us the following circuit diagram:

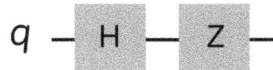

Figure 9.12: 2-gate circuit applying an H gate followed by a Z gate

We can confirm this using a bit of linear algebra. One thing to note is that when we apply gates on a circuit and visualize them, we generally apply them from left to right, as illustrated in the preceding circuit diagram, where we see the **H** gate first, followed by the **Z** gate.

4. However, when calculating the unitary matrix, we place the unitary matrices of each gate we add from right to left. This is the order for the writing convention used to describe the order of applying operations onto an initial state. For example, in this circuit, we calculated the unitary matrix in the following order: first applying the H gate, then the Z gate, so from right to left this results in **ZH = U**, where **U** is the unitary matrix solution. Let's calculate this matrix now:

$$ZH = \frac{1}{\sqrt{2}}\begin{bmatrix} 1 & 0 \\ 0 & -1 \end{bmatrix}\begin{bmatrix} 1 & 1 \\ 1 & -1 \end{bmatrix} = \frac{1}{\sqrt{2}}\begin{bmatrix} 1 & 1 \\ -1 & 1 \end{bmatrix} = \begin{bmatrix} \frac{1}{\sqrt{2}} & \frac{1}{\sqrt{2}} \\ -\frac{1}{\sqrt{2}} & \frac{1}{\sqrt{2}} \end{bmatrix} = \begin{bmatrix} 0.707 & 0.707 \\ -0.707 & 0.707 \end{bmatrix}$$

As you can see from the preceding equation, we have now confirmed that it is the same result we received from the unitary simulator for this circuit.

As with the previous simulators, we can also initialize the unitary simulator with a given unitary matrix. Let's use the results from the previous example as our initial unitary matrix:

```
# Create a quantum circuit
qc_init = QuantumCircuit(1)
# Set the initial unitary using the result from the
# previous example and apply it to q₀
qc_init.unitary(unitary, [0])
# Transpile the circuit
transpiled_qc = transpile(qc_init, simulator)
# Execute and obtain the unitary matrix of the circuit
result = simulator.run(transpiled_qc).result()
# Retrieve the unitary matrix from the result
unitary_result = result.get_unitary(transpiled_qc)
# Print the unitary matrix results representing the
# circuit
print("Unitary of the circuit:\n", unitary_result)
```

The results from the initialized circuit are now the same as the previous circuit, without the need to add any of the gates used to generate this unitary matrix. The output result is represented as a unitary operator:

```
Unitary of the circuit:
 Operator([[ 0.70710678+0.00000000e+00j,  0.70710678+8.65956056e-17j],
           [-0.70710678-8.65956056e-17j,  0.70710678+1.73191211e-16j]],
          input_dims=(2,), output_dims=(2,))
```

We've seen how the unitary simulator is an exceptional component to use should you wish to experiment using a predefined unitary matrix. Using the unitary simulator, we learned how to calculate the unitary operator from a given quantum circuit, and how to create a circuit from a unitary.

Now that we have a better understanding of the various simulators and the differences between them, we'll use them to simulate some of the noise we get when running a circuit on a real quantum device. You've also learned about the various options and parameters each simulator has available to you so you can leverage each one in multiple ways to obtain various results, such as count and state vector information, from the provided quantum circuit. This will help simulate the results from circuits where noise models affect the outcome, as opposed to the results from running on an ideal, noiseless simulator. So, let's generate the noise models in the next section.

Accounting for noise in quantum circuits

Noise models are used to represent various noise effects that cause errors in quantum circuits. The origin of the noise stems from many sources within the quantum system. Based on the currently available devices and those coming in the near future, the number of errors on a device could be significant, depending on the quantum circuit executed on them.

In this section, we will review the various types of errors that can affect a qubit, gates, and readouts. We will also learn how to generate noise models either based on the configuration information from the real devices, or noise models created by ourselves, with which we can simulate the real devices using the Aer simulators.

Implementing an Aer noise model

We'll begin by demonstrating how to implement the various types of noise models that are prebuilt in the Aer noise libraries that will help make our experiments seem more realistic:

1. We'll create the same simple circuit we have used in most of our examples, the Bell state, which includes a Hadamard and CNOT gate, followed by a set of measurement operators, and execute it on an ideal simulator, with no errors. This should result in the expected values of 00 and 11:

```
# Create a 2-qubit circuit
qc = QuantumCircuit(2, 2)
# Add some arbitrary gates and measurement operators
qc.h(0)
qc.cx(0, 1)
```

```
qc.measure([0, 1], [0, 1])
backend = AerSimulator()

# Transpile the circuit
transpiled_qc= transpile(qc, backend)
# Run the circuit on the Aer simulator
result = backend.run(transpiled_qc).result()
# Obtain and counts
counts = result.get_counts(transpiled_qc)
# Plot the count results on a histogram
plot_distribution(counts)
```

The results from this circuit on an ideal simulator are as follows. Notice we only obtain two values, 00 and 11, as expected:

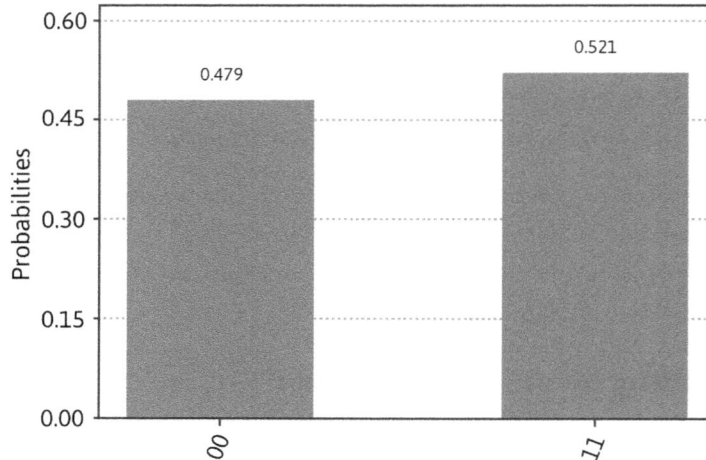

Figure 9.13: Results from an ideal simulator with no effects of noise

2.   Now we will execute the same circuit on an actual device instead of a simulator. To save time, let's find the least busy device that has enough qubits to run our experiment as well. Keep in mind the time to complete this on a quantum system may vary depending on your position in the queue:

```
# Let's set the number of qubits needed and get the least busy
num_qubits = 2
```

```
backend = service.least_busy(min_num_qubits = num_qubits, simulator
= False, operational=True)

# Transpile the circuit
transpiled_qc = transpile(qc, backend)
# Run the circuit
options = Options(optimization_level=0)
shots=1000
with Session(service=service, backend=backend) as session:
    sampler = Sampler(session=session, options=options)
    job = sampler.run(circuits=transpiled_qc, shots=shots)
    result = job.result()
    print('Quasi dist results: ', result.quasi_dists[0])
```

The results are very similar to that of the earlier execution on the simulator, only this time, notice there are some errors in the results. Rather than only obtaining results of **0** and **3**, we see a few instances of **1** and **2**. These are the effects of backend noise on the results of the circuit:

```
Quasi distribution results:  {0: 0.49323295547592433,
1: 0.01753366164023622, 2: -0.009464115736336355, 3:
0.49869749862017565}
```

3. Now, let's do something interesting. Let's make use of a noise model based on the properties of a specific backend device. Aer's `NoiseModel` provides the ability to do this with a simple method call.

In this following code snippet, we will generate a noise model based on `ibmq_kyoto` and its properties: `coupling_map`, which describes how the qubits are physically connected to each other on the physical device, and the available basis gates. When executing the quantum circuit, we will provide the noise model, `coupling_map`, and basis gates. This way, when executing the quantum circuit on the simulator, it will simulate the results as experiencing the same effects that would occur when running the circuit on a real device, noise and all:

```
# Import the NoiseModel
from qiskit_aer.noise import NoiseModel
```

```python
# Obtain an available backend to simulate
backend = service.get_backend('ibm_kyoto')
# Create the noise model based on the backend properties
noise_model = NoiseModel.from_backend(backend)
# Get coupling map from backend
coupling_map = backend.configuration().coupling_map
# Get basis gates from noise model
basis_gates = noise_model.basis_gates
# Get the Aer simulator to apply noise model
noisy_simulator = AerSimulator()
# Execute the circuit on the simulator with the backend
# properties, and generated noise model
result = noisy_simulator.run(transpiled_qc,
                   coupling_map=coupling_map,
                   basis_gates=basis_gates,
                   noise_model=noise_model).result()
# Obtain and print results
counts = result.get_counts()
plot_distribution(counts)
```

The following plot of the results of the preceding code, as you can see, is not as ideal as before. We can observe a few errors here:

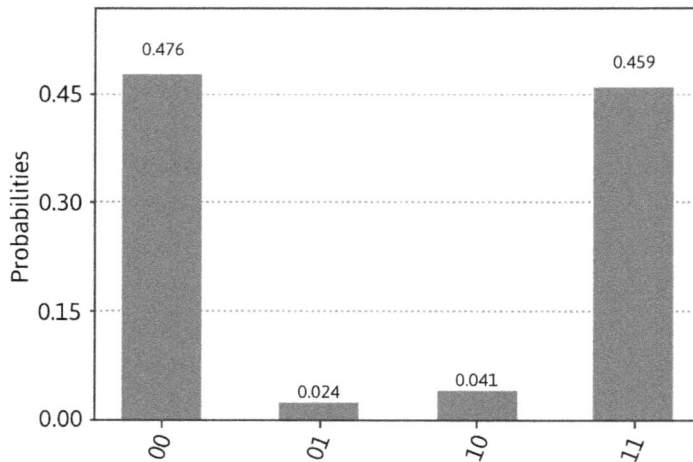

Figure 9.14: Results from a simulator with noise effects based on a specified backend

Now that we can simulate the effects of noise from a backend system onto a simulator, let's develop an understanding of what the cause is of some of these noise effects.

Tracing the source of noise

When executing quantum circuits on a real device, there are various effects that can cause errors in our computations. In this section, we will review some of those effects so that when you're generating or building your noise models, you will have a better understanding of how they affect each qubit.

Understanding decoherence

Decoherence is defined as the loss of quantum coherence due to a quantum system's physical interaction with its environment. Decoherence affects each qubit in many ways, one of which is when each qubit starts in a $|0\rangle$ ground state, and we operate on the qubit to move it from the $|0\rangle$ state to the $|0\rangle$ state. For example, we say the qubit has transitioned from the ground state, $|0\rangle$, to the excited state, $|0\rangle$. An analogy for this is to think of yourself sitting peacefully and perfectly at rest. This peaceful relaxed moment is you in the ground state.

Then, imagine someone jumping out of nowhere and screaming at you! You're immediately startled as your heart rate jumps up and your adrenaline kicks in. This is you now in the excited state. Now, after telling the person who startled you to never do that again, you manage to catch your breath and get your heart rate down. You begin to relax and get your body back down to the grounded state it was in before. The time required to change from the excited state to the grounded state is, coincidentally, called the style **relaxation time**. Of course, one very important thing to note is that while it is ideal for us as humans to quickly get back to our relaxed state, for a quantum system, it is ideal for this time to stay in the set state for as long as possible. This will ensure that whichever state we place a qubit in, it maintains that state as long as possible.

The relaxation time, denoted as T_1, is the time constant of the longitudinal loss (oriented along the z axis) of the signal intensity. Another decoherence effect is **dephasing**, denoted as T_2, where the phase information spreads out widely so that the phase information is lost. We will cover details on how the information is lost in the next chapter. An example of this is if we set the qubit to the $|+\rangle$ state. The dephasing time is a decay constant time where the initial state decays down to a mixed state of $|+\rangle$ and $|-\rangle$, where it is difficult to predict the state of the system and is not perfectly in a superposition state and tends to collapse.

There are two ways to measure T_1 and T_2 decoherence times:

- To measure T_1, you would apply a series of pulses separated by a fixed time delay and capture the statistical results of the state as it moves from $|0\rangle$ to $|1\rangle$. The oscillations that show up in the measurements after applying pulses of varying lengths or amplitudes are called **Rabi oscillations**.

- To measure T_2, you would set the state of the qubit to $|+\rangle$ or $|-\rangle$, and then apply π pulses at sequences to apply a phase rotation. After applying a particular sequence of pulses over time, the state should return to its original position, that is, $|+\rangle$ or $|-\rangle$. If dephasing occurs, then the result will have a lower probability of returning to its original starting position. This technique of measuring T_2 is called a **spin echo**.

Now that we are a bit more familiar with the sources of noise, let's shift our discussion to the contributors to decoherence and how they vary based on their sources. There are generally two source types – **intrinsic** and **extrinsic**:

- Intrinsic noise, often regarded as generic in nature, originates from sources within the system, such as temperature, or defects within the system, so essentially, materials or defects.

- Extrinsic noise originates from environmentally coupled systems such as wave interference, vibrations, and electromagnetic fields.

Let's run a quick example of thermal relaxation on a pair of qubits as this is generally intrinsic to a qubit. In the following example, we will define our T_1 and T_2 values in seconds and apply them to a set of basis gates for all qubits. These values can be set to whatever time constant you wish; the time value provided in the backend properties is stated as an average so it is not likely your results would be the same each time. One thing to note is that the parameters you set must be true for the following, $T_2 \leq 2T_1$, otherwise an error will be thrown. We'll then run a sample circuit with these thermal relaxation errors to see the difference. The circuit that we will create and execute will be the same Bell state circuit we created earlier and ran on a simulator, so we can compare the results:

```
# Initialize your T1 and T2 time constant values in seconds
t1 = 0.0125
t2 = 0.0025
# Apply the T1 and T2 to create the thermal relaxation error
from qiskit_aer.noise import thermal_relaxation_error
t_error = thermal_relaxation_error(t1, t2, 0.01)
# Add the errors to a noise model
```

```
# and apply to all basis gates on all qubits
noise_model = NoiseModel()
noise_model.add_all_qubit_quantum_error(t_error, ['id', 'rz', 'sx','u1',
'u2', 'u3'])
# Print out the noise model
print(noise_model)
#Create the same 2-qubit quantum circuit as before
qc_error = QuantumCircuit(2,2)
qc_error.h(0)
qc_error.cx(0,1)
qc_error.measure(range(2), range(2))
# Set the simulator
simulator = QasmSimulator()
# Transpile the circuit
transpiled_qc = transpile(qc_error, simulator)
# Apply the noise model we created and run the circuit
result = simulator.run(transpiled_qc, shots=1024, basis_gates=noise_model.
basis_gates, noise_model=noise_model).result()
# Obtain result counts
counts = result.get_counts(transpiled_qc)
# Plot the result counts
plot_distribution(counts)
```

The NoiseModel output provides a description of the noise model by indicating which basis gates are available, which gate instructions would be affected by the noise, and which basis gates errors are applied to the qubits. Keep in mind, that the results may vary based on available backend systems:

```
NoiseModel:
   Basis gates: ['cx', 'id', 'rz', 'sx', 'u1', 'u2', 'u3']
   Instructions with noise: ['sx', 'id', 'u1', 'u3', 'u2', 'rz']
   All-qubits errors: ['id', 'rz', 'sx', 'u1', 'u2', 'u3']
```

As you will see, the results after executing this circuit on the simulator with the generated noise are not quite the same as before. In the earlier case, without errors, we had a very close 50/50 split between **00** and **11**. However, as you can see in the following screenshot, the result is more of a 75/25 split between **00** and **11**. This, of course, is due to the thermal relaxation error we added to the simulator, thus causing much of the results to encounter a relaxation from the excited state to the ground state, as illustrated in the following plot:

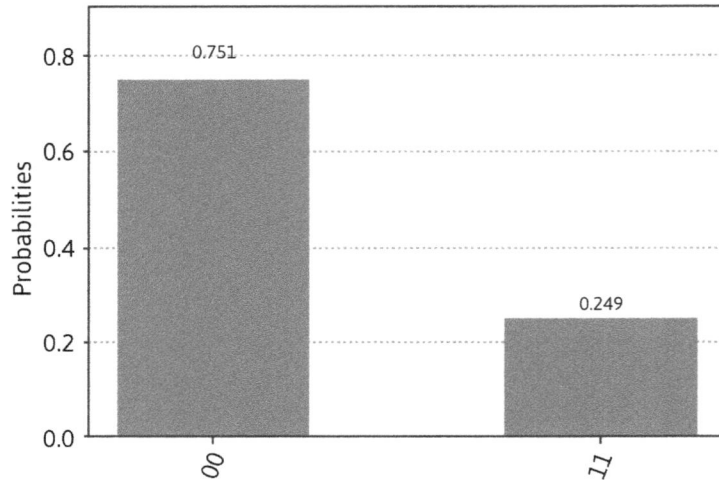

Figure 9.15: Results on a simulator with thermal relaxation errors

Both T_1 and T_2 are environmental effects that act upon the qubits and their ability to maintain their states. Other effects that contribute to the overall noise of a system are contributed by the gates that manipulate the qubits. Let's look at a few of them now.

Understanding single-gate, multi-gate, and readout errors

Single-gate errors and **multi-gate errors** are generally introduced when a qubit is operated upon by the various gates on the system. These errors are based on probabilities that the gate applied to the qubit may not operate exactly as expected. For example, if we apply a 5% gate error probability to a single-qubit gate such as a NOT gate, then the result of the operation has a 5% probability of not resulting in the expected value. The single-gate error could be from poor gate fidelity, whereas the multi-gate error could be from crosstalk or spectator noise from neighboring qubits, or from the physical connection between the qubits. The Aer library has a list of noise model methods to choose from, including **Pauli error**, **depolarizing error**, **amplitude damping error**, and many more for us to use.

Single-gate and multi-gate errors can be applied to all qubits at once using the `add_all_qubit_quantum_error()` method contained in the `NoiseModel` class. This method applies a quantum error object to the noise model for the specified basis gates, which is then applied to all qubits. The first argument is the quantum error, and the second is the list of basis gates to apply the error to.

Readout errors are those that occur when a measurement and acquisition are triggered to read out the value of the qubit. During the operations of measuring and acquiring the signal from the qubit, errors can exist that may interfere with the results of the qubit measurement. The `NoiseModel` class also has methods available to add readout errors to the noise model.

Let's build our own noise model with single-qubit, multi-qubit, and readout errors on a circuit to observe the effects of these errors on our quantum circuit.

Building your own noise model

There may be times when you wish to build your own custom noise models. Whether it's to generate specific errors to test your error-mitigation methods or to create something resembling a specific device, having the ability to customize your own noise model is a handy feature to have available.

In the following steps, we will set the single- and multi-qubit errors and view the results. We will then set the readout errors and run them on the same circuit just to visualize the difference in the results when measurement errors are introduced to an ideal system. The single-qubit error will have an amplitude dampening error, the multi-qubit error will have a depolarizing error, and the readout error will be applied to both qubits in the circuit:

1. We'll begin by defining our quantum circuit and transpiling it with the simulator:

```
# Create quantum circuit
qc_error = QuantumCircuit(2,2)
qc_error.h(0)
qc_error.cx(0,1)
qc_error.measure(range(2), range(2))
# Let's get the qasm simulator
simulator = QasmSimulator()
# Transpile the circuit
transpiled_qc = transpile(qc_error, simulator)
```

2. Next, we'll begin by defining the single- and multi-qubit probability error values, followed by initializing and setting the depolarizing errors, first to the single qubit, and then to the multi-qubit error:

```
# Import the error classes and methods
from qiskit_aer.noise import depolarizing_error
from qiskit_aer.noise import ReadoutError
# Single and multi-qubit probability error
```

```
single_qubit_gate_p = 0.25
multi_qubit_gate_p = 0.1
# Apply the depolarizing quantum errors
single_error = depolarizing_error(single_qubit_gate_p, 1)
multi_error = depolarizing_error(multi_qubit_gate_p, 2)
```

3. Next, we will create our NoiseModel object and add both the single- and multi-qubit errors. The single qubit error will be assigned to the basis gate u2, and the multi-qubit error will be assigned to the CNOT (cx) gate:

```
# Add the single and multi-qubit errors to the noise # model
noise_model = NoiseModel()
noise_model.add_all_qubit_quantum_error(single_error, ['u2'])
noise_model.add_all_qubit_quantum_error(multi_error, ['cx'])
# Print out the noise model
print(noise_model)
```

4. We'll now print out the NoiseModel to confirm out noise model entries are set. As we can see from the output of the noise model, we have a list of all basis gates available, a list of instructions that have been assigned noise, and a list of all the basis states that will affect all of the qubits in our circuit:

```
NoiseModel:
   Basis gates: ['cx', 'id', 'rz', 'sx', 'u2']
   Instructions with noise: ['u2', 'cx']
   All-qubits errors: ['u2', 'cx']
```

5. Now, let's add this to our simulator and run it with both the single and multi-qubit noise model:

```
# Run the circuit on the simulator with the noise model
result = simulator.run(transpiled_qc, shots=1024, basis_gates=noise_
model.basis_gates, noise_model=noise_model).result()
# Obtain the counts and plot the results
counts = result.get_counts(transpiled_qc)
plot_distribution(counts)
```

6. This will result in the following histogram:

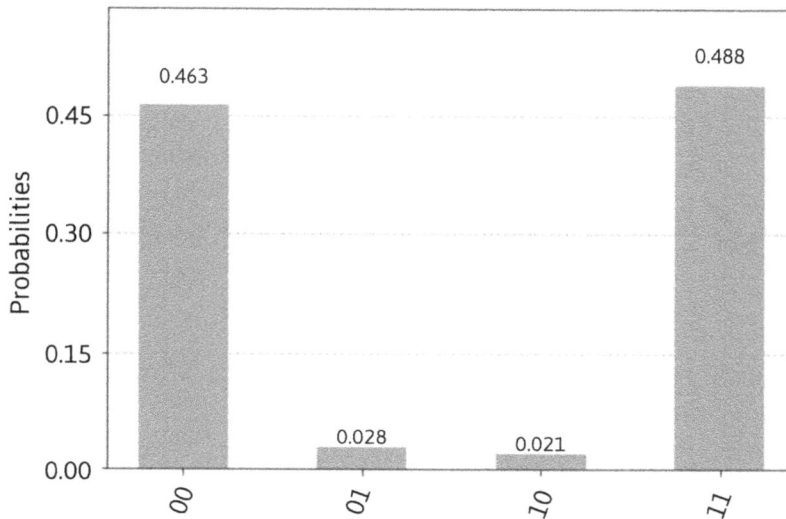

Figure 9.16: Results on a simulator with single and multi-qubit errors

7. As you can see, the errors we introduced had an effect on our results and we now get some unexpected values, 01 and 10, which we didn't expect or see in our ideal case when running on a system with no noise. However, even with the noise, we can see that our results are correct in that we still have a high probability of the states 00 and 11. So here, the noise is minimal so that we can get some good results. Let's try a different error next and increase the noise to see what we get when we have very noisy readout errors.

8. Next, let's include some readout errors. Readout errors are defined in the Aer API documentation as follows:

    Classical readout errors are specified by a list of assignment probabilities vectors P(A|B), where A is the recorded classical bit value, and B is the true bit value returned from the measurement.

    This means that the probabilities of the expected values will be recorded and used to apply readout errors based on the probability values we pass in as arguments to the noise model.

    The equation for a single-qubit readout probability vector is defined as follows:

    $$P(A|B) = [P(A|0), P(A|1)]$$

When constructing the ReadoutError class, P(A|B) is provided as the argument. For our example, we will provide the probability of 0 given 1 as 0.7, and the probability of 1 given 0 as 0.2. We will also add our readout error to the noise model and print out the results, as illustrated in the following code:

> Note, of course, that these values we are setting are very high and do not necessarily need to add up to 1. I'm using them to highlight the impact noise has, in this case, in a very exaggerated yet visually recognizable way to see that the errors are actually pulling the results away from the expected values into the biased values.

```
# Set the readout error probabilities for 0 given 1,
# & 1 given 0,
p0_1 = 0.7
p1_0 = 0.2
p0 = 1 - p1_0
p1 = 1 - p1_1

# Construct a noise model
noise_model = NoiseModel()

# Construct the ReadoutError with the probabilities
readout_error = ReadoutError([[p0, p1_0], [p0_1, p1]])
# Apply the readout error to all qubits
noise_model.add_all_qubit_readout_error(readout_error)
# Print the noise model
print(noise_model)
```

We will see the addition of some instructions and listings of qubits in the result. The first line specifies Basis gates, and the following line is the list of Instructions with noise added to them. Notice that it now only includes the measure instruction. Next, we see the qubits that have been specified for a particular noise – in this case, we added the readout error to all qubit measurement operators:

```
NoiseModel:
    Basis gates: ['cx', 'id', 'rz', 'sx']
    Instructions with noise: ['measure']
    All-qubits errors: ['measure']
```

Now that we have our readout noise model complete, we'll add our custom noise model and run it on the Aer simulator to see the results.

Similar to the previous example, where we included a thermal relaxation noise model, we will provide the readout noise model in the same manner:

```
# Run the circuit with the readout error noise model
result = simulator.run(transpiled_qc, shots=1024,        basis_gates=noise_
model.basis_gates, noise_model=noise_model).result()
# Obtain the result counts and print
counts = result.get_counts(transpiled_qc)
plot_distribution(counts)
```

The results, as you can see in the following plot, are now not as ideal as before:

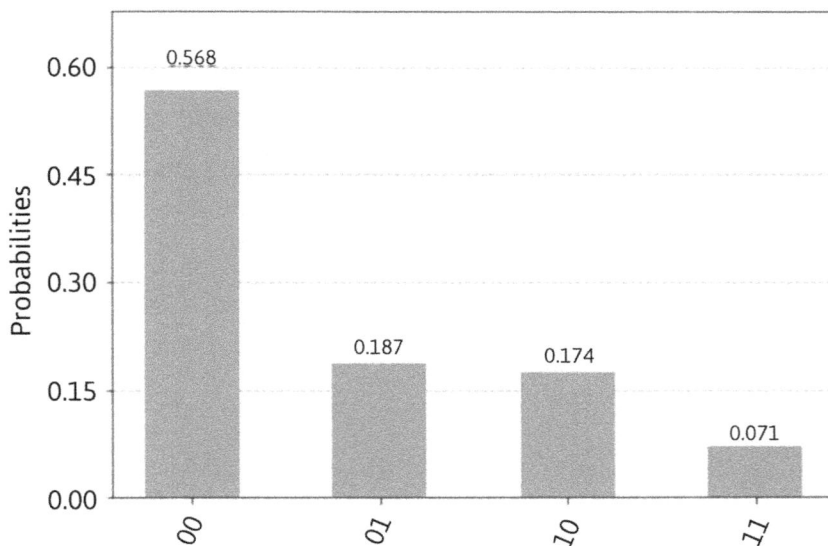

Figure 9.17: Result with effects from our custom noise model on a quantum circuit

We can observe various errors here, caused by the readout noise. First and foremost, our expected results of **00** and **11** are no longer easily visible from our results. In this sense, we see that the readout of each qubit has a higher probability of 0 given 1, which therefore causes the probability results to be higher for the values **00**, **01**, and **10**. This is caused by the readout errors that are applied to all the qubits, which greatly reduces the probability of 1.

The advantage of all this noise is that you have an insight as to the cause of this noise based on the type of noise we included, and the amount of noise applied to a specified qubit(s). This allows you to simulate certain noise effects should you wish to work on some noise-mitigating techniques.

By applying noise and understanding its effects, you can create noise-mitigating techniques and verify the results on a simulator. By doing this, you can test various combinations of noise effects, which can help minimize the error rate on some algorithms, and therefore increase the performance of the quantum computer. We will look at noise-mitigating techniques in the next chapter.

Summary

In this chapter, we covered various simulators. You now have the skills to leverage various simulators to simulate running circuits on a quantum computer and obtain specific content from the circuits, such as state vectors and unitary matrices.

We also covered various visualization techniques. The skills that you have gained will help you visualize the various pieces of information from the simulator, such as visualizing the state and phase information of a qubit using the qsphere and plotting state vector graphs.

And finally, we looked into the noise models that Qiskit provides by either extracting the noise from an existing quantum computer or creating our own noise models and applying them to the simulators.

In the next chapter, we will learn how to characterize and mitigate noise. This will allow us to optimize the performance of the quantum computer and increase its computational power.

Questions

1. Can you list all the simulators found in the Qiskit Aer module?
2. Create a qsphere representation of a qubit on the negative y axis, creating the state $\frac{|0\rangle - i|1\rangle}{\sqrt{2}}$, using only a single Hadamard gate along with the phase gates.
3. When initializing a set of qubits in a circuit, what must the total probability across all states be?
4. Can you use the qsphere to visualize both the phase and probability information of a qubit?
5. What would happen if you set the depolarization error values close to 1?
6. If you applied a readout error equally to all qubits, what results would you expect, and why?

Join us on Discord

Join our community's Discord space for discussions with the author and other readers:

```
https://packt.link/3FyN1
```

10

Suppressing and Mitigating Quantum Noise

In the previous edition of this book, you may recall a chapter which discussed, in a reasonable amount of detail, the different types of noise that affect various quantum systems. Since then, there has been an incredible amount of research that has evolved not only the hardware but the software as well. Due to the changes since then, which includes a few major refactorization iterations of Qiskit, for example, the deprecation of Ignis and its many test circuit libraries, I thought it might be a good time to shift into the latest and not spend too much time on how to test a system, but rather understand how to leverage the latest error suppression and mitigation techniques. Of course, I don't want to leave you too far in the dark, so I will cover some of the fundamentals of what these noises are and how they affect your experiments. However, I do want to ensure we cover the current era of quantum utility (https://www.nature.com/articles/s41586-023-06096-3), which entails using error suppression and mitigation techniques to help you find some useful quantum applications. We should expect to see some advancements as the systems evolve and get wider (more qubits) and deeper (complex quantum circuits with thousands of 2-qubit gates), which can be seen as a great step towards useful quantum applications without needing to wait for fault-tolerant quantum computers.

Early quantum systems were commonly referred to as near-term devices, which generally means they are close to becoming fully fault-tolerant quantum systems. One of the reasons for this is that all current quantum systems, no matter what technology they use to create qubits, are affected by **noise** in some shape or form, which increases the error rates of these systems. To address, and in turn minimize the error rates, it helps to understand what causes these errors and how can we suppress or mitigate them. Keep in mind that the study of errors in any one of the following examples could easily qualify as a research topic, which is why we will simply touch on some examples but if you are interested in more details, I will provide some reference materials at the end of the chapter. For now, this chapter is merely an overview with some examples to help you get an idea on how to create some of these noise models using the functionalities provided to you in Qiskit and how to suppress and mitigate against them using features included in the Qiskit Runtime. The goal here is to help you optimize the effectiveness of your quantum circuits, which in turn helps you design your applications to be as resistant as possible to the various forms of errors.

The following topics will be covered in this chapter:

- Understanding the Qiskit Runtime Service
- Understanding Sessions
- Understanding the Qiskit Runtime Options
- Understanding Primitives
- Understanding the Sampler primitive
- Understand the noise effects of decoherence
- Differences between error suppression, mitigation, and correction

In this chapter, we will cover one of the challenges faced by most quantum systems: noise. By the end of the chapter, you will understand some of the varying noise effects, such as relaxation and dephasing. Then, you'll get an overview of the latest advancements in the Qiskit Runtime Service and learn about the building blocks to run your circuits efficiently on any backend system. Finally, you will learn about the error suppression and error mitigation techniques and how to apply them to your complex quantum circuits.

In previous versions of Qiskit, there was a module titled, Ignis, which was the module that contained libraries to characterize and mitigate against noise. Since then, the Ignis library has been deprecated, so it is recommended that you read the Qiskit Migration Guide on the Qiskit GitHub page (`https://github.com/Qiskit/qiskit-ignis#migration-guide`), particularly if you want to use many of the recent advancements.

In quantum systems, noise originates from various sources: thermal heat from electronics, decoherence, dephasing, crosstalk, or signal loss. Here, we will see how to measure the effects of noise on a **qubit**, and how to mitigate readout error noise to optimize our results. In the end, we will compare the differences to better understand the effects and ways to mitigate them using other techniques such as **dynamical decoupling**, which is used to help reduce noise caused by decoherence of a qubit when its state is left idle for too long.

Before we get started with all of that, we need to first get familiar with one of the newest features that will help bring all these techniques to our fingertips and allow us to adjust them all as needed: the Qiskit Runtime service.

Technical requirements

In this chapter, we will cover some refreshers on simulating noise, so if you have some knowledge of signal to noise theory, this will help. If not, review *Chapter 9, Simulating Quantum Systems and Noise Models*, to get an understanding of the various forms of noise that affect quantum systems. This will help you understand how to suppress and mitigate errors on a quantum computer using the Qiskit Runtime.

Here is the full source code used throughout this book: `https://github.com/PacktPublishing/Learning-Quantum-Computing-with-Python-and-IBM-Quantum-Second-Edition`.

Understanding the Qiskit Runtime service

For those of you who have used earlier versions of Qiskit, you may have been using the `execute()` or `backend.run()` functions to run quantum circuits on a quantum system. This was good to run some basic quantum circuits for learning purposes on small quantum systems with less than 100 qubits. However, if we want to start to think about the future and how we can create circuits for hundreds, thousands, and even millions of qubits, then we will need to think about how to optimally do so without just throwing a large circuit onto a single machine. This is where the **Qiskit Runtime Service** comes in very handy. Not only does it include many new options, such as selecting the optimization and resilience levels, which we will learn about later in this chapter, but it also includes all the transpilation features we covered earlier, so we won't necessarily lose what we have learned so far. In this section, we will cover what the Qiskit Runtime is and how you can execute your circuits using it. Knowing how to use the Qiskit Runtime will also help you later in this chapter, when we learn about the various error suppression and mitigation techniques and how they are applied to your quantum circuit.

Let's begin by learning more about the Qiskit Runtime Service, how is it different from the execute function, and what new features we can use to optimize executing our quantum circuits on a quantum system.

First, let's create a new notebook and import a few Qiskit Runtime objects, functions, and instantiate the QiskitRuntimeService class, using our helper file.

> Note, at the time of writing, there has been a switch from the current Sampler version to SamplerV2. In the following code, it is assumed that the "V2" will be removed. If for some reason it is not, then please update Sampler to SamplerV2 to ensure you are using the latest version of the Sampler.

Another important step is that you must use the token parameter to set either your IBM Quantum or IBM Cloud API token, as illustrated in the following code snippet. If you do not set this, you will likely get an error, and when trying to access the Qiskit Runtime service, it will not work.

```
# Loading your IBM Quantum account(s)
service = QiskitRuntimeService(channel="ibm_quantum", token="API_TOKEN")
```

Now that you have your notebook setup, let's dig into some of the execution mode descriptions..

Understanding Sessions

A **Session** is in essence a collection of Jobs that is guaranteed to run on the backend without any interruptions from other user Jobs, particularly those that require multiple iterations, such as those that are based on variational algorithms: **Variational Quantum Eigensolver (VQE)**, and **Quantum Approximate Optimization Algorithm (QAOA)**. In other words, "without interruptions" means that the Qiskit Runtime will ensure that each Job will complete, including the period where the variables are being adjusted between classical and quantum resources, where in the past this time was used to interleave Jobs from another user in the queue.

To understand the practicality of this format, imagine standing in a long queue waiting your turn to submit a form, like renewing your driver's license. After waiting a few hours, you're finally at the window and handing over your form, only to be told that you need to adjust some values in the form. This is where the difference comes in. In the previous version, you would have to stand off to the side and update the form fields; meanwhile, someone else will move up to the window. Now, if you happen to be ready, you now must wait for that other person to finish before you can continue. This, of course, might take a long time, causing you to wait longer. What Sessions allows you to do is keep that window free and available for you until you finish updating the form and then turn it in.

Regarding what the default and max times are for both the interactive and maximum time values, I would refer you to the Qiskit Runtime documentation https://docs.quantum.ibm.com/api/qiskit-ibm-runtime/runtime_service) as these values might change over time. However, time in the queue does count towards the maximum time of the Session. The idle time could be used to perform any classical operations based on the results of the Job and/or prepare for the subsequent Job in the Session.

Each Job can be set as part of a batch of Jobs to ensure that they run on the same device or closely together to avoid the issues that can occur if they are run on separate systems or far apart, which would introduce strangeness to our results due to device characteristics or device drift. To learn more about device drift, see the *Further reading* section at the end of this chapter. At the time of writing, there are upcoming features that will further optimize execution of circuits, so do keep an eye on the documentation and information feeds for details and examples.

Before we start coding, let's get familiar with the other classes first as this will simplify our coding experience moving forward. In the next section, we will look at the options that we can set to our Session class. The Options class will also be very important later when suppressing and mitigating errors.

Understanding the Qiskit Runtime Options

RuntimeOptions is a class used to set the various parameters for the Qiskit Runtime execution options. Parameters are used to select which quantum system to use and which optimization or resilience levels to use that enable various error suppression or error mitigation features. Below is a list of Options parameters that are used for the various Qiskit Runtime primitives. Keep in mind that, as always, you should check the latest version of Qiskit API documentation to ensure your code is always current:

- Environment parameters such as log_level (DEBUG, INFO, etc.), and callback for any interim or final results, which will receive two positional parameters: Job ID and Job result
- Execution parameters for execution time options, such as number of shots(int), and init_qubits(bool), which will reset the qubits to the ground state for each shot the (default is true)
- max_execution_time is the maximum time, in seconds, after which a job is canceled. If this is not set, the default will be the time limit of the Primitive. If it is set, then the time must be set between 300 seconds and the maximum execution time set for the simulator or device, which can be found in the Qiskit API documentation: https://docs.quantum.ibm.com/guides/max-execution-time.

- `optimization_level` sets the level of optimization to the circuit. The higher the level, the more optimal and therefore longer the transpilation time. These optimization levels also include error suppression such as dynamical decoupling, which we will cover later in this chapter. There are four `optimization_level` settings. The default value is set to the highest, 3:

  - 0 – no optimization, uses basic translation, whichever layout is specified, and routing (uses stochastic swaps by default)

  - 1 – light optimization, routing (uses SabreSWAP, 1Q gate optimization, and dynamical decoupling for error suppression)

  - 2 – medium optimization, layout and routing are the same as level 1, but includes heuristic optimization with a greater search depth and trials of optimization and dynamical decoupling for error suppression

  - 3 – high optimization, layout and routing are the same as level 2 and include further optimization with greater efforts/trials, 2-qubit KAK optimization, and dynamical decoupling for error suppression

- `resilience_level` sets the level of resilience to mitigate errors. The higher the resilience level, the higher the accuracy of your results. Higher results are like that of the optimization level where it will cause longer transpilation time. These resilience levels range from 0 to 2, where level 1 is the default value and is only available for the Estimator primitive. It is important to note that as the technology evolves, so does the implementation and mitigation of these techniques. Please refer to the latest documentation to ensure your code is running the latest version (`https://docs.quantum.ibm.com/guides/configure-error-mitigation`).

  - 0 – no mitigation.

  - 1 – (default) minimal mitigation, which minimizes readout errors. The Estimator primitive uses the Twirled Readout Error Extinction.

  - 2 – medium mitigation, used to minimize bias in a circuit but indicates that it is not guaranteed to be zero, using the same as level 1 and includes Zero Noise Extrapolation.

Now that we're familiar with all the options we can set to optimize and run circuits on our backend systems, let's continue to move forward and learn what the Primitive classes are all about.

Understanding Primitives

Primitives, as defined on the Qiskit documentation, are generally the *"foundational building blocks for designing and optimizing quantum workloads."* At the time of writing, there are two primitives within the Qiskit Runtime: **Sampler** and **Estimator**. Each of these provides a simple way to encapsulate your circuit and leverage each of its features to optimize workloads during execution to optimize running them on multiple quantum systems at scale. If you recall in the previous chapters, when we built and applied optimization levels to our circuit, it involved quite a bit of work, and the optimization was based on a single quantum system that we selected to run on. You can imagine the number of steps and overhead that would require if we needed to do that for each different system that executes our circuit. With the interface provided by the primitives, a lot of that is taken care of for us by applying a handful of option settings and selections. The runtime will then apply these accordingly as it selects multiple systems to execute the circuits. The primitives each perform a specific task and serve as the entry point to the Qiskit Runtime service. Let's look at each primitive to get a little understanding of their functionality and the differences between them. In this chapter, we will focus on the Sampler primitive. The IBM Quantum Learning platform has some very good examples, courses, and tutorials that you can learn from in much greater detail than I can provide in this one chapter.

Understanding the Sampler primitive

The **Sampler** primitive is similar to what we have used throughout this book in that it takes a quantum circuit as its input and generates a quasi-probability result. The result of this is also error-mitigated to ensure that the results are as precise as possible. Example of Sampler primitive circuits are Grover's search and Deutsch-Jozsa. The Sampler can be modified to allow changes such as backends (local simulator or quantum system), which simplifies the management of your circuits and how they are run on the backend in accordance with the needs of your experiments. This is very helpful as each primitive has its own form of operating on the quantum circuit when executed on a quantum system, therefore certain properties or mitigating techniques will not work on some primitives based on the way they perform their tasks.

Well, so far, we've done quite a bit of reading, why don't we get back to some coding. Let's create a new Qiskit notebook and run a simple circuit using the Sampler to try it out. We'll also include the classes mentioned earlier so we can wrap everything together in a simple construct of a circuit.

First, we'll create a simple circuit:

```
# Create a simple circuit:
from qiskit import QuantumCircuit, QuantumRegister, ClassicalRegister,
                   transpile
from qiskit.visualization import plot_distribution

q_reg = QuantumRegister(4, name='qr')
c_reg = ClassicalRegister(4, name='cr')

qc = QuantumCircuit(q_reg, c_reg)
qc.h(0)
qc.cx(0, 1)
qc.cx(1, 2)
qc.cx(2, 3)
qc.draw(output="mpl")
```

This will display the following circuit that we wish to run:

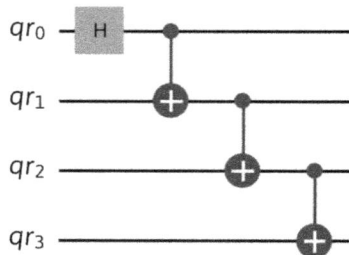

Figure 10.1: Simple circuit to run on the system

Now, here's where the fun starts! Let's begin by following the Qiskit Patterns so we are not only ensuring that our circuits are efficient but also our development patterns.

Qiskit Patterns are a 4-step process that we can use to help integrate our quantum computation circuits into a larger application layer. The 4 steps are Map, Optimize, Execute, and Post-process. We'll go through each of these steps so that you can get familiar with running circuits optimally on a quantum system. We'll start with what we just did: map our problem into a quantum circuit.

Step 1: Map

Mapping a problem to a quantum circuit can be done in many ways. We can probably write volumes of books that could be dedicated to this. This is because it not only depends on the problem we're trying to solve, but also how we can best map our input data and problem solution into a quantum state or initial state. This is similar to planning a trip. If I were to ask you to plan a group trip to New York, there could be many options and even more questions regarding how to get there? Where will everyone be? Are they all in the same location at the beginning of the trip. How long will they be available? These are similar questions we need to consider. How do we get the data to the quantum systems? Where is all the data, at that moment, and how long will the data be there? Once we have obtained the input data the next step is to translate it from classical information into a quantum state or input for our circuit. Let's do this now with a simple example, the circuit we built earlier in this chapter. In *Chapter 13*, we will cover a more sophisticated problem, Grover's search. For now, to allow us to focus on the overall process, we'll stick with the simple circuit, and some random circuits.

So far, we have mapped a problem into a quantum state, in this case the circuit we constructed above. That's step one, Map, done.

Let's now run this circuit using a Statevector class to get the expected results before running on a quantum system. Since this is a small and simple quantum circuit, we can simulate this easily on a classical system such as the one you have at home or in your office. If the circuit or problem involved a large number of qubits that you would be unable to run on a classical system, then the preferred way to do this would be to reduce the problem size to something you can run on a classical system so that you can confirm the expected result at a smaller scale and then run on a quantum system to get the full-scale results.

```
from qiskit.quantum_info import Statevector
# Pass the circuit instructions into the Statevector
results = Statevector.from_instruction(qc).probabilities_dict()
plot_distribution(results)
```

This will display the expected results in the following diagram:

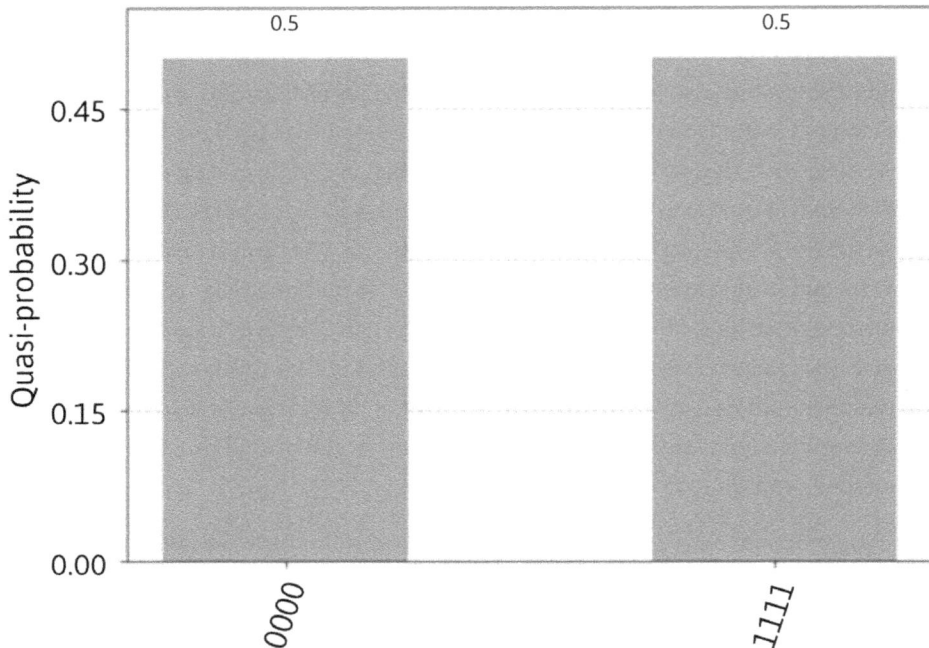

Figure 10.2: Expected probability results from the circuit using Statevector

Next, we can prepare this to run on an actual backend. To do this, we need to include measurement operators in our circuit, which we will do, and then obtain the least busy backend system to run this circuit:

```
# Add measurements to our circuit
qc.measure_all(add_bits=False)

# Select the least busy backend system to run circuit
backend = service.least_busy(simulator=False, operational=True)
print("Least busy backend: ", backend)
```

This will print out the selected backend, which is the least busy at the time it is called.

Step 2: Optimize

Now we can prepare our circuit to run on the backend by transpiling it accordingly. To do this, we will use the new preset_passmanager function, which is a new addition to the Qiskit transpiler library that allows you to set, run, and draw the result of the circuit after transpilation. Aligning a circuit to a target backend is ideal in that it will optimize the circuit to that selected backend by applying not only the general passes available but also AI generated optimizers that introduce further improvements.

```
from qiskit.transpiler.preset_passmanagers import generate_preset_pass_
manager

target = backend.target
pm = generate_preset_pass_manager(target=target, optimization_level=3)

transpiled_qc = pm.run(qc)
transpiled_qc.draw(output="mpl", idle_wires=False, style="iqp")
```

This displays the transpiled circuit specific to the selected backend target. Here, you will note two differences from the original circuit. First, note the qubit mapping has changed; qubit 0 is now assigned to qubit 73. In your case, depending on which system was selected, it might point to other qubits. Next, you'll also note that there are more gates added. This is due to having to use basis gates and connectivity between qubits (using ECR gates: https://docs.quantum.ibm. com/api/qiskit/qiskit.circuit.library.ECRGate) to connect between qubits that might not be adjacent to each other. Results might differ here as your selected backend might have different results.

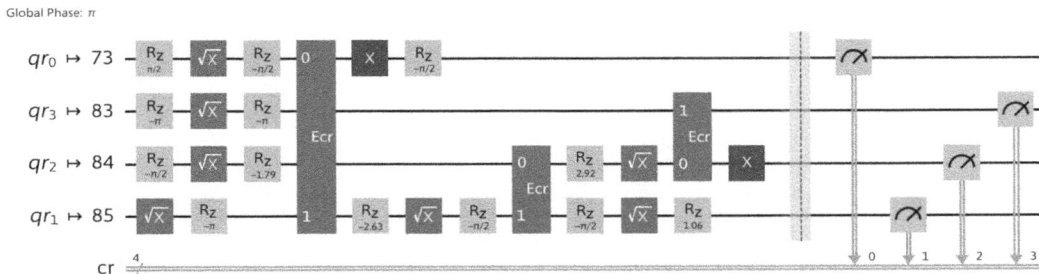

Figure 10.3: Transpiled circuit

Now that we know how to transpile a circuit and set the optimization level values, let's now switch to a bit more complex circuit so we can push the optimizer further and see the differences between the resulting circuits. We'll use a simple Grover operator to generate a circuit. Since we have not yet covered Grover's algorithm in much detail, let's ease into it and just say that we will use it to mark a state we wish the circuit to find. In this case, we will use the binary representation 110. Grover's algorithm will be discussed in *Chapter 13*.

```
from qiskit.circuit.library import GroverOperator

oracle = Statevector.from_label("110")
grover_qc = QuantumCircuit(3)
grover_qc.h(range(3))
grover_qc = grover_qc.compose(GroverOperator(oracle))
grover_qc.draw(output="mpl")
```

This will result in the following circuit, where we have a set of Hadamard gates followed by the Grover operator composite. Note that this is a composite that represents a series of gates into a single block titled Q to simplify the visualization of the circuit. You can run the decompose method a few times to break it down to the basis gates.

In the next steps, we will transpile it with varying optimization level values and compare the two so you can see the power that the `transpiler` optimizers have on the circuit.

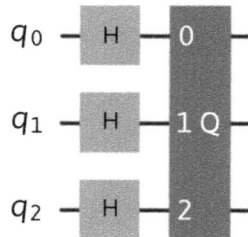

Figure 10.4: Grover operator circuit

The following will highlight the difference between optimization levels with the complexities that accompany many circuits. To be more specific regarding the comparisons, we will be observing the number of **ECR** gates, which is an acronym for **Echoed Cross-Resonance** gate. They're similar to CX gates but with an echoing procedure, which mitigates a few unwanted terms. Details on this gate can be found in the Qiskit Circuit Library. ECR gates, or any multi-source/multi-target gates, are quite complex as they require additional gates to generate connectivity. In this example, we will use the number of ECR gates to compare the circuits.

Let's first capture the Statevector results from the current circuit so we can compare them to the results after transpiling and running on the quantum systems:

```
results = Statevector.from_instruction(grover_qc).probabilities_dict()
```

Next, we'll add measurement gates to this circuit and create multiple copies, each with varying optimization_level values to compare:

```
grover_qc.measure_all()

transpiled_grover_qc = pm.run(grover_qc)
transpiled_grover_qc.draw(output="mpl", idle_wires=False, style="iqp")
```

The result here is a transpiled version of the original Grover circuit we created. I have included a truncated portion of it in the following figure:

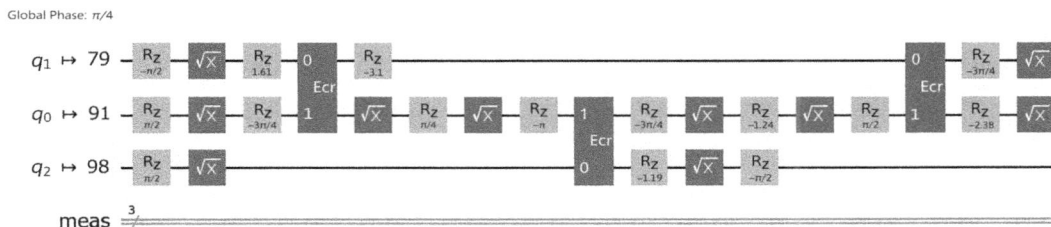

Figure 10.5: Transpiled Grover operator circuit (truncated)

As you can see, it is much more complex and with quite a few extra gates, including ECR gates.

Now, let's go through the circuit and assign a different optimization_level value for each. In this case, we'll compare the extreme levels, one at 0, which is to say no optimization at all, and another at 3, which is fully optimized. We'll then add it to a circuits array to run on a quantum system later.

```
circuits=[]
for optimization_level in [0,3]:
    transpiled_grover_qc = transpile(grover_qc, backend, optimization_
level=optimization_level, seed_transpiler=1000)
    print(f"ECR (Optimization level={optimization_level}): ", transpiled_
grover_qc.count_ops()["ecr"])
    circuits.append(transpiled_grover_qc)
```

This will display the number of ECR gates for each circuit. Note the difference between the two circuits (they will vary based on system) is quite large when compared with no optimization (level 0) and fully optimized (level 3).

```
ECRs (optimization_level=0):  24
ECRs (optimization_level=3):  14
```

Now that we have optimized our circuit by transpiling to the device with specific optimization levels, let's now run both circuits and compare the results, along with the simulated results, on an actual quantum system.

This completes the optimize step and we move onto the next Qiskit Pattern, executing the optimized circuit.

Step 3: Execute

Here, we will now run our circuit on the targeted backend, but this time with a twist. We will use a new feature of the Qiskit Runtime called Batch. This will allow us to provide a batch of operations to run on a quantum system.

To execute the circuits we created, we will first need to create a batch, which is one of the execution modes of the Qiskit Runtime (https://docs.quantum.ibm.com/api/qiskit-ibm-runtime/qiskit_ibm_runtime.Batch), and load it up with our circuit and backend information first, then within the batch, we'll run the Sampler primitive on the backend and print the results.

```
with Batch(service=service, backend=backend):
    sampler = Sampler()
    job = sampler.run(
        circuits=circuits,
        skip_transpilation=True,
        shots=8000
    )
    result = job.result()
```

This might take a while depending on where you are in the queue. But once it's complete, you should see the following results from your experiment, which includes the quasi-probability results and the metadata from the experiment, in this case the number of shots used to obtain the results.

```
SamplerResult(quasi_dists=[{0: 0.136596417234717, 1: 0.057482039100449,
2: 0.03807773583055, 3: 0.051080549862785, 4: 0.028575374054239, 5:
0.068434342226471, 6: 0.540689745421478, 7: 0.079063796269311}, {0:
```

```
0.013241830253957, 1: 0.044991185036454, 2: 0.066493715476242, 3:
0.033981414166734, 4: 0.077452855226391, 5: 0.045273457404358, 6:
0.654480551636603, 7: 0.064084990799261}], metadata=[{'shots': 8000,
'circuit_metadata': {}, 'readout_mitigation_overhead': 1.2784314899265776,
'readout_mitigation_time': 0.03348202304914594}, {'shots': 8000,
'circuit_metadata': {}, 'readout_mitigation_overhead': 1.0800027370262115,
'readout_mitigation_time': 0.0965154911391437}])
```

Let's look at the results a little deeper. First, you will see a set of quasi_dists. These are the results of the quasi-distribution from our experiments. Since we ran a 3-qubit circuit, we should see 8 possible results, 0-7, and the quasi-probabilities for each. This is then followed by some nice information on the readout overhead for each circuit, which is simply the time it took to read out the results for each circuit.

This now helps us move into the final step in the Qiskit Patterns, post-process.

Step 4: Post-process

In this final step of the Qiskit patterns, we will extract the results from the quantum systems and do some post-processing. What exactly is post-processing? Well, simply put, it's whatever you wish it to be. You could extrapolate the results and return them to the next task in your classical application to continue a particular hybrid classical-quantum workflow, or you can simply provide the results as an input to another classical or quantum computational task and continue. In this case, we'll keep it simple and just display the results visually to compare them. We'll compare the state vector results we computed earlier and visualize them in comparison to the results from the two circuits we ran on a quantum system. The following will display the results onto a histogram:

```
qc_results = [quasi_dist.binary_probabilities() for quasi_dist in result.
quasi_dists]

plot_histogram(
    qc_results + [results],
    legend=[
        "optimization_level=0",
        "optimization_level=3",
        "Simulated results"
    ],
    bar_labels=False
)
```

The resulting plot will be as follows:

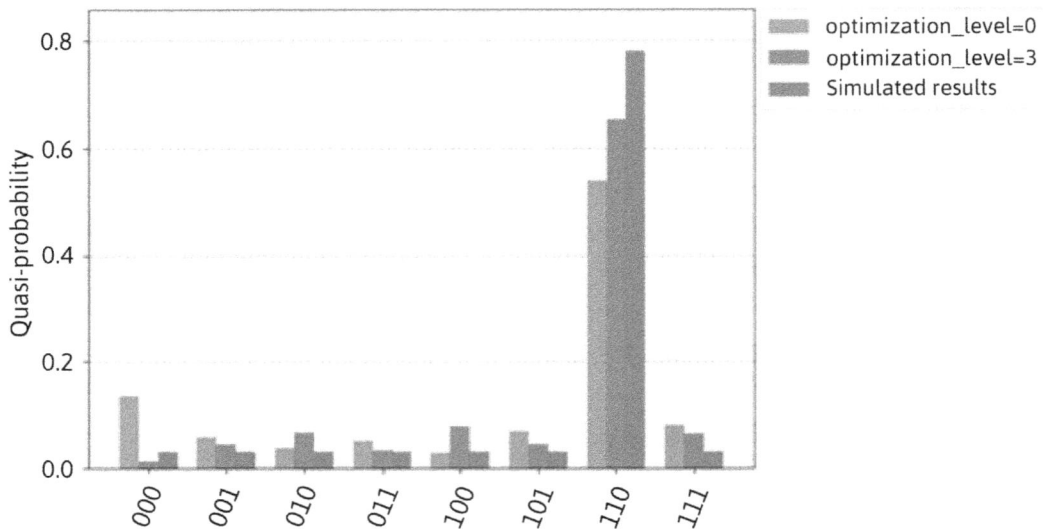

Figure 10.6: Post-processed results, visualization comparison

Here, you can see that our result is as expected, where the results from the optimization at the higher level, 3, are closer to our simulated results, whereas the results from the circuit without any optimization are less accurate.

This brings us to the next topic we need to discuss: noise. All quantum systems, no matter the technology, have some form of noise or effect that the system has that is related to noise. There are some technologies that isolate qubits from any environmental noise; however, this also presents a disadvantage in that when we want to alter the state of the qubit, the speed and fidelity might take longer than other technologies. In this book, since we are using IBM Quantum systems, we will focus on superconducting qubits and the effects that noise has on them. We will, of course, also cover the latest advancements in both error suppression and error mitigation, which over time will potentially provide us with useful quantum applications. In the next section, we'll begin by understanding the differences between the types of noise and how they affect quantum systems.

Understanding the noise effects of decoherence

We learned in *Chapter 9, Simulating Quantum Systems and Noise Models*, that we can generate various noise models that are based on the configuration of a specified quantum computer. After the configuration information is extracted, we can then apply any one of an array of error functions to a local simulator, which will reproduce similar error effects to what we would get from a quantum computer.

In this section, we will expand on that to learn how these errors affect our circuits over time. The two effects we will review here are the two most common issues found in near-term quantum systems: **relaxation** and **dephasing**. These are critical errors as they can affect the quantum state information, which would result in erroneous responses.

Later in this chapter, we will also look at **readout errors**, another common source of noise that originates when the system is applying a measurement pulse, while in parallel, listening in on the acquisition channel. The results and conversion from an analog pulse to a digital value (either 0 or 1) can introduce many errors as well, which we will then try and mitigate.

We will start by learning about one of the most common and important effects of noise in quantum systems: **decoherence**. The three main types of decoherence are **T1**, **T2**, and **T2***. Each of these represents a type of decoherence effect on the qubit. We will begin by looking at each of them individually to understand the differences between them and how to suppress and mitigate against them when they are run on a real quantum device.

If you are deeply interested to learn how to analyze the effects of **relaxation (T1)** and **dephasing (T2/T2*)**, *Chapter 9, Simulating Quantum Systems and Noise Models*, illustrates ways to create circuits that include noise models that replicate each of the three. This will help you run experiments to analyze the characterization of the device.

The next section provides a quick overview of both, just to get you to understand which of them is affected when discussing the mitigation features.

Understanding decoherence errors

T_1, as we covered in *Chapter 9, Simulating Quantum Systems and Noise Models*, is often referred to as the **relaxation time**. Relaxation time refers to the time it takes the energy of a qubit to decay from the **excited state** ($|1\rangle$) back down to its **ground state** ($|0\rangle$), as illustrated in the following graph, where $P(|1\rangle)$ indicates the probability of 1, and $P(|0\rangle)$ is the probability of 0. The T_1 time is defined as the value when $P(t) = 1/e$ (refer to the following diagram):

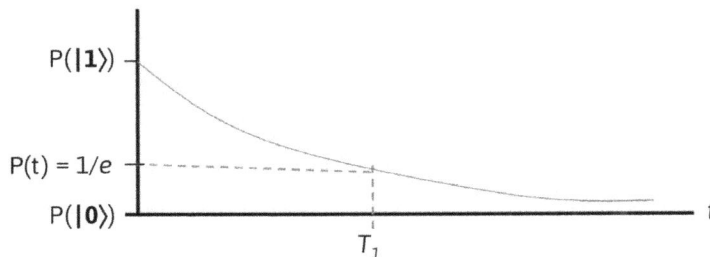

Figure 10.7: T1 defined as the decay time where the probability of the energy state reaches 1/e

When applying this to a quantum system, if you want to determine the amount of time to reach T_1 for any qubit, you would need to create a test circuit that places the qubit in an excited state, $|1\rangle$. We know how to do this by simply applying an X gate to the qubit and then waiting a given amount of time before measuring that qubit. If you were to do this over a set number of time intervals, you will likely start to see the results switch from the excited state transition to the ground state.

So, what does all that mean? Let's dig in a little bit and see how this applies to quantum systems over time and on complex circuits.

We'll start with a simple analogy to provide you with some intuitive understanding of the concepts here. For those of you who already have knowledge of these concepts, feel free to jump to the next section.

Imagine yourself just before or soon after New Year's Eve making that same resolution most of us make, me included, year after year of hitting the gym and getting back in shape, particularly after the feasts we've enjoyed over the holidays. Then, usually on the first or second week of January, we go to the gym and our personal trainer takes us straight to the weights and asks us to pick a weight. Now, one of the things we naturally do is try to pick up where we were the last time we were at the gym and grab a heavy weight. Of course, at first it seems a little heavy, but we power on. Our trainer then wants to test our strength and asks us to hold the weight high over our heads with our arms extended. We then raise the weight confidently over our heads and we're *excited* that this wasn't too bad. Let's call our ability to hold the weight over our heads the excited state. OK, so let's now say our trainer asks us to hold it there as long as we can. What we will notice is that our strength can only sustain this position for some time. We will then begin to feel the fatigue in our muscles, which will then slowly, or in my case rather rapidly, start to lower down towards the original position, which is with the weight down close to the *ground*, where I am no longer feeling the strain of my muscles. Let's call this the *relaxed* position, the ground state.

A qubit pretty much follows this concept in that it will start at a ground state, then sometime later we will amplify the qubit from the ground state to some excited state. Now, just like us, over time we will return to that ground state to relax. This relaxation from excited to ground state is, logically enough, called amplitude relaxation, which may sound familiar because we learned about this in the previous chapter when creating an amplitude dampening noise model to represent decoherence.

Looking back at *Figure 10.8*, you can imagine this is what the effect decoherence (T_1) has on a qubit caused by its environment. What do we mean by environment? I'm glad you asked! A qubit isn't just a single aluminum-niobium component with a Josephson Junction.

Oh no, no, no, it has so much more going on! Of course, depending on the technology that the qubit relies on, superconducting, ion traps, photonics, etc. the qubit is not sitting all alone. It is usually surrounded by various environment variables that can interfere with and even at times speed up the decoherence of the qubit. Superconducting qubits, for example, must sit at a certain temperature, approximately 15 millikelvin, to work properly and make sure that the energy levels between the ground and first excited state are precise to determine the state of the qubit. Then, the pulse sent to the qubit has to have the right amplitude, duration, frequency, etc. in order to place the qubit in the correct state. Keep in mind that this could be difficult as the quantum system might be very complex. For example, we defined one amplitude value as the excited state as just one position earlier in our example: lifting the weight over our heads. But what if we needed multiple amplitudes to encode our data? Then the precision of our gates will need to be very exact, which means that the fidelity of the gates also might influence our system. This is how decoherence, also referred to as the relaxation rate or T_1, if not suppressed, causes us to lose the quantum state information of our circuit, which leads to errors when we read the results of our circuits.

Understanding dephasing errors

T_1, we learned in the previous section, refers to the decoherence or relaxation rate caused when the amplitude of the qubit decays over time. Dephasing errors, on the other hand, occur when the phase of the qubit is blurred, often referred to either T_2 or T_2^*. Dephasing is quite like decoherence in that we will also lose state information over time, only in a slightly different manner.

To define dephasing simply means to lose phase information, of a qubit in this case.

There are many different sources for dephasing noise, each of which has varying properties. A few examples are:

- **White noise**, when there is an equal amount of a signal that is of equal intensity at varying frequencies.

- **Pink noise**, often referred to as flicker noise, occurs usually in electronic devices where the power density decreases with increasing frequency, i.e., 1/f, where f is the frequency.

- **Flux noise**, is found on the surface of **superconducting quantum interference devices**, commonly referred to as **SQUIDS**, the source of which are the magnetic spins on the surface of the SQUID.

Short of converting this from a developer to an engineering book, I will include some references to these as well, should you want to learn more about them, at the end of this chapter.

Now that we have a basic understanding of noise, let's learn what the differences are between error suppression, error mitigation, and error correction and how we can use them to create useful quantum applications.

Differences between error suppression, mitigation, and correction

In the previous section, we discussed some sources of errors that can be introduced to your quantum circuit when running them on a quantum system. Here, we will define the various ways to eliminate these errors from your quantum circuit to obtain optimal results. We'll begin by first defining what the differences between suppressing, mitigating, and correcting errors.

Error suppression is just as the name states, suppressing the noise of a given circuit so that the quantum state remains intact. The specific noise here could be either the decoherence time of a qubit (amplitude dampening) or dephasing. As we learned earlier, if a qubit is placed in a specific state and left there over some long period of time, that qubit will eventually return to the ground state, or some state that is different from the set state. What we would like to do here is suppress this by keeping the circuit in the current state. Of course, this is easier said than done. Let's first think about this intuitively, and then get into the details.

Returning to our gym scenario from earlier, let's now assume you are lifting a very heavy set of weights over your chest from a laying position on the workout bench, bench-pressing. There is a risk here that the weight, over time, starts to feel heavier due to the strain your muscles are feeling. This is why you see most people that do this have, standing very close to the weights, a spotter. This is someone who helps you either when you are fatigued and need a little help, or helps lift the weight off your chest when your muscles just suddenly give up. There are many videos I'm sure you can find online where you can see the terrible results when there's no spotter around, but for now, let's elaborate on what this has to do with error suppression.

If you imagine that you need to sustain the weight over your head for a long period of time, you'll realize that over time your muscles will strain; we aligned this to decoherence earlier. To help with this, your spotter can assist by gently helping you raise the bar back up so you can maintain your initial position, or state in this case. That assistance from your spotter can be seen as error suppression in that it helped maintain your state while not changing the state itself, meaning you're not holding it any higher or lower than expected to count as a lift. Now, let's get out of the gym and switch our context back to quantum and see how this helps us understand error suppression with respect to a quantum circuit.

When a gate or set of gates is applied to a qubit within a circuit, that circuit may, over some period of time, lose its state in many ways, some of which we mentioned earlier. What we need to do is apply a technique in which we can help the circuit maintain its state. Yes, this sounds like the definition of error correction, but let me take a moment to elaborate on that to identify the difference. To do that I'll explain a new Pass (recall that a Pass is an object used to optimize a circuit, such as finding an optimal layout mapping, or optimal qubits) that was added to Qiskit called **Dynamical Decoupling** (**DD**). Dynamical decoupling is a well-known technique that was described back in 1998 by Dr. Seth Lloyd and Dr. Lorenza Viola from MIT (https://arxiv. org/abs/quant-ph/9803057). They describe it as a form of using control pulses to minimize the diffusion of the state of the qubit. This is generally done by applying the same gate operation twice, which mimics an identity gate. We learned about this earlier when we explained that most universal quantum gates are reversible, hence by applying two reversible gates back-to-back, you end up with the identity gate. So, how does this work, you ask? I'm glad you did, here we go!

If you recall from *Chapter 7, Programming with Qiskit; Understanding pulses, and Pulse Library* section when we described that when running your circuit on a quantum computer, you must first create a pulse schedule, which is what dictates to the control systems the pulses to the qubits by following the pulse schedule in order. You may also recall that the pulse schedule includes information regarding the pulse, but also the duration of the pulse and the time gaps in between pulses. Luckily for us, we learned that all of this is done for us with the Transpiler and the PassManager. Once the pulse schedule is created to run on the specific quantum system, the Dynamical Decoupling Pass takes a run through it before running on the system. What the DD Pass looks for is idle time gaps between pulse signals, and it inserts a sequence of gates into those gaps. Remember that since the gates are reversible and we do not want to alter the state or phase of the circuit, it will apply a pair of gates to ensure that it sustains the action of a unitary gate. Let's go to the code and see this in action to get a better idea.

First, we'll import some of the objects and functions we need to get started.

```
%run helper_file_1.0.ipynb
import numpy as np
from qiskit.circuit.library import XGate
from qiskit.transpiler import PassManager, InstructionDurations
from qiskit.transpiler.passes import ALAPScheduleAnalysis,
PadDynamicalDecoupling
from qiskit.visualization import timeline_drawer
```

Let's go over what we are importing here. First, from the Transpiler, we're pulling in `PassManager` and `InstructionDurations`. `PassManager` is what manages the Passes used to optimize our quantum circuits during transpilation. `InstructionDurations` is basically just that; it stores the durations of all the gates, timescales (dt), to the selected backend system. Let's pull the durations for a random backend system to try this out. Check which backends are availale as the systems may change over time.

```
# Select a random backend you have access to, or pick the least busy:
backend = service.get_backend('ibm_kyoto')

# Pull and print the duration times of the backend system for each get per
qubit:
dur = InstructionDurations.from_backend(backend)
print(dur)
```

The following is a truncated example of the outputs, in this case the X gates. Since `ibm_kyoto` is a 127-qubit device, we see that the durations shown are indexed to identify the duration time for the x-gate and its corresponding qubit. Note that the actual results will be a list of all gate durations between all qubits; the following is just a subset of the results:

```
x(0,): 3.5555555555555554e-08 s
x(1,): 3.5555555555555554e-08 s
x(2,): 3.5555555555555554e-08 s
x(3,): 3.5555555555555554e-08 s
x(4,): 3.5555555555555554e-08 s
```

Qiskit also provides you with the ability to set the durations yourself for each gate. This allows you to have a bit more control should you want to modify them for specific devices. The following illustrates how to do this for all gates:

```
# Set the duration times for each gate.
custom_duration_times = InstructionDurations([('x', None, 100),
                                               ('h', 0, 100),
                                               ("cx", [0, 1], 200),
                                               ("cx", [1, 2], 200),
                                               ("cx", [2, 3], 200),
                                               ("measure", None, 500
                                                   )])
```

```
# Print the timescales for each gate we set:
print(custom_duration_times)
```

Here, we have set the following custom duration times for each gate:

Gate	Duration
x	100
h	100
cx[0,1]	200
cx[1,2]	200
cx[2,3]	200
measure	500

Table 10.1: Custom gate duration times

Next, we will visualize the circuit duration in a nice timeline. To visualize the circuit and its timeline, we will need to transpile the circuit using a *scheduling method* to a backend. A scheduling method is how the transpiler will schedule the operations to the qubits, for example, as soon as possible when the qubit is ready for the next instruction, or you can have it scheduled for later, which basically keeps the qubit in the ground state when possible. For these examples, we will use the **alap** scheduling method, which is an acronym for *as late as possible*. You can find details about the various scheduling methods in the Qiskit API documentation.

```
#Let's transpile the circuit and view the default timeline
transpiled_qc = transpile(qc, backend, scheduling_method='alap',
layout_method='trivial')
timeline_drawer(transpiled_qc, time_range=[0,5500], show_idle=False)
```

This will print out a visual representation of the gate duration. It will look very much like the pulse schedule we learned about earlier; however, this is the circuit and not the pulse schedule. You can tell because we see the qubit labels on the left and not the drive channels. Also note that CX gates have taken on the label of **ecr** in this case.

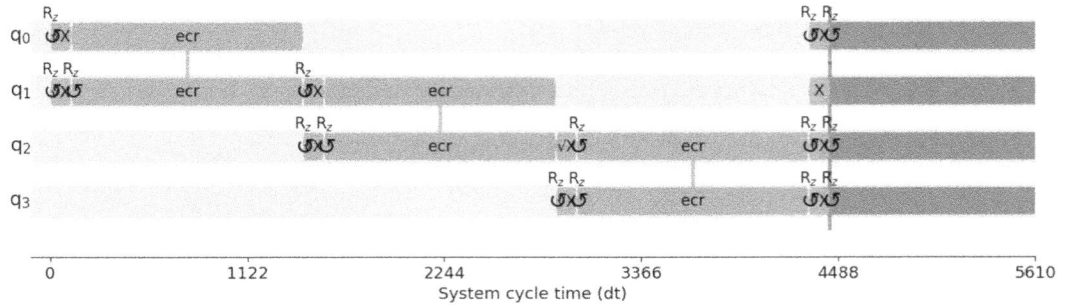

Figure 10.8: Circuit timeline visualization

As shown in *Figure 10.8*, this is the specified duration for each gate that is based on the selected backend. We will use this duration to visualize some of the error suppression features included in Qiskit, particularly Dynamical Decoupling.

The way Dynamical Decoupling works is that it will search for idle time in your circuit and insert a sequence of Dynamical Decoupling gates to those idle time slots to ensure that the qubit's state is not altered. The pair of reversible gates used will operate equally to that of an Identity gate so that it does not alter the state of the circuit. Let's use our custom duration times and a pair of X gates to create the Dynamical Decoupling sequence of reversible gates.

```
# Create the Dynamical Decoupling sequence of reversible gates, let's use
XGates:
rev_gates = [XGate(), XGate()]


# Set the PassManager with the Dynamical Decoupling sequence and custom
duration times
pm = PassManager([ALAPScheduleAnalysis(custom_duration_times),
                  PadDynamicalDecoupling(custom_duration_times, rev_
gates)])
```

What we have defined is the pair of reversible gates that mimic an Identity gate. In this case, we are using a pair of X gates. Then, we instantiated our PassManager, which is what manages which Passes to use to optimize our circuit during the transpilation phase. In this case, we are setting the alap scheduling method and Dynamical Decoupling times to the custom duration times we created earlier. Also included are the reversible gates as an argument to the constructor.

Next, we want to run our transpiled circuit through the PassManager we just created to produce the altered circuit with the Dynamical Decoupling included:

```
# Run the circuit through the PassManager to add the DD to the circuit
qc_dynamical_decoupling = pm.run(transpiled_qc)
```

Now, let's visualize this circuit and compare it to the previous circuit in *Figure 10.9*:

```
timeline_drawer(qc_dynamical_decoupling, show_idle=False)
```

This will draw the circuit with the error suppression of the Dynamical Decoupling added. You can see the X gates that have been added to the first qubit, q_0.

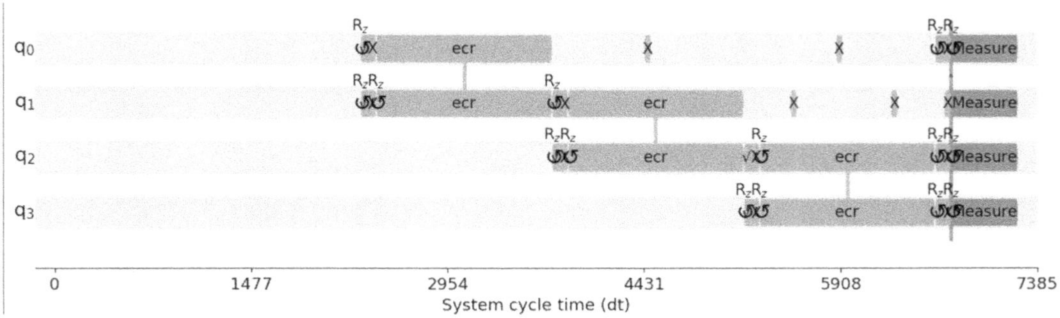

Figure 10.9: Visualization of the Dynamical Decoupling circuit

Here, we can observe a couple of things. First, that the gate durations are smaller due to the custom duration we set when compared to the previous circuit. Next, you will also note that the inserted X gates were added to the first qubit only, and not to the space after the second qubit, q_1. This is because the idle time gap is shorter than that of the two X gates, therefore the gate pairs were not added. Let's make a quick yet significant adjustment to the custom duration time to include a pair of X gates after the second qubit by increasing the duration from 50 to 1500. Since we are only updating the value of one gate, we can just update the value of the gate without restating the other gates by using the update() function, as shown in the following code:

```
# Update durations
updated_values = [('x', None, 1500)]
updated_durations = custom_duration_times.update(updated_values)
print(updated_durations)
```

Now, let's retry and see what we get back this time. Here, we will set the parameters with the updated values and rerun the PassManager and visualize the results:

```
# Set the PassManager with the Dynamical Decoupling sequence and custom
duration times
pm = PassManager([ALAPScheduleAnalysis(updated_durations),
                  PadDynamicalDecoupling(updated_durations, rev_gates)])
qc_dynamical_decoupling = pm.run(transpiled_qc)
timeline_drawer(qc_dynamical_decoupling, show_idle=False)
```

This will now produce two sets of reversible gates, one as before, and now a second set, which we can see after the second qubit. Since we have reduced the duration time, it can now fit in the idle time gap at the end of the second qubit, as shown in the following diagram:

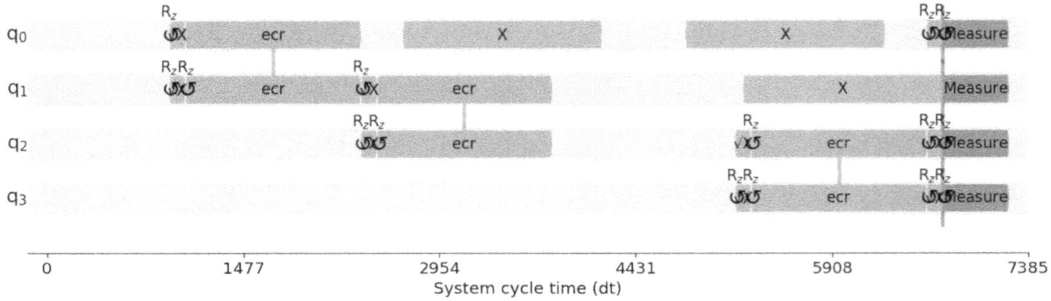

Figure 10.10: Visualization of circuit with updated duration times

As *Figure 10.10* illustrates, we can set the duration time of each gate. In this case, we increased the duration so we can see the changes. However, in many cases you need to reduce it to try to squeeze in our reversible gates to fill in the idle time gaps as needed. But, of course, like anything else, we do not necessarily need to do all this fine tuning ourselves. Thankfully for us, the Qiskit Runtime includes optimization and **resilience levels** that we can set to enable these features for us, as described earlier in this chapter when we discussed the various optimization levels we can set in the Options, which include enabling Dynamical Decoupling.

Now that we have covered an example of error suppression, let's continue and look at error mitigation.

First, before we begin defining what **error mitigation** is, let me cover what **error correction** is and how it is different. Error correction in general is composed of two steps: first identifying that an error has occurred and second, correcting that error using various error correcting techniques. Error mitigation on the other hand uses the errors to calculate and determine an outcome that reduces yet does not necessarily eliminate the error itself.

There are various error mitigating techniques, and much research is still ongoing to find more optimal ways to reduce errors. At the time of writing, three techniques are used to mitigate errors that are included into the Qiskit Runtime resilience level options: **TREX**, **ZNE**, and **PEC**. Details regarding each are linked earlier in this chapter, where we defined the resilience levels. Each of these techniques uses classical resources to perform their tasks. This of course introduces overhead into our application. However, there are advances released regularly that reduce a lot of the overhead to optimize speed, quality, and scalability. By continuing to do this we can surely over time reach a level of quantum utility that will mean the cost to implement a complex quantum circuit may be substantially lower than that of classical simulations.

Thankfully, again, Qiskit makes it easy for us to set the levels of error mitigation using the resilience levels to activate specific error mitigation techniques. In the following code snippet, we will run a circuit first without any error suppression or mitigation techniques, and then we will create one that will use Dynamical Decoupling for error suppression and TREX for error mitigation.

We'll start with no error suppression or mitigation:

```
least_busy_backend = service.least_busy(simulator=False, operational=True,
                        min_num_qubits=transpiled_qc.num_qubits)
# Let's transpile the circuit to this new backend:
transpiled_qc=transpile(qc, backend=least_busy_backend)

options = Options()
options.execution.shots = 1000
options.optimization_level = 0  # No error suppression
options.resilience_level = 0  # No error mitigation

with Session(service=service, backend=least_busy_backend) as session:
    sampler = Sampler(session=session, options=options)
    job_sim_0 = sampler.run(transpiled_qc)
    print(job_sim_0.result())
    session.close()
plot_distribution(job_sim_0.result().quasi_dists)
```

The results are as follows when running the Sampler, and you should see a visual representation of the results as well:

```
SamplerResult(quasi_dists=[{0: 0.463, 1: 0.011, 2: 0.006, 3: 0.008, 4:
0.008, 6: 0.001, 7: 0.009, 8: 0.01, 9: 0.001, 10: 0.008, 11: 0.01, 12:
0.006, 13: 0.014, 14: 0.099, 15: 0.346}], metadata=[{'shots': 1000}])
```

Next, we will enable both Dynamical Decoupling and TREX:

```
options.execution.shots = 1000
options.optimization_level = 3  # Levels 1-3 use Dynamical Decoupling
options.resilience_level = 1  # Level 1 uses TREX for error mitigation

with Session(service=service, backend=least_busy_backend) as session:
    sampler = Sampler(session=session, options=options)
    job_sim_1 = sampler.run(transpiled_qc)
    print(job_sim_1.result())
    session.close()
plot_distribution(job_sim_1.result().quasi_dists)
```

Here, we set the optimization_level to 3, which will enable Dynamical Decoupling, and the resilience_level to 1, which uses TREX for error mitigation. Note the difference in the results are much more refined and the metadata includes the added overhead and mitigation time:

```
SamplerResult(quasi_dists=[{0: 0.4741007821539706, 1:
-0.00328801216329741, 2: -0.006989853410409116, 3: 0.0018169643386157586,
4: -0.005096477885881826, 5: 0.00010104383589854057, 6:
0.0016676295409465852, 7: 0.0017229622606998135, 8: 0.0038884349758400295,
11: -0.0025386992448873155, 12: 0.00141243346088473367, 13:
0.0009761688074426505, 14: 3.0231076968467426e-05, 15:
0.5321963922532457}], metadata=[{'shots': 1000, 'readout_mitigation_
overhead': 1.6922534955446735, 'readout_mitigation_time':
0.059042368084192276}])
```

This and many other error suppression and mitigation methods are increasing in popularity among researchers as they try to understand the effects of noise and determine optimal ways to mitigate against them in the hopes of accelerating our path from quantum utility towards quantum advantage.

Summary

In this chapter, we covered some of the many effects that noise has on a quantum computing system, both specific to the qubit and externally with respect to the quantum system itself via readout errors. We discovered how we can use the Qiskit Runtime service to run our circuits using the fundamental building blocks known as Primitives. Finally, we learned how to apply error suppression and mitigation techniques to our quantum circuits so to filter the noisy results from a quantum device, which significantly reduces errors and provides more accurate results to complex quantum circuits.

In the next chapter, we will learn how to create quantum applications using the many features available in Qiskit. We will look at creating quantum algorithms, and ultimately provide you with all the tools you need to create your own quantum algorithms and quantum applications.

Questions

1. List the three main error mitigation techniques used by the Qiskit Runtime service.
2. Which resilience levels are used for error mitigation?
3. What other reversible gates could you use to fill in the idle time of a qubit using Dynamical Decoupling?
4. Which type of noise contributes to amplitude dampening of a qubit?
5. Which type of noises contribute to dephasing of a qubit?

Further reading

- IBM Quantum Learning platform: https://learning.quantum.ibm.com
- Evidence for the utility of quantum computing before fault tolerance: https://www.nature.com/articles/s41586-023-06096-3
- Quasi-probability decompositions with reduced sampling overhead: https://www.nature.com/articles/s41534-022-00517-3
- Dynamical suppression of decoherence in two-state quantum systems: https://arxiv.org/pdf/quant-ph/9803057.pdf
- Error mitigation in short depth circuits: https://arxiv.org/pdf/1612.02058.pdf
- Sutor, B., *Dancing with Qubits*, Packt Publishing: https://www.packtpub.com/data/dancing-with-qubits

- Nielsen, M. & Chuang, I., *Quantum Computation and Quantum Information*, Cambridge University Press: `https://www.cambridge.org/us/academic/subjects/physics/quantum-physics-quantum-information-and-quantum-computation/quantum-computation-and-quantum-information-10th-anniversary-edition`

- Wootton, J., *What is Quantum Error Correction?*, Medium Series: `https://decodoku.medium.com/1-what-is-quantum-error-correction-4ab6d97cb398`

Join us on Discord

Join our community's Discord space for discussions with the author and other readers:

`https://packt.link/3FyN1`

11

Understanding Quantum Algorithms

If you've been reading the news about quantum computing, you will have noticed many articles from various companies, both large and small, all working on different projects related to quantum computing. The reason is largely based on the potential computing power that quantum systems offer when compared to classical systems. The potential to provide speedup, quality, and scalability are the main areas of interest that most companies and research institutions are looking heavily into now.

By grasping the intricacies of the various quantum algorithms and learning how to apply them to a specific problem set or industry, researchers and developers can then look at extending what they learned about the small problems and apply them to large real-world enterprise solutions. This era of solving real-world problems using quantum computers that are intractable to classic computers is referred to as **quantum advantage**. Currently, most of the work being done centers on understanding and creating quantum computation algorithms, which are usually focused on smaller **toy problems**, as they are commonly referred to.

However, in 2021, IBM Quantum introduced a 127-qubit processor that broke the 100-qubit barrier. This signifies a great move forward as it represents a barrier in which classical simulations may no longer mimic a quantum computer of equal size. Early evidence of this was found in 2023 when a 127-qubit Eagle processor was able to perform exact solutions to computational problems beyond classical brute force. Details about this can be found in the Nature article *Evidence for the utility of quantum computing before fault tolerance* (`https://www.nature.com/articles/s41586-023-06096-3`).

This brings us a step closer to the quantum advantage phase that everyone is racing to achieve. Of course, this will vary as some problems might require more quantum computational power than others, but, over time, different industries will eventually achieve it soon enough. To get yourselves suited up and in the race, you'll need to understand some of the foundational quantum algorithms and how they are applied to solve general problems.

The following topics will be covered in this chapter:

- Understanding the meaning of outperforming classical systems
- Learning about the Deutsch algorithm
- Understanding the Deutsch-Jozsa algorithm
- Learning about the foundational oracle-based quantum algorithm

In this chapter, we will review the various quantum algorithms in use today. One of the most difficult hurdles to overcome while learning about quantum algorithms is that it is not a lift and shift from classical to quantum. Simply implementing a classical algorithm's steps from a classic system onto a quantum system, such as a simple adder, will not automatically make it a quantum speedup algorithm. There's a bit more to it than that.

In *Chapter 5, Understanding the Qubit*, we discussed how quantum states are manipulated, and in *Chapter 7, Programming with Qiskit*, we covered how to run a circuit on a quantum system. We will now put all those pieces together to learn about and create quantum algorithms and illustrate how they can outperform classical algorithms in this chapter. We will begin by providing an example of a quantum algorithm that is foundational and illustrate how quantum systems perform operations much faster by reviewing both the **Deutsch** and **Deutsch-Jozsa** algorithms. We'll follow that up with more generalized algorithms that focus on solving simple problems with the **Bernstein-Vazirani** algorithm.

This is by no means an exhaustive list of quantum algorithms, but this chapter will provide you with the early foundational algorithms that will help you understand the advanced algorithms and how they compare to classical algorithms. Should you want to see a more complete algorithm list, refer to *Appendix A, Resources*, for some links to sites that keep track of quantum algorithms and research. Of course, as the technology and algorithms advance, new algorithms will be discovered that may have different methods than the following, but in all of these, it is ideal to understand the basics to get you up and running without having to delve too deep into the physics.

Technical requirements

In this chapter, it is expected that you have a basic understanding of linear algebra to understand the equations of each algorithm. You should also have some experience in programming basic circuits and executing them on your local simulator and a quantum device available on the **IBM Quantum** platform. Finally, you should be familiar with both classical bit notation and logic, quantum **Dirac notation** (or Bra-Ket notation), and understand the basic quantum computing principles such as superposition, entanglement, and interference that were covered in the previous chapters.

Here is the full source code used throughout this book: `https://github.com/PacktPublishing/Learning-Quantum-Computing-with-Python-and-IBM-Quantum-Second-Edition`.

Understanding the meaning of outperforming classical systems

In this section, we will learn about the potential advantages that a quantum system has over classical systems by studying some of the early examples that illustrate quantum speedup versus classical systems, albeit some of the examples are simple illustrations of the advantages that, in themselves, do not have any practical usage.

Claims such as quantum systems potentially solving equations at rapid speeds over classical systems or having the capability of a larger computation space all sound fascinating. However, recall that, at the time of writing this chapter, there are still no quantum systems available that can outperform current classical systems in solving real-world commercial problems. *"So why all the chatter?"* you ask.

The answer is simple—potential. Theoretically speaking, there are quantum algorithms that describe solutions to problems that illustrate quantum speedup, such as Shor's algorithm. However, it is expected that we will see quantum advantage before we will see quantum breaks in encryption. This is because reaching quantum advantage is based on a specific problem. It will not be specific data for all; it will evolve as the technology is able to compute very large and complex circuits. To implement complex circuits or algorithms, we will require systems that contain error mitigation, suppression, and, eventually, correction in order to obtain accurate results. This, of course, could be similar to most new technologies. A good example of this is **video streaming**.

Multimedia compression has been around for decades, with video streaming invented in the early 1990s. When video compression was first made commercially available, internet bandwidth had increased and was more widely available, albeit the quality of the video and the audio was not as rich as it is today; the resolution was around 150 x 76 pixels, with a refresh rate of around 8–12 frames per second with poor audio quality. The limitation back then was both the compression technique to decrease the quality of the multimedia and the bandwidth to stream the multimedia content to multiple viewers simultaneously.

The infrastructure to ensure proper decompression and minimize information loss was dependent on error correction, and a proper protocol to avoid low-quality and often jittery resolution. Now, of course, just a little over two decades later, we can see the progress: we can stream live multimedia events with low errors and high resolution. Streaming to your home theater system with a large 4K high-definition screen where you don't have to worry too much about the quality of the video is something of a norm nowadays.

Quantum systems share this same *roadmap*, where we have the hardware (quantum systems) and the algorithms to do things at a *medium resolution* now. The difference here is that we have something we did not have back then: a global infrastructure in which anyone, anywhere, has access to a quantum system via the cloud. IBM quantum computers are available for anyone to access by simply registering for a free account.

In the early days of video streaming, very few had access to bandwidth. Those who did were limited by the infrastructure to collaborate. By having cloud-accessible systems, many industries and academic institutions are doing more research on quantum hardware and algorithms. Of course, back in the early days of multimedia streaming, the solutions being solved were classified as toy problems. However, don't let the name fool you. These toy problems are far from just something to play with and show off to your colleagues. They are the stepping stones to real-world solutions.

For example, if you find a solution that illustrates quantum speedup vis-à-vis classical, with just a handful of qubits and very little quantum volume, then that might not be useful for solving many of today's commercial or real-world problems.

What it does provide is the foundational information needed to scale your solution to a system with the necessary quantum volume to solve a real-world problem. To understand what that roadmap to quantum advantage is, where a quantum solution exists that can outperform a classical system in solving a real-world problem, it's important to first understand the foundational quantum algorithms and how they not only differ from classical algorithms but also provide an advantage over them. This will simplify your understanding of other, more complex algorithms and how they are used to solve problems in various industries.

In the next section, we will discuss the various types of foundational quantum algorithms, starting with the original algorithms that demonstrate an advantage over classical systems.

Learning about Deutsch's algorithm

David Deutsch, a physicist at the **University of Oxford**, first discovered a problem that could be solved by a quantum computer faster than a classical computer. The problem itself has no importance or use in any computer problems, but it did serve to illustrate the advantage that quantum computation has over classical computation. Let's understand that problem in the next section.

Understanding the problem

The problem is very simple. We'll use a simple analogy to explain it. Imagine someone is hiding a coin in each hand. Each coin, when revealed, will either be heads or tails. Since there are two coins, one in each hand, there are four possible results, as shown in the following table:

Events	Left hand	Right hand
1	Heads	Heads
2	Heads	Tails
3	Tails	Heads
4	Tails	Tails

Table 11.1: All four possible outcomes

From the preceding list of events, we can see there are two categories. The first and fourth events are an example of a constant outcome, where both the left and right produce the same result of either heads or tails. The second and third events are examples of balanced outcomes.

Here, the event results are the opposite of one another, indicating that if one is heads, then the other will be tails, or vice versa. Using this same analogy, if I were to reveal one hand at a time, let's say the left hand, then by just viewing the results of the left hand, you would not have enough information to determine whether the result will be constant or balanced because you still need to know what is in the other hand.

Now, imagine there were 100 hands in front of you and you had to examine each hand one at a time in order to determine if there are a balanced number of heads and tails, or if all of the hands contain only heads or only tails. In the best-case scenario, you would get it on the first two tries, meaning if the first hand had heads and the second had tails, you can conclude that the results of the other hands will be balanced. On the other hand (pun intended), if the first two hands revealed the same, either heads or tails, then you cannot conclude that it is balanced or constant.

You would have to, in a worst-case scenario, continue until the 51st hand is revealed, because if the first 50 hands are heads, then the 51st would indicate whether the whole set is constant (if the 51st is heads) or balanced (if the 51st is tails). However, we are jumping ahead a little bit, so let's stick to the current scope of the problem of just two events.

Using a quantum algorithm, which is what Deutsch proposed here, to solve this problem is the same as opening all the hands at once and determining whether the first two qubits are constant or balanced. *Interesting, isn't it?* Let's see how this works!

We'll begin by migrating the analogy of the problem to a mathematical equation. This will simplify the description of the solution later:

1. First, substitute heads and tails with binary notations of 0 and 1, respectively.

2. Next, we'll refer to the result of each hand as a function f, where the argument can refer to left or right, $f(0)$ or $f(1)$, respectively.

Therefore, the results are as follows. In this case, the function f is $f(x)$, where the argument x can be either a 0 or 1 (left or right). The results represent each of the events that have a different result, where each one is either balanced or constant:

Events	$f(0)$	$f(1)$	Results
1	0	0	Constant
2	0	1	Balanced
3	1	0	Balanced
4	1	1	Constant

Table 11.2: Mathematical representation of outcomes

As you can see from the preceding table, now we can restate our problem as a function f that maps a single bit {0,1} to a result of either {0,1}, the results of which would be constant if the results for both $f(0)$ and $f(1)$ are the same, such as *Event 1* and *Event 4* (from the preceding table), or the results would be balanced otherwise. Now that we understand the problem, let's figure out the solution.

Defining the problem

We now know that if $f(0) = f(1)$, then we say f is *constant*; otherwise, f is *balanced*. The problem becomes interesting if we were to introduce a **black box**, sometimes referred to as an oracle, that is hidden from us. We don't know whether the function, hidden in the black box, is either constant or balanced, which is the problem we are asked to solve. The following diagram is a graphical example of our input value, x, going into the black box function, f, and outputting the result value, $f(x)$:

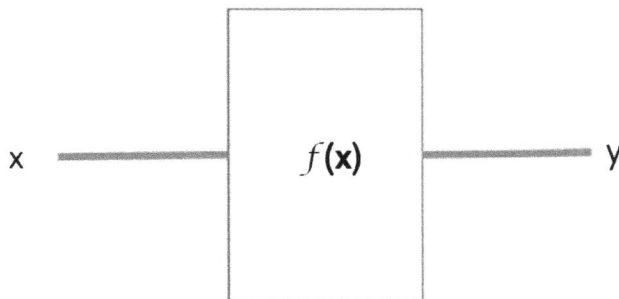

Figure 11.1: Black box representation of our problem

As you can see in the preceding diagram, this problem can be solved classically. However, it will need to have two queries to determine whether f is constant or balanced, where each query would view the results of both $f(0)$ and $f(1)$ to conclude whether it is constant or balanced. When using Deutsch's quantum algorithm, we will see whether we can determine f using just one query that leverages the superposition principle. Let's see how in the next section.

Describing the problem as a quantum problem

Since we are working with quantum computations, we'll have to first switch to representing our functions and values using vectors. Therefore, our constant function, where both inputs result in the same output, can be represented in vector form as follows:

$$f(0) = 0 = \begin{bmatrix} 1 \\ 0 \end{bmatrix}$$

The results of this function with a different input having the same result can be represented as follows:

$$f(1) = 0 = \begin{bmatrix} 1 \\ 0 \end{bmatrix}$$

The function f can therefore be represented by the following matrix:

$$f = \begin{bmatrix} 1 & 1 \\ 0 & 0 \end{bmatrix}$$

Equally, the following is an example of a balanced function, where the results are the opposites of the two input values:

$$f(0) = 1 = \begin{bmatrix} 0 \\ 1 \end{bmatrix}$$

$$f(1) = 0 = \begin{bmatrix} 1 \\ 0 \end{bmatrix}$$

U_f will be our black box, or oracle function. To do this, we will need to extend our previous diagram to include the extra components necessary to create our oracle:

1. First, we will convert our input and output registers into Dirac **ket notation,** $|x\rangle$.

2. Next, we will create two input registers, $|x\rangle$ and $|y\rangle$, where the input registers will feed into our black box, or oracle function, U_f, and the $|y\rangle$ register is used as an ancillary qubit. Ancilla qubits are extra bits used to store information that might be used later or to track information throughout the quantum circuit.

3. Finally, we'll define our two output registers: one that is just the same as the input $|x\rangle$, and the other that is the **XOR** of the input register x and the input register x *XORed* with the function $f(x)$, as $|x, y \oplus f(x)\rangle$.

    Therefore, we can now define the oracle function as follows:

$$U_f : |x\rangle, |y\rangle \rightarrow |x\rangle, \qquad |y \oplus f(x)\rangle$$

This is illustrated as follows:

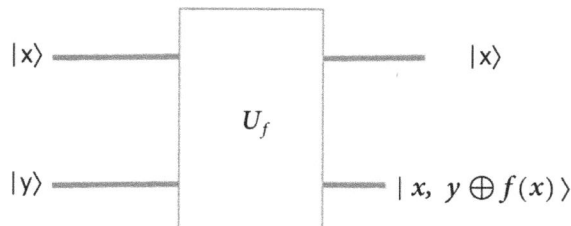

Figure 11.2: Graphical representation of the Deutsch algorithm

Another requirement is that the function should be reversible and we can test to see if it is by working it out in reverse:

$$U_f^{-1} : |x, y \oplus f(x)\rangle \rightarrow |x, y\rangle$$

Now that we have our function defined as a quantum function for our problem, we'll see how Deutsch's algorithm works.

Implementing Deutsch's algorithm

In this section, we will implement the algorithm with a balanced function as an example but will leave it to you to update the code to implement a constant function. We'll examine the Deutsch algorithm and step through each task as we build the algorithm on the IQL as follows:

1. Open a new Jupyter notebook where you have Qiskit installed, and in the first cell, include the helper file:

    ```
    %run helper_file_1.0.ipynb
    ```

2. Next, we will create a 2-qubit circuit and prepare each input, the first to $|0\rangle$ and the second to $|1\rangle$. We will use the identity gate to represent the $|0\rangle$, which is the initial state, and an X-gate to represent the initial state of $|1\rangle$:

    ```
    # Implement Deutsch's algorithm for a balanced function
    qc = QuantumCircuit(2,1)

    # Prepare the input qubits, where q0=0, q1=1
    print('Step 1: Prepare the input qubits, where q0=0, q1=1')
    qc.id(0)
    qc.x(1)
    qc.barrier()
    qc.draw(output='mpl')
    ```

This results in the following circuit diagram:

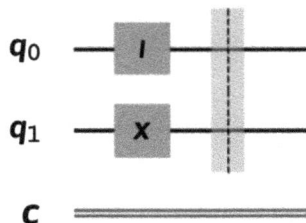

Figure 11.3: Initializing the qubits to 0 and 1

As you can see from the preceding diagram, q_0 is set to $|0\rangle$ and q_1 is set to $|1\rangle$, which creates the first state at the barrier (φ_0) as $|01\rangle$. The use of the barrier is just to indicate checkpoints as we traverse through each operation in the circuit.

3. Now that our inputs are set, we will place them in a superposition state using Hadamard gates. This will allow us to iterate through once while leveraging all four states, rather than iterating through each of them one at a time:

```
# Place each qubit in superposition by applying a
# Hadamard
print('Step 2: Place each qubit in superposition by      applying a
Hadamard')
qc.h(0)
qc.h(1)
qc.barrier()
qc.draw(output='mpl')
```

The result of the preceding code is illustrated in the following diagram. The barriers are used to separate each step so as to simplify reading the circuit:

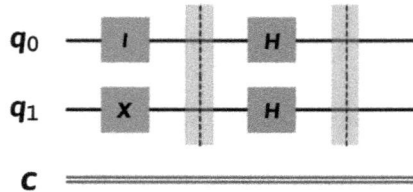

Figure 11.4: Applying Hadamard gates to both qubits

As you can see from the preceding diagram, the Hadamard gate transforms the basis vectors for each qubit as follows:

$$H|0\rangle = \frac{1}{\sqrt{2}}|0\rangle + \frac{1}{\sqrt{2}}|1\rangle = \frac{1}{\sqrt{2}}(|0\rangle + |1\rangle)$$

This generates the following state at the second barrier as φ_1, where $H|1\rangle$ describes a single qubit:

$$H|1\rangle = \frac{1}{\sqrt{2}}|0\rangle - \frac{1}{\sqrt{2}}|1\rangle = \frac{1}{\sqrt{2}}(|0\rangle - |1\rangle)$$

4. After the qubits have applied the preceding Hadamard gates, the resulting value for the quantum registers will be as follows:

$$\frac{1}{\sqrt{2}}\left(\,|00\rangle - |01\rangle + |01\rangle - |11\rangle\,\right)$$

One thing to note here is that we now have the second qubit in a $|-\rangle$ superposition, $H|1\rangle$. This allows us to define the first and second qubit out of U_f, as follows:

$$\left(\frac{(-1)^{f(0)}|0\rangle + (-1)^{f(1)}|1\rangle}{\sqrt{2}}\right)\left(\frac{|0\rangle - |1\rangle}{\sqrt{2}}\right)$$

From the preceding equation, you can see that the second qubit, grouped in the second set of parentheses, has the same value, which is the $|-\rangle$ superposition, $H|1\rangle$.

However, the first qubit we see has an interesting result. Let's dig a little deeper to understand what this means.

Here, we see that if f is constant, we'll have the following:

$$(\pm 1)\left(\frac{|0\rangle + |1\rangle}{\sqrt{2}}\right)\left(\frac{|0\rangle - |1\rangle}{\sqrt{2}}\right)$$

If f is balanced, then we'll have the following:

$$(\pm 1)\left(\frac{|0\rangle - |1\rangle}{\sqrt{2}}\right)\left(\frac{|0\rangle - |1\rangle}{\sqrt{2}}\right)$$

Note that the second qubit is always the same, but the first has a phase kickback from positive if constant, and negative if balanced. This phase kickback is a common trick used in many quantum algorithms, so rest assured we will see this again.

5. Next, by applying a Hadamard gate to the first qubit, we can see something interesting as a result. Let's look at this one at a time.

For a constant function, the first qubit is set to the following:

$$\left(\frac{|0\rangle + |1\rangle}{\sqrt{2}}\right)$$

We recall that applying a Hadamard gate to this superposition state will return us to the $|0\rangle$ state.

For the balanced function, the first qubit is set to the following superposition state:

$$\left(\frac{|0\rangle - |1\rangle}{\sqrt{2}}\right)$$

We can also recall that applying a Hadamard gate to the previous superposition state will return us to the $|1\rangle$ state.

This means that measuring only the first qubit after applying a Hadamard gate to it will provide us with a resulting state of either $|0\rangle$ or $|1\rangle$, constant or balanced, respectively.

6. Let's implement this using our Qiskit notebook.

This is where we wish to set a quantum gate that would operate on q_1, which represents the *y* value, based on the value of q_0, which represents the *x* value. Therefore, this operator, which we'll call U_f, will have inputs (x, y). The gate we will use to represent this will be a **Control-Not (CNOT)** gate. The reason for using this for the balanced function is because it produces the Bell states 01 and 10 with the input qubits. And, of course, this could be switched to the other two Bell states, 00 and 11, by adding an X gate, which would make this a constant function.

In this case, we are working to create a balanced function, one to one, which equates to the following:

$$f(0) = \tilde{f}(1)$$

To accomplish this, we will need to define our state operator, U_f, as follows:

$$U_f = \begin{bmatrix} 1 & 0 & 0 & 0 \\ 0 & 0 & 0 & 1 \\ 0 & 0 & 1 & 0 \\ 0 & 1 & 0 & 0 \end{bmatrix}$$

Now, we will place a CNOT gate with the control on the first qubit, q_0, and the target on the second qubit, q_1:

```
# Add a CNOT gate with the Control on q0 and Target on q1
qc.cx(0,1)
# Draw the circuit
qc.draw(output='mpl')
```

This should now include the CNOT gate that generates the function type (balanced) and renders the following diagram:

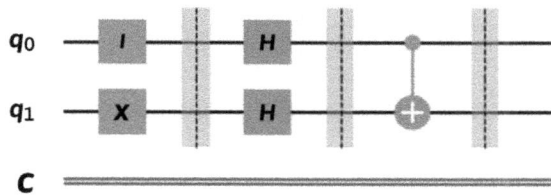

Figure 11.5: Defining the function type (balanced)

7. Next, we'll add Hadamard gates to all qubits and a measurement operator to the first qubit:

```
# Add the Hadamard gates to all qubits
qc.h(0)
qc.h(1)
qc.barrier()
```

As we saw in our equation earlier, we only need to apply a Hadamard gate to the first qubit, as we will only be measuring the one qubit:

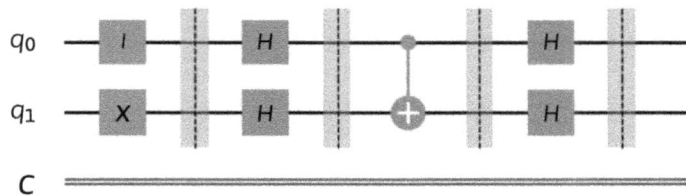

Figure 11.6: Applying the Hadamard gate to the qubits before measuring

This results in the following state, $|\psi\rangle$:

$$|\Psi\rangle = \frac{1}{2}\left[\left(\frac{1}{\sqrt{2}}|0\rangle + \frac{1}{\sqrt{2}}|1\rangle\right)\left(\frac{1}{\sqrt{2}}|0\rangle + \frac{1}{\sqrt{2}}|1\rangle\right)\right.$$

$$-\left(\frac{1}{\sqrt{2}}|0\rangle + \frac{1}{\sqrt{2}}|1\rangle\right)\left(\frac{1}{\sqrt{2}}|0\rangle - \frac{1}{\sqrt{2}}|1\rangle\right)$$

$$-\left(\frac{1}{\sqrt{2}}|0\rangle - \frac{1}{\sqrt{2}}|1\rangle\right)\left(\frac{1}{\sqrt{2}}|0\rangle + \frac{1}{\sqrt{2}}|1\rangle\right)$$

$$\left.+\left(\frac{1}{\sqrt{2}}|0\rangle - \frac{1}{\sqrt{2}}|1\rangle\right)\left(\frac{1}{\sqrt{2}}|0\rangle - \frac{1}{\sqrt{2}}|1\rangle\right)\right]$$

Let's now apply some algebra to simplify our results:

$$|\Psi\rangle = -\frac{1}{2}(|00\rangle + |01\rangle - |10\rangle - |11\rangle)$$

Since we will only be measuring the first qubit, we can throw the second qubit away or just not measure it as it is just an ancillary qubit in this case.

8. Let's take a measurement of the first qubit, shown as follows, the result of which will determine the category of the function as either balanced (1) or constant (0):

```
# Add measurement operator to the first qubit
qc.measure(0,0)
```

We already know from the previous equation that this should equate to a balanced function:

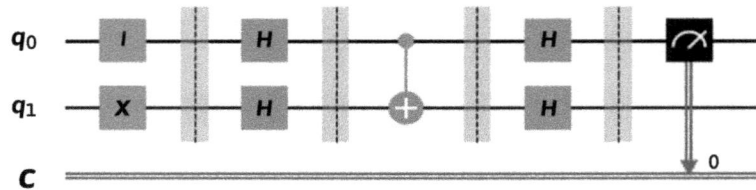

Figure 11.7: Applying the measurement operator to just the first qubit

9. Next, to simplify a few things, let's define a function to run our circuits on a Sampler installed on your local machine. We'll use the following function, which leverages the `StatevectorSampler`:

```
# Run on a Sampler
def run_on_sampler(circuit):
    from qiskit.primitives import StatevectorSampler
    # Construct a Statevector Sampler
    sampler = StatevectorSampler()
    # Run using the Sampler
    result = sampler.run([circuit]).result()
    return result
```

10. Now we can run the preceding circuit and verify our results by using the following code:

```
# Execute the quantum circuit on the simulator first to
# confirm our results.
print('Step 6: Execute the circuit to view results.')
result = run_on_sampler(qc)
counts = result[0].data.c.get_counts()
# Print and plot our results
print(counts)
plot_distribution(counts, title='Balanced function')
```

As calculated previously, the results of this experiment indicate a balanced function, as indicated by the result 1, rather than 0.

This results in the following output:

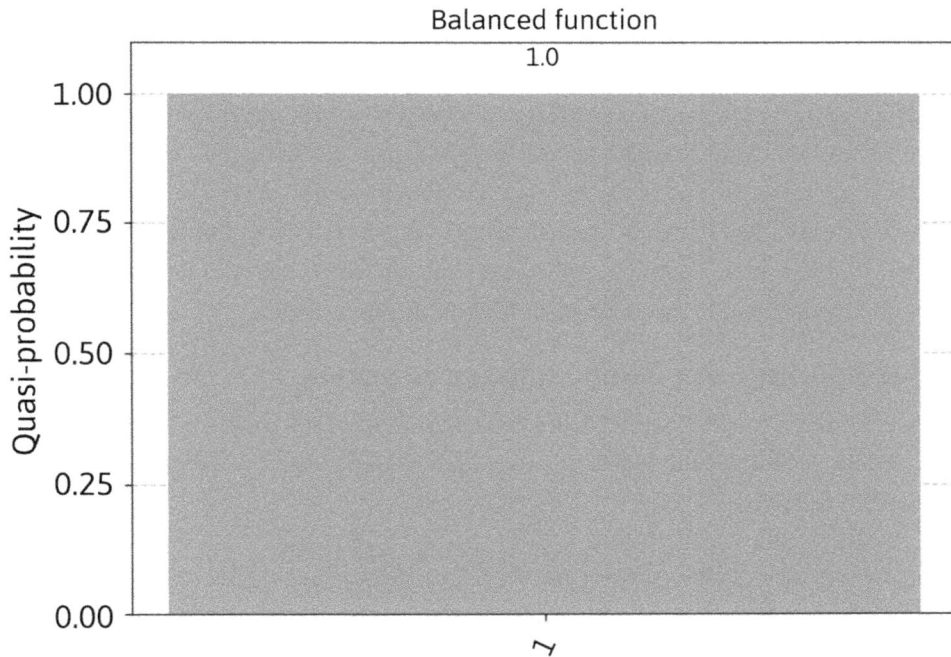

Figure 11.8: Result of value 1, indicating a balanced function

As expected, we see that our result is **1**, indicating a balanced function.

Observe that to retrieve the counts from the results, we need to map to the data object and then to the name of the classical register that we wish to extract the counts from.

From the preceding output, the result shows the same as what we expected for the given function we provided, which, in this case, is the balanced function, where 1 has a higher probability. There is an exercise in the *Questions* section where you are required to create a constant function.

What we have shown here is the potential of a quantum algorithm to perform operations faster than a classical system, which would otherwise need to calculate each function in series for each input. Naturally, this exercise does not offer any real-world applications, but it does help in understanding how these systems have potential speedup properties. In the next section, we will look at generalizing this example by applying it to more than one qubit.

Understanding the Deutsch-Jozsa algorithm

In the previous section, the Deutsch algorithm provided us with an example of quantum speedup where we use two qubits but only measure one qubit. Here, the **Deutsch-Jozsa** algorithm provides a more generalized form of the algorithm. It can be applied to more than one qubit. Originally proposed by David Deutsch and Richard Jozsa in 1992, with improvements by Richard Cleve, Artur Ekert, Chiara Macchiavello, and Michele Mosca in 1998, the problem is still the same, but as we mentioned at the end of the previous section, the problem is now extended to more than just a single qubit. The Deutsch-Jozsa algorithm will operate on multiple qubits at once, and, of course, will still provide a quantum speedup compared with classical computing as it would need to calculate each event in series, as we will see in the next section.

Understanding the Deutsch-Jozsa problem

In this example, we will extend the previous definition of the problem. Previously, we defined our problem on a single-bit value function to determine whether a function was constant or balanced, as follows:

$$f: \{0,1\} \rightarrow \{0,1\}$$

In this case, we will expand the problem to include more than one bit as an input, such that:

$$f: \{0,1\}^n \rightarrow \{0,1\}$$

You can see from the preceding equation that f is *constant* if $f(x)$ is the same for all, that is, $x \in \{0,1\}^n$. Otherwise, f is *balanced* if $f(x) = 0$ for half of x, and $f(x) = 1$ for the other half of x. For example, if we set n equal to 2 in our input values, $\{0,1\}^n$, then this will result in four different input values, that is, 00, 01, 10, and 11.

Based on these four possible input values of x, to create a balanced function, we can set the first half of the results to 0, such that:

Input 1	Input 2	Output
0	0	0
0	1	0

We can set the second half of the results to 1:

Input 1	Input 2	Output
1	0	1
1	1	1

If we were to solve this classically, we would need $2^{n-1} + 1$ queries to determine whether the results are constant or balanced. On the other hand, the Deutsch-Jozsa algorithm will only require one query in order to determine whether the function is constant or balanced, just as in the Deutsch algorithm.

Generating a quantum solution using the Deutsch-Jozsa algorithm

To generate our quantum circuit to implement the Deutsch-Jozsa algorithm, we will use some of the same components as before:

1. Let's start with our inputs to our black box (oracle). The first input register is an n-bit string representing the input X. We denote this with a capital X, as most texts refer to single qubit or bit values with a lowercase variable such as $|x\rangle$, whereas multi-qubits are represented by uppercase variables such as $|X\rangle$.

    The second input register is a single-bit string representing the input y, which, as before, is initialized to 1. This is commonly referred to as an **ancilla qubit**.

2. Next, we define the function of the oracle similar to how we did in the previous form. However, the difference here is that $|x\rangle$ is now a multi-qubit input, $|X\rangle$. U_f is then defined as follows:

$$U_f: |X\rangle|y\rangle \rightarrow |X\rangle|y \oplus f(X)\rangle$$

So, our output would similarly map to two outputs. The first is the same as the first input $|X\rangle$, and the second output is our function $|y \oplus f(X)\rangle$. This results in the following graphical representation:

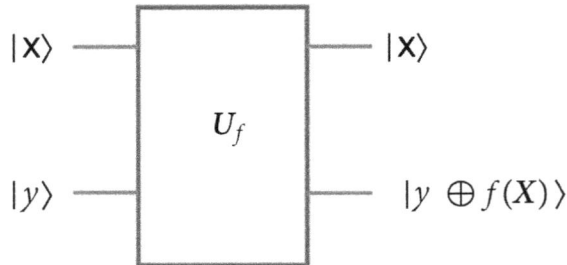

Figure 11.9: Graphical representation of the Deutsch-Jozsa algorithm

Now that we have defined our components, let's implement this block digram as a circuit in the next section.

Implementing the Deutsch-Jozsa algorithm

In this example we will implement the Deutsch-Jozsa algorithm to determine that a given function is constant in one query, whereas determining the same on a classical system will require multiple queries, therefore illustrating how using quantum computing can provide a speedup.

In order to implement the Deutsch-Jozsa algorithm, create a new Qiskit notebook and run the boilerplate cell to load up all our Qiskit modules. Once the setup is complete, let's create our circuit step by step and see how it resolves our problem as we go:

1. First, let's set our input values. We will start by creating a quantum circuit with two inputs, the first set to X, which we will create as a 4-qubit input, followed by a single qubit representing y, which we will initialize to 1. Then we will apply a Hadamard gate to all the input qubits:

```
# Create the quantum circuit with both input registers X,
# and y
input_qubits = 4  # Refers to our X input register,
#4-qubits
ancilla_qubit = 1 # Refers to our y input register,
#1--qubit
# Total qubits in our quantum circuit
total_qubits = input_qubits + ancilla_qubit
# Generate the circuit
```

```
qc = QuantumCircuit(total_qubits, input_qubits)
# Set the X qubits in superposition
for idx in range(input_qubits):
    qc.h(idx)

# Set the y qubit to 1, then apply a Hadamard
qc.x(input_qubits)
qc.h(input_qubits)
qc.barrier()
qc.draw(output='mpl')
```

This will result in the following diagram:

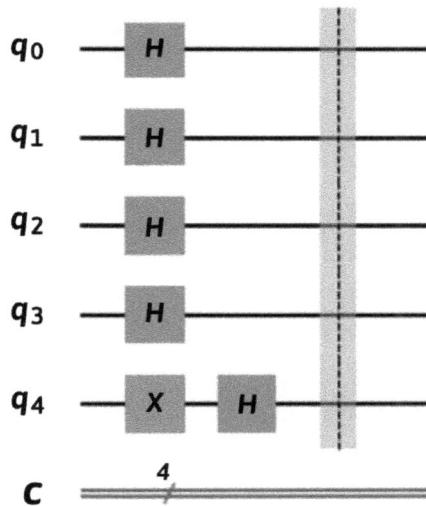

Figure 11.10: Preparing the input values of our quantum circuit

The input state results in the following:

$$|\psi\rangle = |0\rangle^{\otimes n}|1\rangle$$

When we apply a Hadamard gate to the preceding equation, it breaks out into the following:

$$H|0\rangle^{\otimes n} = \frac{1}{\sqrt{2}}\left((|0\rangle + |1\rangle)^0 \otimes (|0\rangle + |1\rangle)^1 \otimes \ldots \otimes (|0\rangle + |1\rangle)^{n-1}\right)$$

When we apply a Hadamard gate to the single qubit $|y\rangle$, this gives us the following equation:

$$H|1\rangle = \frac{1}{\sqrt{2}}(|0\rangle - |1\rangle)$$

Simplifying both $H|0\rangle^{\oplus n}$ and $H|1\rangle$ gives us the following equation:

$$|\psi\rangle = H^{\otimes n}|0\rangle^{\otimes n}H|1\rangle = \frac{1}{\sqrt{2^n}}\sum_{X\in\{0,1\}^n}|X\rangle\left(\frac{|0\rangle - |1\rangle}{\sqrt{2}}\right)$$

2. Next, we will create the oracle U_f function for our circuit similar to how we created it in the previous section on the Deutsch algorithm. We will use the same here, only this time, we have the ket X, which is more than a single bit of information:

$$|\psi\rangle = \frac{1}{\sqrt{2^n}}\sum_{x\in\{0,1\}^n}(-1)^{f(x)}|x\rangle\left(\frac{|0\rangle - |1\rangle}{\sqrt{2}}\right)$$

The value of x is the bit representation of the bit string X of 0 or 1.

3. Let's now set our input state using a bit string to represent the balanced U_f function—in this case, '1010', which we construct by placing an X gate with the set bits and Identity gates with the others. This will allow us to determine whether the input is balanced or constant—in this case, since we have an equal number of 1s and 0s, it is balanced. You can also just not add an Identity gate, but for now, we will add one just to visually indicate the 0 values of the bit string:

```
# Set the bit string which we wish to evaluate,
# in this case set '1010', where I indicates value 0,
# and x indicates value 1.
qc.id(0)
qc.x(1)
qc.id(2)
qc.x(3)

qc.barrier()
qc.draw(output='mpl')
```

This will render the following addition to our circuit, where the added section represents setting the input state $|1010\rangle$ based on the bit string 1010:

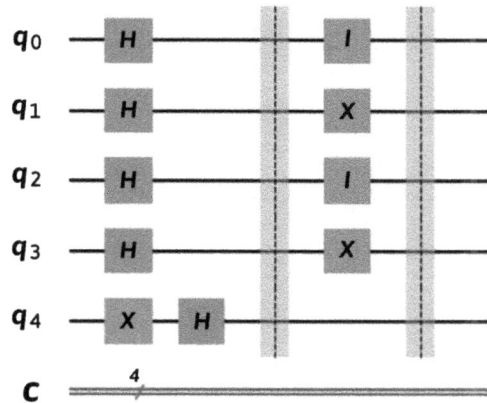

Figure 11.11: State representation $|1010\rangle$ of the bit string 1010

4. Next, we will apply our oracle. In this case, we will set it to a constant output where all outputs should be 1s, with zero probability of 0s. We'll do so by adding CNOT gates, where the Control is applied to each qubit and the Target is set to the last qubit:

```
# Set oracle to either constant (output = 0s)
# or balanced (output = 1s)
# In this example we will choose a balanced function
for idx in range(input_qubits):
    qc.cx(idx, input_qubits)
qc.barrier()
qc.draw(output='mpl')
```

The result of this should be as follows, where we set each Control of the CNOT gate to all qubits and the Target to our ancilla qubit, q_4:

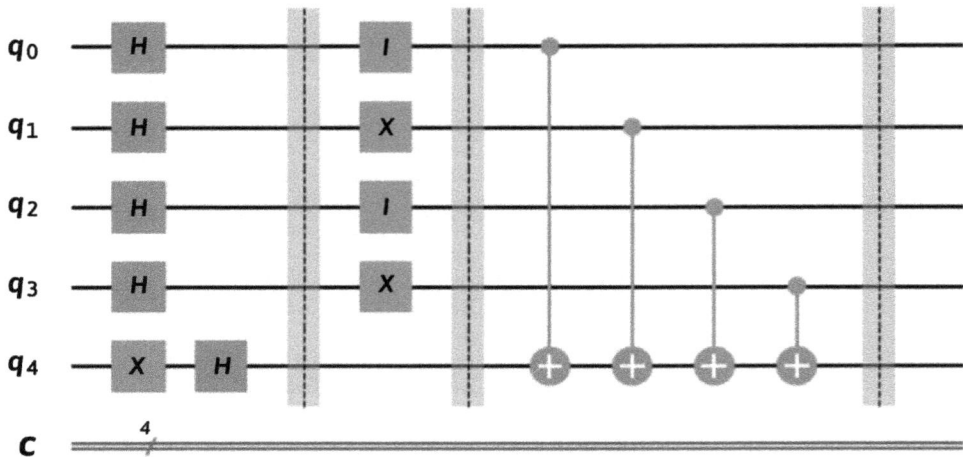

Figure 11.12: Representation of the added balanced oracle

5. Next, we will set the closing bit string, which we use to wrap our oracle—in this case, '1010':

```
# Set the closing bit string we selected earlier to
# evaluate
qc.id(0)
qc.x(1)
qc.id(2)
qc.x(3)
qc.barrier()
qc.draw(output='mpl')
```

The preceding code will give us the following diagram, just as we expected, where the oracle is bound by the bit string:

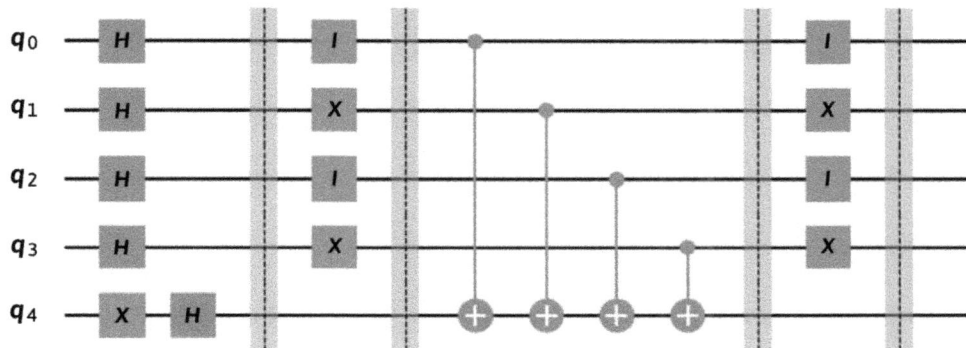

Figure 11.13: Oracle bounded by the bit string representation

6. Next, we will apply the Hadamard gates to all the qubits:

```
# Add the Hadamard gates to complete wrapping the oracle
for idx in range(4):
    qc.h(idx)
qc.barrier()
qc.draw(output='mpl')
```

The result of this is rendered as follows:

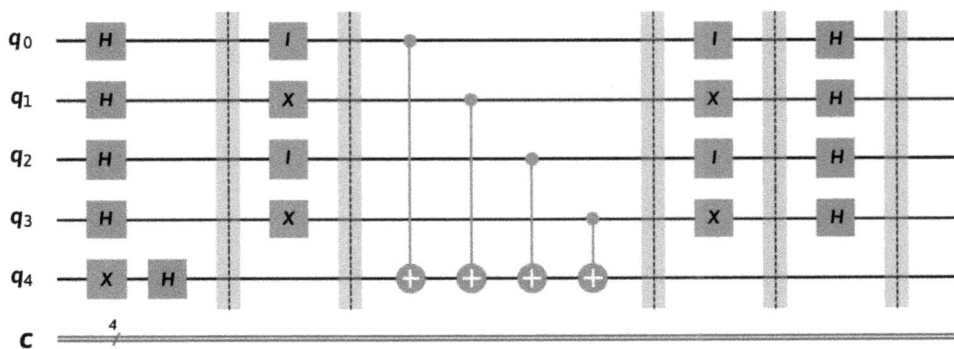

Figure 11.14: A complete quantum circuit of the Deutsch-Jozsa algorithm for a balanced function

7. Finally, we will add our measurements so that we can read out the results. We will apply the measurements only to the first four qubits:

```
# Add measurements only to our inputs
qc.measure(range(4),range(4))
# Draw the circuit
qc.draw(output='mpl')
```

Therefore, our final quantum circuit should be as follows. Each step in creating the Deutsch-Jozsa algorithm is separated by the barriers, where the first is the preparation, the second is to set the bit string 1010, the third is to set our oracle U_f, and then we reverse the first two steps, followed by our measurements:

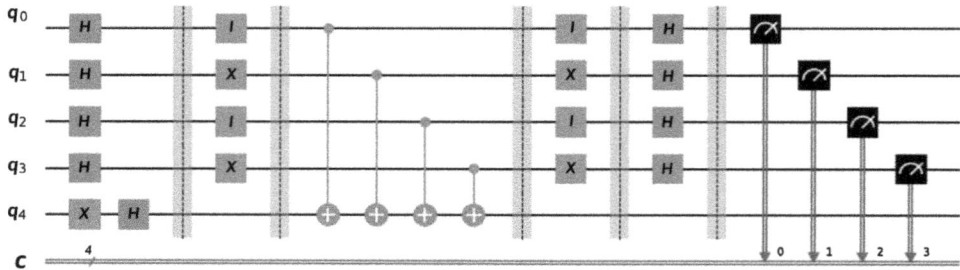

Figure 11.15: Final circuit for the Deutsch-Jozsa algorithm

8. Now that we have created our quantum circuit for the Deutsch-Jozsa algorithm, let's execute the circuit on a simulator first to visualize what results we get back:

```
# Run the circuit
result = run_on_sampler(qc)
counts = result[0].data.c.get_counts()
# Print and plot results
print(counts)
plot_distribution(counts)
```

As expected, our results returned a probability of 100% of 1s for a balanced circuit:

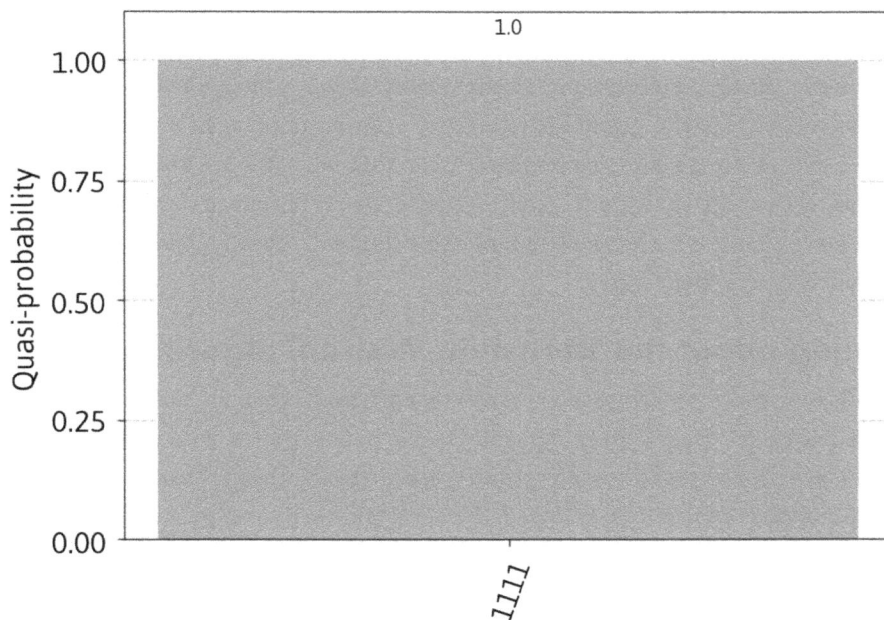

Figure 11.16: Results from the simulator of a balanced function

As expected, we see that we have a high quasi-probability of 1111. This was computed using a single query, as opposed to the multiple queries that we would have needed to compute the same thing classically.

Now that we have completed both the Deutsch and Deutsch-Jozsa algorithms, we can see that there is some speedup when compared to classical systems. However, we can also see that there are no practical or real-world examples where we can apply these algorithms. That said, we have understood how the use of superposition and entanglement can speed up certain functions compared to classical techniques. We'll expand our understanding of algorithms into something that is a bit more of a generalized quantum algorithm, namely, Bernstein-Vazirani, in the next section.

Learning about the foundational oracle-based quantum algorithm

We learned in the previous section that the very early quantum algorithms illustrated quantum speedup vis-à-vis classical systems in relation to a simple problem. In this section, we will expand on this to look at a more complex problem. To do this, we will learn about another oracle-based algorithm, **Bernstein-Vazirani**. The difference between this one and the previous foundational algorithms is that the Bernstein-Vazirani algorithm will identify a hidden bit string using an oracle function in a single query.

Learning about the Bernstein-Vazirani algorithm

Originally invented in 1992 by Ethan Bernstein and Umesh Vazirani, the Bernstein-Vazirani algorithm extends the Deutsch-Jozsa algorithm to a generalization to find an unknown or secret bit string. Where the Deutsch-Jozsa algorithm worked to solve the problem of determining whether a given function is constant or balanced, the Bernstein-Vazirani algorithm works to determine a secret number by applying a function that maps an input to its output.

Understanding the Bernstein-Vazirani problem

The problem that the Bernstein-Vazirani algorithm addresses is straightforward and similar to the previous problem. Given an unknown function, or black box (oracle), similar to the Deutsch-Jozsa oracle, an input string of bits results in an output of either 0 or 1. A simple example could be a logical expression that maps the input values to a single output value of either 0 or 1:

$$f: \{0,1\}^n \rightarrow \{0,1\}$$

For this function f, we are guaranteed that the following applies:

$$f(x) = s \cdot x \ (\mathrm{mod} \ 2)$$

From the preceding equation, s is an unknown or secret string such that:

$$s \in \{0,1\}^n$$

The problem, therefore, is to find the secret value s.

Solving this classically is the same as the previous examples, where we would have to check each value one bit at a time to determine the secret value, s. However, as we have seen in the previous examples, we can solve this with a quantum algorithm executing a single query. Let's walk through the example to see how we can solve this using the Bernstein-Vazirani algorithm.

Generating a quantum solution using the Bernstein-Vazirani algorithm

The Bernstein-Vazirani algorithm is very similar to Deutsch-Jozsa in that it performs the same steps to create the quantum circuit for the algorithm:

1. Initialize all n input qubits to the ground state $|0\rangle$.

2. Initialize the ancilla qubit to the excited state $|1\rangle$.

3. Apply a Hadamard gate to all input qubits and the ancilla qubit, $H^{n+1}|0\rangle^{\oplus n}|1\rangle$.

4. Query the oracle to apply a phase change based on the secret string value using CNOT gates.

5. Apply another set of Hadamard gates to the input qubits.

6. Measure the input qubits to obtain the secret string.

As you can see from the preceding steps, the algorithm is very similar. However, the main differentiator here is *steps 4* and *5*. When a qubit hits the secret key, we then apply a phase shift, that is, when $s_i = 1$, where s_i is the ith term of the secret string. Then, in *step 5*, when we apply the second set of Hadamard gates, the qubit will return from $|-\rangle$ to $|1\rangle$ if $s_i = 1$, or from $|+\rangle$ to $|0\rangle$ if $s_i = 0$.

Let's implement these steps one at a time and review the changes to the state. As before, we will use barriers to separate each step so that we can visualize each step along the way.

Implementing the Bernstein-Vazirani algorithm

The following steps are a step-by-step guide to creating the **Bernstein-Vazirani** algorithm and describe the outcome of each step to help you understand how each step affects the state, which will eventually produce the secret string:

1. Start by creating a new Qiskit notebook with the usual boilerplate cell that will load much of the base Qiskit modules and our account, so that we can execute the quantum circuit on an actual quantum computer.

    First, we will create our quantum circuit, which will be made up of four qubits, and one ancilla qubit, and we will define our **secret bit string** (shh):

    ```python
    # Create your secret number
    shh = '1010'
    # Set the number of qubits to represent secret number and
    # an ancilla qubit
    input_qubits = len(shh)
    ancilla_qubit = 1
    ```

```
total_qubits = input_qubits + ancilla_qubit
# Create the quantum circuit
qc = QuantumCircuit(total_qubits, input_qubits)
```

The preceding code creates our base quantum circuit, qc, which we will use to construct the Bernstein-Vazirani algorithm. The input qubits must be at least the length of our secret string, which, in this case, is the value 1010. Our input register will need to be at least this many qubits in length. We then added an ancilla qubit, which, in the previous examples, we referred to as the output qubit. Moving forward, we will start referring to this qubit as an ancilla qubit in that it is more of a utility qubit that will not be measured or output to our results.

2. Next, we will add Hadamard gates to the input qubits to ensure that all input qubits are set to a superposition state:

```
# Add Hadamard gates to the input qubits
for idx in range(input_qubits):
    qc.h(idx)
# Draw the input circuit
qc.draw(output='mpl')
```

This will render our quantum circuit as follows:

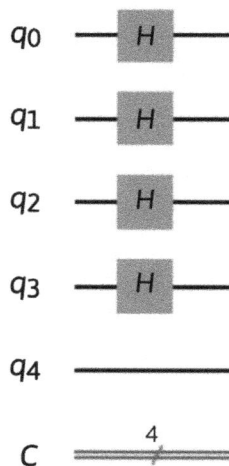

Figure 11.17: Initializing the input qubits' state from $|0\rangle$ *to a superposition state,* $|+\rangle$

3. Next, we will need to prepare our ancilla qubit, q_4, just as we did before, by first initializing it to the state $|1\rangle$, followed by a Hadamard gate, which will prepare the state of the ancilla qubit to $|-\rangle$:

```
# Prepare the ancilla qubit of the circuit
qc.x(total_qubits-1)
qc.h(total_qubits-1)
qc.barrier()

# Draw the prepared circuit
qc.draw(output='mpl')
```

The preceding code will render the following circuit, which we see is the same initialization of our circuit as before. This is how most quantum algorithms are initialized, which allows working with all possible combinations of qubit states. The barrier is added simply to view the various state changes:

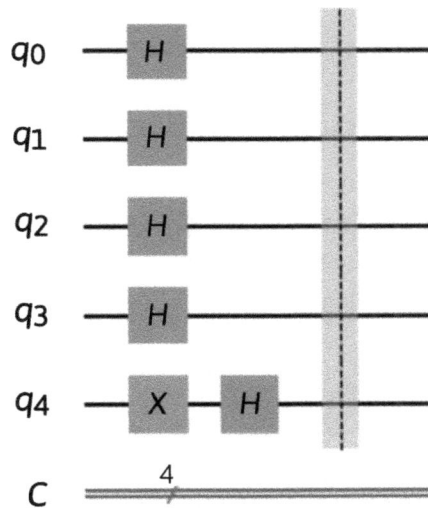

Figure 11.18: Initialization of all qubits

The state at the first barrier is now set to the following, where the input qubits are as follows:

$$|0\rangle^n \to \frac{1}{\sqrt{2^n}} \sum_{x \in \{0,1\}^n} |x\rangle$$

The ancilla qubit is set to:

$$|1\rangle \rightarrow \frac{|0\rangle - |1\rangle}{\sqrt{2}}$$

4. Next, we need to make a quick bit order adjustment before we apply our oracle function. Since the qubits are ordered from right to left, we will need to reverse the order of our secret number:

```
# Before creating the oracle, we need to adjust the
# qubits. Since they are ordered from left to right,
# we will reverse the secret number's current value
print('Secret before reverse: ', shh)
# Reverse order
shh = shh[::-1]
print('Secret after reverse: ', shh)
```

As you can see from the following output, the order is now 0101, so we can now apply our oracle function:

```
Secret before reverse:  1010
Secret after reverse:  0101
```

5. To apply the oracle function, we want to trigger a phase shift each time we hit a '1' in the secret string. To do that, we will apply a CNOT gate to each qubit, where the Control is set to each qubit and the Target is linked to the ancilla. In our case, the secret string has '1' set on **qubit 1** (q_1) and **qubit 3** (q_3):

```
# Now that we have the right order,
# let's create the oracle by applying a CNOT,
# where the qubits set to '1' are the source
# and the target would be the ancilla qubit
for idx in range(input_qubits):
    if shh[idx] == '1':
        qc.cx(idx, input_qubits)
qc.barrier()
qc.draw(output='mpl')
```

The preceding code renders the quantum circuit up to the oracle:

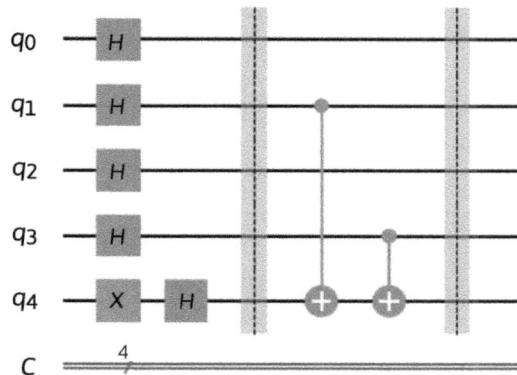

Figure 11.19: Oracle applying CNOT where the secret string is set to '1'

Since all our qubits are in a superposition state, by applying the phase shift based on the secret string $|S\rangle$, we get the following equation:

$$|S\rangle = \left(\frac{|0\rangle + (-1)^{s0} |1\rangle}{\sqrt{2}}\right) \otimes \left(\frac{|0\rangle + (-1)^{s1} |1\rangle}{\sqrt{2}}\right) \otimes \ldots \otimes \left(\frac{|0\rangle + (-1)^{sn} |1\rangle}{\sqrt{2}}\right)$$

Therefore, from the preceding equation, our secret string $|S\rangle$ will apply a phase shift to each qubit where the string is set. This will shift the $|+\rangle$ to $|-\rangle$ whenever the input bit x and the secret string s are equal to 1.

6. Finally, in our last step before applying measurements to the input qubits, we apply another set of Hadamard gates. What this set of Hadamard gates achieves is that it will return the state of each qubit back to either the $|0\rangle$ or $|1\rangle$ state.

This is entirely dependent on whether the qubit experienced a phase shift while passing through the oracle. If it did not, then the state would change from $|+\rangle$ to $|0\rangle$, or from $|-\rangle$ to $|1\rangle$:

```
# Now let's close up our circuit with Hadamard gates
# applied to the input qubits
for idx in range(input_qubits):
    qc.h(idx)
qc.barrier()
# Finally, let's add measurements to our input qubits
qc.measure(range(input_qubits), range(input_qubits))
qc.draw(output='mpl')
```

This will render the following circuit diagram, which completes the steps to implement the Bernstein-Vazirani algorithm along with the measurement operators:

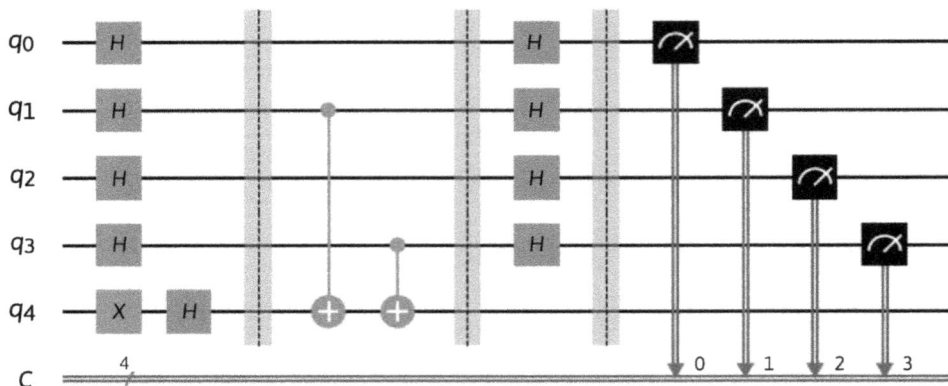

Figure 11.20: Final circuit that implements the Bernstein-Vazirani algorithm

7. Now that the circuit is complete and ready to go, we can execute the circuit on your local simulator and then on a real quantum device:

```
# Execute the circuit and plot the results
result = run_on_sampler(qc)
counts = result[0].data.c.get_counts()
plot_distribution(counts)
```

The results should have a 100% probability for the value of our secret string, as illustrated in the following histogram:

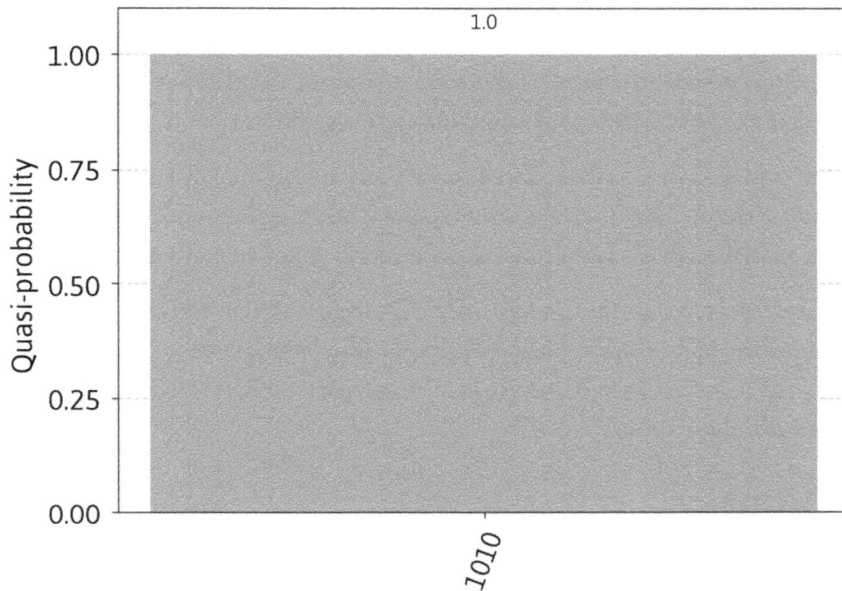

Figure 11.21: Result identifies with 100% probability the value of our secret string

As you can see from the preceding result, like the earlier quantum algorithms, we can solve certain problems in a single query, whereas it would take classical systems a few queries to solve. These problems leveraged **phase kickback**, where we used the phase to solve the question of whether the function was balanced or constant.

Looking back at the step where we applied the last layer of Hadamard gates, it appears as if the control qubit got flipped instead of the other qubit.

In this section, we learned about the foundational oracle-based algorithms and how they illustrate quantum advantage over classical systems to solve problems. We also learned about how oracles and ancilla qubits are leveraged to obtain some of the solutions, which will, in turn, help you understand the more complex algorithms as you expand your knowledge and research. Although these were simple problems that have no commercial value by themselves, they did, however, manage to trigger an interest in the quantum information science field that is still growing to this day.

Summary

In this chapter, we covered some of the many quantum algorithms that employ common techniques that are used in a variety of other quantum algorithms.

The goal of this chapter was to explore each of them systematically so you could have a good understanding of the problem each algorithm solves. The topics here are, of course, foundational and oracle-based, although the techniques are commonly found in many other quantum algorithms.

In the next chapter, we will step away from the oracle-based foundational algorithms and look at another form of algorithm that solves similar problems. However, rather than using phases to identify the solution, they will instead leverage periodicity, which is primarily why they are called **periodic algorithms**.

Questions

1. Which algorithm would you use to determine whether an n-bit string is balanced?

2. Implement the Bernstein-Vazirani algorithm to find the state 170.

3. How many oracle functions are there?

Join us on Discord

Join our community's Discord space for discussions with the author and other readers:

`https://packt.link/3FyN1`

12

Applying Quantum Algorithms

In the last chapter, we considered the fundamentals that highlight the difference between classical and quantum systems, particularly the use of superposition and entanglement. In this chapter, we will focus on algorithms that have the potential to solve more applicable problems, such as periodicity and searching. These algorithms differ from the earlier algorithms as they are used in various domains and are included in many modern quantum algorithms. A few examples of these quantum algorithms are the **quantum amplitude estimation**, **variational quantum eigensolvers**, and **quantum support vector machine** algorithms. Having a good understanding of these algorithms will help you when learning about or creating your own algorithms as the techniques used can be applied in many industries. In this chapter, we will cover some of the fundamental principles and techniques that these more modern, and complex, algorithms leverage, to help you better understand them.

Periodic algorithms can be used to solve factorization or phase estimation problems. **Search algorithms** can also provide some speedup over classical algorithms in how they leverage amplitude amplification to find a specified entry.

The following topics will be covered in this chapter:

- Understanding periodic quantum algorithms
- Understanding the Quantum Fourier Transform algorithm
- Understanding Grover's search algorithm

After completing this chapter, you will be able to grasp the concepts of these algorithms and leverage the algorithms already provided in **Qiskit**, so you can use them without having to *reinvent the wheel*.

Technical requirements

This chapter assumes that you are familiar with some of the basic quantum algorithm components, such as superposition, oracles, phase kickback, and programming with Qiskit. You are also expected to understand basic linear algebra, such as multiplying matrices, the complex conjugation of a matrix, and inner products. Some advanced mathematics, such as an understanding of the **Fourier transform**, is also assumed.

Here is the source code used throughout this book: `https://github.com/PacktPublishing/Learning-Quantum-Computing-with-Python-and-IBM-Quantum-Second-Edition`.

Understanding periodic quantum algorithms

In *Chapter 11, Understanding Quantum Algorithms*, we covered algorithms that use phase kickback to solve various problems.

In this section, we will start by understanding periodic quantum algorithms. Periodic functions are those where values are repeated over time. Your watch, for example, is periodic in that each minute has 60 seconds, each hour has 60 minutes, and each day has 24 hours.

If you have your watch set up with the hours from 1 to 12, then your watch has 2 periods per day, in that your watch will cycle through the numbers 1 to 12 twice in one day. Of course, this is separate from the AM and PM indicators, whether it is before or after midday. Periodic functions occur all around us in many ways, so understanding how to relate them to a quantum circuit is key to understanding many of the quantum algorithms, including one of the most famous, **Grover's algorithm**.

But for now, we will begin by extending our understanding of periodic functions, particularly how we can understand and implement the **Quantum Fourier Transform** (**QFT**) algorithm.

Learning about the QFT algorithm

QFT is related to **Discrete Fourier Transform** (**DFT**) in that it too can transform from one domain to another.

> **DFT** converts a finite sequence of samples into a complex-valued function of frequency that is used to analyze many applications, such as image processing and signal processing, and can also be used to help solve partial differential equations.

DFT is used to transfer signals from the time domain to the frequency domain, or in a more generalized description, mapping one domain, x, to another domain, $F(\omega)$, with the following formula:

$$F(\omega) \ = \ \sum_{j=0}^{N-1} e^{\frac{2\pi i k j}{N}} x_j$$

Similarly, we can define a quantum transformation as a transformation from one basis to another. For example, all the computations we have done in this book so far have been measured according to the Z basis. This means our basis states have been set on the Z-axis of the qubit with the states $|0\rangle$ and $|1\rangle$, referring to the positive and negative ends of the Z-axis on the Bloch sphere, respectively.

There are, of course, other basis states that we can transition to if needed. One example is the X-axis of the qubit, where the basis states there are $|+\rangle$ and $|-\rangle$, which refer to the positive and negative ends of the X-axis on the Bloch sphere, respectively. QFT would transform between these two basis states. The QFT is used by many quantum algorithms, including Shor's, as it has been shown to have improvements over the classical implementation of a discrete Fourier transform.

In this section, we will work through a simple example of a QFT algorithm to extend our understanding of it when we see it used in many other quantum algorithms.

We'll begin by applying QFT to a simple three-qubit quantum state.

Understanding the QFT algorithm

Before getting into the details, let's first get an understanding of what each axis represents. As you recall from the Bloch sphere, one of the visual representations of a qubit, it is made up of three axes, X, Y, and Z. Rotations around the X and Y axes are what we use to adjust the amplitude of the qubit, that is, down along the longitude of the Bloch sphere (the North Pole to the South Pole). Rotation around the Z-axis is what we use to adjust the phase of the qubit, that is, around the latitude of the Bloch sphere.

Each axis is a basis state, named by the axis, i.e. X-basis, Y-basis, and Z-basis. In quantum, the Z-axis is generally referred to as the computational basis and either the X- and Y-axis can be the Fourier basis. In this example, we will set the X-basis as the Fourier basis. The QFT transform is generally a transformation from one basis to another, in this case, from the computational (Z) basis to the Fourier (X) basis.

To transform our quantum function from one basis state to another, we need to apply QFT, as follows:

$$|Z - \text{basis}\rangle \xrightarrow{\text{QFT}} |X - \text{basis}\rangle$$

In the preceding equation, $Z - basis$ refers to the basis states on the Z-axis, $|0\rangle$ and $|1\rangle$, and $X - basis$ refers to the basis states (often referred to as the phase states because rotation around them refers to rotations around the Z-axis) on the X-axis, $|+\rangle$ and $|-\rangle$. The Qiskit documentation (https://docs.quantum.ibm.com/) refers to the Fourier basis with a tilde (~), where *QFT* is the QFT Transform applied to the state $|1\rangle$, given as follows:

$$\text{QFT}\,|x\rangle = |\tilde{x}\rangle$$

This can be equated, where the transformation is represented by the QFT between the amplitudes of x_j and y_k, as follows:

$$\sum_{j=0}^{N-1} x_j\,|j\rangle \xrightarrow{QFT} \sum_{k=0}^{N-1} y_k\,|k\rangle$$

Now, let's see how we can implement QFT in a quantum circuit.

Implementing the QFT algorithm

Let's begin by deriving our implementation based on an input state $|\Psi\rangle$,.

An alternative is to apply it sequentially to the following formula as we move from qubit to qubit. For this example, we will operate as follows; given a state $|\Psi\rangle = |j_{n-1}, j_{n-2}, \ldots, j_1, j_0\rangle$, we will apply a Hadamard gate where we add the phase based on the state $|\Psi\rangle$, where each value, j_i, is appended to the phase, as follows:

$$|\Psi\rangle = \frac{(|0\rangle + e^{2\pi i(0.j_0)}|1\rangle)\ldots(|0\rangle + e^{2\pi i(0.j_{n-2}\,\cdots\,j_0)}|1\rangle)(|0\rangle + e^{2\pi i(0.j_{n-1}\,\cdots\,j_0)}|1\rangle)}{\sqrt{2^n}}$$

In the following exercise, we will implement the QFT of $|\Psi\rangle = |110\rangle$, where $j_2 = 1, j_1 = 1, j_0 = 0$. It's important to note that the fractional parts of the exponents are binary, not decimal:

1. We'll begin by opening a new Jupyter notebook and import some common objects and run our helper file:

    ```
    # Importing standard Qiskit libraries
    from qiskit import QuantumCircuit, transpile
    from qiskit.transpiler.preset_passmanagers import
    ```

```
                        generate_preset_pass_manager
from qiskit.visualization import *
from qiskit_ibm_runtime import QiskitRuntimeService, Sampler,
Estimator, Session, Options


service = QiskitRuntimeService(channel="ibm_quantum")
```

2. Next, we'll create a quantum circuit where the width is equal to the length of our state value, `'110'`:

```
# Initialize the 3-qubit quantum circuit
# Set the state '110'
s = '110'
num_qubits = len(s)
qc = QuantumCircuit(num_qubits)
```

3. Now that we have created our quantum circuit, let's initialize the state, s, to $|110\rangle$. Since we write from the least significant position, we will reverse s accordingly as well:

```
# Set reverse ordering
s = s[::-1]
# Construct the state 110
for idx in range(num_qubits):
    if s[idx] == '1':
        qc.x(idx)
qc.barrier()
qc.draw(output='mpl')
```

The preceding code will initialize and render our circuit as follows:

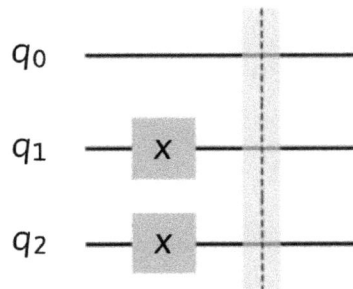

Figure 12.1: Initializing the state, s, to $|110\rangle$

4. Now that we have prepared our state, we can begin transforming it using QFT.

    Let's review our transformation equation with our state $|110\rangle$:

    $$|\Psi\rangle = \frac{(|0\rangle + e^{2\pi i(0.0)}|1\rangle)\ldots(|0\rangle + e^{2\pi i(0.10)}|1\rangle)(|0\rangle + e^{2\pi i(0.110)}|1\rangle)}{\sqrt{8}}$$

    This states that for each qubit where we apply a Hadamard gate, we will need to include rotations while traversing from the qubit down to the least significant qubit—hence, $j_n, \ldots, j_0$. As we traverse down, the qubit states decrease by each degree. This means each of the controlled phase rotations, **Control Rotation (CROT)**, is based on the following matrix representation:

    $$\text{CROT}(\theta)_k = \begin{bmatrix} 1 & 0 & 0 & 0 \\ 0 & 1 & 0 & 0 \\ 0 & 0 & 1 & 0 \\ 0 & 0 & 0 & e^{i\theta} \end{bmatrix}$$

    In the preceding equation, CROT(q)k is the CU_1 gate, and the parameter q is set as follows:

    $$\theta = \frac{\pi}{2^{k-1}}$$

    Therefore, we'll start with the most significant qubit, q_2, from our state $|\Psi\rangle$, as follows.

5. Starting at the most significant qubit, we'll add a Hadamard gate to the circuit:

    ```
    # Import the value pi for our rotations
    from numpy import pi
    # Always start from the most significant qubit,
    # in this case it's q2.
    # Step 1, add a Hadamard gate
    qc.h(2)
    ```

6. Now that we have our first step, the next step is to add CROT(θ) gates starting at $k=2$, which is the index of the most significant qubit position, q_2, and our parameter θ starts at the following:

    $$\theta = \frac{\pi}{2^{k-1}} = \frac{\pi}{2^{2-1}} = \frac{\pi}{2}$$

    We add the CROT gates from most significant to least significant, starting at $\pi/2$, and doubling the denominator of the parameter as we move down each qubit:

```
# Step 2, add CROT gates from most significant qubit
qc.cp(pi/2, 1, 2)
```

7. We then repeat this as we traverse from the current qubit down to the next qubit—in this case, q_0:

```
# Step 3, add another CROT from 2 to the next qubit down,
# while doubling the phase denominator
qc.cp(pi/4, 0, 2)
# Draw the circuit
qc.draw(output='mpl')
```

As we are traversing down, the denominator on the parameter is doubling in size as well, such that the next parameter θ is as follows (note that all qubits are initialized to the state $|0\rangle$):

$$\theta = \frac{\pi}{2^2} = \frac{\pi}{4}$$

This renders the following circuit, which now includes the Hadamard gate and the two CROT gates:

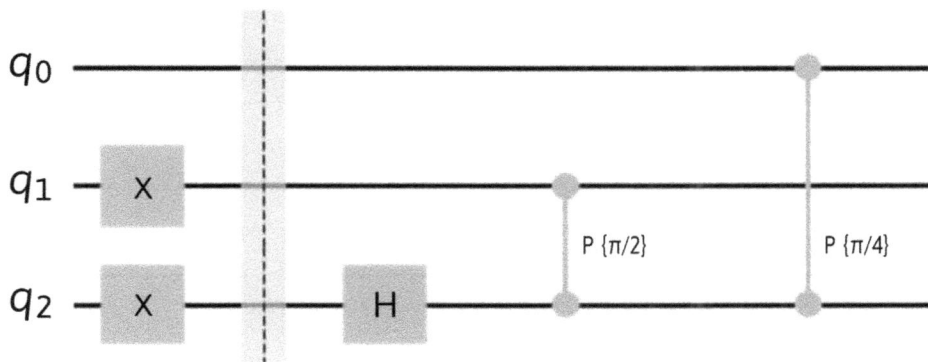

Figure 12.2: The first set of transformations starting from the most significant qubit

8. That completes the first level, which dealt with the most significant qubit. We will now move down to the next qubit (the second most significant qubit) and repeat the process of adding a Hadamard gate, followed by CROT(q) gates, where the phase rotations get smaller as we traverse down each qubit. Let's continue to the next qubit:

```
# Now that we finished from 2 down to 0
# We'll drop to the next least significant qubit and
```

```
# start again,
# Step 1, add a Hadamard gate
qc.h(1)
```

9. This is the same as *step 4* of adding a Hadamard gate; now, we apply the control rotation gate in the same manner as we did earlier and then draw the circuit:

```
# Step 2, add Control Rotation (CROT) gates from most
# significant towards
# least significant starting a pi/2, and doubling the
# denominator
# as you go down each qubit.
qc.cp(pi/2, 0, 1)
# Draw the circuit
qc.draw(output='mpl')
# Now that we finished from 1 down to 0
# We'll drop to the next least significant qubit and
# start again.
```

This will complete the second transformation, which will render the following circuit, which starts with a Hadamard gate and then appends the CROT gates afterward:

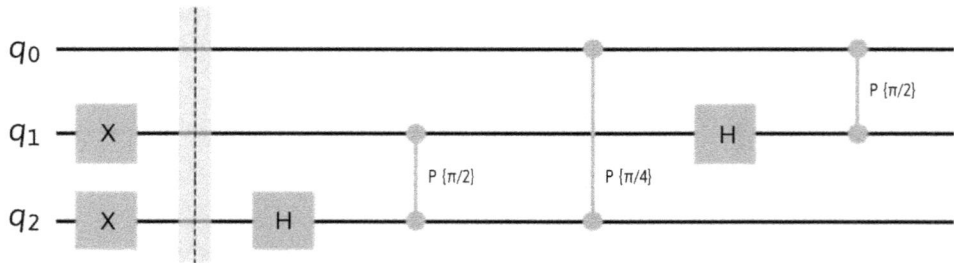

Figure 12.3: The next transformation set starting at the next qubit down

10. Next, we will run our transformation on the last qubit, and then draw the circuit:

```
# Step 1, add a Hadamard gate
qc.h(0)
# Since we are at the least significant qubit,
# we are done!
# Draw the circuit
qc.draw(output='mpl')
```

Since this is the last qubit and the least significant qubit, it has no lower levels, so we complete the CROT phase of the QFT. This renders the following circuit so far:

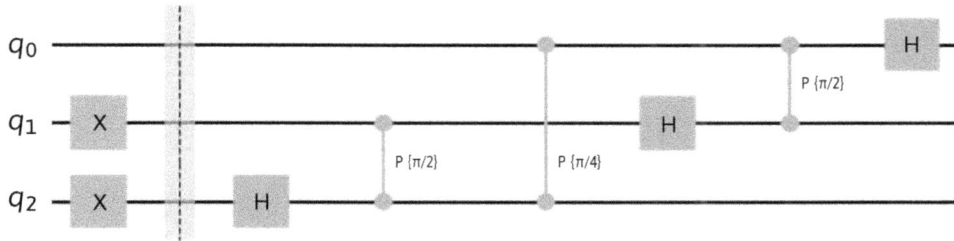

Figure 12.4: The final transformation of our QFT circuit

11. Finally, once we have set all the rotations, we need to apply swap gates to reverse our results. We need to do this to complete the QFT and set the values in the proper order. The swap is performed from the outermost qubits moving inward until you reach the last two qubits in the middle (if the total number of qubits is even), or until you reach the last two pairs with a single qubit in the middle (if the total number of qubits is odd).

To simplify this, we can create a function that will swap the outer qubits and work its way toward the middle. In this case, since we only have three qubits, we will only swap the outer two qubits, as follows:

```
# Define a function which will add the swap gates to the
# outer pair of qubits
def add_swap_gates(qc_swaps, qubits):
    for qubit in range(qubits//2):
        qc_swaps.swap(qubit, qubits-qubit-1)
    return qc_swaps
```

12. Now, we can run our quantum circuit through the add_swap_gates function and complete the circuit:

```
qft_circuit = add_swap_gates(qc, num_qubits)
qft_circuit.draw(output='mpl')
```

This will render our QFT circuit, which encodes our `'110'` value, as follows:

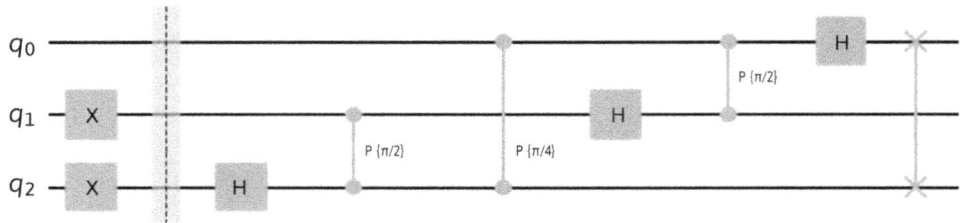

Figure 12.5: The QFT circuit that encodes '110'

13. Let's include some helper functions, similar to the functions we created in the previous chapter, that will run on either simulators or quantum systems. This time, we will include an option to select the number of shots.

```python
# Run on a local Sampler
def run_on_sampler(circuit, shots):
    from qiskit.transpiler.preset_passmanagers import generate_preset_pass_manager
    from qiskit_ibm_runtime import SamplerV2 as Sampler
    from qiskit_ibm_runtime.fake_provider import FakeManilaV2

    # Run the sampler job locally using FakeManilaV2
    fake_manila = FakeManilaV2()
    pass_manager = generate_preset_pass_manager(backend=fake_manila, optimization_level=1)
    transpiled_qc = pass_manager.run(circuit)

    # To ensure we get fixed results, set seed
    options = {"simulator": {"seed_simulator": 10258}}
    sampler = Sampler(mode=fake_manila, options=options)

    result = sampler.run([transpiled_qc], shots=shots).result()[0]

    return result


# Run on the least busy quantum computer
```

```
def run_on_qc(circuit, shots):
    # At the time of this writing we are using the latest version of
    # the Sampler primitive (V2), please review the documentation to
follow updates if you are using a previous version.
    from qiskit_ibm_runtime import SamplerV2 as Sampler2

    # Assign least busy device to backend
    backend =
                    service.least_busy(min_num_qubits=circuit.num_
qubits,
            simulator=False, operational=True)
    #Print the least busy device
    print('The least busy device: {}'.format(backend))
    result = {}

    transpiler = generate_preset_pass_manager(backend=backend,
optimization_level=3)
    transpiled_qc = transpiler.run(circuit)

    sampler = Sampler2(backend)
    job = sampler.run([transpiled_qc], shots=shots)
    job_result = job.result()

    # Extract the results
    result = job_result[0]

    return result
```

14. To visualize our QFT results, we can execute the preceding circuit using the state vector simulator to see our final QFT encoding for each qubit:

```
# Get the state vector simulator to view our final QFT
# state
from qiskit.quantum_info import Statevector

statevector = Statevector(qft_circuit)
plot_bloch_multivector(statevector)
```

The preceding code results in the following encoding for each qubit:

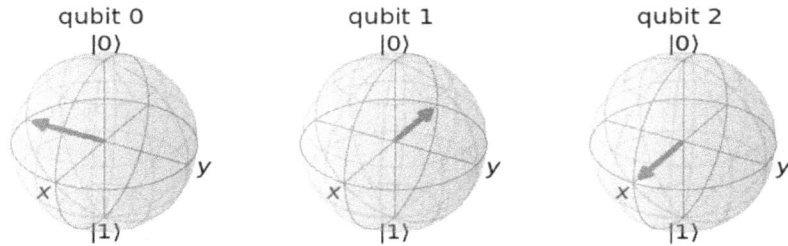

Figure 12.6: A Bloch sphere representation of the '110' QFT encoded value

Note that q_0 (q_2 before the swap) has rotated $3\pi/2$ (which is a Hadamard (H) plus a $\pi/2$ rotation), q_1 has rotated $\pi/2$ (H), and q_2 (q_0 before the swap) has rotated 0, mainly due to q_0 having a value of 0 before the swap because it was initialized to $|0\rangle$).

Note that each qubit is in a superposition state and varies by phase based on the '110' encoded value. We can also represent this using the qsphere object, which will have the same information, only represented in a single sphere object:

```
plot_state_qsphere(statevector)
```

In the following diagram, we can see that the information is encoded into the QSphere and has its encoded representation in the phase and state vector indicated by the color wheel and QSphere, respectively:

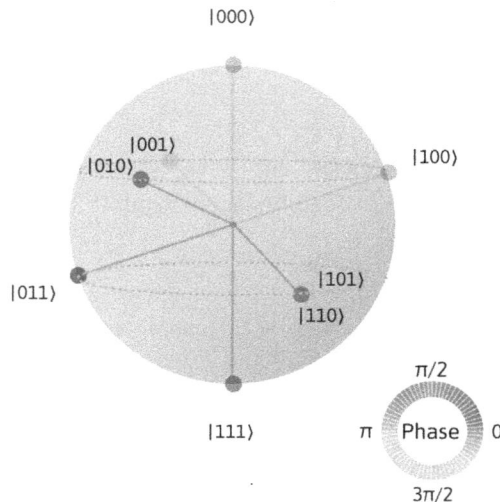

Figure 12.7: A QSphere representation of the QFT representation of the '110' state

Note that the colors indicate the phase of each state specified in the results where, at the time of this writing, green indicates $3\pi/2$-degree phase rotation for rotation states '000' and '100'.

Congratulations! You have just completed encoding your first QFT! This is an algorithm that you will see in many other algorithms that depend on periodic functionality.

In this section, we learned about the QFT algorithm and implemented it as well. One thing we have not covered, but which is important to mention, is that the QFT also has an inverse function called the **Inverse Quantum Fourier Transform (IQFT)**. This is quite simply the reverse of the QFT and in essence transforms the quantum state from the quantum Fourier basis back to the computational basis. This is done, as described, by reversing the functionality which was performed when transforming the QFT which includes reverse rotations. That is to say, if we rotated a qubit $\pi/2$, then when performing an IQFT, we would rotate the qubit by the same angle, only this time in the opposite direction, i.e. $-\pi/2$.

With an understanding of the basis of state transformation, you are now able to leverage this in many periodic functions and algorithms, such as estimating eigenvalues or unitary matrices and factoring discrete logarithms.

Next, we will look at one of the more famous search algorithms: **Grover's algorithm**.

Learning about Grover's search algorithm

Search algorithms are unique in that they can be leveraged by various algorithms to find information, whether in a data repository or a list of values, such as features in an image. The advantage with quantum, of course, is in the potential for speeding up the search. **Grover's algorithm** is one such example. It uses a well-known technique that allows the use of interference to amplify certain states in our quantum circuit in a way that will increase the amplitude of the value we are searching for and decrease those that we are not. Let's start, as always, by describing the problem, where each state is analogous to an entry in an unordered list.

Understanding the problem

The problem here is also very simple: we are given a set of states where all states are set to 0, except one state which is set to 1. We wish to identify which one of those states is set to 1.

Classically, this can be done in, in the best case, 1 step, if the first value is set. In the worst case, it would take N steps, where N is the total number of states and the last state is set. This means that on average, it will take $N/2$ steps to find the value as we would need to check each value individually.

Clearly, this is not ideal if our set is a very large list. We need to find a better way to find our value. This is where, in 1996, Lov Grover came in and discovered a way to solve this problem with his now-famous quantum algorithm. We'll step through the implementation of Grover's algorithm as we try to search for a value in a three-qubit circuit.

To describe this problem using functions, we can state the following, given a function:

$$f\{0,1\}^n \rightarrow \{0,1\}$$

From the preceding equation, $f(x) = 0$ for all cases of x except for a specific case, x^*, such that $f(x^*) = 1$. Find the value of x^*. Since we will be working with qubits, let's select a value N, such that $N = 2^n$.

Now that we have defined our problem, let's step through Grover's search algorithm.

Understanding Grover's search algorithm

Grover's algorithm is similar to the Deutsch-Jozsa and Bernstein-Vazirani algorithms in that it too leverages an oracle. However, note that the example given here illustrates a very simple oracle where we know the tagged state beforehand. This is done for demonstration purposes here; however, in real-world applications, the oracle will not only be more complex, but we will also have no idea which state will be tagged.

Another similarity between Deutsch-Josz0 and Grover's algorithm is that Grover's also leverages interference in a way that it will increase the amplitude of the state we are searching for while decreasing all other states, which in turn increases the speed by $\sqrt{N}$, where N is the number of states to search. This means that rather than iterating through each value within N, we take an exponential speedup, similar to what we did with Deutsch-Josza.

We'll begin by explaining Grover's search process in order to obtain an understanding of how it works. For a deeper description of the mathematics behind this, I recommend the book *Dancing with Qubits* by Robert S. Sutor, which covers this in greater detail.

Grover's search algorithm can be broken down into two main components—perhaps three, if you count initializing all qubits into superposition and adding measurements at the end—but that is something that most quantum algorithms do, so we'll just stick to the two main points. The first is referred to as **Grover's oracle**, and the second is the **Grover diffusion operator**.

In this example, we will describe a two-qubit system that, when placed in superposition by applying a Hadamard gate to each qubit, provides four possible states—**00, 01, 10,** and **11**—as follows:

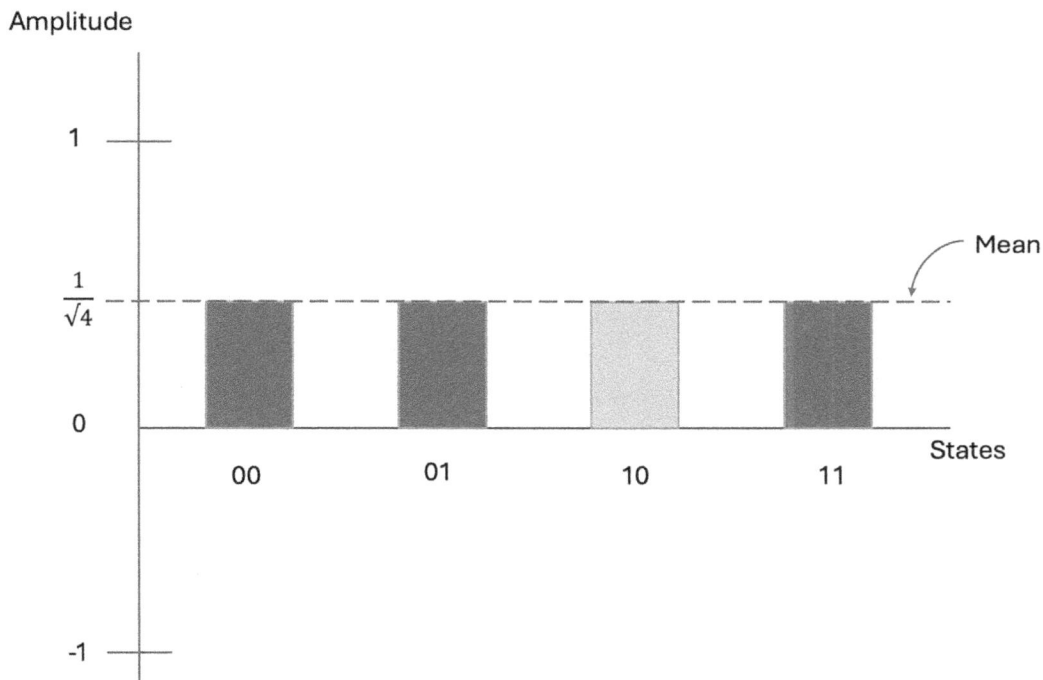

Figure 12.8: Two qubits in a superposition state

When in this state, the average equals the probability amplitude, which in this case is **0.25**, as indicated by the dotted line across the top of each state.

For this example, we'll say the state that we wish to search for is the state '10'.

The first component is the **oracle**, U_f. This is where we generally tag the value we are searching for. By tagging, I mean we will signal that the state that we are searching for will be identified by simply changing the sign of the state from positive to negative. The transition would be as follows:

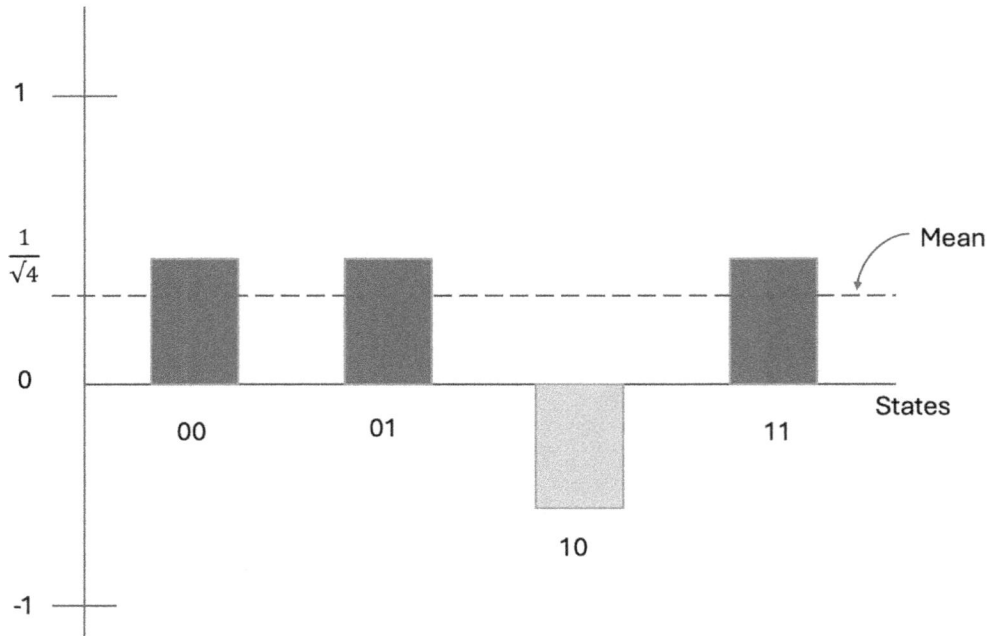

Figure 12.9: Changing the sign of the state to negative

Now that we have changed the sign, we can't, unfortunately, just measure and go at this point—mainly because, as we know, the probability amplitudes are squared, so our results would all still be equal, which does not provide us with any new information about what we are searching for. However, since we are working with amplitudes, we can leverage interference here by increasing the amplitude of the state we tagged and decreasing the amplitude of the other states. *How do we do this?* By incorporating the second component of Grover's search, the **diffusion operator**.

The second component of Grover's algorithm is the **Grover diffusion operator**. Here, we will be performing a mathematical step known as *inversion about the mean*. What this does is invert the distance between the average and the peak of each state. This is analogous to having each state flip reflectively about the average mean. Visually, the transition will be as follows:

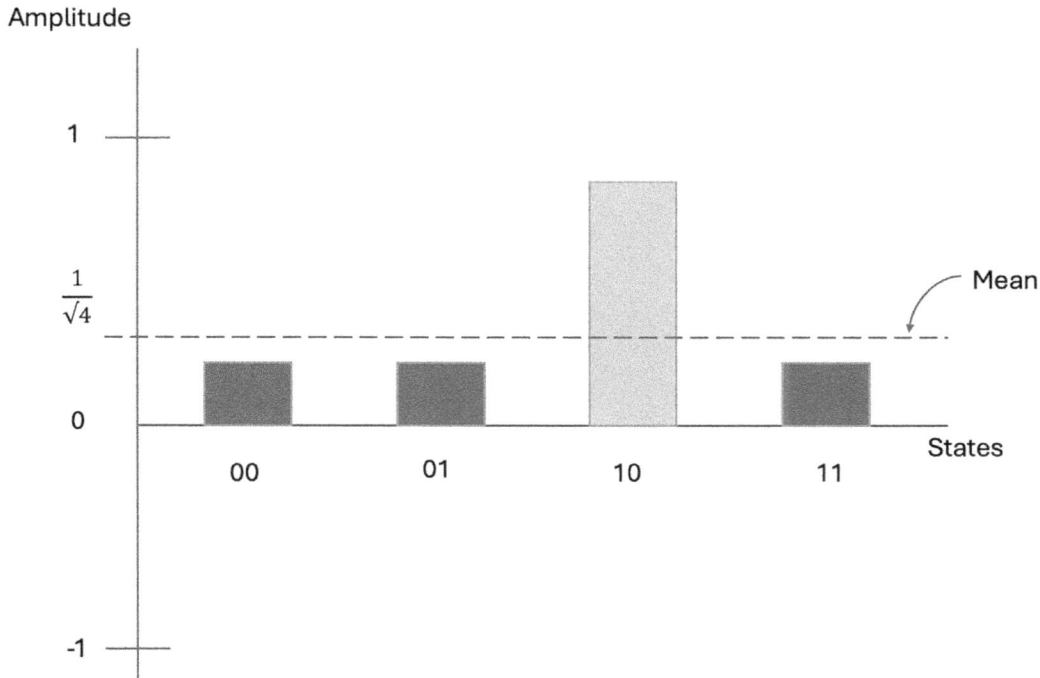

Figure 12.10: Inversion about the mean amplifies the states constructively and destructively

As we can see from the results of performing the inversion about the mean, the amplification of the tagged state is now significantly higher than the other states. If we were to now take a measurement, we would see that the result with the higher probability is the state we are searching for. Keep in mind, of course, that this is all done with a single query to our quantum circuit!

One thing to note is that when the number of states, N, is large, this means we will need to repeat the diffusion operator steps (and not the oracle constructor steps) multiple times, which is what constructs and destructs the amplitudes. The number of times to optimize the results is $\sqrt{2}n$, where n is the number of qubits.

Let's implement Grover's search algorithm next.

Implementing Grover's search algorithm

As usual, we'll explain each step described in the previous section while we work through the algorithm step by step. To start, create a new Qiskit notebook for this example and work through the following:

1. We'll begin by declaring the value we want to set. Let's set the value to 110. This way, we can use a three-qubit circuit to implement Grover's algorithm and place all the qubits in superposition by adding a Hadamard gate to each qubit:

    ```
    # Set the state we wish to search
    N = '110'
    num_qubits = len(N)
    # Create the quantum circuit
    qc = QuantumCircuit(num_qubits)
    # Set all qubits in superposition
    qc.h(range(num_qubits))
    qc.barrier()
    #Draw the circuit
    qc.draw(output='mpl')
    ```

    This will render our initialized circuit:

    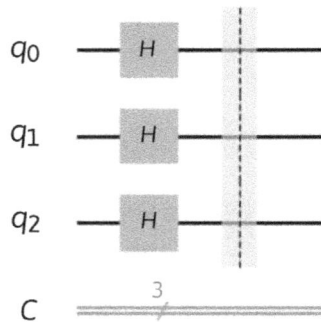

    Figure 12.11: Initialized quantum circuit in superposition

2. Next, we want to encode the state that we want to search—in this case, it is the state |110⟩. Here, we will reverse the state and encode N in the circuit:

    ```
    # Reverse the state so it's in proper qubit ordering
    N = N[::-1]
    ```

```
# Encode N into our circuit
for idx in range(num_qubits):
    if N[idx] == '0':
        qc.x(idx)
qc.barrier()
# Draw the circuit
qc.draw(output='mpl')
```

For each step, we will add a barrier so that we can see the process rendered:

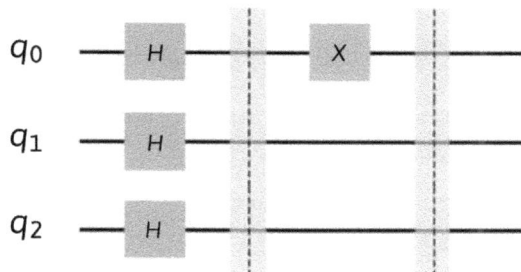

Figure 12.12: Encoding our state '110', we mark the '0' qubits in the state with an X gate

3. Next, we will create Grover's oracle. What we will do here is first set the most significant qubit in a superposition state, followed by a CNOT gate where the target is the most significant qubit, and the source is all the other qubits. Then, place another Hadamard gate on the most significant qubit to complete the oracle. This will negate the state that we set in the previous source cell, $|110\rangle$:

```
# Create the Grover oracle for our 3-qubit quantum circuit
qc.h(2)
qc.ccx(0, 1, 2)
qc.h(2)
qc.barrier()
# Draw the circuit
qc.draw(output='mpl')
```

The preceding code renders the following circuit, which we see sets the two CNOT gates in our oracle surrounded by **H** gates on the most significant qubit:

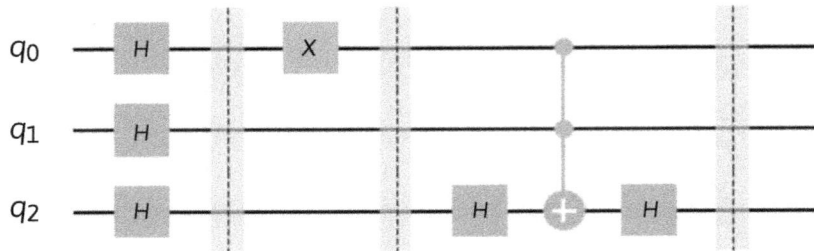

Figure 12.13: Applying Grover's oracle to the circuit

4. Now, we want to reset the state that we are searching in the circuit so that it returns to the superposition value:

```
# Reset the value after the oracle
for idx in range(num_qubits):
    if N[idx] == '0':
        qc.x(idx)
qc.barrier()
# Draw the circuit
qc.draw(output='mpl')
```

The preceding code completes Grover's oracle, which we described earlier as the first component of Grover's search algorithm:

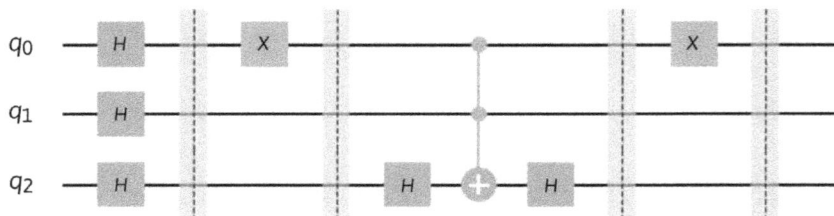

Figure 12.14: The first component of Grover's search algorithm

5. Next, we will implement the second component, the Grover diffusion operator. We start by applying all the qubits in a superposition state:

```
# Set all qubits in superposition
qc.h(range(num_qubits))
qc.x(range(num_qubits))
```

```
qc.barrier()
# Draw the circuit
qc.draw(output='mpl')
```

This renders the following superposition state, followed by Grover's oracle:

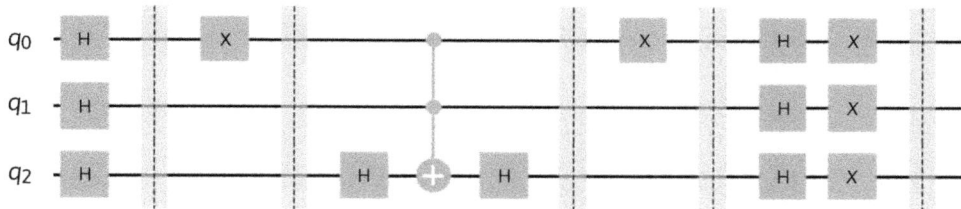

Figure 12.15: The first step in the Grover diffusion operator: apply H gates to all qubits

6. Next, we will flip all the 0-state qubits to their negative phase. Here, the most significant qubit is set as the target of the two CNOT gates:

```
# Apply another oracle, same as the previous
qc.h(2)
qc.ccx(0, 1, 2)
qc.h(2)
qc.barrier()
# Draw the circuit
qc.draw(output='mpl')
```

This renders the next step in the diffusion operator—that is, inversion about the mean:

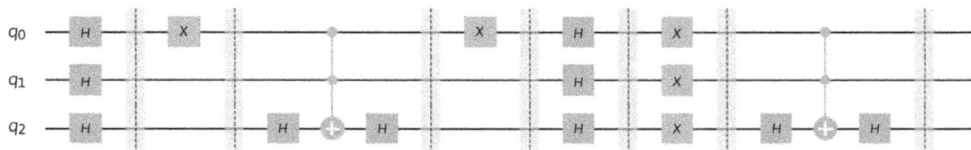

Figure 12.16: The second step of the diffusion operator: to invert about the mean

7. Finally, we wrap up the Grover diffusion operator by applying the first step in reverse. Since we applied a set of H gates across all qubits, followed by a set of X gates, also across all qubits, we will reverse this in the following manner. Apply X gates across all qubits, then apply H gates across all qubits:

```
# Reapply the X rotations on all qubits
qc.x(range(num_qubits))
```

```
qc.barrier()
# Reapply Hadamard gates to all qubits
qc.h(range(num_qubits))
# Draw the circuit
qc.draw(output='mpl')
```

The preceding code completes the Grover diffusion operator component of the quantum circuit:

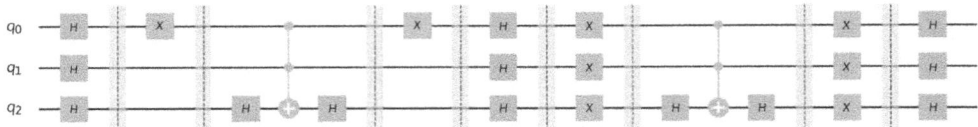

Figure 12.17: The complete Grover's algorithm circuit

To determine the ideal number of times to repeat the diffusion operator, n, we simply need to compute n as follows,

$$n = \pi * \sqrt{N} / 4$$

where N is the number of (log N) qubits N=4 for two qubits; In this example, we should add a second diffusion operator to bring the error down from 3% to 1%.

8. Now, we'll just add measurement operators and prepare to run the circuit on the backend, but first on a local simulator on your device:

```
# Add measurement operators
qc.measure_all()
# Draw the circuit
qc.draw(output='mpl')
```

The preceding code will prepare the following quantum circuit to run on either a simulator or quantum computer:

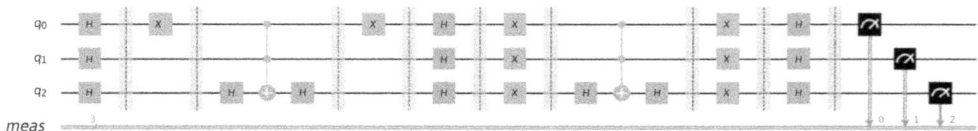

Figure 12.18: The complete quantum circuit ready to run on a simulator or quantum
system

9. We'll start by running the function we created to execute our circuit using the Sampler primitive:

```
# Run on the sampler
result = run_on_sampler(qc, shots=4000)
counts = result.data.meas.get_counts()

# Print and plot results
print(counts)
plot_distribution(counts)
```

After executing the circuit, this will print and plot our results as follows:

```
{'010': 274, '110': 2237, '000': 198, '100': 499, '101': 175, '111':
238, '001': 191, '011': 188}
```

In the following figure, we can see that the state we are searching has the higher probability, a quasi-probability of 0.559%, whereas all the other states have a significantly lower probability of around 0.05%:

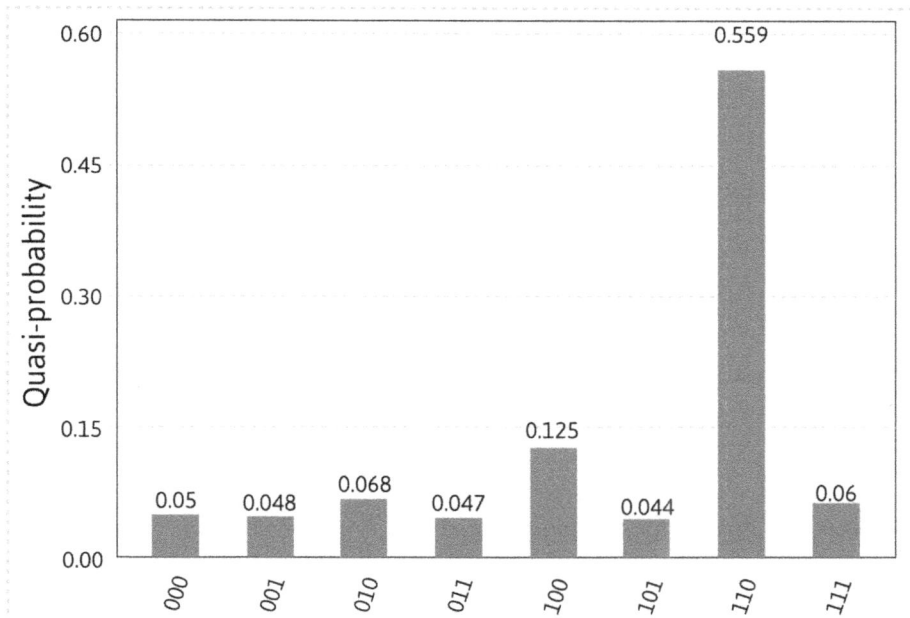

Figure 12.19: Results of executing Grover's search of state 110 on a Sampler

Success! As expected, our Grover's algorithm implementation has found the state within a single query.

10. Now, let's try it on a quantum device. We'll select the quantum computer that is the least busy and operational and has the number of qubits necessary to run our quantum circuit.

```
# Execute the circuit on the least busy quantum computer
backend = service.least_busy(min_num_qubits = num_qubits,
                             simulator = False,
                             operational = True)
print("Set backend: ", backend)
```

The preceding code will print out the least busy quantum computer and assign it to the backend variable.

11. We can now execute this as we did previously with the simulator, then print and plot the results:

```
# Run the circuit on the backend
shots = 1000
results = run_on_qc(qc, shots)
counts = results.data.meas.get_counts()
# Print results
print(counts)
```

12. Once completed, you should see something similar to the following output:

```
The least busy device: <IBMBackend('ibm_osaka')>
{'000': 85, '100': 52, '111': 219, '010': 61, '110': 373, '001': 73,
'011': 71, '101': 66}
```

13. We can now plot the quasi distribution of the results on a graph using the following:

```
# Plot results
plot_distribution(counts)
```

This will display the following output:

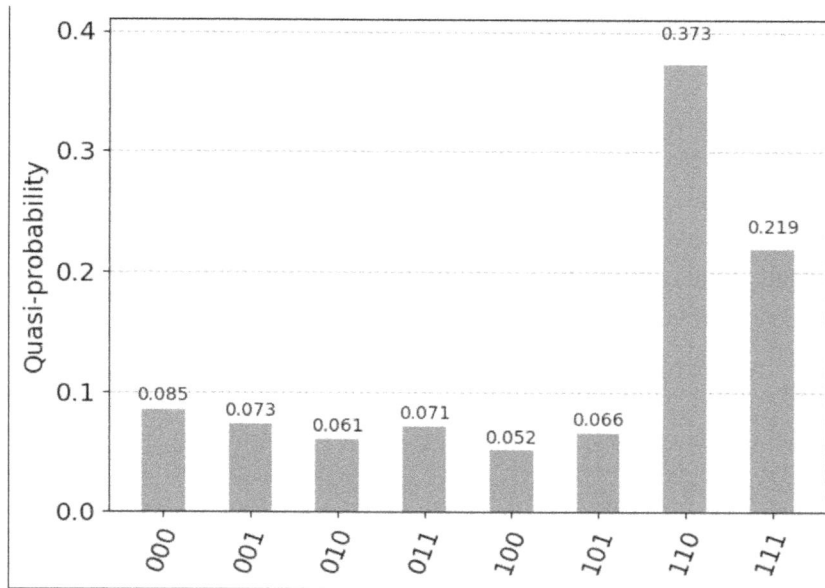

Figure 12.20: Probability distribution

This, of course, depends on the device itself as each system is different from one another. However, the results should be clear that the state with the highest probability is the state that we are searching for—in this case, $|110\rangle$.

As we can see here, the result with the highest probability is the state we are searching for, and the other states have a lower probability. We can see enough of a difference between each state to observe that the Grover's search algorithm that we implemented does indeed identify the state we are searching for. You might also want to try this with a larger value N, just so you can observe the results.

Congratulations! You have successfully implemented a variety of quantum algorithms, which are foundational to understanding how quantum computers are different in how they solve problems compared to classical systems and how they have the potential to solve real-world problems.

Summary

There are many algorithms that implement many of the techniques we covered in this and the previous chapter on quantum algorithms, many of which you will see used in other algorithms, such as the **quantum amplitude estimation** and **variational quantum eigensolver** algorithms, and so on.

I do strongly suggest trying variations of these algorithms yourself to get a better feel and understanding of how they work.

In the next and final chapter, we will look at the features that are built into Qiskit, which allow you as a researcher or developer to leverage them to create your own quantum algorithms. You will gain the skills to integrate these algorithms into your existing research or applications without having to worry about developing circuits, mitigating against noise, or any of the other components that make up an algorithm in Qiskit. This book has already done the heavy lifting for you, so you can simply implement the algorithm and process the results as you see fit.

Questions

1. What other problems can you solve using periodic functions?

2. Implement QFT on a five-qubit state—for example, `'10110'`.

3. Using Grover's algorithm, find the following states: `'101'`, `'001'`, and `'010'`.

4. How many iterations of Grover's diffusion operator would you need to run to find the state $|10101\rangle$?

5. Rerun the Grover's search example. Only repeat Grover's diffusion operator twice and note the difference in the result. What do you see that is different? What would you expect to change if you ran it more than three times?

Join us on Discord

Join our community's Discord space for discussions with the author and other readers:

`https://packt.link/3FyN1`

13

Understanding Quantum Utility and Qiskit Patterns

Here we are, the final chapter. If you've made it this far, then congratulations on keeping yourself focused and determined, your time was well invested! As we close out this chapter, and the book, I want to also make sure I don't just leave you here with some basics and wish you the best. I've found most technical books seem to do that. Not that there is anything wrong with that, but I always felt like most don't provide help regarding next steps or, better yet, any next best action. I thought I would include this chapter as a shift from education to enablement. In other words, where to go from here and *how*. With Qiskit 1.0 (and future updates), we should approach this as a transition to really getting a head start towards enabling you with the proper tools and patterns to evolve your current experiments towards ideal utility application candidates. The goal here is that this book will not only provide you with the education to get started, but will also provide you with some guidance to know what to expect and develop as the technology grows and new features are released.

Up to now, we have covered a *bottom-up approach* to understand quantum computing, where we started with the foundational quantum computational properties, gates, and circuits. We then moved up towards combining those to implement various quantum algorithms. We also covered how to use the various simulators, generate noise models, and mitigate readout errors. All of this helps in understanding the fundamental intricacies of quantum computing and how they are used to create algorithms that are both effective and optimal.

However, it is a lot to ask of a developer, solution architect, or systems integrator to learn all the inner workings just to understand how to integrate quantum computing into their application or workflow. In fact, it is often difficult to find those who want to wander down into the *nuts and bolts* of the quantum algorithm. Generally, most of us would like to just load our data into an algorithm, execute it on a quantum system, obtain the results, and just continue with our experiments.

This *top-down approach* is where Qiskit Patterns comes into the picture.

The following topics will be covered in this chapter:

- Understanding Quantum Utility
- Understanding Qiskit Patterns

In this chapter, you will learn what quantum utility means and why it is key to getting us closer towards quantum advantage.

We'll also cover Qiskit Patterns and how it can simplify your development experience to build complex quantum circuits. As most quantum algorithms and applications become more complex over time, particularly now as we are entering the era of quantum utility, we need to understand what they are and how we can best use these building blocks to create scalable and efficient quantum algorithms.

Finally, we'll wrap up this chapter with a quick example using Qiskit Patterns using Grover's algorithm, which we learned about in the previous chapter, as I do not want to finish this chapter without providing you with some code that combines classical and quantum together.

Technical requirements

For this chapter, it is expected that you have an understanding of creating quantum circuits and general application development using Python.

The following is the source code we'll be using throughout this book: `https://github.com/PacktPublishing/Learning-Quantum-Computing-with-Python-and-IBM-Quantum-Second-Edition`.

Understanding quantum utility

Earlier, I mentioned the term **quantum utility**. I figured I would take the time to describe in a bit more detail what that means and, more importantly, what it doesn't mean. First and foremost, let's start by defining another term, **quantum advantage**. Quantum advantage is a term that describes when a quantum computer can solve a practical use case in science or business that is intractable to classical systems.

One example of this could be Shor's algorithm, which finds the prime factors of an integer. This is currently difficult for classical systems to solve due to the complexity of the task, which is why it is used to encrypt much of our digital content, such as passwords. In the example of Shor's algorithm, where it is estimated to take millions of years to solve the problem using classical computers, some say it could take a few hours on a fault-tolerant system. Quantum advantage, at the time of writing, of course is a few years away, so it is good that you are taking the time now to learn about this new technology so when these systems reach quantum advantage, you'll have a head start on solving interesting problems. It's also important to note that quantum advantage will not happen all at once; it will be incremental and will vary based on the type of problem and cost compared to running on a classical system. As technology advances beyond quantum advantage, so will the solutions to classically intractable problems.

Now that we have an idea of what quantum advantage is, let's look at what quantum utility means. Back in June of 2023, researchers from IBM and UC Berkeley published a paper titled *Evidence for the utility of quantum computing before fault tolerance* (https://www.nature.com/articles/s41586-023-06096-3). In this paper, the authors were able to show that quantum computers can solve problems at a scale beyond brute force classical simulation. Again, this isn't to say that this is quantum advantage, mostly because there are some quantum-inspired classical methods that provided classical approximations using other techniques beyond brute force. The paper used a 127-qubit quantum computer that had almost 3,000 CX gates, which is quite a complex circuit to simulate using brute-force methods. There of course have been a few quantum-inspired classically based papers that were released that managed to reproduce the solution; however, not all the results from each experiment aligned for certain parameters. As a result, accuracy had begun to struggle, some ranging approximately 20% from each other. Furthermore, there have been many other papers that were published afterwards that are over 100-qubits and contain thousands of CX gates. This highlights the fact that we are moving from where we first started, with small-scale circuits, which could very easily be simulated classically, to over 100-qubit circuits with thousands of CX gates. As the size of the circuits, both width (number of qubits) and depth (number of CX gates) grows, so does the cost of simulating the circuit classically. Cost here can refer to loss of accuracy or speed. This era, which is a time before we hit quantum advantage, is what is referred to as **Quantum Utility**. Furthermore, using the error mitigation techniques discussed earlier in this book, allows running these complex circuits on 100+ qubit systems. The era of utility means we can find useful quantum applications to run without having to wait for fault-tolerant quantum computers.

Now that we're familiar with what quantum utility is, let's look at what we as developers should understand to take advantage of this latest move forward in quantum technology to build these more complex quantum circuits.

Understanding Qiskit Patterns

Another announcement at the 2023 IBM Quantum Summit was the introduction to Qiskit Patterns. Qiskit Patterns originated from the idea that as circuits get larger and more complex, computational scientists should not be concerned about what is happening at the hardware level. There is no need for a computational scientist to understand which gate to use on a specific qubit, or which is the ideal optimizer to use when transpiling the circuit to the hardware. Computational scientists should have tools that can be used to provide them with the latest hardware and software and simplify the usage of these 100+ qubit systems. These tools should provide a way for scientists to generate code or functions that will solve a specific problem or set of problems, and not create circuits qubit by qubit, gate by gate. Therefore, the purpose of the Qiskit Patterns is to provide the computational scientist with a way to inject a quantum computational routine into their existing applications and workflows.

Now that we know the purpose of Qiskit Patterns, let's look at what they are and how to use them. Prior to stepping into the details, I do want to stress that this is a new feature that is always being enhanced. There may be many changes to the code and its usage. What I am writing here is what is current at the time of writing. As we know, with all coding languages there are always updates or changes, so I urge you to review the documentation first so you are up to speed on the latest development. Even if there are changes in code, the concept of the overall steps should still be the same.

Simply put, Qiskit Patterns are made up of 4 steps that are used to run algorithms on a quantum computer and provide you with a result to use as part of your application and/or workflow. The four steps are: **map**, **optimize**, **execute**, and **post-process**. We'll learn what each of these steps does and run an example using a simple circuit. Of course, you can use any circuit that you wish.

Step 1, Map

In this step, we want to map the problem to a quantum circuit. This entails encoding the problem and inputs into a quantum circuit or state. A simple example we can use is to encode a binary image. This is an image where each pixel is either black or white, 0 or 1, respectively. It is simple enough to read each pixel and if the pixel is black, we leave the state as 0 and if it is white, we add an X gate to change it to the 1 state. Of course, this means that we would need the same number of qubits as we do pixels, so this is not easy to scale to larger images that have millions of pixels.

So, we would need to find ways to encode these images so that they would not need millions of qubits. This is where encoding comes in handy. If we can find a way to encode pixels into a quantum state, then this will work nicely. There are of course many ways to encode images, too many to list here, but by searching quantum image processing, you should find many forms. A few of the earliest forms are **NEQR**, which stands for **Novel Enhanced Quantum Representation** for digital images, and **FRQI**, which is short for **Flexible Representation of Quantum Images**. The mapping using FRQI maps the intensity value of the pixel, let's say a 256-bit grayscale image, to a single qubit (i.e., pi/256 would represent the pixel value). In NEQR, you would map the values using 8 qubits, where each qubit is set as a binary value, so the qubit intensity is not represented by 1 qubit (as in FRQI), but 8 qubits (8 qubits that map to the 8 binary values needed to represent the numbers from 0 to 256). These are just two, but there are so many more, each of which has its own advantages and disadvantages. What this means is that a lot of the work for you, as a computational scientist, is about selecting the encoding, or mapping, that you believe is best for your experiment. This mapping should ensure that your problem is not just encoded into a quantum state, but encoded in a way where it provides an optimal way to represent the problem you wish to solve. Once you have selected the proper mapping of your problem and input, a circuit is generated. We are now ready to move onto the next step in the Qiskit Pattern, optimization.

Step 2, Optimize your circuit

As we've covered in previous chapters, optimizing a circuit is not just one step of mapping the circuit to the quantum hardware; there are many different aspects to it. Thankfully, most of this is done automatically for us, but it also provides us with ways to alter them, either by setting `optimization_level` option values to specify the type of optimization to perform, but the recently added `resilience_level` option values, which allow us to also select the type of error suppression and error mitigation to apply to our circuit. As most of these require some classical resources, this provides us with a way to set how much of those classical resources to use. The result of the transpilation and optimization is called **Quantum Instruction Set Architecture (QISA)**. This optimized circuit is specific to the quantum hardware we select to execute this circuit on, which leads us to the next step, execute.

Step 3, Execute your circuit

One thing to note is that when we say execute a circuit, this is not to say we will execute this circuit on a quantum system, particularly when running a variational quantum algorithm that requires some classical interactions during execution. This is why primitives like the Estimator and Sampler are great building blocks as they provide the necessary context needed to execute these circuits to allow classical and quantum interactions during execution time. Executing a circuit can use one of many modes, such as Sessions, Jobs, and Batch.

We discussed these in *Chapter 10, Suppressing and Mitigating Quantum Noise,* where we covered how circuits are run on a quantum system. Now that we have executed our circuit on a quantum system, we now have reached the final step in the Qiskit Pattern, post-processing.

Step 4, Post-process

This is just a matter of obtaining the results we received from executing our circuit and processing them into what our classical application or workflow expects. Up to now, we've been displaying our results as either graphs or as text so we can view them and understand what the results mean. But when integrating with an application or workflow, the results might need to either be formatted in a certain way or aggregated with other results from various other systems as a collection. In either case, the post-processing step is just a matter of handling the results and passing them back to the calling system in a way that will facilitate its integration into the application itself in a very robust way. This of course would be dependent on how the results would be used in the next step or displayed.

In essence, those are the 4 steps, straightforward and quite simple. But then again, that is the point! Ideally, you, as a developer, computational scientist, or quantum enthusiast, should not have to struggle with how to create, execute, and obtain results from a quantum system. The process should be very straightforward and simple. Speaking of simplifying the process, another announcement during the Summit was that there will soon be AI included, which would be able to auto-generate quantum code as well. It has not been announced when this, and other AI features, will go live but the code will soon include this. This should help those who are new and just getting started as it could serve as a tool to ask how to create certain circuits, i.e. Grovers, Simon's, etc. and of course should also help those experienced researchers who would like to scale their existing circuits into these larger complex circuits, which could advance their solutions towards a path to quantum advantage.

Now, that all being said, I will not let you down! I did leave a little programming for you here so to not have a chapter without any coding. We will implement something that we built in the previous chapter, a simple logical expression to determine the optimal result using Grover's algorithm. This is a simple example where we will start with a logical expression, which we can say is the classical data coming in. Then we will proceed to use the Sampler primitive so we can run it locally, define the problem, and use the Grover algorithm class to solve the problem. This time, we will use the methods to input the problem and provide us with the optimal result, which we will then print out and display visually, hence completing the hybrid classical-quantum application. Here we go!

Implementing the logical expression oracle

Logical expressions are commonly used to describe problems, particularly those that have some constraints. These logical expressions can be used to construct a circuit and execute it on various algorithms. Let's begin with a simple problem. Note that the names have been changed to protect the identities of bands who have trouble staying together.

Melba, a music producer, has been tasked to put together the next big rock band, based on the musicians who currently have a contract for a record company. The following musicians are available:

- **Ivana** is a singer who has a great voice and is available to tour as soon as possible.

- **Karla** is also a singer with a great voice and is also available to tour right away.

- **Lex** is a guitar player that can play any genre and has his own tour bus.

- **Leo** is a drummer that gets along with everyone and is very liked in the industry.

Now, here is the problem you have been asked to solve by the music producer: Ivana and Karla tend to not get along on tour and have been known to have creative differences when writing music. Lex and Leo, on the other hand, get along fine together both in the studio and on tour. However, Ivana and Lex recently broke up after the last time they toured together so we can have one of the following options: only Ivana or Leo can participate, or neither and simply replace them both.

What you need to do is determine which combination of these four musicians is best for you to put together as a band, and then have them tour with minimal issues based on their history together.

To solve this, let's write this out as a logical expression:

1. We'll map each musician to a variable such as: A = Ivana, B = Karla, C = Lex, and D = Leo.

2. Next, we'll create a logical expression using logical operators to illustrate the constraints. To start, we know that Ivana and Karla do not get along, so this we can represent as follows, where $\wedge$ indicates XOR. This means we need at least one of them to participate, but not both at the same time: $(A \wedge B)$.

3. Next, we know that Lex and Leo get along fine together, so we can represent them with an AND operator as follows: $(C\&D)$.

4. Finally, we know that Ivana and Lex have just ended their relationship, so they might not be open to working and touring together. We will represent them as a NAND as follows. This indicates that they cannot work together, but it will allow for both not to participate at all: $\sim(A\&C)$.

5. By putting these all together, our complete logical expression for this example is as follows: $(A \wedge B)\&(C\&D)\&\sim(A\&C)$.

    Now that we have defined our logical expression, let's create an oracle on the logical expression so that we can use **Grover's algorithm** to search for the optimal result.

6. We'll begin by importing all the necessary modules and classes needed for the rest of these steps and defining our logical expression:

    ```
    # Import the necessary modules and classes
    from qiskit import QuantumCircuit
    from qiskit.visualization import *
    from qiskit_algorithms import Grover, AmplificationProblem
    from qiskit.circuit.library.phase_oracle import PhaseOracle
    # State the SAT problem into a logical expression
    # A = Ivana, B = Karla, C = Leo, D = Lex
    expression = '((A ^ B) & (C & D) & ~(A & C))'
    ```

7. Now that we have defined our problem as a logical expression, let's use this logical expression to create our oracle, which as you recall is what we use to describe the problem we wish to solve. In this case, it represents the logical expression. Note that in the code I included a cell that would install a dependency for using PhaseOracle (pip install tweedledum), as you will likely also have to install Qiskit algorithms (pip install qiskit-algorithms). I've commented the line out to install just in case you already have it installed; however, if you get an error when executing a cell that requires the dependency, simply install onto your development environment using the command-line instruction, and restart the kernel. This will then complete the installation and you can then run the code without the dependency error:

    ```
    # Create a PhaseOracle based on the logical expression
    oracle = PhaseOracle(expression)
    ```

8. Now that we have created an oracle from the logical expression, we can create the problem by calling the AmplificationProblem() method and passing the expression we wish to solve as its argument:

    ```
    # Construct the amplification problem from the oracle
    problem = AmplificationProblem(oracle,
                    is_good_state=oracle.evaluate_bitstring)
    problem.grover_operator.oracle.draw()
    ```

The preceding code calls the oracle from the Grover operator which contains the quantum circuit representation of the oracle which is illustrated as follows:

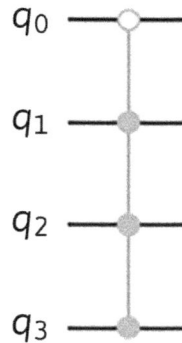

Figure 13.1: Quantum circuit representing the logical expression oracle

9. We can see that this oracle describes the logical expression, where q_0, q_1, q_2, and q_3 represent our logical expression, where q_0 = Ivana, q_1 = Karla, q_2 = Lex, and q_3 = Leo. Observe that the control in q_0 is not filled in. This is to indicate that it is triggered when the state value of q_0 is $|0\rangle$, as opposed to the others, which are triggered when the qubit is in the $|1\rangle$ state. We can now use this oracle on any oracle-based (oracular) algorithm. Since we are searching for the solution to this rock band problem, let's use Grover's algorithm. First, we will set up a session and use the Sampler primitive for this example, and then create the Grover's algorithm class using the sampler as the primitive. We'll then pass the problem we defined in the previous cell into the amplify method, which will in essence run Grover's algorithm, provide us with the result, and display it:

```
# Using the Sampler to run circuit
from qiskit.primitives import Sampler
# Set the Options
sampler = Sampler()
grover = Grover(sampler=sampler)
result = grover.amplify(problem)
plot_distribution(result.circuit_results[0])
```

The preceding code results in the following output, which represents the value we are searching for: 1110. Keep in mind that the qubit at position 0 is represented by the least significant bit (far right). This means that the result, 1110, is equal to D=1, C=1, B=1, A=0:

We also obtain the following quasi-distribution:

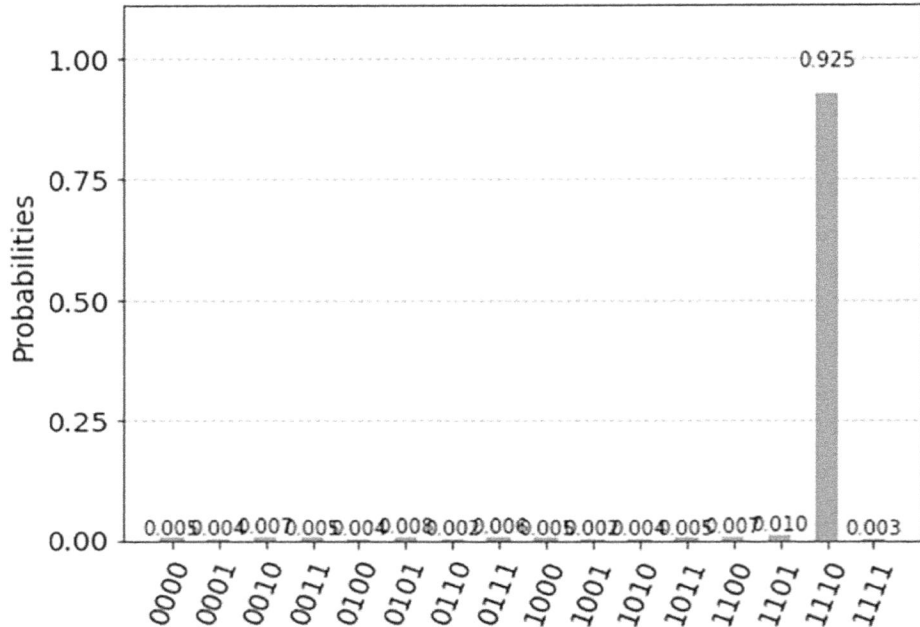

Figure 13.2: Grover solution results based on the logical expression oracle

As shown by the preceding results, the algorithm indicates our solution is **1110**. This states that Karla, Leo, and Lex are the three ideal musicians to recruit into the next band project. Melba has then decided to recruit Ivana as a solo career singer.

This, of course, is a simple example. As you can imagine, if your expression is more complex, then the Grovers search would help determine that in just a few lines of code. As you can see, you can take a problem that's defined by a logical expression on a classical system and then, by leveraging the Qiskit Runtime and Grover's algorithm class, prepare the problem in a variety of ways, all of which can be executed on a quantum system. All of this can be done without having to delve into the lower layers of the quantum algorithm, i.e., quantum gates, operators, error mitigation, etc.

As Qiskit continues to add many more features, algorithms, utilities, and other artifacts, this will help you create flexible yet modular quantum applications that suit all your needs.

Summary

In this chapter, we covered Qiskit Patterns, which are focused on helping you quickly develop robust quantum circuits to include into your applications and workflows. With the release of Qiskit 1.0 and future changes, I also highly recommend you keep up with the latest changes. Qiskit 1.0 has a nice roadmap filled with updates to primitives, patterns, and many features that not only help you get up to speed with the development process but also ensure that your circuits can scale up to larger utility sized circuits.

Now that you have the general skills to understand how to start creating quantum applications and using Qiskit Patterns in a way that simplifies the creation process, you can start applying these features into your existing circuits, or in new circuits if you are just starting out.

Finally, we looked at a problem that we needed to solve using Grover's quantum algorithm, without having to really understand how they are constructed, meaning we did not have to create a quantum circuit, an oracle, or diffusion operators to run the algorithm. The focus was on how to represent the problem, in this case as a logical expression, and apply it via a combination of available classes and methods of the algorithm to present the problem and solve it. Just keep in mind that as we are moving towards quantum utility, there will be more efficient and modern ways to implement this and future algorithms. As mentioned throughout this book, these are just the principles and general programming practices to help get you started, but as quantum computing evolves, so to will the algorithms and the way we think about how to program. It's with this that you should take away from this book, it's a place to start for you to take the code and keep on pushing towards the outer bounds of your ingenuity and imagination. But for now...

Congratulations! You've taken a very large step towards getting yourself started with learning and building quantum applications. Initially, we followed a bottoms-up approach, which is to start by creating and running quantum circuits on both a locally installed simulator and on a quantum computer. Doing this helped you understand the inner workings of how a quantum circuit is built and executed on a quantum system. Next, you reviewed the various algorithms and quantum computing principles that differentiate between classical and quantum applications. By running these applications, you also visualized the results and of course the effects caused by various environmental effects, which in turn helped you learn about the various features that mitigate the noisy effects of the quantum computer. And finally, you looked at a top-down approach offered by the Qiskit Runtime to help you quickly see how some of these algorithms in various domains are used to solve small problems. The hope here is that this book has provided you with a simple gateway to simplify your journey into the quantum computing world and, as always, I look forward to reading your research papers or perhaps your own textbook!

Welcome to quantum!

Questions

1. What are the four steps of Qiskit Patterns?

2. Which Qiskit Pattern handles mapping a quantum circuit to the hardware?

3. When encoding your problem to a quantum state, which Qiskit Pattern step are you on?

4. Why did we use a Sampler and not an Estimator primitive for the Grover example?

Join us on Discord

Join our community's Discord space for discussions with the author and other readers:

`https://packt.link/3FyN1`

Appendix A: Resources

In addition to this book, there are many other resources available that I highly recommend you use to get a deeper understanding of quantum computing and where to find the latest research. As you will notice, quantum technology is evolving at a very rapid pace, so much that it was rather difficult to keep up as this book was written. Believe it or not, it took longer to update and keep up with the updates for this edition than it took to write the first edition! But believe me, it was well worth the wait, as the current state of quantum has not only changed how we program but how we build and run circuits. Things which were challenging in the past such as creating circuits at the gate level are now much easier using primitives and other features of the Qiskit Runtime.

The following resources should help guide you to understanding not only the fundamentals and the technology, but will keep you up to date with the latest features and releases. In fact, Qiskit 1.0, which was released during the writing of this book, has so much that it would likely need a book all on its own! The contents of this appendix is far from an exhaustive list of resources, but it does have key links and information:

- **IBM Quantum Learning Platform**: This is where you can find a variety of learning resources for all levels: `https://learning.quantum.ibm.com`. Here, you will find various learning materials, tutorials, and online courses, which include topics beyond quantum computing, including an introduction to quantum cryptography. All courses are perfect for beginners and experienced researchers and developers; each course walks you step by step from the basics all the way up to advanced topics.

- **The documentation**: The link for the full documentation is `https://docs.quantum.ibm.com/`. This is the main documentation page for all the topics discussed in this book. This link is one you'll want to bookmark as it will be your guide and at times a great time-saver to help you migrate code to new versions or to get familiarity with new features.

- **The Qiskit GitHub repository**: The GitHub repository link for Qiskit is `https://github.com/Qiskit`. This is the Qiskit GitHub repository where you will find the open-source code for Qiskit. Like most other open-source GitHub projects, you can fork and contribute to the open-source project by either mitigating any issues or implementing a design request. You can also submit requests for enhancements or issues you may find. If it is your first time, it is recommended to work on issues labeled *good first issue*.

- **Qiskit Slack community**: The link to join the Qiskit Slack community is `https://qisk.it/join-slack`. This is the Qiskit community's worldwide Slack channel. It is here where the real fun begins! You'll not only find quantum researchers, professors, students, and quantum enthusiasts, but you'll also find various channels that discuss all aspects of quantum and Qiskit, from hardware to software, to practically any quantum project you can think of. This is where you can meet others like you who are either just getting started or looking to advance their knowledge.

- **Quantum Algorithm Zoo**: As the welcome page indicates, *this site is a comprehensive catalog of quantum algorithms.* It provides details about the algorithm type, speedup, and a description of the algorithm. They are grouped by types such as *algebraic and number-theoretic, oracular, approximation and simulation*, and several others. This is very useful should you want to get a quick overview of an algorithm and how it works. The link for this page is `http://quantumalgorithmzoo.org/`.

- **Arxiv: Quantum Physics**: This is an open-access documentation repository for scholarly papers and articles, at `https://arxiv.org/archive/quant-ph`. This resource is for articles that specifically cover the topic of quantum physics, a topic that also includes many quantum computation papers.

- **IBM Quantum Network quantum papers**: This resource provides a list of all research papers that were published by the IBM Quantum research team and **IBM Quantum Network** partners and members: `https://ibm.biz/quantum-network-arxiv`.

  The link is to an **AirTable**, an online hybrid spreadsheet database, which lists the industry domains to which a given project is relevant, such as *finance, optimization, chemistry, machine learning, error mitigation, quantum utility*, and so on. It also lists the name of the company and which quantum computers they used during their research. Arxiv links to all the papers listed are also included. This is a great resource to have to ensure you keep up to speed on the latest research and the wider quantum research landscape.

- **The Qiskit YouTube channel**: The URL for this channel is `https://www.youtube.com/Qiskit`. This is the official Qiskit YouTube channel, on which there are several series on research and development with frequently scheduled uploads to keep viewers up to date on the latest content and research from the IBM quantum research team, and IBM Quantum Network partners and members.

- **SciRate:** This site (`https://scirate.com/`) gathers the top-rated Arxiv papers in each category, including quantum physics. It's a good resource should you have time to read what most people are reading about from Arxiv.

Join us on Discord

Join our community's Discord space for discussions with the author and other readers:

`https://packt.link/3FyN1`

Appendix B: Assessments

Chapter 1 — Exploring the IBM Quantum Tools

Question 1

Which Application contains your API token?

Answer

There are two places to obtain your API token. The first is the **Account settings** view, where the API token is available and where you can regenerate a different token if needed. The other is on the main dashboard.

Question 2

Which device in your resources list has the fewest qubits?

Answer

The availability of the device with the fewest qubits will vary based on the quantum devices available. However, at the time of writing, there are systems with no less than 127 qubits. The next systems will be of sizes 133 qubits and higher. This is due to the recent shift to the IBM Quantum Platform to provide quantum utility systems (over 100 qubits).

Question 3

Which Application would provide you a qubit map of a quantum system?

Answer

The **IBM Quantum Platform** provides the **Compute Resources** application view, which displays all available quantum systems.

Chapter 2 – Creating Quantum Circuits with IBM Quantum Composer

Question 1

From the Composer, where would you find the time it took to run your circuit on a quantum computer?

Answer

You would find it in the **Status Timeline** view of the **Composer Jobs** view.

Question 2

How would you remove or add a qubit to your circuit on the composer?

Answer

You would click on a qubit and select either the + or the trashcan icon to add or remove a qubit from the circuit, respectively.

Question 3

On which view would you specify which quantum system to run your circuit?

Answer

You would use the **Setup and run** view, which is accessible from the **Composer** view, to select the system.

Question 4

Which sphere would be ideal to view the quantum state of three qubits in a single sphere?

Answer

You would use the qsphere to represent multiple quantum states in a single sphere.

Chapter 3 – Introducing and Installing Qiskit

Question 1

In your own words, describe the difference between a kernel developer and an application developer.

Answer

In general, the kernel developer can be seen as a developer that creates the specific circuit for a quantum system. It is analogous to a classical assembly developer. An application developer would integrate a quantum algorithm into a classical application or workflow.

Question 2

If you wanted to obtain the unitary matrix of a circuit, which simulator would provide the unitary matrix result?

Answer

The unitary simulator from the Qiskit Aer library.

Question 3

Can you name and describe in your own words each of the five simulator categories that are provided by Aer?

Answer

The details of each are described in the chapter; this question is to check that you have an intuitive understanding of each simulator. For example, a state vector simulator does not need a measurement as it only computes the final state of the circuit.

Question 4

Which module would you need to import to plot a histogram?

Answer

The Qiskit Visualization module.

Chapter 4 – Understanding Basic Quantum Computing Principles

Question 1

How would you create a circuit that entangles two qubits where each qubit is different (that is, 01, 10)?

Answer

We can use the following code to create a circuit that entangles two qubits:

```
qc = QuantumCircuit(2,2)
qc.h(0)
qc.x(1)
qc.cx(0,1)
qc.measure([0,1], [0,1])
qc.draw()
```

Question 2

Create a circuit with a multi-qubit gate, such as a controlled-Hadamard gate.

Answer

The circuit will just need to be ensured to have two qubits and include a controlled Hadamard gate (**ch**). In the following example, the first qubit is the control and the second qubit is the target. We add a Hadamard gate to the control qubit to ensure we will get either a 0 or 1; otherwise, the control will never be set:

```
qc = QuantumCircuit(2,2)
qc.h(0)
qc.ch(0,1)
qc.draw()
```

Question 3

Create all 4 Bell states in a circuit.

Answer

The circuit will just need to have two qubits and include a controlled-X gate (cx), where the first argument is the control and the second is the target. In the following example, the first qubit is the control and the second qubit is the target. We add a Hadamard gate to the control qubit to ensure we will get either a 0 or 1; otherwise, the control will never be set:

```
qc = QuantumCircuit(2,2)
qc.h(0)
qc.cx(0,1)
qc.draw()
```

Subsequent circuits will just alter the direction of the **cx** gate's control and target, and ensure that the Hadamard gate is on the same qubit as the control.

Question 4

What are the three quantum computation principles?

Answer

The three quantum computation principles are superposition, interference, and entanglement. Superposition and interference are described in classical physics, and entanglement is described in quantum physics.

Chapter 5 – Understanding the Qubit

Question 1

Which would provide visual information about the phase of a qubit—the Bloch sphere or the qsphere?

Answer

Both do. The Qiskit sphere (q-sphere) includes a checkbox to visualize the phase information. The Bloch sphere illustrates the phase by the position of the vector when it is out of phase, which is to say it is rotated about the z axis.

Question 2

Can you visualize multiple qubits on the Bloch sphere? If not, then describe why you wouldn't.

Answer

No, we can't visualize multi-qubits on the Bloch sphere as we can on the qsphere. The Bloch sphere is generally leveraged to illustrate a single qubit vector position for a given state, whereas the qsphere includes the phase. To represent multiple qubits using the Bloch sphere, you will need to have one Bloch sphere for each qubit.

Question 3

Write out the tensor product of three-qubit states in all forms.

Answer

The resulting basis states for a three-qubit system are $|000\rangle, |001\rangle, |010\rangle, |011\rangle, |100\rangle, |101\rangle, |110\rangle, |111\rangle$.

Question 4

What is the probability amplitude of a three-qubit system?

Answer

The amplitude of a three-qubit system is $\frac{1}{\sqrt{2^n}}$, where n is the number of qubits, which results in $\frac{1}{\sqrt{2^3}} = \frac{1}{\sqrt{8}}$.

Chapter 6 – Understanding Quantum Logic Gates

Question 1

For the multi-qubit gates, try flipping the Source and Target. Do you see a difference when you decompose the circuit?

Answer

No, there is no difference that can be seen, only that the source is now assigned to the opposite qubits.

Question 2

Decompose all the gates for both single- and multi-qubit circuits. What do you notice about how the universal gates are constructed?

Answer

The single gates are now displayed by their respective basis gate, including rotation values, if any. Multi-qubit gates, such as the Toffoli gate, are also broken down into specific gates that are used to construct the operation of the Toffoli gate between the assigned qubits.

Question 3

Implement the Toffoli gate where the target is the center qubit of a three-qubit circuit.

Answer

Use the following code to implement the Toffoli gate where the target is the center qubit of a three-qubit circuit:

```
qc = QuantumCircuit(3)
qc.ccx(0,2,1)
qc.draw()
```

Question 4

Decompose the Toffoli gate. How many gates in total are used to construct it?

Answer

When decomposing the Toffoli gate down to Hadamard, T, T dagger, and CX gates, there are a total of 15 gates, and it runs 11 operations deep. It's good to note that the depth might change if a more efficient way of composing the Toffoli gate is developed.

Question 5

Apply the Toffoli gate along with a Hadamard gate to a state vector simulator and compare the results to that from the Sampler primitive. What differences do you see and why?

Answer

The Sampler primitive, since it runs 1024 shots by default, will produce a result of approximately 50% 000 and 50% 001, assuming placement of the Hadamard gate is in the first qubit. On the other hand, the state vector simulator, which only runs a single shot, will either result in the state 000 or 001; the results of which will vary depending on the qubit in which you placed the Hadamard gate.

Question 6

If you wanted to sort three qubits in the opposite direction, which gates would you use and in which order?

Answer

You can use the swap gate to switch the value of each qubit from one qubit to another (for an example of two qubits):

```
qc = QuantumCircuit(2)
qc.x(0)
# current state is '01'
qc.swap(0,1)
# current state is reversed, '10'
```

Chapter 7 – Programming with Qiskit

Question 1

Construct a random quantum circuit with a width of 4 and a depth of 9.

Answer

```
from qiskit.circuit.random import random_circuit
#Circuit with a width = 4, a depth = 9
qc = random_circuit(4, 9, measure=True)
```

Question 2

Create another random quantum circuit with the same width as the circuit you created in *Question 1* and concatenate it so that it is added before the random quantum circuit you created.

Answer

```
qc1 = random_circuit(2,2)
qc_combined = qc.compose(qc1, [0,1], front=True)
```

Question 3

Print the circuit properties of the concatenated quantum circuit from *Question 3* and specify the total number of operators, not including any measurement operators.

Answer

```
qc_combined.draw()
qc_combined.count_ops()
```

Question 4

Create a circuit with a parameterized R_Y gate that would rotate by an angle of $\pi/2$.

Answer

```
import numpy as np
from qiskit.circuit import Parameter
param_theta = Parameter('θ')
qc = QuantumCircuit(2)
qc.rz(param_theta,0)
```

```
qc = qc.assign_parameters({param_theta: np.pi/2})
qc.draw()
```

Chapter 8 – Optimizing and Visualizing Quantum Circuits

Question 1

Can you name two components of the transpiler?

Answer

Pass and **PassManager**.

Question 2

Which component allows you to specify the passes to use?

Answer

PassManager is used to specify which passes are used and which passes can communicate with other passes.

Question 3

What is the default `optimization_level` value when running the transpile() function?

Answer

Optimization level 1.

Question 4

Name the three Layout Selection Passes.

Answer

Trivial, Dense, and Sabre.

Chapter 9 — Simulating Quantum Systems and Noise Models

Question 1

Can you list all the simulators found in the Qiskit Aer module?

Answer

The list of simulators can be generated using the `Aer.backends()` function.

Question 2

Create a qsphere representation of a qubit on the negative Y axis, creating the state $\frac{|0\rangle - i|1\rangle}{\sqrt{2}}$, using only a single Hadamard gate along with the phase gates.

Answer

In order to accomplish this, you will need to set the qubit in a superposition state. This can be done using the Hadamard gate (H), which will place the qubit in the state $\frac{|0\rangle + |1\rangle}{\sqrt{2}}$. After that, we will have to run a phase shift from the $|+\rangle$ state to the $\frac{|0\rangle - i|1\rangle}{\sqrt{2}}$ state, which would mean we need a phase gate to shift the state by a phase of $-\pi/2$, as follows:

```
qc = QuantumCircuit(1)
qc.h(0)
qc.sdg(0)
simulator = Aer.get_backend('statevector_simulator')
transpiled_qc = transpile(qc, backend=simulator)
result = simulator.run(transpiled_qc).result()
statevector = result.get_statevector(transpiled_qc)
statevector
```

Question 3

When initializing a set of qubits in a circuit, what must the total probability across all states be?

Answer

The sum of the squares of the total param values in the `initialize` function argument must add up to 1, as in the following example, where $\frac{1}{\sqrt{2}}$ is set twice. So, if you take the sum of the squares, it will be equal to 1:

```
import numpy as np
qc = QuantumCircuit(2, 2)
init_qubits = [0, 1]
qc.initialize([1, 0, 0, 1] / np.sqrt(2), init_qubits)
```

Question 4

Can you use the qsphere to visualize both the phase and probability information of a qubit?

Answer

Yes, the phase is given by the color of the state vectors and the probability is visualized by the size of the tips of the state vectors. The larger the diameter, the higher the probability.

Question 5

What would happen if you set the depolarization error values close to 1?

Answer

This will set the λ value to 1, therefore completely depolarizing the channel.

Question 6

If you applied a readout error equally to all qubits, what results would you expect and why?

Answer

When running on a simulator, rather than resulting in an ideal condition (no errors), you will instead see errors, where the significance of the errors is based on the set ReadoutError() parameters.

Chapter 10 – Suppressing and Mitigating Quantum Noise

Question 1

List the three main error mitigation techniques used by the Qiskit Runtime service.

Answer

Minimal mitigation, medium mitigation, and heavy mitigation.

Question 2

Which resilience levels are used for error mitigation?

Answer

Levels 0 through 2, where level 1 is the default.

Question 3

What other reversible gates could you use to fill in the idle time of a qubit using Dynamical Decoupling?

Answer

Any reversible gate, XGate or YGate, for example.

Question 4

Which type of noise contributes to amplitude dampening of a qubit?

Answer

Decoherence.

Question 5

Which type of noises contribute to dephasing of a qubit?

Answer

White noise, pink noise, and flux noise.

Chapter 11 – Understanding Quantum Algorithms

Question 1

Which algorithm would you use to determine whether an n-bit string is balanced?

Answer

The Deutsch-Jozsa algorithm can be used to determine whether a function is constant or balanced.

Question 2

Implement the **Bernstein-Vazirani** algorithm to find the state 170.

Answer

To create the circuit, you need the binary representation of 170. Then, after applying a Hadamard gate to all the qubits, except the ancilla qubit, to which you will first apply a NOT gate followed by a Hadamard gate, apply a CX gate to each qubit that is represented by the binary value for 170, which is represented by the value 10101010. So, you would apply a CX gate to each of the odd qubits, where the control of each CX gate should be set to qubit 1, 3, 5, and 7 and the target of each CX gate is the ancilla qubit. Then, apply a Hadamard gate followed by a measurement operator to all qubits except the ancilla qubit.

Question 3

How many oracle functions are there?

Answer

In general, most algorithms have one oracle function; however, there are some algorithms that require more than one, or multiple runs of a function, such as the Grover algorithm, which repeats the oracle and diffusion operator function based on the number of qubits of the circuit.

Chapter 12 – Applying Quantum Algorithms

Question 1

What other problems can you solve using periodic functions?

Answer

The **Quantum Fourier transform** (**QFT**) is one of the more popular algorithms to solve periodic functions.

Question 2

Implement QFT on a 5-qubit state—for example: '10110'.

Answer

Using the same example in the book, simply extend another **swap** gate repetition by adding another qubit.

Question 3

Using Grover's algorithm, find the following states, '101', '001', and '010'.

Answer

Simply change the numerical value on the argument to the values above, then observe the change in the circuit's oracle representing each of the three values. Since all are 3 qubits in length, the repetition will be the same for each value (just once).

Question 4

How many iterations of Grover's diffusion operator would you need to run to find the state $|11010\rangle$?

Answer

Use the following to determine the number of times to repeat the function, $4/\pi(\sqrt{N})$, where N is the number of qubits. Here, N=4.

Question 5

Rerun the Grover's search example. Only repeat Grover's diffusion operator twice and note the difference in the result. What do you see that is different? What would you expect to change if you ran it more than three times?

Answer

The amplitude difference between the value we are searching for and the other values will vary differently, either increasingly or decreasingly.

Chapter 13 – Understanding Quantum Utility and Qiskit Patterns

Question 1

What are the four steps of Qiskit Patterns?

Answer

Map, optimize, execute, and post-process.

Question 2

Which Qiskit Pattern handles mapping a quantum circuit to the hardware?

Answer

The optimization step handles mapping the circuit to the hardware.

Question 3

When encoding your problem to a quantum state, which Qiskit Pattern step are you on?

Answer

You are mapping the input values of your classical data into a quantum state.

Question 4

Why did we use a Sampler and not an Estimator primitive for the Grover example?

Answer

We did not have to use any observables to solve Grover's algorithm. Simply returning the quasi-distribution of the results provided the answer.

Join us on Discord

Join our community's Discord space for discussions with the author and other readers:

https://packt.link/3FyN1

‹packt›

`packt.com`

Subscribe to our online digital library for full access to over 7,000 books and videos, as well as industry leading tools to help you plan your personal development and advance your career. For more information, please visit our website.

Why subscribe?

- Spend less time learning and more time coding with practical eBooks and Videos from over 4,000 industry professionals
- Improve your learning with Skill Plans built especially for you
- Get a free eBook or video every month
- Fully searchable for easy access to vital information
- Copy and paste, print, and bookmark content

At `www.packt.com`, you can also read a collection of free technical articles, sign up for a range of free newsletters, and receive exclusive discounts and offers on Packt books and eBooks.

Other Book You May Enjoy

If you enjoyed this book, you may be interested in these other books by Packt:

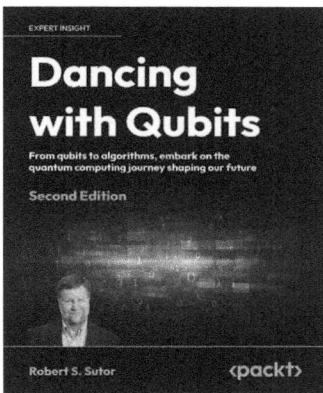

Dancing with Qubits

Robert S. Sutor

ISBN: 9781837636754

- Explore the mathematical foundations of quantum computing
- Discover the complex, mind-bending concepts that underpin quantum systems
- Understand the key ideas behind classical and quantum computing
- Refresh and extend your grasp of essential mathematics, computing, and quantum theory
- Examine a detailed overview of qubits and quantum circuits
- Dive into quantum algorithms such as Grover's search, Deutsch-Jozsa, Simon's, and Shor's
- Explore the main applications of quantum computing in the fields of scientific computing, AI, and elsewhere

Packt is searching for authors like you

If you're interested in becoming an author for Packt, please visit `authors.packtpub.com` and apply today. We have worked with thousands of developers and tech professionals, just like you, to help them share their insight with the global tech community. You can make a general application, apply for a specific hot topic that we are recruiting an author for, or submit your own idea.

Leave a Review!

Thank you for purchasing this book from Packt Publishing—we hope you enjoyed it! Your feedback is invaluable and helps us improve and grow. Please take a moment to leave an Amazon review; it will only take a minute, but it makes a big difference for readers like you.

`https://packt.link/r/1803244801`

Scan the QR code below to receive a free ebook of your choice.

`https://packt.link/NzOWQ`

Index

Download a free PDF copy of this book

Thanks for purchasing this book!

Do you like to read on the go but are unable to carry your print books everywhere?

Is your eBook purchase not compatible with the device of your choice?

Don't worry, now with every Packt book you get a DRM-free PDF version of that book at no cost.

Read anywhere, any place, on any device. Search, copy, and paste code from your favorite technical books directly into your application.

The perks don't stop there, you can get exclusive access to discounts, newsletters, and great free content in your inbox daily.

Follow these simple steps to get the benefits:

1. Scan the QR code or visit the link below:

https://packt.link/free-ebook/9781803244808

2. Submit your proof of purchase.
3. That's it! We'll send your free PDF and other benefits to your email directly.

www.ingramcontent.com/pod-product-compliance
Ingram Content Group UK Ltd.
Pitfield, Milton Keynes, MK11 3LW, UK
UKHW012241170225
4635UKWH00015B/726

9 781803 244808